Tears of the Lotus

TEARS *of* *the* LOTUS

Accounts of Tibetan Resistance to the Chinese Invasion, 1950–1962

Roger E. McCarthy

McFarland & Company, Inc., Publishers
Jefferson, North Carolina, and London

The present work is a reprint of the library bound edition of Tears of the Lotus: Accounts of Tibetan Resistance to the Chinese Invasion, 1950–1962, *first published in 1997 by McFarland.*

Library of Congress Cataloguing-in-Publication Data

McCarthy, Roger E., 1927–
  Tears of the lotus : accounts of Tibetan resistance to the Chinese invasion, 1950–1962 / Roger E. McCarthy.
    p.   cm.

  ISBN-13: 978-0-7864-2847-2
  ISBN-10: 0-7864-2847-3 (softcover : 50# alkaline paper) ∞

  1. Guerrillas — China — Tibet.   2. Tibet (China) — Politics and government — 1951–   3. Tibet (China) — History.   I. Title.
DS786.M385   2006
951'.5 — dc21   97-6131

British Library cataloguing data are available

©1997 Roger E. McCarthy. All rights reserved

No part of this book may be reproduced or transmitted in any form or by any means, electronic or mechanical, including photocopying or recording, or by any information storage and retrieval system, without permission in writing from the publisher.

On the cover: The Potala Palace in Lhasa, Tibet *(Photodisc)*

Manufactured in the United States of America

McFarland & Company, Inc., Publishers
  Box 611, Jefferson, North Carolina 28640
  www.mcfarlandpub.com

Contents

Preface	1
Prologue	9
1 The Past Forms the Present	11
2 The Imperialist Invasions	36
3 Agreement by Duress	63
4 Deeds of Deceit	77
5 Thunder in the East	98
6 Honey on a Knife	115
7 The Gold Throne	131
8 The Volunteer Defense Force	141
9 The Pendulum Swings	165
10 The Red Devils Unmasked	177
11 Four Sides of the Story	191
12 The Blood of Patriots	216
Epilogue	253
Appendices	
A. Text of the Dalai Lama's Cable to the U.N., September 9, 1959	261
B. U.N. General Assembly Tibet Resolution, October 21, 1959	263
C. Statement of H. H. the Dalai Lama on the 20th Anniversary of the Tibetan National Uprising of March 10, 1959	265
D. Text of September 7, 1995, Letter to President Clinton Written by a Trusted Representative of the Dalai Lama Protesting the State Department Statement Broadcast by *Voice of America* on August 24, 1995	269
Glossary	271
Notes	273
Bibliography	281
Index	283

This book is dedicated to Tibet and those magnificent Tibetans who fought so courageously for over two decades, against all odds and with little help, for their freedom, their religion and their country against a barbaric and merciless invader. Many of these fighters died, but many survived.

It is also dedicated to those who, nearly fifty years later, still remain subjugated against their will and against all reason by a heartless, pseudonymous "People's Republic" of China.

Although one of the leaders of the Chushi Gangdrug, Gompo Tashi Andrugtsang, provided most of the details of the resistance efforts waged against the People's Liberation Army described herein by him and his fellow Khambas, some of the extraordinary accomplishments of other tribal people both before and at the same time as those of Gompo Tashi Andrugtsang are also related.

Over the centuries there have been many warriors in many lands who chose to risk all in the cause of freedom or in defense of their country. The Freedom Fighters of Tibet clearly demonstrated their right to stand shoulder to shoulder in equal honor with the bravest of them.

Be they from one of the Kham tribes, or Golok, or Amdo, or Lolo, or U, or other, those who fought for Tibet will not be forgotten. Because of the efforts by the resistance forces, many tens of thousands of Tibetans were able to escape their Chinese executioners and have since been able to carry on under His Holiness, thus insuring that there will be another tomorrow with hope and honor in Tibet's long and fascinating history.

Preface

Tibet. Shangri-La. Theocratic state. Roof of the world. Once but a large lake in early geological times. Three-fourths of its 900,000 square miles are 14,000 feet above sea level. Land of the yak, the yeti and the dzo—and of a fiercely independent, freedom-loving people. Until invaded by multiple thousands of the People's Liberation Army in 1950, Tibet, under the theocratic rule of the fourteenth Dalai Lama, had been a land of peace and promise.

Uniquely positioned above the three most populated areas of the world—China, India and what was the Soviet Union—Tibet had been courted and attacked as an independent country by her neighbors for centuries. Even the mighty Mongol chieftains Genghis, Kublai, Altan and Gushri Khan were drawn to and fascinated by Tibet's Buddhist religion and came to respect and befriend the fiercely independent Tibetans. At times, the Mongols fought in defense of Tibet and her Dalai Lamas. The fourth Dalai Lama was born in Mongolia, a grandson of the Mongolian Prince, Altan Khan.

Whether as a conqueror or conquered, Tibet has remained devout in her Buddhist religion and practices. Ecclesiastically aligned with India, drawn to China only by ancient and profitable trade routes, and strong in her own heritage, for centuries Tibet managed to maintain an isolation and uniqueness that few other countries in history have matched.

As described in 1900, "The Thibetans [sic] are a warlike race, but their military tendencies are subdued by an extreme religious devotion, which, far from being exclusively Buddhistic, seems among their educated men to be as broad as it is among the most scholarly philosophers of Europe and America."[1] A good description then and now as well, but the Tibetans are currently a diminishing and disadvantaged minority in their own country. According to China, Tibet is simply a Chinese province, totally governed and controlled by the Chinese. Conceivably, Tibet could become only a name if the Chinese occupier continues to gradually eliminate and absorb the Tibetans remaining in Tibet—a simple and devious but effective practice of genocide. Sadly, the Dalai Lama's requests for an investigation by the United Nations, or any other internationally composed group, of the Chinese practices in Tibet continue to be ignored. Why? Because few, if any, in the free world care or dare to challenge the People's Republic of China.

This book is primarily about the resistance by the Tibetans to the forces of the People's Liberation Army that Mao Tse-tung sent into Tibet, first into western Tibet and the eastern province of Amdo in 1949, and then massively into the eastern province of Kham in 1950. Ill-prepared, disorganized, vastly outnumbered and with very limited fire power, the few Tibetan army forces and the tribesmen in eastern Tibet were no match for the invaders.

At first the smiling Chinese persuaded many Tibetans that their intent was merely to help Tibet and to have Tibet share in the future greatness and wealth of China that Mao had promised all in the so-called Chinese family. However, as the numbers of Chinese rapidly increased, controls tightened, and the smiles and promises of the Chinese changed dramatically to demands for full compliance. Then came forced labor gangs, collectivization and increasing abuses of Tibetans politically, religiously and personally. The Tibetan tribesmen and most monastics finally realized that Mao's promises and practices were intended to destroy Tibet, her religion and their freedom. Despite the repeated urging by the Dalai Lama and others in Lhasa that there be no resistance to the Chinese, the decision to fight was made by the tribals in the mid-1950s in order to save their individual freedom, their religion and their country.

In 1947 the State Oracle of Tibet had prophesied that in the Year of the Iron Tiger (1950) Tibet would experience extreme difficulty from the east. In 1949 a horse-tailed comet appeared in the sky over eastern Tibet for weeks. This same phenomenon had preceded the attempted armed invasion of Tibet by China in 1910. In August 1950 there was a monstrous earthquake in eastern Tibet. Villages were destroyed, the course of the mighty Brahmaputra River was changed and the eastern horizon reportedly glowed red for hours. All these signs were interpreted by most Tibetans as evil omens and dire threats emanating from her enemy, China.[2] They were 100 percent correct.

The history of Tibet has been one of turmoil with many peaks and valleys. It is summarized herein for the reader, as is the how and why Tibet had arrived at the critical points that she faced when the Chinese troops crossed Tibet's borders. At best, Tibet is now a province totally controlled and exploited by her haughty military conqueror. Tibetans find themselves without representation or a meaningful voice and with little real hope. At worst, Tibet will be totally absorbed by the Chinese and eventually exist only as another Han province. Tibet will have disappeared.

Well over a million Tibetans died in the 1950s because of Chinese military and civil actions, and another million Tibetans lost their true identity when China realigned and swallowed the provinces of Tsinghai and Sikang, in which Tibetans had historically enjoyed distinct majorities. Since 1960 many thousands have died of starvation, or in prisons, or have simply been executed by the Chinese. Fortunately, scores of thousands of Tibetans have escaped to neighboring countries, especially into India where the Dalai Lama keeps alive the flame of hope of returning to Tibet.

But there is disagreement between those in exile who would seek an accommodation with China and those who do not support any such accommodation, insisting instead that the Tibetan leadership press for the granting to Tibet of the independence and freedom that she enjoyed from 1910 to 1950. The Dalai Lama, an openly declared admirer and advocate of Marxist socialism, appears inclined to accept an accommodation with the PRC in which Tibet would be given at least a semiautonomous status with control over most if not all of her internal (but not external) affairs, while others, particularly the "young Turks," want and expect a Tibet free of most, if not all Chinese influences, controls and presence. Unfortunately, these differences have caused some fragmentation of unity and little progress in or positive negotiations with the PRC. This is to the benefit of China, time being on her side as the total assimilation process continues in Tibet.

The thirteenth Dalai Lama had predicted in 1932 that "Unless we can guard our own country it will now happen that the Dalai and Panchen Lamas will disappear and become nameless ... that the rule of the law will be weakened ... that monks and their monasteries will be destroyed ... that the lands and property of government officials will be seized ... that all beings will be sunk in great hardship and overpowering fear."[3] He had favored seeking a close relationship with the British, including the gradual establishment of a small but effective army of some fifteen to twenty thousand with British assistance. He was strongly resisted in this by some high-ranking monastics, and some government officials as well, who saw a strong military as a possible threat to their own powers and influences. The grasp and need for a capable Tibetan army did not surface again until just before the Chinese invaded, by then far too late.

Whether it has yet or will be recognized that the Theocratic State is no longer feasible in this day and age is another vital consideration. As Tibet has experienced, forms of government can and do change, but her Buddhist religion remains strong. It is the single thread that those in Tibet cling to, but Tibet's religion did not and cannot serve as her only strength.

This book is not a religious treatise, nor does it examine the involved politics and polemics of Maoism. It does provide examples of the many treacheries of the Chinese and that of some of the collaborating Tibetan officials. It also describes and provides considerable information on the brutalities inflicted on the Tibetans by the Chinese. And it relates in detail a number of the actions between the resistance forces and the Chinese. It discusses many of the problems the resistance experienced, including lack of support from the Dalai Lama. It also describes the difficulties experienced by the Freedom Fighters and the escape of the Dalai Lama from Lhasa in 1959, closely guarded and made possible by the resistance forces. It notes the changing role and relocation of the resistance as overwhelming numbers of Chinese soldiers were posted to Tibet. It also addresses many of the errors and misconceptions that

The author with some Tibetan trainees in Colorado (1959).

have been printed regarding support by the Central Intelligence Agency to the Tibetan resistance.

Early in my thirty-year career with the CIA, it was my good fortune to train, get to know and infiltrate the first six Tibetan (Khamba) trainees in 1957. Prior to this I had known little about Tibet beyond its location. Assisted by Thubten Jigme Norbu, oldest brother of the Dalai Lama, and Jentzen Dhondrup, who had been with Mr. Norbu in the Kumbum Monastery in Amdo in eastern Tibet, the six-days-a-week training of the Tibetans conducted by myself and a few selected CIA officers went very well despite the long hours the extensive curriculum demanded of the trainees. By the fall of 1957 — and the infiltration by parachute of the Khambas into Tibet — I had learned considerably more about Tibet and Tibetans and formed the opinion that I still hold that there are none finer or braver.

From a very modest and successful beginning, the program expanded over the following years, including providing training of Tibetans in the United States, not only in subjects directly related to resistance but others as well. For example, the functions and benefits of representative government and the basic requisites of government infrastructure, etc., were given to some of the trainees, including special guided visits to Washington, D.C., the United Nations in New York, and to other cities in order to broaden their horizons and knowledge of government.

In the early fall of 1959 I met with and debriefed Gompo Tashi Andrugtsang, one of the key resistance leaders, and also three of the original six trainees who had just exfiltrated from Tibet, in Darjeeling, India. The majority of the resistance actions related are based on the lengthy discussions during those many long and interesting days of the Darjeeling debriefings. I remained in charge of the Tibetan program for the CIA until late 1961 when I was again posted overseas, leaving behind me many unforgettable memories, a number of dedicated Tibetans undergoing training in Colorado, and the outstanding and highly motivated staff of CIA officers that had been carefully chosen for this program. We were agreed that as the British who had worked with them decades earlier had noted, the Tibetans were quick learners, high spirited, quietly confident, direct, friendly, capable and totally dedicated.

I have often been asked why I waited so long to write this saga. The simple explanation is procrastination, for Tibet, and the Tibetans, were never forgotten. Their achievements against the forces of Chinese evil personified by Mao and the PLA deserve to be made a part of the record available to all to read. Thus I have tried to provide insights on the resistance; to describe the countless and unforgivable Chinese brutalities, excesses, and deceits; to outline the sorry role of the Free World — the United Nations and that of Prime Minister Nehru — when Tibet desperately needed help; and to relate the story of the near demise of a unique country simply because of the demoniacal ambitions of Mao Tse-tung.

This is not a story about the CIA or its assistance to the resistance. It is not about many of the Abbots, Lamas and monks and many government officials, especially in Lhasa, believing that prayer alone would keep the Chinese from invading. Nor is it about the petty jealousies within some monasteries or in the Tibetan government, or the traitorous acts of a few, nor about the monastics hurriedly empowering a young teenager with the impossible task and responsibilities of government in order to escape that responsibility themselves. Nor is it a story that religious faith alone is incapable of maintaining and protecting freedom. Nor is it about the myth of Mao as a great and enlightened leader or about the myth of an all powerful Chinese army that so many world statesmen chose to believe at the time. The book does include a number of comments about these but in succinct perspectives.

The research involved in this book took me to a number of excellent sources, as indicated in the notes at the end of each chapter and in the bibliography. I found Melvyn Goldstein's *A History of Modern Tibet, 1913–1951* exceptionally well detailed and informative. John Avedon's *In Exile from the Land of Snows* was both learned and interesting. Peter Fleming's *Bayonets to Lhasa* provided insights on the British role in Tibet and India. Chanakya Sen's *Tibet Disappears* proved to be a storehouse of information on the debates in the Indian Parliament on Tibet and China in the 1950s. The others listed were also useful in providing insights and viewpoints.

Unfortunately, I was unable to locate objective sources that could provide meaningful insights from the Chinese point of view on the events related, particularly regarding the Tibetan resistance. This would have been most useful, for the official releases, such as those in the *Peking Review*, offer little other than party dogma. And unfortunately, Phala, the Dalai Lama's Lord Chamberlain and advisor, died in Switzerland without having left a public record of his views. Such a record would have added greatly to any story about Tibet during the period of time involved.

As earlier noted, my days with Gompo Tashi Andrugtsang and the three survivors of the original six trainees, Wangdu, Athar and Lhotse, in Darjeeling provided most of the resistance stories related here. Other helpful discussions include those with Geshe Wangyel, a high-ranking Kalmuk monk who was in the Drepung Monastery in Lhasa before relocating to the United States to settle in New Jersey. He would talk for hours about Tibet. He contributed extensively to the success of the program, including completing a Tibetan telecode book vital to the program's radio communications. Geshe was a key link in the communications process, requiring that he commute regularly to Washington, D.C. He had an uncanny ability to intuit solutions to what often appeared to be difficult problems in communicating and exchanging information via radio with the resistance teams in Tibet. Lhamo Tsering and his sustained efforts over many years in India and Nepal on behalf of the resistance program were vital and are well remembered and appreciated, as is my conversation with his son who visited me in Nevada in 1993 and provided answers to many questions I had. Gyalo Thondup, older brother of the Dalai Lama, urged and prompted me to write the story of the Tibetan resistance during a conversation we had while he was visiting San Francisco that same year. Especially rewarding was my visit to Thubten Jigme Norbu in 1995 at the Tibetan Cultural Center in Bloomington, Indiana, and the renewing of our earlier friendship. His recollections, insights and ready answers to my many questions have been especially valuable.

And to my CIA colleagues who have helped to sort the details and sequence of events from those earlier days, I again say thank you. Sadly, I was advised that you must remain nameless.

But it is those many fine and brave Tibetans who on blind faith chose to volunteer to undertake training without knowing where they were destined, or what their fate might be, and those thousands of other Volunteers who fought so desperately to free Tibet of the Chinese invader that are collectively the centerpiece of this book. All of you deserve high praise in the history of your country and are certainly well remembered and honored by those of us who came to know you and, through you, your fellow volunteers.

Hopefully the thoughtful views expressed by the Dalai Lama in a column carried by the *New York Times* on August 9, 1985, will prevail. He wrote, "We Tibetans are not against the Chinese people. All we demand is that which is rightfully ours.... China does not possess any right whatsoever to decide the fate of the Tibetan people.... Not a single Tibetan record states that Tibet has at any time been a part of China.... Stronger powers have, and still do, at times use their influence in an aggressive way to advance claims of sovereignty over weaker nations. But such claims have no basis and such actions cannot confer sovereignty. ... In the final analysis, it should be for the concerned people themselves, in this case the Tibetans, to decide what they want. I have always believed that human determination and any cause that is truly just will ultimately triumph."

May it be so.

Prologue

I am an old man now. Age has robbed me of my strength and fate has stolen all that was ever dear to me. From this lofty peak of my old age, I look back towards the memories of my young days, and they still stand before me, vivid and clear as the crystal streams of my land Nyarong. It was a beautiful land, and the lives we led there, though simple and hard, were happy.

Then the Chinese came. At first with soft words and bright silver, and later with guns and death. They took away my fields, my animals and my home. They looted, desecrated and burnt the temples and monasteries I worshipped in. Like vermin, they slew my friends, relatives, lamas, and all the people dear to my heart. On a frozen wasteland, thinly covered with wind-swept snow, I left behind me the twisted, bullet-ridden (bodies) of my family and my only little daughter.

I was forced to live in the high mountains like an animal, and like a thief to hide by day and to move by night. Hunger and thirst, exhaustion and pain were my constant companions. Bullets ripped and tore through my flesh and muscles. My wounds putrefied [sic] and rot ate the flesh until my world was a haze of dull pain and the overpowering stench of gangrene. So much sorrow, so much pain and death.... Not only did it prey upon my life and the lives of my countrymen then, but still now it exists and feeds on my poor people back in Tibet. They live in despair night and day, in a country that has become an endless nightmare. Everything has been taken away from them: their faith, their dignity, their manhood and their freedom ... except perhaps, the freedom to starve, to slave and to die. Yes, I remember it all. Pain and bitterness have etched every moment and event forever into my mind.

Rapten Dorje (Aten), from *Warriors of Tibet* (1974)

The foregoing describes the world of Aten (Rapten Dorje) as he knew it before the Chinese invaded, then as it was under the Chinese, and as he viewed it as a refugee in India. His story is especially unique because he was appointed by the Chinese in 1951 as an assistant administrator in his subdistrict in Wulu, (Nyarong District) in Kham in eastern Tibet. In 1955 he was selected by the Chinese for training at the Southwest School for National Minorities in Chengtu, after which he worked for the Chinese in Kham until 1958 when, seizing an opportunity, he fled with his family to join the resistance. Aten escaped from Tibet in 1960. Of the 16 who left their village in 1958 to join the resistance, only Aten and three others made it safely to India. All other members of his family were killed in Tibet.

CHAPTER 1

The Past Forms the Present

Although long identified as a theocratic state, Tibet's history has been volatile, violent and involved. It includes periods of her being a powerful and vast empire, as well as periods when she was vanquished and occupied. Tibet has also experienced and endured unending religious and political turmoil, complete with extensive intrigues among and between competing and ambitious religious and government figures. Although these problems have been the rule rather than the exception, she also has a heritage and record of impressive cultural and religious accomplishments. While never a distinctly divided land in the modern sense of geopolitics, Tibet, bonded together by the Buddhist religion, was seldom a closely knit country led by a strong central government respected both in her capital, Lhasa, and in her provinces. To the contrary, her provinces and her many tribals were more often openly scornful and antigovernment in general, understandably hostile to the selfish, avaricious, and zealous attitudes and practices of most of the ambitious Lhasan bureaucrats who usually viewed the provinces and districts simply as sources of tax revenues. Because of the land holdings of their own monasteries and their religious ties to Lhasa, many of the prominent abbots and lamas in monasteries located in rural areas held similar views of the tribals. Be they farmers, nomads, businessmen or traders, those in the provinces were viewed by Lhasa primarily as money sources. There was keen ecclesiastical competition for favored positions in Lhasa, some of which were subject to manipulation of religious influences and available to those able to make a well-placed financial gift or donation. These factors have played a significant role throughout Tibet's history, particularly in periods of time when there was less than a strong Dalai Lama leading the country, or when there was no enthroned Dalai Lama and Tibet was governed by a Regent who chose to follow his own dictates.

Even a brief review of earlier periods in Tibet's history provides many insightful backdrops to the particularly sad and brutal events that transpired in Tibet at the hands of Mao Tse-tung and the People's Liberation Army beginning in 1949. The remainder of this chapter offers a summary of those periods.

Despite the lack of completeness of records from earlier times, most

Tibetan scholars agree that Tibet's recorded history begins with the enthronement of Son-Tsan Gam-Po in A.D. 620, and his reign until A.D. 650. He married a Nepalese princess, a devout Buddhist, which helped to further promote Buddhism in the area. His armies conquered upper Burma and western China. The Emperor of China, after his army was defeated by the Tibetans, was forced to send a daughter, also a Buddhist, to marry him as part of the truce agreement. His Buddhist wives assisted him in the subsequent spreading and acceptance of Buddhism throughout Greater Tibet and in contiguous areas. Although Buddhism had come to Tibet some two hundred years earlier, it had not previously become widely practiced, so King Son-Tsan Gam-Po sent scholars to India to return with Buddhist scriptures so that Buddhism could then be distributed further and more quickly. He also established laws, including that murder, robbery and adultery were to be punished. Under his leadership a Tibetan alphabet and grammar were developed and, as previously noted, Buddhism was strongly supported and encouraged. He also wrote that "those on high should be kept under control by law, and those from below should be governed according to reason; that land should be cultivated, people should be taught to read and write, and to follow good manners." He ordained that "those who quarrel should be fined; murders should be compensated for; thieves should pay nine times the amount of the stolen property; those who commit rape should be banished; the liar should have his tongue cut; people should worship God, respect the elders and repay the kindness of loving mothers and old fathers; good should be returned with good; scriptures should be read intelligently; one should believe in karma, the doctrine of retribution; debts should be paid; good actions bring back good, evil actions bring evil; and if there be a doubt between yes and no, take advice from the gods." He also built a palace on the Red Hill three miles outside of Lhasa, and until those days in March 1959 when the Chinese pillaged and looted Lhasa and all nearby places, religious services were still held there whenever a threat of war was perceived.[1]

Shortly after the death of King Son-Tsan Gam-Po, the Chinese, believing Tibet was weakened, invaded Tibet in A.D. 650 and captured Lhasa, but they could not sustain their presence there in the hostile environment, so they soon returned to China. However, border skirmishes between Tibetans and Chinese continued over the years, becoming the rule rather than the exception in the eastern provinces of Tibet.

In the second half of the eighth century, under the reign of King Thi-song-deu-tsen, Tibet again became a very powerful nation, so much so that in A.D. 763 its army captured Chang-an, then the capital of the Chinese T'ang Dynasty. Tibet's empire crossed the Pamirs and touched the domains of Arabs and Turks. Considerable efforts were devoted to the translation of Sanskrit works during this period, an undertaking that continued thereafter except for the brief period of time when King Lang-dar-ma reigned in the early part of the tenth century.[2]

Lang-dar-ma was the jealous brother of King Ral-pacen, and was strongly anti–Buddhist. Lang-dar-ma arranged to have his brother assassinated and then assumed the throne. His reign was described as Tibet having sunk into utter darkness. Lang-dar-ma lasted only three years. "A lama, having smeared his white horse with black soot and donning a pitch black garment, with a white lining, rode into the presence of the king. The lama danced fantastically, and, while prostrating himself, drew out a bow and arrow and shot the king dead. Mounting his fast steed, the lama then rode through a river which washed the soot off the horse. Then, turning his garb inside out, the lama escaped to safety. The dance of the lama became known as the Black Hat dance, and has been reenacted in Lhasa ever since during national celebrations. Lang-dar-ma was the last king of Tibet. After him petty chiefs exercised sway through their forts on commanding hills."[3] Thus the previous strong control of the central government was broken, and replaced largely by provincial war lords. That Tibetans had little tolerance for those in high positions in Tibet who chose to shun or oppose Buddhism was clear, and centralized government control was weakened.

Also in the eighth century, the following inscription was made on the western face of a large stone pillar near the temple in Lhasa, marking an agreement reached between Tibetan and Chinese forces:

> The Sovereign of Tibet, the Divine King of Miracles, and the great King of China, Hwang Te, the Nephew and the Maternal Uncle, have agreed to unite their kingdoms. Having made this great Agreement, that it may be held faithfully and never be changed, all gods and men were invoked to bear witness to the oath. That it may remain from generation to generation, the sacred terms of the relationship have been duly inscribed on the pillar.
>
> The King of Miracles Ti-de-tsen and the Chinese King Bun-Pu-He-u-Tig Hwang Te, Nephew and Uncle, united their kingdoms, considering the mutual welfare of Tibet and China, and thus conferred great benefits upon the people of the inside and outside, making many and all happy and prosperous for a long time. They agreed to hold as sacred the respect of the old relationship and the happiness of the neighbors. Tibet and China shall guard the land and frontier, of which they have hitherto held possession. All to the east of the frontier is the country of Great China. All to the west is certainly the country of Great Tibet.
>
> Henceforth, there shall be no fighting as between enemies and neither side will carry war into the other's country. Should there be any suspected person, he can be arrested, questioned, and sent back. Thus the great Agreement has been made for uniting the kingdoms, and the Nephew and Uncle have become happy. In gratitude for this happiness it is necessary that travellers with good messages should go backwards and forwards. The messengers from both sides will also travel by the old roads as before. According to the former custom, ponies shall be exchanged at Chang-kun-yok on the frontier between Tibet and China. At Che-shung-shek the Chinese territory is met; below this, China will show respect (supply transport and other assistance). At Tsen-shu-huan Tibetan territory is met; above this Tibet will show respect.
>
> The Nephew and Uncle, having become intimate, will respect each other according to custom. No smoke or dust shall appear between the two countries.

> There shall be no sudden anger and the word "enemy" shall not even be mentioned. Not even those guarding the frontier shall feel apprehension or take fright. Land is land and bed is bed (land will not be violated and men will be able to sleep carefree in their beds without having to watch for enemies), thus happiness will reign. Happiness will be established; prosperity will be gained for ten thousand generations. The sound of praise shall cover all the places reached by the Sun and Moon.
>
> This Agreement that the Tibetans shall be happy in Tibet and the Chinese happy in China and the great kingdoms united shall never be changed. The Three Precious Ones (Buddha, the Buddhist scriptures and the Buddhist priesthood), the Exalted Ones (The Celestial Buddha, Chenrezi, etc.), the Sun and Moon, the Planets and Stars have been invoked to bear witness. Solemn words were also uttered. Animals were sacrificed and oaths taken and the Agreement was made.
>
> Is this Agreement held to be binding? If this Agreement be violated, whether Tibet or China violates it first, that one has committed the sin. Whatever revenge is taken in retaliation shall not be considered a breach of the Agreement. In this way the Kings and Ministers of Tibet and China took oath and wrote this inscription of the Agreement in detail. The two great kings affixed their seals. The Ministers, considered as holding the Agreement, wrote with their hands. This inscribed Agreement shall be observed by both sides.[4]

Another inscription in Lhasa, dated A.D. 763, badly damaged by the Chinese as they tried to obliterate the names of towns in China that Tibet had acquired, reads

> King Thi-song-deu-tsen considered and ascertained the affairs of the kingdom of China. He gave instructions to the military commander who first took his armies to Kar-tsen. Being versed in strategy he marched slowly. He subdued Ha-sha in the domain of China. China shivered with fear. The Chinese King He Hu Hik Wang Te and his ministers were struck with terror and bought peace by offering a perpetual annual tribute of 50,000 rolls of silk. Soon after the king died and his son, Wang Peng Wang, considering it degrading, stopped the tribute. Two great commanders were then ordered by the Tibetan king to carry war up to the new Chinese king's palace of Keng-shi. A great battle was fought on the ford of Chi Hu Chir. Many Chinese were killed. The Chinese king also fled from his castle. Keng-shi was captured.

The remainder of the inscription has been hammered and rubbed out by the Chinese.[5]

These inscriptions are especially interesting in that even in this early period they reflect the distrust and enmity between the Tibetans and the Chinese, the emptiness of Chinese promises, the disdain by the Chinese for Tibetans and the long lineage of Chinese deceits. Unfortunately, the events that have followed in Tibet repeatedly underscore these points.

Buddhism, with its messages of love, friendship, tolerance, kindness, and ardor for peace, generally and gradually reduced and replaced the previous practice and spirit in Tibet of militarism and her willingness and determination to defend herself, her religion and her freedom. Tibet became markedly less secular, more religious, distinctly more isolationist and very vulnerable.

The wisdom of the Tibetan government's decision to abandon a centralized military capability in favor of relying solely on Buddhism for protection is questionable but understandable because with the passage of time there was little real authority in Lhasa beyond that directly related to the powerful abbots, lamas and monasteries. However, delegating authority to her provinces and reducing her army to a ceremonial guard all but insured that Tibet would be repeatedly threatened and attacked by her covetous neighbors, especially China, for decades to come, for Tibet's days as a strong military power were now over. The rural areas were largely left to manage their own affairs although the system of taxing land holdings and monasteries remained. Control and influence often became more or less a Tibetan version of the Chinese system and tolerance of war lords. However, Buddhism became stronger throughout Tibet, as well as in Mongolia, Nepal, India and in China with the passage of time. High-ranking Tibetan religious figures exerted considerable influence in Lhasa, directly via their supporting monasteries as well as by riches accumulated from lands, as did their civilian government counterparts who also held extensive land and taxing privileges. These forces and factors have had considerable effect and impact on the ebb and flow of Tibet's fortunes through the years, from the early Dalai Lamas to the present one. Pivotal of course has been the strength and leadership of the individual Dalai Lamas.

In the year 1270, Kublai Khan, then the first Mongol emperor of China and the grandson of the mighty Genghis Khan, unified Tibet and China in the world's largest ever land empire. This was the first time that Tibet can be said to have become a true vassal of China—but in turn Kublai Khan was conquered by Tibetan Lamaism. He also became captivated by the Tibetan tribals, whom he likened to his fellow fiercely independent and freedom-loving Mongolians. He readily embraced Buddhism and then offered the sovereignty of Tibet to the Abbot of Sa-ca, thereby beginning the rule of priest-kings in Tibet. Tibet's history as a unified country with a recorded chronicle of developments begins with Kublai Khan.[6]

In 1358 Tsong-kha-pa, founder of the Buddhist Yellow Hats, was born in Amdo in northeastern Tibet. He reformed the church, forbade the monks to marry or to drink wine and founded the powerful lamaseries at Ganden and Sera, which, together with the Drepung monastery, became known as the "Three Pillars of State." The Yellow Hat monks came to defeat (and for a time forced out) the Red Hat sect that had previously controlled Tibet. The Yellow Hats also enforced stricter vows among all monks—such as chastity and the forbidding of marriage—and enforced stricter religious practices and values than those of the Red Hats. The successor of Tsong-kha-pa, Ganden-tru-pa, is recognized as having been the first in a unique system of reincarnation, his spirit having been passed into his successor, an infant born in 1476, two years after his death.[7]

Sonam Gyatso, now identified as the third Dalai Lama, visited Mongolia in 1578 and again in 1587. On his first visit he received the title of Vajradhara Dalai Lama, Holder of the Thunderbolt and Ocean Lama, from the Mongol king, Altan Khan. Sonam Gyatso is credited with having extended laws in Tibet and into Mongolia, and it was he who converted Altan Khan to Buddhism.[8] These close and natural ties between Tibetans and Mongolians continued for centuries and still endure.

Dalai is a Mongolian term meaning ocean, or vast, indicating extensive wisdom. Combined with the Tibetan word *lama*, which means "the superior one," Dalai Lama can be literally defined as one with an ocean of knowledge. Tibetans prefer to use the term "His Holiness," or "Chenrezi," which means one who has acquired the right to Nirvana but chooses to work on earth for the good of all. However, the term *Dalai Lama* is used widely, especially outside of Tibet, and the succession of Dalai Lamas continues, with the present one, the fourteenth, presently living in exile in India.

The fifth Dalai Lama, Lobsang Gyatso, is one of the most famous of the Dalai Lamas. To him Tibet owes its present secular and monastic practice. History records that he called on the Mongol prince Gushri Khan to help him subdue the older Buddhist sect, the Red Hats, which had again become powerful and unruly. Gushri Khan did so and then conferred the Tibetan kingdom on him, along with the title of Dalai Lama, after which Lobsang Gyatso became known as the Great Fifth throughout Tibet. He was able to establish a strong central government in Lhasa and continued the close bonds that had been established with the Mongols. He also respected and in turn was respected by the Manchus in China, the latter treating him as an independent Sovereign. By Imperial Order, the Chinese declared Lobsang Gyatso as the Dalai Lama and a "relationship described as one between the patron and the Chaplain was established. It could work only so long as the patron was capable of exercising effective patronage and the chaplain was content with his status."[9] He was also responsible for erecting the immense and commanding Potala Palace, used since by his successors. The Great Fifth held his teacher in such high esteem that he made him the Grand Lama of Tashilhunpo and declared him to be a reincarnation of Amitabha, The Boundless Light. Successors of this teacher have since become known as Panchen Lamas.

The Great Fifth Dalai Lama died in 1680. His successor, Tsang-yang Gyatso failed to maintain the disciplines established by his predecessor, and eventually parts of Tibet were again occupied by the Chinese. He himself was captured and put to death by the Chinese. This era basically marked the beginning of constant interference by or involvement of the Chinese in the affairs of Tibet. In 1788 the Nepalese invaded Tibet for the second time in three years. Defenseless, Lhasa asked the Chinese for help. This time the Chinese Emperor Ch'ien Lung sent two of his ablest generals from Sining in northwest China with a very large army (estimated to have been in the many thousands) and,

A caravan of yaks and dzos being formed, with the Potala in the background.

actively supported by the Tibetans, defeated the Nepalese Gurkhas. However, in doing so the Chinese again established an excellent political foothold in Tibet.[10]

In the second half of the nineteenth century the Chinese empire again became weakened because of internal struggles and disagreements, but this did not reduce Tibet's problems. Britain and Russia were quick to compete to fill the power gap left by China, each hoping to assume the position of overlord of the Himalayan region. The British had long realized the importance of the Himalayas and by a number of political ploys and military actions they soon extended their power to Burma, Nepal, Ladakh, Bhutan and Sikkim, all of which had been part of the Chinese Empire at the height of its power and much of which had belonged to Tibet in her earlier days as a strong power. Bhutan, Sikkim and Ladakh were actually a part of geographical Tibet, and as the British extended their power over these territories, their relations with Tibet became estranged. In 1856 Nepal imposed a treaty on a weakened Tibet, securing additional territorial rights and an annual payment of 10,000 rupees, marking the further deterioration of relations between the two countries and underscoring China's inability to "protect" Tibet as China had claimed she would. In 1876 China and England agreed in a treaty to the latter's right to send a small scientific exploration to Tibet, but the Tibetan reaction to this was so strong that the Chinese withdrew their permission, much to the consternation of the British. In 1890, after a series of small military clashes between the British and Tibetans over Sikkim, a still weak China confirmed British protectorate power over Sikkim. This brought further conflict between Britain and Tibet and led the thirteenth Dalai Lama, who feared the expansionist policy of Britain, to seek from Czarist Russia possible protection against the British. The timing for Tibet was poor, for it was at this time that the Russo-Japanese war began, leaving Tibet without what she perceived as a protector.[11]

In 1904, citing intelligence reports that the Dalai Lama was allegedly plotting with the Russians to keep the British out of Tibet, the British sent a military mission to Lhasa under Sir Francis Younghusband. Lord Curzon, Britain's Viceroy in India, recognizing the collapse of Chinese influence in Tibet, described Chinese sovereignty over Tibet as "a political affectation" and a "constitutional fiction." With Russia engaged in a war with Japan and China weakened, Britain's timing in expanding its influence was excellent. Tibet resisted this incursion, and the mission soon became more of a military expedition. After a series of 16 skirmishes, however, during which an unknown number of Tibetans were "shot down like partridges," the British made a triumphant march into Lhasa. The British were impressed and surprised by the bravery of the Tibetans, but resistance by the hastily formed, ill-equipped (muzzle loaders), ill-trained and totally outgunned Tibetans was doomed before it began. The Dalai Lama had fled to Mongolia and then to western China, leaving his representatives and his National Assembly to sign with Britain the Lhasa Convention of 1904. In it Britain established a precedent of direct negotiation with Tibet over and above that right claimed by China. The Convention also established Britain as a most favored nation with "special interests" in Tibet. In the Peking Convention of 1906 a still weak China confirmed the Lhasa Convention. In the St. Petersburg Convention that followed in 1907, Russia recognized the special interests Britain had acquired. Both agreed that Tibet was to enjoy full autonomy and that each would keep hands off Tibet. It was in the St. Petersburg Convention that the word *suzerainty* was first used to describe China's relation with Tibet, but it should be noted that unlike the Lhasa Convention, Tibet was not a signatory to either the Peking or St. Petersburg Convention. The British government did not allow Lord Curzon to apply his policy with regard to Tibet but chose instead to accept Chinese sovereignty over Tibet, providing that there would be no concessions in Tibet without Britain's consent.[12]

The British mission had been designed as "a preventative campaign, aimed at averting a perceived Russian menace to Tibet; but this menace proved a myth, and little credit can be claimed for preventing something which was not going to happen anyhow. Limited gains had, it is true, been made in ancillary matters. Tibet had been 'opened up' to the extent that the trade-marts existed and were connected with India by telegraph. A great deal of surveying and other scientific work had been done.... And, rather surprisingly, the foundations of a genuine friendship between the British and the Tibetans had been laid."[13] As Sir Charles Bell noted in summarizing the British Mission, however, "The Tibetans were abandoned to Chinese aggression, an aggression for which the British Military Expedition to Lhasa and subsequent retreat were primarily responsible."[14]

The British withdrew from Tibet without leaving a permanent representative in Lhasa, creating in effect a political vacuum for the Chinese to fill, which they attempted to do again by military means. The Tibetans again resisted the Chinese, killing the Chinese Deputy Resident in Lhasa in the process. In turn the Chinese sent into Tibet increased numbers of their Imperial troops, led by Chao Erh-feng, a very capable but ruthless commander. After subduing the Tibetans, and much like what the Chinese were to do some 45 years later, Chao appointed Chinese magistrates in the place of Tibetans, introduced new laws limiting the number of lamas and depriving monasteries of their temporal power, and inaugurated schemes for having the land cultivated by Chinese immigrants. Backed by the heavy presence of Chinese soldiers in Lhasa and Central Tibet, the Chinese Amban in Lhasa began to take all power into his hands, reducing the Tibetan ministers to puppets. Failing to come to any agreement with Peking, the Dalai Lama fled hastily to India in February 1910. Confident that the British dared not interfere, China then claimed Nepal as a feudatory, and referred to her "sovereign" rights in Tibet, a vice "suzerainty."[15] The British, not wishing to further irritate China, remained largely quiet and discouraged all efforts by the Dalai Lama to foment resistance against the Chinese in Tibet.

An interesting story at the time was that the Dalai Lama received a secret query in India from a Tibetan monastery asking what should be done with a certain Chinese captain who had arrived with two hundred armed men. The Dalai Lama is reported to have replied: "If they are stronger than you, send them on with soft words; if you are stronger, cut them off by the root."[16]

Many challenges faced the thirteenth Dalai Lama, but the earlier remark that there were times when Tibet had no Dalai Lama to lead her, and that during these periods Tibet did not prosper, needs to be addressed. From 1750 until 1876, the ninth, tenth, eleventh and twelfth Dalai Lamas died very young, either in their teens or early twenties. Many believe that the Chinese Ambans (Minister residents) were involved in these early deaths, although others believe the Tibetan Regents were involved. It is likely that both views are correct, for not all Regents were fully willing to turn over their many powers to the young Dalai Lamas as they became eligible to assume their duties. Collusion between a corrupt Regent and a similarly inclined Amban was not unknown.[17]

Regardless, Tibet was badly led and poorly served for more than 125 years. This changed under the guidance of the thirteenth Dalai Lama. Born in 1876, he lived until December 1933. Throughout his rule, Tibet experienced multiple problems as she faced an amazing array of political, diplomatic and military turbulence. During this period Tibet was recognized by Russia, Britain,

India and China as having considerable tactical value, and each attempted to play Tibet accordingly. Tibet aroused the special interest of the Russians and British, yet both were hesitant to challenge China, nor did either wish to challenge the other over Tibet, so in the final analysis both abandoned Tibet when she most needed one or the other. The Chinese revolution in 1911 and the fall of China's imperial system gave Tibet nearly forty years of independence and freedom from China, but unfortunately Tibet did not take her place alongside other nations as an independent country during this period. Shed of China, Tibet became more a vassal of England than truly independent, and clearly, for a number of involved reasons, she was never able to become master of her own ship of state.

The Chinese revolution of 1911 against the Manchus began a significant chapter in the history of Tibet. The thirteenth Dalai Lama recognized that Chinese suzerainty over Tibet was more fiction than fact, and he and his government began to think in terms of an independent Tibet. Tibet was assisted primarily by Britain, whose motivations probably included concerns about Russia as well as her concerns about protecting India's borders against China. When news of the revolution and the overthrow of the Manchu dynasty reached Lhasa, mutiny broke out among the Chinese soldiers and extensive fighting erupted between their competing factions, as well as with the Tibetans. The thirteenth Dalai Lama fled to Darjeeling in India and was granted political asylum by the British. The Chinese then issued a proclamation deposing the Dalai Lama, but the Tibetans and the British simply ignored it. According to Sir Charles Bell, then Britain's Viceroy in India, "The Government of China also informed the British Minister that they had no intention of altering the administration of Tibet, still less of converting it into a province of China, which, as they were careful to point out, would be a contravention of treaties. Both promises were soon to be broken."[18]

While in Darjeeling, the Dalai Lama had the opportunity for extensive conversations with representatives of the British government on a wide range of subjects, including the possibility of military support. He returned to Lhasa in 1912 and declared Tibet independent, following which the remaining Chinese officials and soldiers were required to leave Tibet.[19] Unfortunately, Tibet did not take the necessary additional diplomatic actions to seek and gain recognition by others of her independence. It was obvious that China was no longer in a position to meet her self-appointed obligation to protect Tibet from foreign aggression, and that "suzerainty" existed only legalistically, but Tibetan attempts to get rid of it did not find encouragement from other countries.

Despite China's many problems, she continued to harass Tibet, both by armed skirmishes on her western borders and politically with proclamations such as that by the Presidential Order of Yuan Shih-kai, Provisional President of China, that Tibet was "to be regarded as on an equal footing with the provinces of China proper." This served only to infuriate the Tibetans. And when the British learned that Tibet had contacted Mongolia to seek assistance, and suspecting that the Dalai Lama may have engaged in similar discussions while briefly in exile in Mongolia, she demanded that a tripartite conference be held on Indian territory, with Tibetan plenipotentiaries participating in the discussions on an equal footing with British and Chinese delegates. The conference was held in Simla, India, in October 1913. After protracted discussions, the agreement recognized Chinese suzerainty over Tibet and was signed by the participants, except for China which initialed the document. However, the Chinese subsequently refused to ratify and sign the Treaty; thus they never formally recognized themselves as being the suzerain power. (Tibet later raised this point in 1950 in its appeal to the United Nations to no avail.) The Chinese then resumed attacks along the Sino-Tibetan border, but the Tibetans defeated the Chinese forces in 1917 and recaptured many parts of Tibet that had previously been annexed by China, including the areas in eastern Tibet near Tachienlu.[20] Fearing the Tibetans might seek to gain more territory, the Chinese asked the British Consul to draw up a truce. After agreeing to the truce, frontier engagements between China and Tibet were, at least for a while, much reduced.

During this same period there were a number of communications between the Dalai Lama and the Chinese addressing respective problems. Two of these are particularly interesting, not only because of the tone and charges they contained but because of the many similarities of the Chinese behavior following their invasion of Tibet in 1950. Setting the stage for the exchanges was the deposition posted on February 25, 1910, in Lhasa by order of the Chinese Amban, quoted in part as follows:

> The Dalai Lama of Tibet has received abundant favours from the hands of Our Imperial predecessors. He should have devoutly cultivated the precepts of religion in accordance with established precedent in order to propagate the doctrines of the Yellow Church.
>
> But, ever since he assumed control of the administration, he has shown himself proud, extravagant, lewd, slothful, vicious and perverse without parallel, violent and disorderly, disobedient to the Imperial Commands, and oppressive towards the Tibetans.
>
> In July 1904, he fled during the troubles and was denounced by the Imperial Amban (in Lhasa) to Us as lacking in reliability. A Decree was then issued depriving him temporarily of his Titles. He proceeded to Urga (Mongolia), whence he returned again to Sining. We, mindful of his distant flight, and hoping that he would repent and reform his evil ways, ordered the local officials to pay him due attention. The year before last he came to Peking, was received in Audience, granted new Titles, and presented with gifts.
>
> On his way back to Tibet he loitered and caused trouble; yet every indulgence was shown to him in order to manifest Our compassion. In Our generosity we forgave the past. Szechuan troops have now been sent into Tibet for the special purpose of preserving order and protecting the Trade Marts. There was no reason for the Tibetans to be suspicious of their intentions. But the Dalai Lama spread rumours, became rebellious, defamed the Amban, refused supplies, and would not listen to reason.

> When the Amban telegraphed that the Dalai Lama had fled during the night of February 12 on the arrival of the Szechuan troops, We commanded that steps be taken to bring him back. At present, however, his whereabouts are unknown. He has been guilty of treachery and has placed himself beyond the pale of Our Imperial favour. He is not fit to be a Reincarnation of Buddha. Let him, therefore, be deprived of his titles and his position as Dalai Lama as punishment. Henceforth, no matter where he may go, no matter where he may reside, whether in Tibet or elsewhere, let him be treated as an ordinary individual. Let the Imperial Amban at once cause a search to be made for male children bearing miraculous signs and let him inscribe their names on tablets and place them in the Golden Urn, so that one may be drawn out as the true Reincarnation of previous Dalai Lamas. Let the matter be reported to Us, so that Our Imperial favour may be bestowed upon the selected child, who will thus continue the propagation of the doctrine and the glorification of the Church.
>
> We reward Virtue that Vice may suffer. You, lamas and laymen of Tibet, are Our children. Let all obey the laws and preserve the Peace. Let none disregard Our desire to support the Yellow Church (Yellow Hat Sect) and maintain the tranquility of Our frontier territories.[21]

The Chinese soon learned how difficult it would be for them to replace a living Dalai Lama; thus in September 1910, the Dalai Lama received an offer from the Chinese Amban to rescind the deposition order if the Dalai Lama would return to Tibet. He would not be punished, nor would he be restored to his political position, but he would be allowed to live in the Potala and resume his temporal duties. The Dalai Lama responded as follows:

> On the tenth day of the ninth month of the Iron Dog year (1910), I received an urgent message from the Peking political and military departments asking me to return to Lhasa. In reply, I have the following to say: The Manchu Emperors have always shown great care for the welfare of the successive Dalai Lamas, and the Dalai Lamas have reciprocated these feelings of friendship. We have always had each other's best interests at heart. The Tibetan people have never had any evil designs on the Chinese.
>
> In the Wood Dragon year (1904), when the British expedition arrived in Tibet, I did not consider taking any assistance except from Peking. When at Peking, I met the Emperor and his aunt, and they showed me great sympathy. The Emperor committed himself to taking care of the welfare of Tibet. On the strength of the Emperor's word, I returned to Tibet, only to find that on our eastern borders, large bodies of Chinese troops had massed and many of our subjects had been killed. Monasteries were destroyed and the people's rights suppressed. I am sure that you are fully aware of this.
>
> Furthermore, the Amban at Lhasa, Lien-yu, had been reinforcing his troops with the object of occupying Lhasa. On several occasions, I objected to this; he turned a deaf ear to my appeals. When the troops were on their way to Lhasa, I sent my representative, Khenchung, to meet them and explain my position; but the military officers executed Khenchung and seized all his possessions.
>
> While on their march, Chinese troops had exploited the people and the monasteries to such an extent that my subjects and the monastery monks requested permission to retaliate. Had they done so, it would not have been impossible for us to defeat your army, owing to our knowledge of the terrain. However, a fight by my subjects against your troops might have been construed as against

the Manchu Emperor. I therefore asked my ministers to negotiate with your officers and to protect your representatives in Lhasa. I also wrote to the Emperor asking him to withdraw these troops. All this is clear in the records held by both the Chinese and the Tibetans. I have several times explained this by wire to the Peking Political Department; but I have received no reply.

At Nagchuka, on my way from China to Lhasa, I wrote several notes to the Amban, informing him that China and Tibet must continue their long-standing friendship; but instead of listening to my appeal, he insisted on bringing more troops to Lhasa. The advance of the Chinese troops coincided with the Monlam festival being held at Lhasa, at which thousands of monks from different monasteries had come together. In order to avoid a clash, the Nepalese representative at Lhasa called on the Manchu Amban to prevent trouble from arising. The Amban refused to do anything about it; instead, he sent his bodyguard out to meet the advancing troops. On the way, they fired on the Lhasa police, killing some of them. They also fired on the Jokhang Temple and Potala Palace.

The Eleventh Dalai Lama's nephew, Teiji Phunkhang, and Tsedron Jamyang Gyaltsen, were Tibetan government officials assigned to administer the Monlam festival. On their way to the Jokhang Temple, they were met by the troops, who fired on them and Tsedron Jamyang and Teiji Phunkhang's servant and horse were killed. Teiji Phunkhang was then beaten and taken away to the military camp. The people of Lhasa were so outraged that they wanted to take revenge; but I restrained them from doing so. I still hoped we could negotiate with China and avoid unnecessary bloodshed. Not knowing what would happen if I were captured, I appointed a representative in Lhasa to continue negotiations and I then crossed the border of Tibet and India in order to personally conduct negotiations with China.

My ministers had appealed to me to remain in Lhasa; but had I done so a situation similar to the Muslim invasion of India might well have taken place, which resulted in many religious institutions being destroyed. As I did not want this to happen in Tibet, I came here especially to negotiate for my country, not caring what hardships I might have to endure. When I arrived in Phari, I was asked by the Chinese official of Yatung to remain at the Phari monastery and negotiate with Peking with the Manchu Amban in Lhasa by wire. I thought this arrangement would be ideal; but when troops arrived to take me alive or dead, I had no choice but to cross the Indian border.

At Kalimpong, I came to know that the Manchu Emperor had already issued orders that I had been deposed from office. This was published in the Indian newspapers, and even in Lhasa posters were put up announcing that I was now an ordinary person and a new Dalai Lama would soon be chosen. Since the Emperor had done everything on the recommendation of the Manchu Amban in Lhasa, without considering the independence of Tibet and the religious relationship between our two countries, I feel there is no further use in my negotiating directly with China. I have lost confidence in China and in finding any solution in consultation with the Chinese.

I have contacted the British because the 1904 Convention permits us to deal directly with them. The Chinese are responsible for this action of mine.

During my stay in India, Amban Lien-yu has moved Chinese troops all over Tibet and has exploited Tibetan subjects to extremes. They have stopped my supplies and censored my letters from Tibet. They have seized the treasury in Lhasa, emptied our armory, and seized our mint factories. Khenche Khenrab Phuntsok, assistant to my representative in Lhasa, aged seventy years, who was completely innocent, was imprisoned without cause and sent to Tachienlu. Judicial cases that have already been settled were reopened. Tibetan Government property and the property of Tibetan officials and monasteries have been illegally seized.

You are fully aware of this inexcusable illegal action taken by your troops; yet you inform me and my ministers that the situation in Tibet is peaceful and the status quo is being maintained. I know that this has been said to persuade me to return and also I know that this is false.

Because of the above, it is not possible for China and Tibet to have the same relationship as before. In order for us to negotiate, a third party is necessary; therefore we should both request the British government to act as an intermediary. Our future policy will be based on the outcome of discussions between ourselves, the Chinese and the British. Are you able to agree to the participation of the British in these discussions? If so, please let me know.

In case you are not agreeable to this, I am handwriting you a letter containing the above facts, written in both the Manchu and Tibetan languages, which I would like you to forward to the Emperor. Please explain carefully to the Emperor the contents of my letter. (dated: Thirteenth day of the ninth month of the Iron Dog year. [1910] Seal of the Dalai Lama)[22]

Shortly after, the Chinese rose up against their non–Chinese rulers, and the Manchu garrisons were slaughtered as a republican form of government was created in China. The Tibetans, encouraged by the Dalai Lama still in India, rebelled against the Chinese, capturing some three thousand troops and officers, which were then allowed to leave Tibet via India. The Dalai Lama returned to Chumbi, Tibet, in 1912 and in January 1913 to a Lhasa free of Chinese for the first time since the eighteenth century.[23]

Some three weeks following his return to Lhasa, the Dalai Lama issued the following proclamation:

To all officials and Tibetans: I, the Dalai Lama, most omniscient possessor of the Buddhist faith, whose title was conferred by the Lord Buddha's command from the glorious land of India, speak to you as follows:

I am speaking to all classes of Tibetan people. Lord Buddha, from the glorious country of India, prophesied that the reincarnations of Avalokitesvara, through successive rulers from the early religious kings to the present day, would look after the welfare of Tibet.

During the time of Genghis Khan and Altan Khan of the Mongols, the Ming dynasty of the Chinese, and Ch'ing dynasty of the Manchus, Tibet and China co-operated on the basis of [a] benefactor and priest relationship. A few years ago, the Chinese authorities in Szechuan and Yunnan endeavored to colonize our territory. They brought large numbers of troops into central Tibet on the pretext of policing the trademarts. I, therefore, left Lhasa with my ministers for the Indo-Tibetan border, hoping to clarify to the Manchu Emperor by wire that the existing relationship between Tibet and China had been that of patron and priest and had not been based on the subordination of one to the other. There was no other choice for me but to cross the border, because Chinese troops were following with the intention of taking me alive or dead.

On my arrival in India I dispatched several telegrams to the Emperor; but his reply to my demands was delayed by corrupt officials at Peking. Meanwhile the Manchu Empire collapsed. The Tibetans were encouraged to expel the Chinese from central Tibet. I, too, returned safely to my rightful and sacred country, and I am now in the course of driving out the remnants of Chinese troops from Do Kham in eastern Tibet. Now, the Chinese intention of colonizing Tibet under the patron-priest relationship has faded like a rainbow in the sky. Having once again achieved for ourselves a period of happiness and peace, I have now allotted the following duties to be carried out without negligence:

(1) Peace and happiness in this world can only be maintained by preserving the faith of Buddhism. It is, therefore, essential to preserve all Buddhist institutions in Tibet....

(2) The various Buddhist sects in Tibet should be kept in a distinct and pure form. Buddhism should be taught, learned and meditated upon properly. Except for special persons, the administrators of monasteries are forbidden to trade, loan money, deal in any kind of livestock, and/or subjugate another's subjects.

(3) The Tibetan government's civil and military officials, when collecting taxes or dealing with their subject citizens, should carry out their duties with fair and honest judgement so as to benefit the government without hurting the interests of the subject citizens. Some of the central government officials posted at Ngari Korsum in western Tibet, and Do Kham in eastern Tibet, are coercing their subject citizens to purchase commercial goods at high prices and have imposed transportation rights exceeding the limit permitted by the government. Houses, properties, and lands belonging to subject citizens have been confiscated on the pretext of minor breaches of the law. Furthermore, the amputation of citizens' limbs has been carried out as a form of punishment. Henceforth such severe punishments are forbidden.

(4) Tibet is a country with natural resources; but it is not scientifically advanced like other lands. We are a small, religious and independent nation. To keep up with the rest of the world, we must defend our country. In view of past invasions by foreigners, our people may have to face certain difficulties, which they must disregard. To safeguard and maintain the independence of our country, one and all should voluntarily work hard....

(5) Tibet, although thinly populated, is an extensive country. Some local officials and landholders are jealously obstructing other people from developing vacant lands, even though they are not doing so themselves. People with such intention are enemies of the State and our progress. From now on, no one is allowed to obstruct anyone else from cultivating whatever vacant lands are available. Land taxes will not be collected until three years have passed; after that the land cultivator will have to pay taxes to the government and to the landlord every year, proportionate to the rent. The land will belong to the cultivator. Your duties to the government and to the people will have been achieved when you have executed all that I have said here. This letter must be posted and proclaimed in every district of Tibet, and a copy kept in the records and offices in every district.

From the Potala Palace. (Seal of the Dalai Lama)[24]

The Dalai Lama also had problems other than the Chinese to resolve, not the least of which was the Panchen Lama. When the Dalai Lama had fled Lhasa for Mongolia (1904–1906), the Chinese had recommended that the Panchen Lama take his place, a recommendation that was not refused by the Panchen Lama but one that the Tibetan people made clear as being totally unacceptable. In 1909, when the Dalai Lama fled to India, he issued a written invitation to the Panchen Lama to join him, believing that this showing of solidarity against the practices of Chinese brutality in Tibet would enhance support for Tibet. However, the Panchen Lama refused and instead accepted an invitation of the Chinese Amban in Lhasa to stay in the Dalai Lama's quarters in Lhasa. And the Dalai Lama was further angered in 1911–1913 when the Panchen Lama did not assist in expelling the Chinese from Shigatse, the Panchen Lama's home area. Nor did the Panchen Lama assist when many of the monks of the Drepung monastery refused to help fight the Chinese, and in fact sided more with the Tibetan officials who orally defended the Chinese than supporting the expulsion of the Chinese.[25] The dispute between the two continued to deepen until finally "... in 1923 the Panchen escaped to China, where he was accorded a state welcome, when he should have been turned over to Tibet."[26]

Among eight questions put by the Chinese government to the Dalai Lama, and his answers to them received in Nanking on August 30, 1930, the following quotes underscore the thirteenth Dalai Lama's firm view that Tibet did not consider the Panchen Lama a figure of authority, or Tibet to be a vassal of China.

>Question: How shall the autonomy of Tibet and its scope be defined?
>
>Answer: As from now on, the patronage relationship between the central government and Tibet is going to be faithfully observed and the central government is to show sincerity to make Tibet feel safe and secure; the area over which autonomy is to be exercised should naturally be the same as before. It is expected that the central government will return to Tibet those districts which originally belonged to it, but which are not (now) under its control so that a perpetual peace and harmony will surely be the result.
>
>Question: Shall the relative position of the Dalai and the Panch'en Lama and their respective jurisdiction in political as well as religious affairs be maintained as before or new provisions be made?
>
>Answer: Political and religious affairs have always been administered by the Tibetan government at Lhasa. The Panch'en Lama has had only the Tashilhunpo monastery (in Shigatse) in his control. Actually, the Tashilhunpo monastery was built by the first Dalai Lama. It was the second Dalai Lama who entrusted the administration to a fellow monk and conferred upon the latter the honorary title, when he moved his seat to Lhasa. Later, in view of the tutor-disciple relationship existing in turn through generations between the Dalai and the Panch'en, the fifth Dalai Lama awarded this monastery to the fourth Panch'en Lama. If this age-old practice were to be continuously observed, all Tibetans would be only too pleased.
>
>Question: How shall the Dalai welcome the Panch'en back to Tibet and how shall the Central Government escort him?
>
>Answer: Among the Panch'en's retinue, many employed the terms "anterior" and "ulterior" Tibet with intent to sow discord. They disobeyed orders of the Tibetan government and acted frequently against their superiors. Both their thought and conduct are corrupt. In the year Chia Ch'en (1904), the Panch'en went to India and conspired with the British, but all his efforts were of no avail. In the year Hsin Hai (1911) he intrigued with the Resident (Chinese) Lien-yu and made an attempt to seize the reins of government and control of the church

during the absence of the Dalai Lama. But his efforts were thwarted by the opposition of the people and especially the clergymen of the three leading monasteries. According to established practice, the Panch'en should contribute one quarter of the provision for the Army. Not only did he fail to make such contributions, but also committed acts in violation of law. Had the offenders been punished strictly in accordance with the letter of the law, there would have been no such state of affairs as now exists. It is only in consideration of the long-standing and close tutor-disciple relationship between the Dalai and the Panch'en through generations that a policy of tolerance and forgiveness has been followed. Yet these people not only remained unrepentant, but further advised and urged the Panch'en to flee away from Tashilhunpo. A dispatch inviting him back was sent to the Panch'en, but he refused to accept. He then fled to Urga and had secret dealings with the communists. Only upon the death of the Chief Lama of Mongolia, Che-putsuntanpa, was he obliged to come to China proper. Consequently, the Tibetan government dispatched officials to Tashilhunpo to take proper care of the monastery. Now these offenders are still conspiring and making trouble. As the matter stands, Tibet would find it very difficult to welcome them unless they can give satisfactory explanation as to their reason for taking to flight.[27]

The unexpected death of the Panchen Lama in 1937 as he was en route from China to Tibet resolved the long-standing problem, and prevented what would likely have been armed resistance by Tibetans to his return. The Panchen Lama had been in exile in Peking since his hasty departure in 1923, but with the death of the thirteenth Dalai Lama in 1933 the Chinese are believed to have decided to force the return of the Panchen Lama, thereby undermining the Tibetan government from within. As negotiations for his return proceeded, the Tibetan authorities said that the Panchen should make no attempt to enter Lhasa. Then they declared that "no official deputation would be sent to welcome the Panch'en Lama to Tibet, nor was there any intention of doing so in the foreseeable future."[28] When the Chinese chose to ignore these obvious hints, the Tibetans formed plans calling for armed resistance to his return, and moved their limited forces into positions along the border to intercept the Panch'en Lama and his retinue. His sudden death, reportedly from pneumonia, as he neared the border reduced tensions and, for a time, eliminated what had become a serious source of friction. (The role and fate of the tenth Panchen Lama vis-à-vis the fourteenth Dalai Lama and the PRC is told in Chapter 12.)

To return to the period immediately following the rebellion in China, the new Chinese government did not agree at all that Tibet was to be free. The Presidential Order by Yuan Shih-kai that Tibet was to be regarded as on an equal footing with the other Provinces of China was in contradiction to the declarations of Sun Yat-sen that the non–Han territories should have the right of self-determination, with those wanting to be part of China being welcome and those choosing not to be then left to govern themselves. But Yuan Shih-kai's order totally ignored Sun Yat-sen, and Tibetan autonomy was thus swept away. All previous admissions and promises were fully and frankly broken.

The British feared that this might prompt Tibet to seek assistance from Mongolia and possibly through Mongolia from Russia.[29] The nervous British again agreed to open negotiations with China.

As a backdrop to the discussions at Simla, "At the end of 1912, Russia concluded an agreement with Mongolia by which Russia agreed to assist in the preservation of Mongolian autonomy and in return obtained economic and political privileges." Towards the end of 1913 there was another agreement concluded between Russia and China by which the Russians acknowledged Chinese suzerainty over Mongolia and in return the Chinese recognized the autonomy of Mongolia, adding they would refrain from colonization and military occupation. In January 1913 there was a treaty between Mongolia and Tibet and under its terms the two countries agreed to aid each other. Aid by Mongolia might have meant aid by Russian troops. Russian rifles had already been coming into Lhasa by the well-established ancient Urga (Ulan Bator)–Lhasa route. Britain was frightened and attempted to establish Chinese suzerainty over Tibet once again. According to the Tibetan Prime Minister Lonchen Shatra, "The Dalai Lama wanted Tibet to manage her own internal affairs, to have no Chinese Amban, no other Chinese officials and no Chinese soldiers in Tibet; only Chinese traders could come in and lastly, Tibet was to include Nyarong, Derge, Bathang, Lithang and the country as far as Tachienlu, the districts (in eastern Tibet) that had been snatched away by the Chinese during the last two hundred years. The National Tibetan Assembly even desired the posting of a representative of the Indian Government at Lhasa."[30]

Tibetan, British and Chinese plenipotentiaries met at Simla in October 1913.

> Lonchen Shatra, the Tibetan plenipotentiary, brought with him loads of documents bearing on the Tibetan relationship with China during the past few centuries and repudiating the Chinese claim to Tibetan provinces and districts which China had militarily occupied from time to time. The Chinese plenipotentiary, I Fan-chen, had little evidence to oppose the loads of register, laws, executive orders, tax accounts, bonds of allegiance, militia lists, etc., that proved clearly and decisively the claim of Lhasa to rule their own countrymen. Sir Henry McMahon, the Indian Foreign Department Secretary, served as the British plenipotentiary. It was he who would play the leading role in guiding deliberations and arriving at decisions. The discussions extended over six months, and it was on the 27th April 1914 that the Convention was initialled by the three plenipotentiaries. According to its provision Tibet was divided into two zones: the zone contiguous to China was styled Inner Tibet, the zone far removed from China but contiguous to Inner Tibet was styled Outer Tibet. It is Outer Tibet whose southern boundary formed the northern boundary of India. (The eastern part of this boundary is the McMahon Line.)
>
> The division of Tibet into two zones has a parallel in the two zones of Mongolia, Inner Mongolia and Outer Mongolia. Inner Mongolia is that part of Mongolia which is contiguous with China. Like Inner Tibet, Inner Mongolia has been absorbed as a province of China. Chinese officials and troops are aided by Chinese colonists in progressively converting Inner Tibet and Inner Mongolia into Chinese territories.

The British and the Chinese had this parallel before them. So they provided in the Convention that Inner Tibet was to be a free region for Chinese troops and colonists. Lhasa would retain only the control of the monasteries and would be allowed to appoint local chiefs. Keeping Outer Mongolia in mind, they provided for autonomy of Outer Tibet, allowing the Chinese suzerainty over Outer Tibet but not allowing her to station troops or establish colonies.

In the case of Outer Mongolia, Russia was able to exert her influence to the extent of ousting China altogether. Now Outer Mongolia is an independent sovereign state.

The provisions of the Convention were only initialed by the three plenipotentiaries. Two days after, on 29 April, 1914, the Chinese government disowned the action of her plenipotentiary. China's disowning was caused by disagreement on the borderline between China and Inner Tibet, as established in 1727.

The breakdown of the Convention gave the Tibetans freedom from the grip of the British and the Chinese. In March 1919 the Chinese proposed the resumption of negotiations initiated at Simla. But the Tibetan government rejected all Chinese proposals, and no discussions were held. From 1912 onward there had been no Chinese Amban at Lhasa and the government of Tibet had stopped referring its affairs to Peking.[31]

Feelings between Tibet and China were strong and the respective position papers presented at the Simla conference made it clear that there would be no truly satisfactory solution. In her paper, Tibet recounted the numerous incidents caused by the Chinese when, in 1903–1904, under the guise of bringing soldiers into Tibet to protect Tibet, the soldiers "picked unnecessary quarrels with the people on the road, and robbed and destroyed villages and monasteries without provocation ... [and] on their arrival at Lhasa, without any consideration for any agreements either verbal or in writing, they killed and wounded Tibetan officials ... [and] they violated the treaties and forcibly took possession of all powers from the Tibetans ... [and] killed and robbed the people in U and Tsang and destroyed their houses and property ... [and] attacked the monastery of Sera without any provocation, set fire to the city of Lhasa ... [and] tried their best to destroy the upper and lower Palaces (the Potala and Norbulingka), the Cathedral (Jokhang) and other places held sacred by Tibetans ... [and] the Chinese officers and troops, devoid of shame as a nation, came to Kham where they set fire to many monasteries and many thousands of houses of our subjects, killed the people and robbed them of their property. Tibet and China have never been under each other and will never associate with each other in the future. It is decided that Tibet is an independent State and the precious Protector, the Dalai Lama, is the Ruler of Tibet, in all temporal as well as in spiritual affairs. Tibet repudiates the Anglo-Chinese Convention concluded at Peking on 27 April 1906 ... as she did not send a representative for this Convention nor did she affix her seal on it. It is therefore decided it is not binding on the three Governments.... In future no Chinese officials and troops will be allowed to stay in Tibet. Their staying there is only an expense to the Chinese, who obtain no revenue from Tibet. In order therefore to ensure peace between the two countries in future no Chinese Amban or other officials and no Chinese soldiers or colonists will be permitted to enter or reside in Tibet."³²

The Chinese in turn presented their views:

> What sacrifices China has made in money and lives for the sake of protecting the Tibetans and their territory! ... but the Tibetans aggravated the situation by their brutal murder of Amban Fung and many Chinese officials, who were skinned to death. From what has been related it is evident the claims presented in the Tibetan statement are inadmissible, and in answer to them the following demands are made as the only basis for the negotiation of the Tibetan question:
>
> (i) It is hereby agreed by the undersigned that Tibet forms an integral part of the territory of the Republic of China, that no attempts shall be made by Tibet or Great Britain to interrupt the continuity of this territorial integrity, and that China's rights of every description which have existed in consequence of this territorial integrity shall be respected by Tibet and recognized by Great Britain. The Republic of China engages not to convert Tibet into a Chinese province, and Great Britain engages not to annex Tibet or any portion of it.
>
> (ii) The Republic of China has the right of appointing a Resident to reside at Lhasa ... he is entitled to have an escort of 2,600 Chinese soldiers...
>
> (iii) Tibet undertakes to be guided by China in her foreign and military affairs and not to enter into negotiation with any foreign Powers except through the intermediary of the Chinese Government....
>
> (iv) Tibet agrees to grant an amnesty to all those Tibetan officials and people who have been imprisoned by the Tibetan authorities merely on account of their well-known sympathy for the Chinese and also to restore to them all [their] property.
>
> (vii) The frontier boundary between China Proper and Tibet is now roughly indicated in the accompanying map (this map placed the boundary point a mere hundred miles from Lhasa).³³

Although the charade of negotiations continued for some six months, with little or no real belief on the part of either China or Tibet that a satisfactory agreement would result, the British concern that its position and influence in the area not be damaged was the engine driving the talks. Both China and Tibet were politically and militarily weak during this period; thus the collapse of the talks did not poorly serve either, other than to harden their respective positions.

The following fairly describes the situation at the time and at least some of the problems that would continue between Tibet and China for the next few decades. "The Chinese Government, however, did not for a moment regard Tibet as anything but an integral part of the Empire. Not only was there in Tibet a powerful section of the Lamas who wanted to have cordial relations with China, the rivalry between the thirteenth Dalai Lama and the ninth Panchen Lama which came to a showdown in 1924 gave the Chinese munitions of interference. The Panchen fled (in 1924) with his court to China where he lived until his death in 1937. Since 1924 the Panchen Lama has been traditionally an ally of China and an instrument of China's Tibetan policy."³⁴

As for Great Britain and Tibet, the British maintained extraterritorial powers in the trade marts, control over the lines of communication between the trade marts and the Indian border, and access to all of Tibet for British and Indian traders. There was also the agreement that moved the Indo-Tibetan border from the foothills of the Himalayas to their crests, creating the large segment called the Northeast Frontier Agency, now known as Arunchal Pradesh. Most of the other boundary delineations in the area, identified as the McMahon Line, remain contested by China.

The Dalai Lama recognized upon his return to Tibet in 1913 that he needed to control the internal threats to his government as well as the external ones. He understood that to do this he needed to have both an effective and supportive government as well as an effective military capability. Without both, he realized that Tibet could not withstand China's political threats or those posed by the surprising numbers — although still a minority — of high-ranking lamas and bureaucrats who had by their actions indicated their willingness to align themselves with China.

"Before 1913, all of Tibet had only about 3,000 regular troops. These were a sorry lot, untrained in modern techniques, with out-of-date arms; moreover, many of the soldiers were old and infirm.... More often than not, however, these 'taxpayer' serfs hired substitutes to serve their obligations."[35] Plans were made to retire the unfit and to recruit and train young and fit soldiers, led by able officers recruited from the middle and upper classes, to a new level of 4,000 soldiers, and to increase this number gradually to some 10,000 — and then to 15,000 and possibly more — if the British would help by providing weapons and training. Maintaining the force even at the lower numbers posed a financial burden, for the tax base was limited. In the interim, the British finally agreed in 1914 to provide 5,000 new rifles and a half a million rounds of ammunition that were eventually used effectively in driving the Chinese from the positions they had gained in attacking areas in Kham in 1917. Repeated requests by Tibet to the British for machine guns and other more powerful weapons (mortars, etc.) were initially refused, even though the British officers most closely involved with the Tibetans supported the idea. "This response reveals a fundamental British ambivalence towards Tibet that persisted until the end of the Lamaist State in 1951. British officers on the spot were always highly sympathetic to the needs and concerns of the Tibetan government; the government of India in Delhi was less concerned; and His Majesty's Government in London generally cited strategic interests that were more important than Tibet's."[36]

"Interest in Tibet languished during the First World War. The country's eastern marches were still under military pressure from China, but the Dalai Lama, mindful of the kindness he had been shown in India, offered a thousand soldiers to fight on the British side against Germany. The offer was declined, but throughout the war special services to invoke divine aid for

Britain's cause were held in the main monasteries of Tibet. This was not a perfunctory gesture. These services were a charge, and not a light one, on public funds, and the Tibetans believed firmly in their efficacy and importance — so much so, indeed, that the Dalai Lama privately transferred to, as it were, the British account a number of services ostensibly held on behalf of the Tibetan government."[37]

As remarked earlier, both Tibet and China were less than strong during this period, yet China remained intent on bringing Tibet to heel and did not hesitate to attempt to take advantage of any perceived military, political or religious weakness on the part of the Tibetans. Even during the 1930s, when she was beset by the Japanese — and the beginning of the military threat from the Chinese communists — the Republic of China continued to try to gain more geography from, and political and religious influence in, Tibet. The Dalai Lama became intent on modernizing Tibet, at least in those areas of government where it was abundantly clear that Tibet was very weak, and looked to England for assistance. "Insofar as Tibet was subject to any foreign influence, she was subject to Britain's. Tibetan youths went to school in India — four even went to England; the Tibetan army was trained and equipped on British lines, and was soon able to hold its own against the Chinese in the fighting which flickered on in eastern Tibet."[38]

However, Tibet was beset by political problems that involved ecclesiastical and civil matters, as well as military. The latter impacted the other two, caused at least in part by the strong support the Dalai Lama gave to reorganizing and strengthening Tibet's weak army. The new military commanders believed that Tibet's army, even as ineffective a force as it had previously been, not the prayers of monks or negotiations by civil servants, had made it possible for the Dalai Lama to return to Tibet in 1912. "Relatively young, energetic, and modern in their attitude, this new breed of Tibetan soldier possessed an esprit de corps unique in Tibet. However, because they were committed to modernization, others considered them to be a threat to the religious domination of the Gelugpa (Yellow Hats) State. Ostentatious in their adoption of Western (British) uniforms, dress and customs such as sweet tea, shaking hands, and playing tennis and polo, and generally secular in orientation and demeanor, the commanders appeared to challenge the very essence of the monastery-dominated political system.... The apparent unity of purpose and camaraderie of the military commanders made them an extraordinarily dangerous force in Tibetan politics. Although not a political party in the normal sense, they shared the view that the ultraconservative monks had brought Tibet to its knees in the past and would do so again unless the central government developed its own power."[39]

Increasingly opposing this revitalization of Tibet's army were the monks and the government officials. The very strong monastic view was that Tibet's military only served to draw resources that otherwise should go to themselves and the furtherance of Tibetan Buddhism. Civil officials saw the military as bringing in foreign practices and ideologies that might change the government of Tibet. Both entities saw the new military program as becoming stronger as an entity and thus a potential threat to what each had long enjoyed under the theocratic state. Neither of these two factions would publicly acknowledge that an effective army would serve as a real benefit to Tibet, and both began to undermine wherever and whenever they could the Dalai Lama's intention to further modernize and strengthen Tibet's army. Both also expressed concerns and complained regularly about the costs of the proposed expansion of the army and the economic hardships that would result, disregarding entirely that the proposed buildup to the figure of a 15-to-20,000-man army was to be reached over a twenty-year period and at a rate of 500 new recruits per year.

Between 1922 and 1925 the British sold the Tibetans "… 10 mountain guns, 20 Lewis guns, and 10,000 rifles with ammunition. Moreover, 4 officers and over 300 noncommissioned officers received military training in Gyantse … [and] 4 officers and 20 noncommissioned officers received training in the use of mountain guns in India; and others were trained as armorers, and in gunnery, infantry, and cavalry work…. The British provided technical assistance in building a telegraph line between Lhasa and Gyantse, and some Tibetan youths were trained as telegraphers. Machinery for a 40,000-rupee hydroelectric plant was purchased from England, and work on the plant began. A survey for mineral wealth was conducted in Tibet by an Englishman, and an English school was started in Gyantse in 1924 with several dozen aristocrats' sons in attendance. And a Sikkimese police officer from Darjeeling was hired to establish a modern police force in Lhasa."[40]

But behind these promising scenarios of modernization all was not well. The monasteries and the civil servants were openly critical of the money being invested in the "westernization" of Tibet, citing the poverty and limited resources of Tibet to pay for such "luxuries" and seriously worried that there would be less money available to them. And the military and police forces were not in harmony, each believing that the other was being paid and outfitted better. There were incidents between the two, just as there were confrontations between the army and monks, especially those of Drepung Monastery who remained strongly supportive of a large Chinese presence in Tibet, and between the police and monks with it not unlikely that certain lamas and high ranking civil servants were behind at least some of the "incidents" that occurred at the time. That the jealousies were increasing and the support of the Dalai Lama for modernization was decreasing was evident to all. A letter dated August 26, 1927, from a Tibetan official to the British political officer in Sikkim described the decline as follows: "The military are drilling daily but their uniforms are practically all torn, many of them have got one boot on one foot and the other is naked and they always beg me whenever I pass

Norbulingka and Chenselinga (in Lhasa). The police are about 100 in number and they are worse than the military. I find everyone either in the police or military desire to run away from here if can manage to do so."[41] Sadly, the Dalai Lama's decision to weaken the military and to retreat from the program of modernization only played into the hands of China and the British policy in the area, which was based primarily on its fear of China.

On December 17, 1933, at age 58, the thirteenth Dalai Lama, as he had predicted a year earlier, died in Lhasa after a brief illness. For seventeen years after his death, "Tibet was ruled by two regents. This period was characterized by a preoccupation with internal political affairs and intrigues which, to a significant degree, consumed the vitality of the political and monastic elite."[42] Sadly, Tibet's fate was already cast, due in part to the nearsightedness and cowardice of both Britain and India, as well as, and substantially, the self-centered and pious attitudes of those Tibetans, especially the lamas, who failed to put Tibet's needs above their own. There were many leading Tibetans, religious and government figures alike, who shared and supported the visions of the thirteenth Dalai Lama to improve and secure Tibet, but they were too few in number to overcome those who chose to pursue courses of action that would lead only to the detriment of their country's future. Unfortunately for Tibet, and as clearly predicted by the thirteenth Dalai Lama, there was far more tragedy to come.

At the death of the thirteenth Dalai Lama, the Chinese government informed the Tibetan government that they wished to send an official mission to Lhasa to convey their condolences and to make appropriate ceremonial offerings. The Kashag wanted to deny them entry, but in response to the strenuous objections of the monastic segment, the Kashag agreed to convene the National Assembly to discuss the issue. The dominant opinion among government officials in the assembly was that under no circumstances should the Chinese be granted permission to enter Tibet. The monastic segment emphatically disagreed, arguing that the proposed Chinese visit was purely religious. They contended that the Chinese would be religious pilgrims and that Tibet, a Buddhist country, could not refuse them permission to pay their condolences. As was usual in the assembly, the monastic viewpoint dominated. As can be seen from the following report of the *Times of London*'s correspondent in Shanghai, the Chinese view of this mission was clearly political: "It is reported from Nanking that the leading Lamas and people of Tibet welcomed the proposed dispatch of a Chinese High Commissioner to Lhasa and will continue to be loyal to the Chinese Government. The Tashi (Panch'en) Lama who fled from Tibet several years ago and has since been a highly honoured guest in this country is being consulted by the Government with a view to the restoration of China's influence in Tibet."[43]

Some of the other dire predictions made in 1932 by the thirteenth Dalai Lama were also beginning to emerge. He had warned that the lessons of the past were to be well remembered and used wisely as a guide for the future, but those responsible for Tibet remained in near total disagreement and turmoil, thereby weakening Tibet to the point that its government began to border on helplessness.

CHAPTER 2

The Imperialist Invasions

In November 1949 only some seven weeks after the People's Republic of China was formally inaugurated, Radio Peking announced that the tenth Panchen Lama had appealed to Mao Tse-tung to "liberate Tibet from the imperialists." That the twelve-year-old tenth Panchen Lama had lived in China since his birth and never traveled outside of China since the Chinese selected and declared him to be the reincarnation of the ninth Panchen Lama only made the obvious fig leafs of political deceit and propaganda that much more evident. However, in Tibet, the Regent, the Kashag (Cabinet), and the National Assembly understood and were all but paralyzed by the blatant threat. The Dalai Lama was but 14, some four years short of the age when he was expected to assume his dual role as head of the theocratic state. Since early 1949 there had been increasing numbers of reports received in Lhasa regarding elements of the soldiers of the People's Liberation Army prowling along the borders of and into Amdo and Kham in eastern and northeastern Tibet and of skirmishes in those areas between the Tibetan tribals and Chinese soldiers. However, Lhasa had attached little significance to them, for it was not uncommon for clashes to occur between the Chinese and the Khambas in eastern Tibet, and such events in Kham were not very important to Lhasa. But this broadcast was different. It obviously was a declaration by the People's Republic of China of its intention to soon invade and occupy Tibet with large numbers of Chinese soldiers, spearheaded by combat-experienced elements of the People's Liberation Army. And Lhasa would be directly impacted, not just the border areas.

In the minds of most Tibetans the reasons given by the Chinese in these radio announcements for the invasion were quite silly, even ridiculous, for there were no "imperialists" in Tibet; in fact, there were hardly any foreigners in Lhasa, only a very few, perhaps a dozen or two, mostly the few Indians, British and Nepalese posted to Tibet by their respective governments and the German, Heinrich Harrer, who everyone in the area knew had served only as a special tutor to the young Dalai Lama. The question on the streets of Lhasa was basically, "How could anyone label this small, disparate grouping of foreigners as an imperialist force?" And the broadcast also ignored other very basic points: the tenth Panchen Lama was younger than the fourteenth Dalai

Lama and had never been in Tibet; he had been selected by the Chinese, not the Tibetans, and had been raised in China; thus he knew nothing about Tibet. The Panchen Lama had no authority in Tibet and could not speak for Tibet since the Regent and the Kashag were responsible for the affairs of state until the fourteenth Dalai Lama, not the Panchen Lama, was enthroned as the spiritual and secular power at age 18. How could the Chinese think that the Panchen Lama would have any authority in Tibet beyond the little that previous Panchen Lamas had been allowed in Shigatse, the historically designated locale of the Panchen Lama? Even the majority of the lamas who had previously supported the idea of a Chinese presence in Tibet became increasingly concerned, for the stories that had reached Lhasa from eastern Tibet and western China about the harsh practices of Mao's Chinese Communists were ominous. Recalling the warnings by the thirteenth Dalai Lama, Tibet rapidly became a very troubled land, for the Chinese ploy to use the Panchen Lama was easily transparent. Although Peking's surprise announcement had little impact on the outside world — except for India, which must have recognized what China intended — it was seen as a fearful warning in the minds of most of the Tibetan government officials and the people.

The dire prophecies of the thirteenth Dalai Lama in regard to Tibet's future and that of her people were indeed soon to become fact, and Tibet was ill-prepared to handle them.

The thirteenth Dalai Lama's "Political Last Testament," written shortly before his death, warned that Tibet faced the danger of a Communist takeover and the destruction of her religion, such as had befallen Outer Mongolia. His testament became a major policy statement for the entire interregnum period:

> You must develop a good diplomatic relationship with our two powerful neighbors: India and China. Efficient and well-equipped troops must be stationed even on the minor frontiers bordering hostile forces. Such an army must be well trained in warfare as a sure deterrent against any adversaries.
>
> Furthermore, this present era is rampant with the five forms of degeneration, in particular the "red" ideology. In Outer Mongolia, the search for a (the Grand Lama of Urga) was banned; the monastic properties and endowments were confiscated; the lamas and the monks were forced into the army; the Buddhist religion destroyed, leaving no trace of identity. Such a system, according to reports still being received, has been established in Ulan Bator (the capital of Outer Mongolia). In the future, this system will certainly be forced either from within or without on this land that cherishes the joint spiritual and temporal system. If, in such an event, we fail to defend our land, the holy lamas, including the "triumphant father and son" [the Dalai Lama and the Panchen Lama] will be eliminated without a trace of their names remaining; the properties of the incarnate lamas and the monasteries along with the endowments for religious services will all be seized. Moreover, our political system, originated by the three ancient kings, will be reduced to an empty name; my officials, deprived of their patrimony and property, will be subjugated like slaves by the enemy; and my people, subjected to fear and miseries, will be unable to endure day or night. Such an era will certainly come.

> At the present time, when we enjoy peace and happiness as well as the admiration of others, inerrable common cause of religion and polity still remains in our hands. The political stability depends on the devotion of the ecclesiastic and secular officials and upon their ability to employ skillfully every diplomatic and military means without any possibility of regret or failure in the future.[1]

Unfortunately, the interim government had done little over the years since the death of the thirteenth Dalai Lama in December 1933 to prepare Tibet and Tibetans for what they were to face over the next decades, nor had there been political stability. The threat posed by the anticipated but unwanted return of the ninth Panchen Lama in 1937 had motivated the lay officials to move again towards upgrading the status of the Tibetan military, especially after alert Tibetan border guards intercepted an advance shipment of goods sent by the ninth Panchen Lama from China and discovered it contained large amounts of rifles, hand grenades and ammunition. In response to the protest note sent him by the Tibetan government about these weapons, the Panchen Lama simply but strongly protested the seizure of his arms.[2]

At this time in eastern Tibet about 10,000 regular and militia troops in roughly 20 detachments occupied the border area, "with about 5,000 good Lee-Enfield .303 rifles and 6 Lewis guns. The militia had a motley collection of other foreign guns and old Tibetan rifles. They had no machine guns.... In Lhasa, there were only the 600 troops of the Bodyguard Regiment, 400 armed police, and 300 soldiers from regiments stationed in Kham who were learning to use mountain guns. There were 6 mountain guns in Lhasa, 2 good Lewis guns, and 5,000 modern rifles with the Bodyguard Regiment. The Tibetan government had about 4,000 new rifles in the armory as well as 4 machine guns. A few regular troops were stationed on the Nepal border; all the other districts, including those bordering on Ladakh, were defended entirely by militias with ancient matchlock rifles."[3]

In 1936 a British brigadier in Tibet gave the following summary of the state of the Tibetan military: "It is clearly apparent that the Tibetans as a nation are absolutely unmilitary, all their thoughts and energies are devoted to their religious life. The Tibetan government has absolutely no idea of military organization, administration or training. The military authorities, even if they had the knowledge, have no power to apply it. These troops are untrained, unreliable, and unpopular with the country. The Tibetan official hierarchy are quite indiscriminately pitchforked into civil or military jobs regardless of their qualifications. No regular soldier of experience can rise beyond the rank of Rupon, a lower grade of commissioned officer. In fact, it is justifiable to say that, except for the fact that they possess a certain number of modern weapons, the army has advanced but little from its condition in 1904."[4]

Despite this grim review, British advisors in Tibet made repeated recommendations that the Tibetan army be upgraded, much along the lines the thirteenth Dalai Lama had originally intended. However, there was still considerable opposition, not only from the monastics in Lhasa but from the Indian Foreign and Political Department as well. By this time Tibet owed India 600,000 rupees for arms and ammunition previously provided, and so India asked British support for requiring cash payments for any further military supplies provided Tibet. In addition, the Indian Foreign and Political Department noted: "We are by no means satisfied that it is in India's interest to have a well-trained, well-armed and highly organized army in Tibet. Such an army might encourage the Lhasa Government to undertake adventures on the Tibetan-Chinese frontier which would cause further complications, and, if we bring such an army into existence, we shall be committed not only to continual inspections on the military side but also to some responsibility for control of Tibet's foreign policy."[5] Earlier reports to London from India had noted that: "(a) [the] Regent and Kashag are incapable of taking [a] strong line about anything or of following any consistent policy except of waiting on events ... [and] ... (b) [the] Tibetan army required complete reorganization and elaborate training before it could be regarded as of any military value even if additional armament now asked for is supplied."[6]

In January 1937 the Kashag advised the British of its decision to decline the offer of military assistance, "with due acknowledgement and with regret that preoccupations on the eastern frontier necessitate its postponement for the time being."[7]

"The issue was never again raised during Reting's regency. (Reting had become Regent following the death of the 13th Dalai Lama). The legacy of the military-monastery conflicts of the early 1920s still cast its shadow over Tibetan politics. Tibetans made excellent troops when properly led and armed, but the political implications of a modern and efficient army continued to threaten the religious elite and precluded the development of such a force. The Tibetan government continued purposely to maintain an ineffective army."[8]

In the summer of 1936 the Tibetan National Assembly finally approved the sending of three search teams to the East to locate the "new" (fourteenth) Dalai Lama. The assembly made its decision despite concerns that should the new Dalai Lama be found in Chinese territory it could provide the Chinese with unwanted leverage in Tibet. More important than these concerns were the interpretations of various signs and visions that pointed eastward. Three state oracles had, while in trance, on numerous occasions clearly indicated that the new Dalai Lama was to be found in the East. Also, following the death of the thirteenth Dalai Lama, his body had been placed in state on a throne facing south, but twice attendants found his head turned toward the East.[9]

In 1937 the fourteenth Dalai Lama was located in Taktse in Amdo province, which was then controlled by Ma Pu-feng, the Chinese Nationalist and Moslem warlord who commanded the Tsinghai area from his headquarters in Sining. The son of farming parents, born in July 1935, the young candidate passed all tests conducted by the search team without flaw, leaving no doubt in the minds of each of the members of the team that indeed, they had located the fourteenth Dalai Lama. The problem facing them was to gain his release for the return to Lhasa. The large and nearby Kumbum Monastery was not able to provide much help, even though the oldest brother of the newfound Dalai Lama was already at the monastery as a reincarnation of a previous high deity there.

Ma Pu-feng controlled all travel in the area. Despite the efforts of the search team to not let him know that they had located the fourteenth Dalai Lama, Gen. Ma Pu-feng first demanded 100,000 silver coins (equivalent to 7,000 to 8,000 pounds sterling), then later raised the ante an additional 300,000 silver coins to allow the departure of the newfound Dalai Lama for Lhasa. The tests, and the long negotiations of the demands by General Ma — and those of the Kumbum monastery — and the communications with Lhasa which took months to complete, resulted in delays. It was July 1939 before the return trip to Lhasa began. Moslem traders, who had also provided the ransom money demanded by General Ma, served as bodyguards for the travelers. On August 23, the full National Assembly declared the Taktse boy to be the fourteenth Dalai Lama, and he and the search party arrived in Lhasa on October 8, 1939. The enthronement ceremony, dictated by astrological calculations, took place on February 22, 1940, with both Chinese and British dignitaries in attendance.[10]

During this period China's war against the ruthless Japanese invader was not going well, and Japanese successes included the severing of most of China's traditional supply routes. After consulting with the British in Chungking, Chiang Kai-shek "issued orders in February 1941 to begin construction of a motorable highway from southwest Szechuan Province through southeast Tibet to the NEFA (Northeast Frontier Agency) border."[11] Such a road would have taken a very long time to complete under the best of circumstances and would not have solved China's supply problem, but unlike British views from New Delhi, London did not oppose the idea, fearing that a collapse of China would mean a much longer war for the Allies against Japan. New Delhi noted that China should also gain Tibet's support and approval, which it had not done. The Chinese belatedly informed the Tibetan government of its intention to build such a road, but the Tibetans, in keeping with their established policy, refused permission and ordered their border officials to turn back any Chinese survey parties. Reportedly Tibetans killed the head of one such party.[12] In February 1942 China, India and Britain agreed to build what became famous as the Ledo road from Assam in India to northern Burma to Yunnan Province in China. And Tibet again notified China, India and Britain that Tibetan territory was not to be violated. Tibet also advised the British that it intended to remain neutral in the war, a stance that the British had earlier urged Tibet to take. Interestingly, in the spring of 1943, the Chinese advised the British "of reports of Tibet's aggressive intentions toward China and of unconfirmed rumors that the Japanese were sending munitions to Tibet and were preparing airfields in Kham (in eastern Tibet) for Japanese aircraft."[13] Tibet then complied with Britain's formal request to give official assurances to China that the rumors were false and that Tibet did not intend to attack China.

In 1942 the U.S. Office of Strategic Services (OSS) proposed to send two intelligence officers to Tibet to survey the terrain and then to proceed to China to join General Stillwell. Initially the Chinese were asked by the U.S. to gain approval from the Tibetans, but this request was rejected by the Tibetans. The request for permission was then made to the British in New Delhi, and the head of the British Mission in Lhasa gained the approval from the Tibetan Foreign Affairs Bureau. Captain Ilia Tolstoy and Lt. Brooke Dolan arrived in Lhasa in December 1942 with gifts (assessed by the British as being too inexpensive to impress the Tibetans) and a letter dated July 3, 1942, from President Roosevelt to the Dalai Lama:

> Your HOLINESS:
>
> Two of my fellow countrymen, Ilia Tolstoy and Brooke Dolan, hope to visit your Pontificate and the historic and widely famed city of Lhasa. There are in the United States of America many persons, among them myself, who, ... greatly interested in your land and people, would highly value such an opportunity.
>
> As you know, the people of the United States, in association with those of twenty-seven other countries, are now engaged in a war which has been thrust upon the world by nations bent on conquest who are intent upon destroying freedom of thought, of religion, and of action everywhere. The United Nations are fighting today in defense of and for preservation of freedom, confident that we shall be victorious because our cause is just, our capacity is adequate, and our determination is unshakable.
>
> I am asking Ilia Tolstoy and Brooke Dolan to convey to you a little gift in token of friendly sentiment toward you.
>
> With cordial greetings,
> Franklin D. Roosevelt[14]

Tolstoy's remarks to Tibetan officials — that he would recommend to his government "that Tibet be represented at the Peace Conference at the end of the war, and that the U.S. government was in full sympathy with weak and small countries that wished to retain their independence" — excited the Tibetan Foreign Affairs Bureau and the Kashag. In turn Tibetan officials urged that America support Britain in her effort to maintain Tibet's independence. The British viceroy of India was furious about the remarks by Tolstoy and those of the British political officer in Sikkim supporting Tolstoy's view. In a note to the Secretary of State for India in London he commented, "I regard with apprehension amateur efforts of two Americans who have recently been in Lhasa. Indications indeed are that they are impressed with Tibetan claim for autonomy, but suggestion ... that Tibet should be represented at Peace Conference seems to me strangely inept.... American enlightenment in matters

Tibetan may come in due course, but I would judge it unsound that we from here should attempt to hasten [the] process."[15]

Also in the spring of 1943 London officialdom began to rethink its China and Tibet policies. A May 1943 letter from the India Office, London, to the Foreign Office, London, noted in part: "Chinese plans and propaganda for a post-war settlement in the Far East aim at securing independence from British rule for such territories as India, Burma and Malaya. The real motive, so far as the two latter are concerned, is undoubtedly to clear the ground for Chinese political and economic domination, which the people of regions would be in position to resist if left to themselves. The Chinese are the least sentimental and altruistic of nations but they are shrewd propagandists and have been clever enough to present their aspirations as an unselfish desire to secure for their neighbours the same freedom from foreign imperialism that they themselves desire. Chiang Kai-shek has said that 'China has infinite sympathy for the submerged nations of Asia, and toward them she has only responsibilities, not rights.' ... The Atlantic Charter is invoked on behalf of the British, Dutch and French colonies; but when it comes to Tibet and Mongolia, who have successfully emancipated themselves from Chinese domination, it would seem that the case is different. We are expected to accept an ex parte statement that these territories form part of the Chinese republic, and that any tendency to contest this would be offensive to the Chinese.... I see no reason why the Chinese should be allowed to get away with it as easily as that."[16]

The brief period that such noble thoughts were given serious consideration by the British quickly gave way to the continuation of their old policy, which conceded that while Tibet was an autonomous state it was under the suzerainty of China. Britain's Prime Minister Anthony Eden confirmed this to T. V. Soong, China's Foreign Minister, in a memorandum dated August 5, 1943, in which the main concern was the question of the boundary areas (McMahon Line) that had remained unresolved since the Chinese-Tibetan-British convention of 1914. Because the memorandum noted that Great Britain considered Tibet to be part of China, the Chinese were satisfied and did not bother to respond to it.[17]

In a joint press release in Chungking on June 24, 1944, Chiang Kai-shek and U.S. Vice President Henry Wallace recognized "the fundamental right of presently dependent Asiatic peoples to self-government, and the early adoption of measures in the political, economic and social fields to prepare those dependent peoples for self-government within a specified practical time limit."[18] In turn, the Kashag, prompted by the comments of Tolstoy and Dolan when they were in Lhasa in 1943, asked for British "... help in giving Tibet a voice in the postwar peace conference ... in order that [the] whole world may be aware that Tibet is autonomous ... and that [the] Tibet government desires help of His Majesty's Government in order to send a Tibetan delegation to the postwar peace conference."[19]

Tibet's hopes that the British would intercede on her behalf, or would at least agree to be her political protector against China, proved illusory. Although Tibet had been discouraged by the British to take any meaningful role in World War II, now London advised the Tibetans that they could not be considered as participants in the postwar peace conference because Tibet had not participated in the war. Although Tibet had rejected an early invitation from the Japanese to "join the Great East Asia Co-Prosperity Sphere" and to provide Japan religious (Buddhist prayer) support; and had warmly received and assisted the American OSS mission (including the promise to assist in rescuing any Allied pilots and crewmen downed in Tibet); and had fought the Chinese Communists in eastern Tibet as early as 1934; and had publicly supported the British; Tibet received no credits. Thus her orphan status was again underscored.

The Tibetans had repeatedly told the British that as long as Chiang Kai-shek was occupied fighting the Japanese that Tibet would not be invaded by the Chinese army, although skirmishes between Tibetans and Chinese along China's western border were to be expected. This had proved to be a correct estimate. As late as August 25, 1945, Generalissimo Chiang Kai-shek was forced to grant that "if and when the Tibetans attain the stage of complete self-reliance in political and economic conditions, the Chinese Government would like to take the same attitude as it did toward Outer Mongolia, by supporting their independence.... However, Tibet should be able to maintain and promote its own independent position in order that the historical tragedy of Korea might not be repeated."[20] In his book *China's Destiny*, which he wrote before Japan's surrender, Chiang Kai-shek noted, "If only the Manchus could have done away with the boundaries that separated the Chinese, Manchus, Mongols, Mohammedans and Tibetans, and recognised that our five branches are, in fact, one unified body, it would have been hard to find fault with them."[21]

Chiang's dream was to restore the so-called Celestial Empire. He failed. Mao Tse-tung, who had similar dreams and ambitions, came much closer but still fell short of success.

In 1946 Tibet sent Gyalo Thondup, an older brother of the Dalai Lama, and Phuntso Tashi, the Dalai Lama's brother-in-law, as representatives to the Victory Celebrations ceremonies, first in India and then in China. On their arrival in Nanking in April, the "Chinese press did not give them much notice, but described them as arriving to attend the coming National Assembly ... and to represent Tibetans in paying respects to President Chiang Kai-shek for his leadership in the war of resistance against Japanese aggression."[22] "In the past only Tibetans from areas under Chinese control (Sikang, Tsinghai, and Yunnan provinces) attended national assemblies. Now, for the first time, the Chinese were on the verge of having delegates from the Tibetan government participate in a Chinese National Constitutional Assembly.... For Kuomintang

China, the propaganda value of this participation was immense ... [and] by attending the National Assembly and being displayed in Chinese newspapers, the mission had given the Chinese a choice propaganda victory which they were to use in the United Nations debates over Tibet in 1950."[23]

On August 15, 1947, India became independent, and the British Union Jack was also replaced in Pakistan, Ceylon and Burma. They, along with the other countries of Central Asia and the Himalayas, were now, at least ostensibly, under the political protection of India. British interests in the area became primarily economic, and her policy of course was not to anger China in any way. Beyond that, London's political influence in the area waned and soon was little more than financial and academic, for no longer was there a strong British military to provide backbone to her diplomatic presence. And while India's concerns were primarily internal, she was also worried about her external borders, especially in Ladakh, Sikkim, and Bhutan — all of which had very close ties with Tibet — and with China, for India's borders were both vulnerable and extensive. India was far from a unified country, and she also had a very limited capability to protect herself. As for Nepal, it was the only country that continued to have extensive trade contacts directly with Tibet and geographically represented a semblance, if not the illusion, of a buffer between Tibet and part of India. That China would soon consume Tibet and become India's neighbor had been assumed by the British well before India was given her independence, so this too was an unwanted concern of the new government of India.

"The entire basis of Britain's Tibetan policies crumbled down. The leaders of New India had no inclination to shoulder any imperial burden, or to inherit any imperial legacy. They had more difficult immediate problems to handle."[24] Amaury de Reincourt, author of *Lost World — Tibet, Key to Asia*, was then in Lhasa (August 15) and wrote, "Looking at this map [of Tibet], ... I was struck by the strategic potentialities of the Roof of the World, of this colossal natural fortress standing in the heart of Asia and almost inaccessible by land.... The radio broadcast (just) announced that Chinese Turkestan was being attacked by Soviet Outer Mongolian troops (July 1947). There was little doubt in my mind that Tibet was destined to become one of the borders of the expanding Soviet empire. And this was the time chosen by the British to withdraw from Tibet and from Central Asia! ... Communist infiltration has definitely taken place in Tibet since the end of the Second World War. I became convinced that if even Tibet was taken over by the Soviets or the Chinese Communists, the whole of India and of south-east Asia would become strategically untenable and left wide open to an invasion."

The surrender of Japan left the Chinese Nationalists alone to continue the fight against the Chinese Communists. For years the Communist forces had been intent on evading and seldom allowed themselves to be caught in a position where they had to fight either the Japanese or the Chinese Nationalists during WWII, and by the end of the war they were well armed and prepared to fight the war-weary and increasingly disparate forces of Chiang Kai-shek. In 1934 the Chinese Nationalists had repeatedly and soundly defeated the Chinese Communists, finally driving some 87,000 of the pro–Soviet faction of the Chinese Communist army and party from Yudu, marking the beginning of the 6,000-mile trek that Mao proclaimed and communist propaganda celebrated as The Long March, but in reality it more accurately qualifies only as The Long Retreat. Regardless, Chinese Communist forces, often reported to have received supplies from the Soviets, retained their military and political organizations and remained disciplined during the years of evading combat. The People's Army fought only when cornered or only when opportunities were strongly favorable to them to ambush Nationalist forces as the latter sought and fought the Japanese invaders. There is no question that Mao's forces added to Chiang's woes and also reduced the effectiveness of the Nationalist forces who were in essence forced to fight a two-front war. Despite what Mao and his followers later claimed, unless they were cornered or ambushed by the Japanese, the Chinese Communists usually succeeded in avoiding the Japanese. They gladly left that unwanted task to Chiang Kai-shek's armies.

The Long March (Retreat) took some of the Chinese Communist forces into and through Tibetan areas, which in turn prompted numerous fire fights with Tibetan tribals. Tibetan resistance ranged from engaging the Communists, to ambushing stragglers, to rolling boulders onto them when they could not engage them in a firefight. Edgar Snow wrote that Mao had told him in 1936: "To the Tibetans, the Red Army was just a hateful tribe that came to rob them of their food." And Tibetans in the area reported that "the Red Army is in a state of poverty. Its actions in searching for food and other supplies is worse than that of Liu Wen-hu (the ruthless former Chinese Nationalist commander in the area)."[25] In the Chengtu area, Gen. Zhang Guo-tao reported "The people were Tibetans. They didn't speak our language and we were there and had to eat and we took their sheep and cattle — how could we have a good relationship?"[26] The Red Army "broke into Buddhist temples, smashed the huge idols, stole the grain contributed to the temples by worshipers and devoured the wheat; Mao took the Red Army through 50 kilometers of Yi (Lolo and Kham) territory; the Fifth Army (rear guard) did not do so well as Lolos continued to seize stragglers and to fire on lagging elements. Some of the food was paid for, mostly by IOUs, while most food and animals were simply seized; there was trouble with the minorities: the Tibetans, the Miao and the Yi."[27] The Red Army took thousands of Chinese prisoners and also missionaries for the purpose of gaining ransoms in order to finance the Long March, with one group held for $700,000. "The Red Army arrested these people and held them until the landlords paid a suitable fine. When the fine was not paid the hostages were often executed. Two American missionaries, John and

Betty Stam, Presbyterians, were captured and executed in Anhui on September 6, 1934, and their baby left unattended until found a day later."[28]

It is interesting to note that Mao studied Buddhist philosophy in 1920. He totally rejected it as it did not serve his views, as he later indicated in conversations with the fourteenth Dalai Lama in Peking, wherein he likened religion to a poison that undermined the races and retarded the development of many countries, including Tibet and Mongolia. Mao is also quoted as having often told his many foreign visitors that "We are eagerly looking for the doom of the old world. Its destruction will eventually lead to the establishment of a new one. And will it not be better than the old world? Destruction is the elemental method of social change."

When Japan surrendered in August 1945, the Chinese Communists claimed to have some 915,000 regular army troops and a militia of 2,200,000. Chiang Kai-shek's forces were estimated by the United States at 3,000,000. The inauguration four years later of the People's Republic of China on October 1, 1949, brought China a powerful government for the first time in the twentieth century. The Chinese Communist party's ideology emphasized reunification of China, one of the prime targets of which was the liberation of Tibet and her reintegration with the "motherland." The Chinese Communists believed that Tibet's desire to be separate from China was caused by Western imperialist interference in Chinese affairs. The Chinese did not believe it to be coincidental that the thirteenth Dalai Lama had expelled all Chinese from Tibet and severed relations with China in 1913 just after he had spent two years in India where he developed a close friendship with the British diplomat Sir Charles Bell. The Chinese viewed British policy as an attempt either to eliminate or to reduce to token status all Chinese influence in Tibet and believed the elimination of British "imperialism" (i.e., influences) as critical to the restoration of what they considered China's traditional hegemony over Tibet. Thus it followed that in 1950 the Chinese would repeatedly broadcast, in both Chinese and Tibetan, that the Chinese People's Liberation Army had as a priority the "liberation" of Tibet from the imperialists.

In turn, the Tibetan replies protested that there were no imperialists in Tibet, that there was no need for any liberation and that the proper relationship between Tibet and China was one of priest and patron, not one in which Tibet was but a part of China. The Tibetan government also sent letters dated November 4, 1949, to the British and the United States in which they referred to a letter that had been sent to Mao Tse-tung on November 2 regarding the seizing of Tibetan territories along the Lanchow, Chinghai and Sinkiang borders, asking that China refrain from sending Chinese troops into Tibet. The letters to Britain and the United States asked that both countries render extensive civil and military aid should the Chinese Communist government ignore Tibet's request to Mao. Neither Britain nor the United States responded favorably, which prompted Tibet to decide to send missions to China, India, Britain and the United States seeking resolution of the problem posed by China's declared intention of forcibly returning Tibet to the control of China. These missions also failed. "Radio Peking and the Soviet Union's TASS (repeatedly) stated that the Tibetan missions to the United States and Britain were illegal and that any country receiving such an 'illegal mission' will be considered as entertaining hostile intentions with regard to the Chinese People's Republic. They claimed that the people of Tibet demanded to join the People's Republic of China and said that if the Lhasa authorities sent representatives to Peking for negotiations in accordance with this wish, they would be received."[29]

In response to Tibet's request for modern arms, the Indians indicated a willingness to sell mortars and mortar shells, some small arms and ammunition, but nothing else (the Tibetans had also requested antiaircraft weapons and machine guns). The Indian foreign secretary K. P. Menon told the British, "If the Communists were really determined to take Tibet, nothing could stop them from doing so and there was no question of India giving Tibet any direct military support."[30]

Following the defeat of the Chinese Nationalist forces in Lanchow in 1949, and the flight of Ma Pu-feng to Taiwan, the People's Liberation Army moved into Amdo in considerable force as early as July 1949.

As described by Thubten Jigme Norbu, oldest brother of the Dalai Lama, then Takster Rinpoche, Abbot of the Kumbum Monastery, "The Chinese were at first very respectful and friendly, not just to me in my position as Abbot of the Kumbum Monastery, and the lamas and monks of my monastery, but to all. They talked constantly of the benefits of communism that Mao Tse-tung was bringing to everyone and the benefits of the totalitarian state of China under his guidance. The Chinese political officers promised there would be land for all and no more poverty, that everyone would share in the ownership of all the good things. Because the Chinese government would be taking care of all the needs of the people, they said, the future was very bright for all. They said everyone would share in the work and also in the benefits of that work, and there would no longer be a division between the rich and poor. Of course, they did not give details about the type of work or how the system of communes was to work. The Chinese came with presents, such as cloth, blankets, tools and candy and with smiles and many speeches. At first the candy was given freely to the children, then more sparingly, then as a reward to those children who answered their questions and volunteered information. For example, they used the children extensively as informants to learn who had the most land and the most animals, who had weapons, who was unfriendly to or spoke against the Chinese, who had fought against the Chinese, who the village leaders were, who the teachers were, and with such information they then questioned the others, and arrests and beatings began. Most of those who had been foolish enough to believe the lies and smiles soon became angry. We in the monastery quickly understood what those who had fled from western

Thubten Jigme Norbu (middle) at the Kumbum Monastery in Amdo, Tibet, where he was the abbot until 1951.

China and had earlier sought asylum with us had tried to tell us when they described the terrible things the Communists had done to the civilians in nearby areas. We knew, of course, what had happened to our fellow Buddhists in Mongolia and China, and it was evident by the lies and propaganda of the Chinese Communists that they were an evil threat to our religion, our freedom and our country. The abusive and vulgar language used by these Chinese when talking about the Chinese Nationalists was the same as had been used against our Mongolian friends, and we knew it would also be used against us, for the Han Chinese have never respected others.

"One of the first orders by the Chinese was that all weapons were to be turned in, including those belonging to the monasteries. To make their point, the Chinese arranged for a mob to attack one of the nearby (Shartsong Ritro) monasteries and burn it to the ground after it had been plundered. Other monasteries were also looted and burned. More Chinese decrees followed, and each took more freedom away. By October, the smiles were gone, and the earlier promises and expectations had disappeared. And resistance against the Chinese had started by some of the Amdo leaders, including some of the monks whose monasteries had been destroyed.

"I went to Siling to talk to Gen. Ye Chun-tang. As I wrote in my book, I did not want to give him any excuse to attack us, so I went to him to discuss the situation. He said we Tibetans had nothing to fear, for now we were free of the threat of imperialists and could practice our religion in peace. It was useless to talk to him about there being no imperialists in Tibet. I also met with the new Governor of Tsinghai, Tang Tu-shi, who told me that all of Tibet would soon be free, not just Amdo. Free of what? I asked. He stressed that with the redistribution of land all of the problems would be solved, for everyone, including monks, would share in the labor process, and that even the education of all the Tibetan children would be performed by the motherland (China), relieving the parents of that burden.

"And then two Chinese political officers were assigned to me under the guise of helping me and the others in nearby monasteries to assist in implementing the Chinese programs. They were obviously assigned to watch me and to report any misdeeds by me or by my fellow monks. And they tried to lecture me constantly. For example, they repeatedly told me that Buddhism was nothing, and that our gods were powerless, as evidenced by their being there. They said that Chairman Mao and Stalin were the true leaders of the world and that it was they who put food in the stomachs of millions of people, not Buddha, and that the Tibetan monks were worse than parasites. There was no reasoning with such robots of propaganda.

"As I said in my book, I was a prisoner in my own monastery, and I knew that as the brother of the Dalai Lama I would always be a hostage of the Chinese so long as I was in Tibet. I realized that I had no choice but to escape, but the question was how.

"Amazingly, the most shocking of the Chinese proposals also permitted me to escape. The Chinese chairman of the Tibet Commission, and then the secretary to the Chinese governor, suggested that if I persuaded the Tibetan government to welcome the entry of the People's Liberation Army into Tibet as liberators and to accept China as its leader I would be appointed governor general of Tibet. The governor (of Tsinghai) and the Chinese military commander repeatedly confirmed this proposal in subsequent meetings and conversations, and I was told that if the Dalai Lama resisted or disagreed then I should find ways and means to change his mind or to get rid of him. And it was made clear that if I did not agree to this plan then I would remain in the Kumbum Monastery the rest of my life, or, I concluded, perhaps I would not live very long. It was a very difficult time. Not only was I shocked with what they had said, but I knew that somehow I had to let His Holiness know of the Chinese plan and of the danger to him.

"I had almost no time to myself in the monastery, and so took short trips in the area in my capacity as Abbot to give me the opportunity to think of an answer. I concluded that if I quickly agreed or if I asked that I be sent to Lhasa right away the Chinese would probably not believe me and would not let me go, so I decided to insist on being sent to Peking soon so that I could better study and learn the programs and plans of China and Chairman Mao before going to Lhasa to carry out their plan. It was clear that they did not expect such an answer and finally rejected my demand to go to Peking because they knew it could result in a long and unnecessary delay. They insisted instead that I proceed to Lhasa. So, in the summer of 1950 the Chinese agreed that I resign as Abbot of Kumbum, and permitted me to set out on the long trip to Lhasa on what the Chinese believed was the mission they had assigned me."[31]

The Chinese had not attempted to keep secret their intentions to "liberate" Tibet; quite the contrary. "On September 2, 1949, the official Communist news agency, NCNA, announced that Tibet must be liberated, and that the Communist regime would not permit a 'single inch of territory' to remain outside the rule of the Chinese People's Republic." On November 24, 1949, Radio Peking broadcast appeals from the Chinese-sponsored Panchen Lama to Mao Tse-tung and the Communist Chinese Army requesting the "liberation of Tibet." And on January 1, 1950, an official announcement was made "that it would be one of the major tasks of the People's Liberation Army to 'liberate Tibet.' General Liu Po-chen and Teng Hsiao-ping had met in Chunking earlier to complete the invasion plans and they tasked subordinates to complete all plans by September ... and Gen. Liu Po-chen then announced the Chinese decision to bring Tibet back into the Motherland's big family."[32] Then, "On May 22, 1950, Peking Radio addressed an appeal to the Tibetan Government and people calling on them to achieve 'the peaceful liberation of Tibet.' The broadcast declared that Tibet was part of Chinese territory and that its geographical remoteness would constitute no obstacle to the Chinese Liberation Army. It advised the Tibetan government not to count on British or American aid and not to be 'misled by slanders of the British and American imperialistic bloc aimed at sowing discord between [Chinese] nationalities.'" And "on August 5 the New China News Agency circulated a statement by Gen. Liu Po-chen, then Chairman of the Southwest China Military Affairs Commission and Commander of the Second Field Army, in which he declared that the Chinese forces would soon enter Tibet to liberate the territory to drive out 'the aggressive influence of British and American imperialism,' to bring Tibet back into the 'motherland's big family,' and to consolidate China's 'line of defence.' The declaration also said that Tibet would be allowed regional self-government and freedom of religion, that her institutions would be respected, but her army incorporated in 'the national defence forces of the Chinese People's Republic.'" On September 30, Prime Minister Chou En-lai announced in Peking, on the eve of the first anniversary of the founding of the Chinese People's Republic, (China's) determination "to liberate the people of Tibet and stand on guard at the Chinese frontiers."[33] In early October 1950 tens of thousands of Chinese troops that had trained for six months for the invasion of Tibet crossed the Yangtze (Drechu) River and entered Kham in eastern Tibet.

On October 8, 1950, United Nations forces in Korea crossed the 38th parallel, unknowingly but further insuring that Tibet's plight would remain isolated as Free World forces devoted their efforts to the Korean War. From information provided her by many well-placed sources and by noting that there had been no real objection raised to her many and repeated announcements that she intended to seize Tibet, China accurately assessed that little, if any, attention would be paid to Tibet, and that no one would come to Tibet's assistance or provide Tibet with support.

Peking's messages that promised Tibet "religious freedom" and "regional autonomy" if the Tibetans agreed to a peaceful liberation proved false. By Chinese design, there had been no direct discussions between the two countries before the massive invasion by China. Tibet had been given no options beyond the incredible plot that had been presented to the Dalai Lama's oldest brother. There had, however, been a number of fire fights between Tibetan and Chinese forces on the eastern borders. It is possible that the Chinese had concluded that there could be no peaceful liberation, but it is more likely that China intended to invade and exert her will regardless. The 5,000,000-man Chinese army had little to worry about from the maximum force of less than 8,000 lightly armed and poorly trained Tibetan soldiers or the smaller number of unprepared and ill-equipped Tibetan militia and tribesmen.

The Chinese soldiers that had infiltrated into Kham and Amdo in 1949 and in early 1950 had apparently done so in order to locate and assess Tibet's defenses. In so doing the Chinese had often been ambushed and beaten when they were detected by the fierce Amdos and Khambas who historically detested the Chinese. For example, in one instance, a Chinese force numbering about 600 attacked and seized Dengko, a small town in Kham in July 1950, some 100 miles northeast of Chamdo. A Khamba leader by the name of Muja Dapon rallied his men, then counterattacked and recaptured Dengko with some 700 Khambas. They simply eliminated the entire force of Chinese and lost no more than 15 men in the brief time it took. Some of the other probing efforts by the Chinese were similarly unsuccessful. It may have been that the Chinese hoped

Yak-skin boat

there would be no resistance, or, more likely, and as time has confirmed, the Chinese had made the offer merely in order to deceive, meaning that they had no intention of honoring their own proposal, just as they failed to keep other promises.

In any event on October 7, 1950, General Liu Ba-ting sent more than 80,000 troops of his First and Second Field Armies into Tibet, including sending most of them across the Yangtze to seize Chamdo in Kham. After crossing the river (in the yak-skin boats that are used in Tibet and western China) the Chinese soldiers then attacked six locations in Kham to the north and south, simply overwhelming the Tibetans who at best were poorly organized and totally unprepared to fight such a force. One by one the towns fell, although Tsakhalo in the south and Dengkog, 250 miles to the north, held firmly against the Chinese for a few days. In fact, Muja Dapon succeeded in forcing the Chinese back across the Yangtze in the north, again inflicting heavy casualties on them. But finally the towns of Riwoche and Jyekundo and Markham Gartok fell, leaving Chamdo all but defenseless. Only a small contingent of about 3,000 or so of the Tibetan army was left as a protective force, but it was not combat trained, nor was it adequately armed to fight such a vastly superior enemy. Unfortunately, not all Khambas supported Muja's efforts, and some of the monks in one of the nearby monasteries who were sympathetic to the Chinese traitorously deceived Muja, which resulted in many of his men being ambushed and killed by the Chinese. The battle continued for two days, with heavy casualties on both sides. It was a moral victory for Muja and the Khambas, but given the limited numbers of Khamba combatants available, it was far more costly to the Tibetans.[34]

The Governor General located in Chamdo, Lhalu Shape, had worked hard all the summer of 1950 attempting to recruit and train Khambas and had devised a defensive system for the entire area designed to take advantage of the terrain. His task was not easy, for the tribals in Kham and Amdo did not trust those who came from Lhasa. The government brought little to the provinces but taxes and service demands, and the years of abuse had done little to change these feelings. But the religious ties remained very strong, as did their distrust and dislike of the Chinese.

This disaffection and dissatisfaction with Lhasa had led to an unsuccessful attempt in 1934 to separate Kham from Tibet, led by members of the wealthy Pandatsang family, one of the wealthiest and most influential families in Kham. They believed that the archaic policies of the government in Lhasa would never change its stifling isolationist practices and that the provinces, particularly Kham with its profitable trade routes to China, Nepal, India and Sikkim, needed to go their separate ways. With Tibet virtually leaderless at this point in time, dissent and plotting among and between government and monastic figures continued for months, both in Lhasa and in the provinces. Another Pandatsang member founded the Tibet Improvement Party in 1939, also known as the Western Tibet Reform Party, whose members believed it necessary to liberate Tibet from the "existing tyrannical government" in order to undertake the revolutionary restructuring of the Tibetan government and society. The Tibet Improvement Party believed in the ideology of Sun Yat-sen and wanted change to come to Tibet as it had to China following the overthrow of the Ch'ing Dynasty, for without change Tibet would remain ill-suited for the modern world.[35] A separation of State and Church was intended, but otherwise the religious role of the Dalai Lama was to remain basically the same. Popular support for the party and its platform was absent, probably because of the support role it expected of the Nationalist Chinese, including the party proposal that Tibet would be autonomous under the protection of China. That was less than persuasive to most Tibetans, and the party leaders eventually located in India. The party was forced to disband.

To return to Lhalu Shape in Chamdo, his three-year term ended in August 1950 before he had completed his plans to defend Kham and Chamdo and before he had recruited and trained the numbers of Khambas that he had set as a goal. Unfortunately for Tibet,

Lhalu was replaced by another official from Lhasa named Ngapo Ngawang Jigme who, upon arrival in Chamdo, spent most of his time attending parties and bragging about how brave and able he was, and how strong an army the Chinese had. Ngapo had previously served in Kham and even then had earned the reputation of being less than able among the Tibetans there, and especially among the Khambas, but the Kashag either ignored those reports or chose not to believe them. And when the invasion began, the cabinet members were attending a five day holiday celebration in Lhasa, so no communications from the east were answered in a timely fashion. In the meantime, there was no organizing of forces or any defensive preparations by Ngapo of any kind in Chamdo. To the contrary, Ngapo ordered the defenses torn down that Lhalu had constructed. There was no leadership. The townspeople were frightened, and simply circled the Lingkhor Monastery's Holy Walk, praying that the Chinese would not arrive. Others burned effigies of Chinese soldiers, trying to thwart the evil of the Chinese. Ngapo Ngwang Jigme officially recommended surrender, but Lhasa said no. Upon receiving this word, Ngapo changed from the yellow silk robes of his high office into the dress of a minor official and fled his residence in Chamdo with a few of his close officials and without letting others know that he was fleeing, including not advising Robert Ford, the British radio operator in Chamdo under contract to the Tibetan government. His only order before he left was to two officers of the Tibetan garrison in Chamdo to destroy the ammunition dump, which they did. This meant that the Khambas and Tibetan soldiers had no ammunition with which to fight the Chinese. There was total confusion, and panic increased. The Khambas were enraged at the destruction of the ammunition dump and the cowardly betrayal by Ngapo. They tried to find him to force him to order the Tibetan forces to resist the Chinese, but could not locate him. As he fled west from Chamdo, Ngapo met a column of Tibetan soldiers, armed with artillery, which had been sent by Lhasa to help defend Chamdo. He ordered these soldiers to throw away all their weapons and surrender — which they did. Then, ironically, Ngapo encountered Muja Dapon and his four hundred or so mounted soldiers as they arrived from the northeast to help defend Chamdo ... and he ordered them to put down their arms and surrender.[36]

So it was that only eleven days after the attack across the Yangtze began, the Chinese, ably assisted by the confusion and the orders and actions of Ngapo Ngawang Jigme, had vanquished the key towns in eastern Tibet and effectively neutered the Tibetan army and the resistance forces there.

The New China News Agency announced on October 24 that the People's Liberation Army had entered Tibet to free her from imperialist oppression: "A political mobilisation directive had been issued ordering the Chinese liberation forces to advance into Tibet to liberate three million Tibetans from imperialist aggression, to complete the unification of the whole of China, and to safeguard the frontier regions of the country." And on October 28 it was announced in New Delhi that official confirmation had been received from Lhasa that Chinese troops had entered Tibet from the east. There was no word about what had actually transpired, or the size of the Chinese forces, or of the fighting, or of the demands of the Chinese. Communications in the border areas were very poor at best, and with the capture of Chamdo the Chinese effectively controlled all communications in Tibet, except for India's wireless with her consulate in Lhasa, and Lhasa's own fragile links. Except for Tibetan couriers on horseback, there were no other channels. And with the fall of Chamdo, Lhasa was now but 300 miles west of elements of the People's Liberation Army.

In early November "two officials sent by Ngapo Ngawang Jigme arrived in Lhasa from Chamdo with a message from him that he and some others were being held in a prison in Chamdo, and that the Chinese had promised to release him and the others, and that there would be no further military advances, if Lhasa agreed to discuss peace terms. The Kashag quickly approved, with no one thinking yet to question Ngapo more closely. It is still not known if the Chinese had recruited Ngapo in earlier years, or if it was just ignorance on the part of the Kashag in not readily recognizing that Ngapo was an opportunist as well as a fully willing collaborator. But they did not, and we suffered for it — dearly."[37]

"A delegation had been sent to New Delhi in April 1950 and then Calcutta, to meet with Chinese representatives to settle any differences, but there were no meetings. The Chinese stalled and simply refused to meet. Then the Chinese said on Radio Peking in May that Tibet should send our representatives to conduct peace talks in Peking 'to save the Tibetan people from unnecessary losses.' That same broadcast also warned the Tibetan government not to count on British or American assistance. The Tibetan delegation tried to fly to Hong Kong in June 1950, but the British refused to grant visas to the delegation because of the so-called 'delicate situation in Hong Kong.' The British also questioned the diplomatic status of the delegation, even though the members had Tibetan passports, which had previously been honored by the British when Tibetans traveled abroad. So the delegation sat in New Delhi that summer until September, when the Chinese Ambassador to India suddenly agreed to begin conversations. Of course, even this pretense ceased in October when the Chinese invaded Tibet, and our delegation simply returned to Lhasa. It was very discouraging and confusing…. We were like puppets on a string trying to satisfy the various whims of the Chinese — and with little hope of success or for support. We had not yet realized that all this was just a game being played by the Chinese."[38]

India did not pretend to stand by Tibet during this period. There was an exchange of notes between India and China in October, including a mild one to the Chinese "regretting China's military action," and pleading for "slower but more enduring methods of peaceful approach." The tone of the Indian notes made it clear that India had no intention of siding with Tibet or of helping Tibet or of taking any action of consequence. The Chinese response was that "Tibet is an integral part of Chinese territory and the problem of Tibet is entirely a domestic problem of China," and accused India of working under "foreign influence."[39]

When Tibet asked India to raise the question of Tibet at the United Nations, Mr. Nehru refused. On November 17, however, El Salvador bravely called on the United Nations to condemn the People's Republic of China for "unprovoked aggression against Tibet," and asked the General Assembly to consider the problem, including creating a special committee to study what measures could be taken by the United Nations to assist Tibet. India's instruction to her ambassador to the United Nations was that the question of Tibet should not be considered at all and that India did not support Tibet. The Tibetan government also sent an appeal to the United Nations on November 7: "The attention of the world is riveted on Korea where aggression is being resisted by an international force. Similar aggression in remote Tibet is passing without notice."[40] Based on the strong position of the Indian representative, and the silence of Britain and the United States, the United Nations Steering Committee ultimately set aside the Tibetan complaint indefinitely. That Tibet had been declared independent by the thirteenth Dalai Lama in 1910 and had functioned since then as an independent country, including having its own currency, postal service, trade regulations, travel documents, standing army and, obviously, its own government was ignored by the rest of the world.

"We were very disappointed, especially when India argued so strongly against us behind the scenes at the United Nations. Tibet had also hoped for at least some British support and had expected the support of the United States and perhaps from others such as Canada and Australia, ... but it was soon apparent that the British did not want to antagonize China for fear of losing her last colony, Hong Kong. We knew the United States was already deeply concerned about South Korea and probably did not want to risk the possibility of China committing her huge army to help North Korea. But the United States was also supposed to be the leader of the free world, the one country that was a beacon of hope for the other less-fortunate countries. Our disappointment was very deep, for without at least some support from the United States we were quite certain that no other country would dare help us. It was terribly difficult to understand, for everyone knew that the Soviet Union was openly supportive of China — and North Korea. But Tibet had no help. And now the United Nations continues to be largely inept, particularly in its so-called police actions around the world under the banner of 'One World' or 'New World Order,' which is simply Socialism cleverly masked. And Socialism, like Communism, has never been of real or enduring benefit to any country or people. The many different religions, the cultural differences, the basic economic differences between countries, as well as the deeply rooted political differences can and should live in general harmony, but only if not injudiciously disturbed by those who seek to eliminate or drastically revise the differences. Greed and self-aggrandizement can thrive only when manipulation is an available tool. Like air and water without which we humans die, freedom and independence are equally necessary and vital. There is no acceptable substitute. How dearly we Tibetans have learned that lesson!"[41]

On November 17, 1950, following the instructions that two State Oracles had given to the Tibetan government in October while they were in trances to answer the question posed to them as to what the government should do in this period of crisis, the Dalai Lama accepted the request of the Tibetan government to assume the powers of government. Although only 15 years of age, and himself hesitant to assume the responsibilities involved because of inexperience and youth, the Dalai Lama was given full temporal authority in addition to the ecclesiastic authority given him before. He was now the theocratic leader of Tibet.

On November 24 the General Committee of the United Nations General Assembly met to consider the Tibetan appeal. The Indian delegate, Jam Saheb of Nawanagar, argued that India believed that the best way to obtain a peaceful settlement was for the United Nations not to discuss the Tibetan pleas but to abandon it as had been proposed by the United Kingdom representative. The Russian representative "agreed with the United Kingdom proposal." In explaining his delegation's view on the substance of the question, which he described as an extremely simple one, the Russian said, "Tibet was an inalienable part of China and its affairs were the exclusive concern of the Chinese Government."[42] The United States joined the other members in unanimously voting to adjourn consideration of the El Salvador proposal. Tibet had desperately sought a life ring, but to no avail.

While abandoned politically by those she had trusted most, Tibet's plight was covered extensively in India, both in the press and especially in debates in both houses of her government. For example, Prime Minister Nehru said in December 1950,

> Ever since the People's Government of China talked about the liberation of Tibet, our ambassador told them, on behalf of the government of India, how the latter felt about it. We expressed our earnest hope that the matter would be settled peacefully by China and Tibet. We also made it clear that we had no territorial or political ambitions in regard to Tibet and that our relations were cultural and commercial. We said that we would naturally like to preserve these relations and continue to trade with Tibet because it did not come in the way of either China or Tibet. We further said that we were anxious that Tibet should maintain the autonomy it has had for at least the last forty years. We did not challenge or deny the suzerainty of China over Tibet. We pointed all this out in a friendly way to the Chinese government. In their replies, they always said that they would very much like to settle the question peacefully but that they were, in any event, going to liberate Tibet. From whom they were going to liberate Tibet, is, however, not quite clear. They gave us to understand that a peaceful solution would be found, though I must say that they gave us no assurance or guarantee to the effect. On the one hand, they said they were prepared for a peaceful solution; on the other, they talked persistently of liberation. We had come to believe that the matter would be settled by peaceful negotiations and

were shocked when we heard that the Chinese armies were marching into Tibet. Indeed, one can hardly talk about war between China and Tibet. Tibet is not in a position to carry on war and, obviously, Tibet is no threat to China. It is said that other countries might intrigue in Tibet. I cannot say much about it because I do not know. It is certain, however, that there was no immediate threat.[43]

Following Nehru's presentation, Professor N. G. Ranga, a member of the Congress Party, asked, "Can we be quite so confident that the China that we talk about is the same today as it used to be ten years ago, one hundred years ago, two thousand years ago, when Lord Buddha's teachings were being carried to China through our missionaries? ... Could we be also indifferent to the fact that China, the modern China, the present-day China, was sending her own troops in order to assert the sovereignty over Tibet? And in the minds of people on that side of the world, sovereignty makes no other meaning than expansion of their own control, political, economic and social, over other people. Now, when we talk again and again on the sovereignty of the Chinese people over the Tibetan government or country, what is it that we are doing? Are we not giving a blank cheque to be signed on our behalf by somebody else in order to spread their own imperialist tentacles? ... Should we not keep these things in our mind? Instead of that, I found, to my utter surprise, our government and their spokesman both in India as well as abroad, repeatedly professing their friendship not only to China's people, not only to the Chinese government but to China's sovereignty over Tibet. This beats anybody and everybody. These are days when we would be ready with the aid of the United Nations and other factors to counter this menace of sovereignty of one country over another. Instead of that, we go about accepting it, admitting it and apologizing for it. This is one criticism that I am obliged to make against our foreign policy."[44]

Dr. S. P. Mukherjee, who resigned from the Cabinet in 1950 and a cabinet colleague of Nehru's, said, "Along with China, we have to take up the question of Tibet because both are interlinked. Now the Prime Minister naturally reminded the House of the part which India had played progressively in the matter of recognition of the legitimate rights of the present Chinese government. How has China reciprocated? When it comes to the question of Tibet, there may or may not be some sort of loose suzerainty of China over Tibet, but historically this is not so easy a matter and yet, what is the reply that China sent to India, when India asked China not to proceed on the path of violence in the matter of Tibet? The reply that China has sent has shocked, surprised and has given sorrow to the government of India.... But here again, what is the definite policy of the government of India in regard to Tibet? ... Just as in the case of Korea, each country for which this so-called liberation starts is the worst sufferer. It is like the old story of the operation being fully successful and the patient succumbing. The sufferings of the people themselves are indescribable.... With regard to Tibet, we sent frantic appeals to

China asking her not to be violent, but did China listen? What is the policy behind China's action? It is no use our trying to gloss over things because these are matters which affect not only the people of Tibet but also the security of India. It is a fact that the boundary between India and Tibet is yet to be definitely defined. The Prime Minister said the other day that we stand by the McMahon Line, but the maps of China which are in circulation even now include portions of Assam, Ladakh and Leh territories in which India is vitally interested. The reply which China has sent to India on the question of Tibet definitely indicates that China will do everything necessary for the purpose of keeping in tact what it considers to be China's border and when it refers to the Chinese border, it includes Tibet as well and the undefined boundary of Tibet so far as it touches the Indian border. Similarly with regard to Nepal."[45]

Mr. Acharya Kripalani, then leader of the Praja Socialist Party in the Lok Sabha, in talking about China's admission into the United Nations and India's having strongly supported the admission, but having rejected Tibet's plea, said, "The Raja of Nepal, who is our guest, his theoretical claim to the crown of Nepal is greater than the theoretical claim of China on Tibet. And moreover, today, every nation has a right to democratic rule.... Now there are newer kinds of tyrannies that are possible; there are newer kinds of totalitarian regimes that are possible. Today, if you deny a people democracy, all that they will get will be communism."[46]

Next, Mr. Masani, once a Socialist, said, "May I remind the House that some months ago, after we had shown our friendliness to Communist China, a message was sent by Mao Tse-tung to Ranadive, the Secretary of the Communist Party, which was engaged in trying to overthrow our government by force — a message of greetings and good wishes 'for the liberation of India' and their hope that India would soon go the Chinese way.... I read a statement of the New China News Agency a few months ago, that the 'anglo–American imperialists' and their running dog, Pandit [i.e., Jawaharlal] Nehru, were plotting a coup in Lhasa for the annexation of Tibet.... By the one act of attacking Tibet and deceiving the Indian government after their assurances given repeatedly, they have shown utter contempt for the idea that we embraced, namely, of a free and united Asia. They have cut Asia into two—Communist and non–Communist Asia. Those of us who are not prepared to go all the way with them must fall on the other side of the fence. In that setting and in the face of this remark which comes from the New China News Agency in the last few weeks, that 'the Chinese People's Liberation Army will hoist the Red Flag over the Himalayas,' what are we to think of the friendship that we may expect from them?"[47]

Mr. Ayyangar spoke: "Tibet is one of the most peace-loving countries in the world. Both by tradition and religion, Tibetans never waged war. In the European continent they can have Switzerland. Can we not have a similar Switzerland in the form of Tibet to our north? What is this 'liberation'? As our Prime Minister rightly pointed out, there is no question of liberation. It is all a myth, it is a hoax. China ought not to have marched on Tibet. Sir, as against 450 millions of Chinese, if we with our 350 millions had armed ourselves and were ready for an offensive, if necessary, China would not have ventured on Tibet."[48]

Mr. Anthony, a representative of the Anglo-Indian community, asked, "But what excuse — unless it be an utterly unworthy and dishonest excuse — can anyone assign for the cynical, unprovoked attack on Tibet? India has assumed the treaty obligations and rights which existed between Britain on the one side and Tibet on the other. According to these treaty obligations while there was some recognition of Chinese suzerainty there was definitely this condition that India recognised the complete autonomy of Tibet. I do not think this point has been brought sufficiently to the notice of the Chinese government. We have not told them sufficiently that this cynical and unprovoked attack on Tibet has outraged the conscience of every self-respecting Indian."[49]

Mr. Joachim Prasad of the Congress Party in Parliament, and a strong supporter of the United Front idea (of a united India, China and Soviet Union) said, "I hold there will be no war if we ally ourselves with China and Russia. There will be peace and stability in Southeast Asia. From the point of view of both military strategy and geo-politics, it will be physically impossible for any alien power to land troops in Southeast Asia. If we want peace, we must join hands with Russia and China. I am quite sure that whatever Hon. Members of this House may feel now, events will justify the stand I have taken in this House today."[50]

In responding, Nehru said, "The House knows very well what the policy of the government of India has been in regard to communist activities in this country. It has not been a tender policy and it is not going to be a tender policy. We must look at the world as it is and recognize that mighty forces are at work and millions of people have come under their influence.... The point at issue is that China is a great nation which cannot be ignored, no matter what resolution you may pass. Nor can you ignore the United States of America. Some people talk of American imperialism and American dollars in a hostile fashion. You cannot condemn or ignore the whole nation just because you do not approve of some aspect of the myriad shapes of American life. We have to take facts as they are.... I beg this House to consider Asia specially — Asia in a tremendous ferment of change. One does not know whether that change is good or bad.... I have spoken of China and, more particularly, of Tibet. Professor Ranga seems to have been displeased at my occasional reference to Chinese suzerainty over Tibet. Please note that I used the word suzerainty, not sovereignty. There is a slight difference, though not much.... The real point to be made is that it is not right for any country to talk about its sovereignty or suzerainty over an area outside its own immediate range. That is to say, since Tibet is not the same as China, it should ultimately be the wishes of the people of Tibet that should prevail and not any legal or constitutional arguments. That, I think, is a valid point. Whether the people of Tibet are strong enough to assert their rights or not is another matter. Whether we are strong enough or any other country is strong enough to see that this is done is also another matter. But it is a right and proper thing to say and I see no difficulty in saying to the Chinese government that whether they have suzerainty over Tibet or sovereignty over Tibet, surely, according to any principles, the principles they proclaim and the principles I uphold, the last voice in regard to Tibet should be the voice of the people of Tibet and of nobody else."[51]

As stirring and insightful as such statements may have been in parliament and in the newspapers in New Delhi at the time, they did not alter in any way the events that had happened in Tibet or those that were to follow there. In time, however, many of these statements came to haunt both India and those that spoke that day.

In Tibet, China chose not to advance rapidly towards Lhasa from Chamdo, primarily because of the time of the year and the difficult terrain between eastern Tibet and Lhasa. On the other hand, her propaganda efforts were extensive, including radio broadcasts, posters and pamphlets stressing the "peaceful liberation" of Tibet. All stressed the theme(s), "With serious concern for the people of Tibet, who have suffered long years of oppression under American and British imperialists and Chiang Kai-shek's reactionary government, Chairman Mao Tse-tung of the Central People's Government and Commander in Chief Chu Teh of the People's Liberation Army ordered the People's Liberation Army troops to enter Tibet for the purpose of assisting the Tibetan people to free themselves from oppression forever.... With the entry of the People's Liberation Army into Tibet, life and property of the Tibetan lamas and people will be protected. Freedom of religious belief will be safeguarded and lama temples will be protected. Assistance will be rendered to the Tibetan people in the direction of developing their educational, agricultural, pastoral, industrial, and commercial enterprises, and their living conditions will be improved.... All lamas, officials and chieftains may remain at their posts. Matters relating to reforms in Tibet will be handled completely in accordance with the will of the Tibetan people and by means of consultation between the Tibetan people and the Tibetan leaders.... The People's Liberation Army is a strictly disciplined army which will faithfully carry out this policy of the Central People's Government. They will respect the Tibetan people's religious beliefs as well as their traditional habits and local customs. They will be polite in their speech, fair in business transactions, and will not take a single thread from the people. In borrowing any articles, they will obtain the owner's consent; in cases of damage, compensation will be paid at market price of the article concerned. In hiring hands or animals, appropriate remuneration will be paid. No person will be drafted; no livestock taken away."[52]

Although the New China News Agency had announced in November that

4,000 men and officers had been killed or taken prisoner by the Chinese in the Chamdo area, many of the local people were persuaded by these promises, for the Chinese were on their best behavior. They released a number of the Tibetans that had been taken prisoner, including Tibetan soldiers, who were given money by the Chinese and told simply to go home. However, most Tibetan leaders of elements that had fought the Chinese, as well as many others who had been captured, were sentenced to prison in western China. The Chinese obviously were trying to insure that the Tibetans who had resisted would not do so again. In December the Tibetan government sent one last appeal to the United Nations and formed a delegation to travel to the United States to present Tibet's case. After noting the political waffling and realizing that they would receive no support from either the United States or Great Britain, plus the very strong negatives they continued to receive from India, Tibet reluctantly abandoned its plan to send a delegation to Lake Success, having finally recognized that their only option was to try to negotiate directly with Peking.

CHAPTER 3

Agreement by Duress

As noted in the last chapter, after his capture in Chamdo, Ngapo spent several weeks in conversation with his Chinese captors, then communicated to Lhasa that the Chinese would release him — and some of the other officials that had been captured there — if the Tibetan government agreed to negotiate with the Chinese. He noted that the Chinese had assured him that the role and authority of the Dalai Lama and other high officials in Lhasa would not be changed, and he volunteered to join in the negotiations if Lhasa agreed. Lhasa responded favorably, including designating Ngapo as head of the delegation.[1] Apparently Lhasa was still unaware of the relationship that had been formed in Chamdo between the Chinese and Ngapo. "In early 1951, long before the Tibetan delegation signed the Seventeen Point Agreement, a 'People's Liberation Committee' was begun in Chamdo. Empowered to administer the area without reference to Lhasa, it was headed by Ngapo, who, although still a Kalon [a high-ranking official] in the Dalai Lama's administration, was working for the communists through the local [Chamdo] Chinese military headquarters."[2] Obviously, Ngapo's self-interests were being well served, but Tibet's were not.

As it became increasingly evident that there would be no support from the United Nations and that it was the intention of the Chinese to occupy all of Tibet, the Kashag ordered that a plan be prepared to move the Dalai Lama and part of the government to Yatung, a small frontier city some 15 miles from the Sikkim-Indian border, until such time it was more clear as to what the intentions of the Chinese really were. The frightening report that the brother of the Dalai Lama, the former Abbot of the Kumbum Monastery in Amdo, had provided the Kashag of the Chinese proposal regarding the Dalai Lama was a major factor in this precautionary move, for the safety of the Dalai Lama was of the utmost concern of all Tibetans. The plan included the option of the Dalai Lama seeking asylum in India if it appeared that by staying in Tibet his life would be in danger. A live Dalai Lama provided hope for all Tibetans; other alternatives were obviously not acceptable.[3]

As part of the contingency plan, the caravan also included pack animals carrying a large amount of gold and silver bullion under the care of Kenrup Tenzin and a number of very precious religious items to insure their preservation.

The silver and gold was to insure that in the event exile was necessary there would be some funds available to the Dalai Lama to support it.[4] The large caravan of some 1,500 pack animals also included selected government officials and monastery representatives, nobles, some family members, aides-de-camp, 250 men of the Dalai Lama's bodyguard, household servants — and Heinrich Harrer, the Dalai Lama's now famous Austrian tutor who had fled India to Tibet to escape internment and who, the Dalai Lama feared, if seized by the Chinese would be imprisoned or worse. Leaving behind two Prime Ministers with plenipotentiary powers, one a monk and the other a layperson as was customary, the caravan left Lhasa on December 19 and arrived at Yatung on January 7, 1951. The gold and silver bullion and the priceless religious items continued on to Sikkim. The Dalai Lama's oldest brother, known by his honorific name, Takster Rinpoche, as well as by his family name of Thubten Jigme Norbu, was ordered by the Dalai Lama to proceed to India for his own safety. (When the Chinese first invaded, it had been decided that Gyalo Thondup, the older brother of the Dalai Lama should leave Tibet.)[5]

Ngapo and two other Tibetans "arrived in Peking on April 22 or 23, and two other Tibetans representing the Dalai Lama arrived from Yatung on April 26. Chou En-lai himself came to the railway station to meet the former group, while Chu Teh, the commander-in-chief of the People's Liberation Army, welcomed the latter. The delegation (sent by the Dalai Lama) from Yatung brought a ten-point written statement that was to be the basis of the Tibetan position. They were instructed to use their judgment but were to accept the status of Tibet as part of China only in a token sense. They were instructed to establish a wireless link between Peking and Yatung so that other important issues could be discussed. They were clearly not authorized to make major decisions on their own."[6]

"Ngapo suggested that certain points should be kept in mind during the upcoming talks, but that the statement should not be presented to the Chinese.... Ngapo also believed that they should not refer important issues back to Yatung but should take the responsibility upon themselves. He argued persuasively that the abbots and other conservatives in the assembly had no idea of the modern world and the Chinese Communists; that they would refuse to accept the wording and terms the Chinese were going to present and would insist on talking about the patron-priest relationship and independence; delays would result; etc. However, if the negotiators assumed the responsibility, Ngapo said, an agreement could be reached quickly and in a spirit of friendship ... [and] Ngapo said he would take full responsibility."[7]

At the first meeting on April 29, Li Wei-han, chairman of the National Minorities Commission and head of the Chinese delegation, asked Ngapo if he had a position statement, and when Ngapo answered no, Li offered to prepare an agenda. At the next meeting, Li presented "the same 10 points that the Chinese had broadcast and posted on the walls in Chamdo and Kham ... and politely asked the Tibetans to read it over carefully." At the start of the third meeting, Li asked Ngapo "what special instructions he had received regarding the Panchen Lama. When Ngapo told him that he had none, Li remarked that 'This is one of the most important concerns and events for Tibetans everywhere.' ... Over the next six or seven meetings the meetings focused exclusively on the question of the Panchen Lama, but without the slightest sign of change in the attitude of either side.... Finally, Li presented an ultimatum, explaining that because the Panchen Lama had accepted Mao as the new leader of China before the liberation of Tsinghai and Mao had accepted the candidate as the true incarnation of the late Panchen Lama, the 'face' of Mao and China were at stake.... Ngapo told Li he would have to wire Yatung ... [and] made it clear in his communiqué that the Chinese would not begin the real negotiation until the Tsinghai candidate had been officially recognized by the Tibetan government.... The Dalai Lama and his advisors now relented and quickly conducted a lottery divination which conveniently reported that the candidate in Peking was the true incarnation of the late Panchen Lama."[8] The so-called negotiations then resumed, with the Chinese obviously in full command.

"The Chinese presented (the Tibetans) with a ready-drafted ten-point agreement and told them to sign it. It was drafted on the assumption that Tibet was a part of China, which raises the interesting question of why the Chinese found in necessary to negotiate: if they really were the sovereign power, what need was there to negotiate? ... The Tibetans resisted this farcical 'agreement,' but the only effect of this was that the Chinese then reworded it so that there were 17 points instead of ten, and then increased pressure on them to sign. Nor did this pressure stop, including veiled threats that Chinese troops were prepared to advance further into Tibet. The Tibetan delegation recalled the Chinese behavior of nearly eight hundred years before when Genghis Khan had sent ambassadors to the Chinese; the Chinese simply returned their mutilated bodies. Eventually, after prolonged meetings and mental duress, the Tibetan delegation was prevailed upon to sign the 'agreement.' Even then, they refused to affix seals, for they did not have government seals with them, ... but this did not delay the Chinese for long: they forged duplicates forthwith."[9]

Following the signing on May 23, 1951, by both delegations in the former Imperial Palace, the Tibetans met Mao Tse-tung for the first time. Mao told them that "now that they had accepted to be part of one big family, the People's Liberation Army would go to Tibet and because they would be with the People's Liberation Army day to day their doubts would be cleared away."[10] On May 26, Ngapo Ngawang Jigme then went on Radio Peking, announcing the 17 points, among them: "The Tibetan people shall return to the big family of the Motherland, the People's Republic of China; The Tibetan people shall unite and drive out the imperialist aggressive forces from Tibet; The local government of Tibet shall actively assist the People's Liberation Army to enter Tibet and consolidate the national defense; The Central People's Government shall have centralised handling of all external affairs of the area of Tibet; In order to ensure the implementation of this Agreement, the Central People's Government shall set up a Military and Administrative Committee and a Military Area Headquarters in Tibet." This was the first that the Tibetan government — and the rest of the world — heard of the agreement. The Kashag sent Ngapo a telegram stating that the agreement seemed unfavorable; that Tibet seemed to have lost all powers; and reminded him that he had been instructed to seek approval from Yatung for major issues. And, for the first time in history, with Ngapo signing the Seventeen Point Agreement, Tibet acknowledged Chinese sovereignty.[11]

This so-called peaceful liberation avoided the international stigma that might have resulted from a military liberation, and paved the way for a massive infusion of Chinese troops into Tibet. It also precluded the possibility of support or interference from anti-Communist countries should fighting in Tibet resume. The Chinese had achieved a masterful victory. That Ngapo had exceeded his authority, or that the Tibetan delegation had virtually been forced to sign the Agreement, no longer really mattered, for in the eyes of the world, Tibet had publicly and officially agreed to become a part of China.

The Dalai Lama and the Tibetan officials with him in Yatung had expected that the negotiations would be an extended affair, that they would very likely become stalemated over various issues and perhaps even broken off because of issues that could not be reconciled. At the very least the Tibetans had thought to have time to make additional pleas to the United Nations and to other free world countries for at least political support. Delegations had been organized to travel to Britain, to the United States and the United Nations, and to India. Britain and India gave responses that made it very clear that they were in no position or inclination to assist, but the United States evidenced increasing interest and made a number of specific offers to the Dalai Lama in trying to assist Tibet both at the United Nations and in the event that the Dalai Lama decided to seek asylum. Key to this equation was the Dalai Lama publicly disavowing the Agreement that had been signed under duress in Peking and without his authority. There was a flurry of exchanges between Yatung, Calcutta, New Delhi and Washington addressing the possibilities of exile, assistance, support at the United Nations and related issues. The Dalai Lama's oldest brother was heavily involved, urging his young brother to leave Tibet. For a period of time it appeared that he would do so, but suddenly, whereas the Dalai Lama had previously urged his brother to travel to and seek help from the United States, and had provided him letters substantiating that he was acting on the Dalai Lama's behalf, "on 2 July (1950) Takster received a brief letter from the Dalai Lama advising him not to go to the United States, presumably because this would irritate the Chinese. Takster telegraphed back, again urging the Dalai Lama to disavow the Agreement and leave Tibet at once. However, as no statement issued from Yatung, Takster became less optimistic and commented that the Dalai Lama was surrounded by Communist sympathizers and agents who might obtain control at any time. Correspondence continued well into July between the Dalai Lama and U.S. officials, but the U.S. Consulate in Calcutta received telegraphic word in late July that the Dalai Lama was returning to Lhasa." Those with the Dalai Lama in Yatung had heatedly debated the question of the Dalai Lama going into exile, accompanied by some 100 others to be determined by the Dalai Lama, or whether he should return to Lhasa. The two sides were divided largely between those representing the monasteries and those that were government officials. Most of those with monastic connections and the State Oracles, believing that the Communists intended to destroy Buddhism, insisted that the Dalai Lama should return to Lhasa and thereby preserve the Lamaist state, while the majority of the government officials urged him to renounce the Seventeen Point Agreement and leave Tibet enabling the Tibetan government to continue to resist the Chinese from a safe location. Given the failures of the Tibetan delegations to India and Britain, the negative response from the United Nations and the very cold attitude of Nehru, the religious arguments held sway. The Dalai Lama decided to return to Lhasa.[12]

The Dalai Lama, in recalling some forty years later his communications with his eldest brother at the time, said, "Again he urged me to come to India, saying that the Americans were very anxious to make contact with Tibet. He suggested that if I were to go into exile, some arrangement for assistance could be negotiated between our two governments. My brother concluded his letter by saying that it was imperative that I should arrive in India as soon as possible, adding that the Chinese delegation was already in Calcutta en route to Dromo (Yatung). The implication here was that if I did not make a move immediately, it would be too late. A pact with America or anyone else meant war. America was thousands of miles away, [and] China had numerical superiority.... There was a likelihood of years of struggle. America, a democracy, therefore would not put up with unlimited casualties, then Tibet would be on her own again, and China would have her way ... and in the interim only heavy losses to China, Tibet and America. I therefore concluded that the best course of action was to stay put and await the arrival of the Chinese general."[13]

On July 14 the Dalai Lama met with Gen. Chang Ching-wu, the newly appointed commander of the Military and Administrative Committee of Tibet, as the general transited Yatung en route to Lhasa from China (by way of India). The general presented the Dalai Lama a letter from Mao Tse-tung welcoming Tibet into the People's Republic of China. The formalities were brief, polite, and restrained but correct, including the representatives of the monasteries and the Tibetan government officials in Yatung with the Dalai Lama all formally dressed and resplendent in their colorful robes of office. For the Tibetans, and especially those that had favored the Dalai Lama seeking asylum, it was a somber occasion, not a festive one. His Holiness, now 16 years old, could only hope that he could find a way to salvage the future of Tibet. Thus, after nearly nine months away from Lhasa, uncertain but hopeful, he prepared to return. General Chang arrived in Lhasa on August 8, the Dalai Lama on August 17, per their agreement to travel separately. A month later, the first elements of the several thousands of Chinese troops that were to follow began arriving in Lhasa.

There was considerable debate in the National Assembly following Ngapo's presentation describing the negotiations leading to the Seventeen Point Agreement. He stressed the might and strength of the Chinese military, and the futility of considering resistance, as well as the many benefits that would come to Tibet now that it was an integral part of China. The debate began in late September, and, led by the monastics who believed strongly that the Chinese would not dare to interfere with Tibet's religious practices under the Dalai Lama or reduce the strength of the monasteries, the National Assembly, despite the strong opposition of many officials, voted to accept the agreement. On October 24, the Dalai Lama sent official confirmation to Chairman Mao as follows: "Chairman Mao Tse-tung. At the end of April 1951 there arrived in Peking a special delegate, Kalon Ngapo and four other plenipotentiary representatives sent by the local Tibet government. They held peaceful negotiation with the plenipotentiary delegates appointed by the Central People's Government. The representatives of both sides, on May 23, 1951, signed on a friendly basis an agreement relating to the measures for the peaceful liberation of Tibet. The local government of Tibet, the monks and the entire Tibetan people express their unanimous support for this agreement. Under the leadership of Chairman Mao Tse-tung and of the Central People's Government they are actively helping units of the People's Liberation Army which entered Tibet for the strengthening of the national defences, the driving out of imperialist forces from Tibet and the guaranteeing of the sovereignty of the entire territory of the motherland."[14] Obviously, it had not taken long for the Dalai Lama and most of the bureaucrats and the monastics to complete the capitulation process, including adaptation of the Chinese verbiage.

The entry into Lhasa of 3,000 soldiers from the 18th Route Army in early September, complete with drums and marching band, and huge portraits of Mao Tse-tung and Chou En-lai, and hundreds of red Chinese flags carried by the soldiers was described as a time of bitter sadness and little hope. And when more Chinese troops arrived over the next three months, with the total reaching in excess of 20,000 in the Lhasa area, most Tibetans became very angry. The people lined the streets, throwing stones and spitting at the Chinese soldiers as they marched through the streets of Lhasa. They openly labeled the soldiers "Red Barbarian Devils," a term that is still used when Tibetans refer to the Chinese. That the Chinese had also brought some 30,000 animals with them only increased the concerns of Tibetans, for there was the unanswered question of where was the food and fodder going to come from to feed these two- and four-legged unwanted invaders? The Chinese had said that they would provide completely for themselves, but it was soon learned that this meant that Tibet was to provide the tons of supplies that the Chinese demanded. At first the term used was "loan," but that was soon replaced by demands to "give," despite Point 13 of the Agreement, which stated "The People's Liberation Army entering Tibet shall abide by all the above-mentioned policies and shall also be fair in buying and selling and shall not arbitrarily take a single needle or thread from the people" or of article 16 of the Agreement, which said "Funds needed by the military administrative committee, the military headquarters, and the People's Liberation Army entering Tibet shall be provided by the Central People's Government. The local government of Tibet will assist the People's Liberation Army in the purchase and transport of food, fodder, and other daily necessities." Nowhere did it say that Tibet had to give everything to the Chinese. The vast stores of grain were soon gone, taken without pay by the Chinese, and meat, vegetables and household items became very scarce, with prices spiraling ten to twenty times what they had been for years and years. For the first time, Lhasa experienced famine. The Tibetans in Lhasa became increasingly open and bold about their resentment, and anti–Chinese demonstrations of one kind or another became a daily happening.[15]

"Petitions demanding that the Chinese leave Tibet were circulated and even sent to the Chinese military officials. Posters attacking and ridiculing the Chinese were to be seen throughout Lhasa, and anti–Chinese songs were sung openly in the streets. But the Chinese soon reacted and made their own demands, the first of which was that the Tibetan army was to be integrated into the People's Liberation Army immediately, and that the Dalai Lama's two Prime Ministers were to resign. One of them had incurred the anger of the Chinese when, during a meeting to discuss the rough treatment of the Tibetans and the problems the Chinese were experiencing in Lhasa, he told the Chinese commander that '... if you hit a man on the head and break his skull, you can hardly expect him to be friendly.' And five of the Tibetans that had participated in the petitioning efforts in Lhasa were also put in prison by the Chinese. The fear of arrests reduced some of the more insulting actions by Tibetans, but not very many for these were quickly becoming angry times. The Chinese promises had again proven to be false; Lhasa was starving; oppression was increasing; and even the pretension of the Chinese assistance referred to in the Seventeen Point Agreement had proven to be but more empty words. And there were also increasing reports that in eastern Tibet the Chinese were again treating the Tibetans badly ... and in turn the Khambas and Amdos were resisting and fighting the Chinese as best they could. The pot was beginning to boil over."[16]

Nehru was to often refer to the Tibet-China problem as "a conflict of will" and soon spoke in a manner less supportive of Tibet's plight than he had originally. In defending China's actions, Nehru explained to his Parliament that, "In granting Tibet regional autonomy, the Chinese Central Government only recognized that Tibet, on account of its cultural, linguistic and historical and social differences from China proper, deserved special treatment under the Chinese constitution. Tibet is not the only autonomous region in the Chinese People's Republic; autonomy has also been given to places like Inner Mongolia, and Sinkiang. If anything, it only meant that in introducing radical social and economical changes, the Chinese Communist leaders would take into consideration special conditions prevailing in Tibet and would not force the pace of reforms.... But the Communist revolution in China meant a great human upheaval affecting one-fourth of the entire mankind. For the first time in history, the whole of China was under the effective control of a powerful central government which was anxious to take up positions at the far-flung frontiers of the Chinese Republic. Along with the rest of China, Tibet was in for great changes."[17]

Tibet's fears that the government of India would provide no help were well founded. It was abundantly clear that Nehru feared China's military might and was in awe of Mao. The decades of India being the quasi-protector of Tibet ended with the departure of the Union Jack from India.

"The Chinese authorities soon began to prepare the ground carefully for introducing far-reaching political and economic changes in Tibet. In 1952 they took two important steps to integrate Tibet. First, they divided Tibet into three separate administrative zones and in so doing established a strong, separate military area in Tibet. The central and western portions of Tibet were ostensibly placed under the administration of the Dalai Lama, whereas the Shigatse area (south of Lhasa) was placed under the Panchen Lama. The eastern region of Tibet came directly under a Chinese military commander. Second, the Chinese began to open up Tibet — but only to China. It no longer remained the Forbidden Land. New roads were built, and these roads brought truck-loads of Chinese troops. Airfields were constructed. Hundreds of Tibetans were taken to China for education and then returned to Tibet trained in party doctrine and communism. A Tibetan branch of the Chinese Communist Party was set up. A network of grade schools and basic dispensaries was established, with the schools teaching Chinese and Maoism and the dispensaries serving the Chinese. Some waste-lands were reclaimed and new agricultural techniques, such as the use of tractors, were introduced. Simultaneously, the Chinese authorities began to encourage the Chinese people to migrate to Tibet in large numbers. In 1952 Mao Tse-tung told a Tibetan

Opposite: "Welcome" to the Chinese in Lhasa. Mao's picture is prominent — there is *no* picture of the Dalai Lama.

delegation in Peking that Tibet's population must increase by six million in the first instance and then to ten million. This could only happen with large-scale Chinese migration ... and in December 1955, the Chinese Communist Party decided to introduce land reforms in Tibet. The Tibetan land system is one of the most primitive in the world, with most of the arable land owned by a handful of lamas and government officials. The majority of the rural people lead the life of serfs. The Communists began to encourage farm cooperatives which threatened to disturb the very basis of Lamaism and its pastoral aristocracy. Temple lands were either confiscated or nationalized and the monasteries were left without their vital and traditional incomes."[18]

China had discovered the secret of rendering Tibet's Lamaistic powers and influences to near zero. It became obvious to all that China had cracked, if not broken, Tibet's rice bowl, and the days of extensive monastic power were numbered.

And there were many other questions that went without answers. For example, who would feed these ten million Chinese, or even half or a quarter of that number? Agriculture in Tibet could not begin to meet such a demand. And how would they be housed? What would they use for transportation? Would the People's Liberation Army provide vehicles and shelters? How would the Chinese be employed? What was the real purpose of such a massive increase of Chinese? What was to become of the Tibetans? The Tibetans asked, but the Chinese did not answer.

The arguments began to increase in the National Assembly as conditions worsened in Lhasa and as it became more evident that the Chinese had no intention of coordinating their plans with either the religious or government leaders of Tibet. The powers of the Dalai Lama were to be considerably reduced. Street talk was strongly anti–Chinese, and comparisons were again drawn to what had happened to Mongolia and that which was beginning to happen in Tibet. Such questions as Who had given the Chinese the right to claim Mongolia? were asked. What natural bonds had existed between them? Had not the Mongols demonstrated their attitude toward the Chinese in previous times? Had not Tibet made clear its opinion of China? Or did China believe that those few Tibetans who had willingly accepted Chinese bribes to be representative of all Tibetans? Did history not record Mongolia's independence and strength? Had it been forgotten that the Mongols had a strong bond of friendship with Tibet and had been protective of Tibet and previous Dalai Lamas, such as the Fifth Dalai Lama? No such linkage existed between China and Mongolia, not even when the Mongols defeated and ruled China. How would the many famous Mongolian Khans react to the claims of the Chinese that there was a strong bond between Mongolia and China? While it is true that Mongolia no longer possessed the ability to resist the Chinese, or the Russian military strength, do not the Mongols remain proud, united and strong? As for Sinkiang or Tsinghai, the people there had never considered themselves an integral part of China, yet its people were trampled militarily by the Chinese Communists in the name of the so-called Han motherland. Is this to be the fate of Tibet? Does military conquest equate to cultural, historical, or social ties? An executioner (China) and prisoners (Mongolia, Tibet, Sinkiang, Tsinghai, etc.) are not and never will be friends. And what of religious ties? Is Tibet connected in any religious way to Communist China? What natural linkage is there between Tibet and modern China? By what right does China still claim Tibet? Trade was the single main connection for many decades; and since early 1949 that too diminished drastically because of the problems caused by the Chinese in the traditional trading centers. In fact, trade disappeared in most areas, and for quite a period of time the Chinese were not even allowed to set foot in Tibet. "A Tibetan king once married a Chinese princess, but certainly Mao Tse-tung and Chou En-lai should not be angry at Tibet because neither of them had any royal or famous ancestors. Almost all of our Dalai Lamas have been born to poor families. A humble beginning — or an exalted one — is not a meaningful measure, it only matters what the person does in his or her lifetime. That is the only basis of judgement."[19]

"Did these men (in the National Assembly) speak and act and vote simply to appease the Chinese ... or is it possible that such ignorance can truly exist among men who, at least in theory, are educated and aware? And had the leaders of India forgotten so soon what it was to be but a colony with no hope and shattered dreams? How could those who studied the teachings of Gandhi and who had just achieved independence and freedom simply look the other way while bowing to Chairman Mao? These things are very difficult to understand."[20]

The restructuring of Tibet into three administrative zones was simply a first step to insure increased control by the Chinese over the Tibetans in those areas that the Chinese were most concerned about. The Panchen Lama was given the Shigatse area to the south and southwest of Lhasa simply as an extension of the powers that historically had been given to the Panchen Lama there. Since he was returning to Shigatse from China, it followed that the Chinese would trust and designate him to be in charge of that area and because this Panchen Lama had been "selected" by the Chinese, and raised and trained by them most of his life, they expected him to do their bidding. The Dalai Lama was given some of the remaining western area as well as southern and central areas, with the western area having the fewest Tibetans. And central Tibet, primarily Lhasa, was already under the military and political control of the Chinese. Thus the Dalai Lama, the Kashag and the National Assembly were effectively, at least in the minds of the Chinese, neutralized. Eastern Tibet, the vast areas where the Khambas, Amdos and Goloks lived, and where the Chinese had experienced resistance since late 1949, was seen as a threat by the Chinese, and so was placed under a high-ranking Chinese military commander who had considerable military resources under his command. "They thought that the Tibetans would not dare to attempt to resist again with such a Chinese presence there. They believed this was a good plan."[21]

"Then the Chinese started to build roads and airfields, using Tibetan labor. At first the Chinese paid the workers a small sum of money for their labor, but gradually the payments stopped, but the demand for Tibetan labor continued, and soon became nothing but forced labor under increasingly brutal Chinese supervision. But there were a number of roads completed, including the Sikang-Tibet highway which went into Chang-tu and then to Lhasa, built by more than 4,000 Tibetan laborers. These projects were not to help Tibetans, but to make it easier for transportation between China and Tibet for the Chinese. Certainly no Chinese migration was going to take place if the Chinese had to walk to Tibet.... Few if any Chinese would have survived such a difficult trip. Airfields were built so that the senior Chinese officials and military officers would be able to travel quickly, and to map Tibet, as well as to enable the Chinese to locate from the air the location of resistance groups. Nothing of benefit to the Tibetans from the airfields was intended. And forcing 20,000 Tibetan children to attend schools in China was not for the benefit of Tibet, but to indoctrinate the children in the ways of Chinese Communism, and to learn Chinese. The Chinese taught Marxism and Maoism to the Tibetans, but they did not teach them to be doctors, nurses, teachers, engineers, or craftsmen ... only to be Chinese Communists, like robots. Some learned Chinese methods of farming, and some learned to drive trucks, or to repair them, but not many."[22]

The Chinese also tried to develop agricultural programs, primarily because of the necessity to feed the thousands of Chinese troops already in Tibet and the additional thousands of soldiers and civilians that the Chinese Communists intended to send to Tibet. The grain reserves in Tibet were gone, food prices in Lhasa had sky-rocketed, and famine and starvation was spreading. The Chinese made countless mistakes in trying to implement Chinese farming practices in Tibet, most of which turned into disasters, but never admitted as such by Chinese officials in Tibet or Peking. For example, wheat replaced barley as the main crop under the Chinese agricultural program, with dismal results. "On 29 April 1953, the *Times* of India reported from Kalimpong that the price of food had risen 50% in the last fortnight. Grain is beyond the reach of the common man. Butter, meat and other foods have increased steeply and are hard to get. Forcible procurement of grain has resulted in discontent against the Communist regime.... Many instances of clashes are reported between peasants and Communist Chinese grain requisition officials in various parts of Tibet." And earlier, on April 22, the same paper had reported under a Kalimpong dateline that "Members of the secret Tibetan People's Party, whom Chinese occupation authorities describe as agents of an underground 'reactionary' movement, were arrested in Lhasa after they had submitted a multi-point memorandum to the Chinese through the Dalai Lama's office. The memorandum demanded: (1) That the Dalai Lama be given full control over Tibet; (2) That the overall strength of the Chinese occupation troops be minimized; (3) That conditions in Tibetan monasteries be made much better; (4) That the food situation in the land be improved."[23]

With great fanfare, the Chinese had arranged for the Panchen Lama to visit the Dalai Lama in Lhasa. This was a historical and important event for Tibet, for it had been many decades since the Dalai Lama and the Panchen Lama had met publicly. The streets were filled with thousands of Tibetans celebrating the occasion. It soon became evident to all in Lhasa that the Dalai Lama and the Panchen Lama had formed a real friendship, far exceeding the niceties of a religious meeting or a ritual protocol between two high-ranking religious leaders, but a sincere mutual bond was established between the two young religious leaders. There is little doubt that the Chinese had intended this meeting to underscore the differences between the two highest lamas, and that they expected disagreement and jealousy to emerge. The result was quite the opposite, and years later, after the Dalai Lama had fled Tibet, this friendship came to haunt the Chinese, as related in Chapter 12.

Also in 1952 was the command invitation issued by the Chinese government to a delegation composed of Tibetan officials and certain influential Tibetan civilians to visit China to learn firsthand the progress that the Communist leaders had brought to China. "This delegation was to visit Peking and several other cities in China, Inner Mongolia, and Sinkiang to see how well the people there were treated, and how prosperous China had become. The delegation members were received with elaborate ceremonies throughout their travels, and also constantly reminded of the military strength of China, for there was usually a series of military parades or a demonstration of military strength in each area visited. And in case that was not enough, there was the constant presence of Chinese soldiers everywhere the delegation traveled. The intended message of Chinese military strength was unmistakable. Pamphlets and photos were also given the members throughout the trip, as were constant lectures about the benefits of Chinese Communism and the wisdom of Chairman Mao Tse-tung. It was soon apparent to all members of the delegation that despite the extensive efforts of the Chinese, and behind the facade of a happy China, there was extensive fear, oppression and poverty. Living conditions were very poor; there was no sign of freedom and few smiles or laughter.... The Chinese people were but slaves of the Chinese government and very fearful of the soldiers and Communist cadres and the uniformed and secret police that were also present everywhere in large numbers. China was an unhappy land. It was this message that members of the delegation brought back. Other delegations also visited China, but they too were not fooled. In the minds of the Tibetans who had seen it in practice, Chinese Communism already had rot that could not be hidden. But matters were made worse, for it was also at this time that the Chinese began to forcefully take more and more Tibetan children to China to train them in Chinese schools. This action only served to further harden the resolve of many Tibetans to take revenge against the Chinese, for our children are very precious to us Tibetans and hate was only a natural reaction to such Chinese practices."[24]

CHAPTER 4

Deeds of Deceit

While on the surface it may have appeared that the Chinese were making headway in their plans towards bringing Tibet to heel and to communize her with minimum problems, the Tibetan venture was not going well for either China or Tibet. Resentment among the Tibetans was increasing; bureaucratic disagreements in Lhasa, while not widespread, were growing; armed conflicts were expanding in the east; and Tibetans ridiculed the Chinese soldiers publicly, in printed leaflets and in songs, as well as in shouted slogans telling the Chinese to leave. Children threw stones at the Chinese soldiers, and Tibetans of all ages began to spit at the Chinese on the streets of Lhasa. These actions were not what the Chinese political cadre had expected, and General Chang demanded that the Dalai Lama issue a proclamation banning any criticism of the Chinese. The Dalai Lama did so, but it had little effect. The anti–Chinese posters continued; the jokes continued; the insulting songs continued. Very few Chinese understood Tibetan so the Chinese remained largely ignorant of the insults; the spitting changed from on, to the direction of, or at the backs of the Chinese. Only the rock-throwing diminished. Obviously, Chairman Mao's "Motherland" was not being embraced by the Tibetans, with some noteworthy exceptions such as Ngapo Ngawang Jigme and certain other officials and Lamas that had been swayed by the various inducements offered them by the Chinese.[1]

The trips to China by various Tibetan delegations, which had been organized by the Chinese to impress, or perhaps frighten, the various strata of Tibetans, including government officials, merchants and students, had failed to do either. In fact, the vast majority of those who traveled to China returned with descriptions of conditions in China that were not at all flattering or favorable to Mao's new China and Marxism. The extensive poverty, the heavy atmosphere of resignation and unhappiness, and the overwhelming presence of Chinese soldiers to insure control over the population could not be hidden. The trips soon became the subject of extensive ridicule, much to the embarrassment and chagrin of the ranking Chinese military and political cadre in Lhasa.

One of the more amusing examples was that in the course of viewing the photographs that had been taken of and presented to the different Tibetan delegations that had visited China over a period of time, two of the Tibetan government officials that had been involved in preparing each of the trips on the Tibetan end made an interesting discovery that they shared with a number of their colleagues and friends. They pointed out, one by one, many of the same faces of Chinese in their same costumes and uniforms in many of the photos, not only with the different delegations, but some even in the different areas visited by the delegations as well. "At first the Tibetan officials could not believe their eyes, but given the proof in the photos before them it was evident that the Chinese had not wanted to leave anything to chance, so used many of the same guides and security people, both army and police, over and over. It was simply a matter of transporting them and loyal cadre personnel not traveling with the delegations from one place to another in advance of the Tibetan visitors, thereby insuring the presence of the many smiling faces they wanted to show, and making sure there were no problems in controlling the visits. One has to admire the thoroughness of such preparations. However, despite the elaborate requirements and precautions that were obviously needed for this illusion, there was no way that the Chinese could conceal the abject poverty, the regimentation, the unhappiness of the people, and the tight control over all aspects of life that the Chinese government exercised. Many delegations went, including officials, merchants, religious leaders and students. They all basically formed the same conclusions and had the same observations despite the many cosmetic efforts made by the Chinese to make a favorable impression on their 'guests.' The Tibetans particularly noted the presence of the Chinese soldiers everywhere, and remarked upon returning to Tibet how this was particularly disturbing, as was the obvious fear of the Communist cadres and soldiers by the villagers and farmers."[2]

"After many of these pictures had been displayed publicly on a wall in Lhasa for everyone to admire, some of the monks and others eventually noticed the duplication, perhaps helped by some of the faces having been lightly marked by those who had made the discovery. Nothing was said directly to them, but the Chinese were very embarrassed when, in the course of pretending to admire the many various photos the Chinese displayed in Lhasa of the delegations, some of the Tibetans would remark in the presence of Chinese, first on the general appearance and dress of the Chinese groups escorting the delegations and then to note loudly and repeatedly on the 'amazing likenesses' of the same Chinese from one picture to another. These attempts to deceive the Tibetans soon became the subject of many street jokes in Lhasa, much to the chagrin of the Chinese, such as 'It is no wonder that there are so many of the Chinese, for I have seen photographs with my own eyes that most of them have twins living in different areas of China. Is that not remarkable?'... or ... 'Did you know that the Chinese have mystical powers that enable them to fly from one photograph to another? You may not believe this possible, but it is so, for I have seen it.'... Another was ... 'I talked to one of the delegation members the other day and he told me of the incredible powers of the Chinese that he had seen while in China. He said that many Chinese are able to magically move themselves long distances from one place to another. He said that often persons are seen in one area one day, and then, as if by magic, in a very distant area the next day. This is truly a special power, is it not?' There were others, but those give you an idea. And while the Chinese efforts to deceive us were often quite funny at the time, they were also warnings of how devious the Chinese are and how far they will go to deceive if they believe it of use to them."[3]

Far more serious problems for Tibet were on the horizon for 1953, the Year of the Water Snake. It was not long before Peking had to admit that their puppet government experiment in Tibet was not succeeding. The rate of progress was far behind what the Chinese had planned, and much of what was supposed to have been accomplished had not even begun. Above all, the presence of the Chinese had not been accepted, and in fact it was being rejected daily, nor had Tibetans shown any indication of accepting China as the "motherland." On the contrary, resistance to the Chinese was on the rise throughout Tibet, ranging from many passive forms in the cities and villages, to guerrilla warfare in the more rural areas.

Concurrent with the above, there were increasing problems of inflation in Lhasa and of famine in some parts of the countryside, along with many stories of Chinese atrocities against Tibetan peasants and farmers as communes were formed. Early vestiges of thought control began to be enforced in various parts of Tibet, mirroring the efforts that were ongoing in China as Marxist readings. And as in China "Large accusation meetings would be organized. It all resembled a giant, coerced program of religious conversion."[4] Family denunciations were encouraged, and all were expected to cite their deep appreciation to the Chinese invader for having saved and brought enlightenment to Tibet. "Since that time [the 17 Point Agreement] the Tibetans have suffered untold agonies. The Chinese Communists have gradually deprived us of all our political rights. Our government, right from the top to the provincial and district offices, has been made powerless and today we are governed completely by the Chinese.... Economically Tibet used to be self-sufficient for its food supply. But today millions of Chinese are living on our people and our food situation is desperate. The people in the east and northeast are facing famine. The Chinese, beside laying hands on our current crops, have forced our people to open our centuries-old granaries. They have also taken away our reserves of gold and silver bullion. In the southern and central regions they have destroyed thousands of acres of agricultural lands by giving priority to 'national highways' and to the building of barracks and arsenals."[5]

There were also increasing numbers of reports of wanton stealing by the Chinese soldiers from Tibetan farmers; stories of Chinese raping and beating Tibetans in rural areas; stories of Tibetans, including monks, being forced at gunpoint to labor on building roads and airfields for the Chinese; and continuous stories of the Chinese forcibly taking Tibetan children by the hundreds from their families to send them to schools in China.

"The reports of 'difficulties' in Tibet were confirmed later by Gen. Chang Ching-wu, Peking's chief representative in Tibet. General Chang told the State Council in Peking in 1955: 'Due to communications and transport difficulties and many other factors ... what we have achieved is very little, as far as the construction of Tibet and the consolidation of national defense is concerned. There have been grave misunderstandings among the nationalities (Han and Tibetan). This coupled with the unthorough education on the implementation [of] the Agreement (treaty) of 1951 ... caused misunderstandings and doubts on the part of Tibetan personnel, thus hindering the smooth progress of our work."[6] All of these so-called "misunderstandings" served only to reenforce the deep resentments long held by Tibetans against the Chinese.

Some of the Tibetan officials protested these stories of abuse and mistreatment to the Chinese officials, but they reportedly said they knew nothing of any such happenings. "This was obviously a lie, for some of the Chinese officials in Lhasa had often been overheard talking and laughing about these same reports."[7] The Tibetans then decided to make these issues public. "There were even public denouncements of the People's Liberation Army, much to the chagrin of the Chinese officials," and of course to the embarrassment of the senior Chinese political and army officers. The Tibetan People's Assembly in Lhasa, the Mimang Tsongdu, dispatched a six-point petition to the Tibetan government via the Kashag, and to the Chinese Army command in Lhasa, urging in very clear language all Chinese to withdraw. And, by this act of direct defiance, the Mimang Tsongdu demands became popularly known as the first official resistance group. As reported in the *Times* of India on April 22, 1953, "Members of the secret Tibetan People's Party, whom Chinese occupation authorities describe as agents of an underground 'reactionary' movement, were arrested in Lhasa after they had submitted a multi-point memorandum to the Chinese through the Dalai Lama."[8]

That the efforts by the Mimang Tsongdu were doomed to failure was not important, for its symbolic value remained priceless to the Tibetans long after the Chinese ordered the Mimang Tsongdu to be dissolved. Because of the many unexpected oppositions and inability to move their plans forward, the Chinese Politburo decided to intervene directly; thus even the illusion of any meaningful Tibetan participation in the government began to dissolve. The People's Assembly (formerly the National Assembly) was effectively stripped of all real powers, as was the Kashag. "Only the office and religious position of the Dalai Lama remained between the Chinese and the Tibetans. All other real buffers were now gone."[9]

The Kashag and a modified People's Assembly remained as organizations but in name only. Under the circumstances of the time, they existed only because the Chinese thought they served some useful purpose, such as helping to pacify the monasteries and the general public, and to present the illusion of a Tibetan government functioning in support of the Dalai Lama. This charade was soon to end.

In late 1953, the Dalai Lama was "invited" to China to attend the first Chinese People's National Assembly, which was to meet in September 1954 to adopt a Chinese Constitution. It was made very clear by the Chinese that the Dalai Lama was expected to attend, and, despite strong urging from nearly all Tibetans not to go, he announced he would accept the Chinese invitation. "He believed he might be able to influence the Chinese leaders while learning more about them, and thereby be better able to protect his people. He also believed that if he refused, the Chinese would only increase the suffering of the Tibetan people. It was a very difficult time for the people of Tibet, for now they feared that they might never see him again. In the minds of most, he would be but a hostage to be used by the Chinese to work their will in Tibet. Petitions were sent to the Dalai Lama urging him not to go, and thousands of Tibetans were on the streets of Lhasa protesting the Chinese invitation. But the Dalai Lama had made up his mind that there was no other choice, and that it was imperative that he make the trip to see China for himself ... and to meet the leaders of China."[10]

It was clear to most Tibetans at this point that they had only their religion to sustain them, along with the hope that the Dalai Lama would return, for without the Dalai Lama there was no Tibetan government, it having been effectively replaced by the Chinese. With his departure for Peking, Tibetans were totally at the mercy of the Chinese Liberation Army. Before leaving, the Dalai Lama gave sermons to the people, urging them not to despair. He promised that the Lord Buddha would look after them, and after him as well, and that he would return. "In private audiences with some of the leading Tibetans who had been rumored to be in favor of organizing resistance groups, he urged that no such action take place during his absence, for it would only encourage the Chinese to retaliate without mercy and result in the slaughter of thousands of Tibetans. He told them that a peaceful way had to be found. In turn, he received promises from these leaders that they would exercise restraint and follow his words, but some also voiced clearly their doubts that the Chinese would keep whatever promises they made to him. It was pointed out to him that in eastern Tibet the Chinese soldiers had already broken all the promises made earlier and that there was really no other option but to fight back. The tribal leaders noted that the Chinese understood only too well that conciliation and appeasement on the part of the Tibetans served well the purposes of the Chinese, but not Tibet's. His Holiness did not argue, but continued to urge patience. From their questions to and statements from the Dalai Lama, and from quiet rumors circulating in Lhasa, it was clear that some of the leaders would use the time until his return to plan and scout the countryside in preparation for what they saw as the inevitable coming of extensive armed resistance against the Chinese."[11]

In mid-1954, the Year of the Wood Horse, the Dalai Lama, now 19, left Lhasa for Peking with a retinue of some 500 government and religious leaders and servants. Such a sizable group was, in the minds of the Tibetan officials, necessary to properly impress the Chinese. Of more practical value, it was also a security measure in the sense that even the Chinese would not likely want to have to explain publicly the disappearance of the Dalai Lama and a retinue of 500. This large number was initially upsetting to the Chinese, who thought such a big group to be very pretentious but finally agreed to it because, for political and propaganda reasons, they needed the Dalai Lama to willingly attend the People's Assembly. Also, in their minds, it provided the opportunity to publicize the goodwill of the Chinese, as well as time for them to achieve more converts to their cause should they find such vulnerabilities among the many Tibetan government officials and religious leaders accompanying the Dalai Lama. Along the way, at Sian, the Dalai Lama was joined by the Panchen Lama, now 16 years old, and his more modest retinue. The roads, built largely by Tibetan forced labor, made the early part of the journey one of weeks rather than the months previously required, with the final stages of the journey completed by "train and airplane, which were new experiences for both the Dalai Lama and the Panchen Lama, and for most of the other Tibetans in the retinue. The Dalai Lama and the Panchen Lama were greeted with great fanfare in Peking, like visiting heads of state,"[12] but again it was more a staged event than one of sincerity. Two days later the Dalai Lama met Mao Tse-tung.

The timing of this meeting was quite unusual. The Dalai Lama was not a visiting head of state but merely a representative to attend the People's Assembly. However, Mao later said that he was very curious about the Dalai Lama and that he had determined to establish his influence right away. He reportedly had often referred to the Dalai Lama simply as "that pretentious boy King," or the "King of Tibet," when talking to others about the Dalai Lama, and usually referred to Tibet as "that pastoral aristocracy." It was obvious that Chairman Mao was confident that he would have no trouble in converting the Dalai Lama into being a useful political supporter of his, and he wanted to begin that process right away. In this first meeting he asked the Dalai Lama if there were any complaints against any of his officials or representatives in Tibet. This was a question intended to test the Dalai Lama, daring him actually, more than one actually seeking information. The Dalai Lama answered it with diplomatic generalities relative to having high expectations for the future under the leadership of Chairman Mao, and that both the Tibetans and the Chinese should present their views openly and frankly in future discussions. The purpose of these general responses has been described by the Dalai Lama as twofold: one, to assure that Chairman Mao would have no reason to suspect that the Dalai Lama was in opposition to him, and, two, he wanted to be certain that Chairman Mao would continue to want to meet and discuss matters with him. In this way, the Dalai Lama has explained, he believed the Chinese would have no excuse to take further actions against the Tibetans in his absence, and continued meetings would give him the opportunity to better know and understand Mao. This, then, raises the question: was the Dalai Lama simply naive, or was this just the reaction of a young man faced with the presence of the most powerful man in Asia? Whichever, it is understandable.

During a series of meetings, the Dalai Lama came to understand many of the contradictions inherent in Chairman Mao, the dictator of the largest nation in the world. At one meeting, Mao reportedly said, "I understand you [the Dalai Lama] very well ... but of course, religion is poison. It has two great defects. It undermines the race, and secondly it retards the progress of the country. Tibet and Mongolia have both been poisoned by it."[13] Comments about his discussions with Mao made by the Dalai Lama years later (1989) are interesting and revealing. For example, he has said that the more he looked at Marxism, the more he liked it. He described Marxism as a system based on equality and justice for everyone, which in turn could be a panacea for all the world's ills. He noted that "From a theoretical standpoint, its [Marxism's] only drawback as I could see was its insistence of a purely materialistic view of human existence. This I could not agree with."[14]

The Dalai Lama also noted his concern that the methods used by the Chinese in pursuit of their ideals were too rigid. Despite these reservations, and what the Chinese were doing to Tibet, the Dalai Lama asked to become a party member. He has explained that he felt then that it would be possible to work out a synthesis of Buddhist and pure Marxist doctrine that would be an effective way of conducting politics. He has often repeated that he still holds that opinion.

The question that immediately comes to mind after reflecting on these words of the Dalai Lama (written in 1989) is how could he have arrived at such a conclusion, for Maoism, and Mao's Marxism, had devastated Tibet and her people. History reveals that there was never an indication of any kind that China ever intended any good or benefit to accrue to Tibet, regardless of Mao's claim of pursuing enlightened Marxist ideology. Even the thirteenth Dalai Lama had provided clear and strong warnings to Tibet's secular and monastic leaders of what China intended, although few heeded them.

And by the time of the Dalai Lama's first meeting with Chairman Mao there was already an abundance of evidence of what China intended to do and how it was going to do it, including the use of famine, starvation, restrictions on religious practices and forced labor in Tibet. And there was ample evidence available from the visits of the many Tibetan delegations to China as to what Marxism had already brought to the Chinese people. Also, there were — and are — the lessons from the historical experiences of those countries that had previously tried Marxism. Marxism's track record was then — and remains — one of unbroken and abject failure. Stalin and Mao both spoke glowingly of Marxism, but both also knew that without applying extensively the terrorist and control practices initiated and used effectively by Lenin and Stalin and Mao, it was not possible for Marxism to endure.

It is readily understandable that the very young Dalai Lama was likely all but overwhelmed by Mao and the vast power that he represented. However, it is difficult to understand how the Dalai Lama could make remarks supportive of Marxism thirty years after fleeing Tibet. Perhaps he has not yet studied extensively about the evils that have accompanied Socialism and Communism. Perhaps he simply forgot that the Marxist-Leninist approach to the problem of nationality and nationalities provides for self-determination, and the right to secede, as does Communist theory. That neither of these latter two provisions have ever been granted in any Socialist or Communist state are also worth contemplation.

It is also worth noting that the Dalai Lama has readily stated that he had been inspired by Mao and in those first meetings that "every time I saw Mao he inspired me again." In turn, these inspirations led to the Dalai Lama composing and dedicating a lengthy poem eulogizing Mao, much to the dismay of most Tibetans.

From his conversations with Chou En-lai and Liu Shao-chi the Dalai Lama concluded that Liu was a man of few words and little laughter, but he was very determined and tough. Chou En-lai was described as pleasant, smiling, intelligent, overly polite, but not necessarily to be trusted. In defense of his favorable impression of Mao, it is obvious that the Dalai Lama was not the first nor the last to misread or be fooled by Chairman Mao.

During one of their meetings, Mao told the Dalai Lama and the Panchen Lama that the Chinese intended to colonize Tibet at a ratio of more than five to one.[15] Obviously, this would make imposition of Chinese rule on Tibet much easier and at the same time would help solve China's chronic overpopulation problem. Of much greater consequence to Tibet was the obvious intent by the Chinese to simply outnumber and assimilate Tibetans, insuring that Tibetans would be but a small minority in their own country.

There is little detail about the meetings between the Dalai Lama and Mao. No doubt Mao talked persuasively of the benefits of Marxism and all the wonderful things that he and Marxism had brought and would bring to China. He very likely convinced the Dalai Lama that Marxism would similarly benefit Tibet as well. One thing that Chairman Mao did reveal in his remarks to the Dalai Lama was his deep disdain for religion, but he also remarked to the Dalai Lama that Buddhism served a purpose in that it was a good religion for the common masses, implying perhaps that Buddhism serves primarily as a useful opiate to Tibetans in their theocratic society. Another impression the Dalai Lama formed was that Chairman Mao tried to pay attention to all governmental details yet was very impatient with delays, even though it was Mao himself who had created the cumbersome centralized government in China that by design could not function quickly.

It is also clear that Mao managed to convince the Dalai Lama that China would not dispatch more military forces into Tibet to achieve what China wanted. The Dalai Lama seemed to cling to that belief, even after it was obvious that Mao had misled him, just as he believed that Mao did not know the details of the terrible things the Chinese soldiers and cadre had done, and were continuing to do, in Tibet. However, most Tibetans believe that Mao — and Chou En-lai and many other leaders — knew full well what was happening, and that indeed Mao had approved of and authorized what the Chinese were doing in Tibet. This is not to say that Mao or Chou En-lai had specifically directed the extensive and reprehensible abuses of Tibetans by the Chinese in Tibet, but it needs to be remembered that it was more degree than difference between what the Chinese were doing in Tibet and that which they had done and were doing in most of China. In general but simple terms, the Han Chinese have historically had little or no regard for others and often not even for each other, as Mao later clearly demonstrated in purges of his formerly close companions.

There is a saying: "If it is not easy to explain, it is much harder to understand." And so it is in trying to reconcile what the Dalai Lama says now about Marxism and Communist China with that which had happened and was happening then in Tibet, and with what happened following his meeting with Chairman Mao. Certainly most Tibetans would classify Mao as a monster, as would most Chinese who suffered under him. As for Chou En-lai, he too is believed to have been fully cognizant of the events in Tibet, including the brutal treatment of the lamas and the other excesses of the Chinese. However, Chou En-lai is credited with having done the most to restrain and reduce the carnage and destruction in Lhasa following the Tibetan uprising there in March 1959. Reportedly, it was because of his influences that at least some of the great buildings of Lhasa, such as the Jokhang, were saved and not reduced to rubble.

While in Peking, the Dalai Lama had some opportunities to meet various other political figures and visitors, although the Chinese discouraged anything more than the briefest social encounters at diplomatic parties and dinners. For example, he did not have an opportunity to talk at any length with the Russian ambassador or with Pandit [Jawaharlal] Nehru when he made a state visit to Peking. He did meet the Indian ambassador, but the conversation was constrained by the Chinese not allowing him to use his own Tibetan-English translator. Instead, the Chinese insisted on a circuitous translation from Tibetan into Chinese, and then Chinese into English by Chinese interpreters so that they could keep full control of what was being said.

Following the dutiful rubber stamping in September 1954 by the "delegates" to the 1st National People's Congress of the new constitution that had been completed — and announced publicly well before any of the so-called delegates had even arrived in Peking — and after the ensuing and requisite speeches by some of the delegates praising Chairman Mao, most of the "delegates" departed Peking for their homes. The Dalai Lama and many of his retinue remained at the insistence of the Chinese to study the wonders of Marxism and to travel in China on arranged trips to learn more of (Mao's) China and, unexpectedly, to learn the details of a new governmental structure for Tibet that Mao had told him the Chinese had devised called the Preparatory Committee for the Autonomous Region of Tibet (PCART).

PCART was described to the Dalai Lama by Mao as an organization designed to expand the authority of the Dalai Lama and to increase the numbers of Tibetans in his government. Not mentioned by Mao was the fact that as an autonomous region per the recently signed Agreement, Tibet was but a province of China and, as stated in the Communist Chinese constitution, an integral part of the People's Republic of China under the leadership of the Central (Peking) Government. In simple terms, China had simply again broken her own rules as set forth in the Seventeen Point Agreement, while using that Agreement to do so.

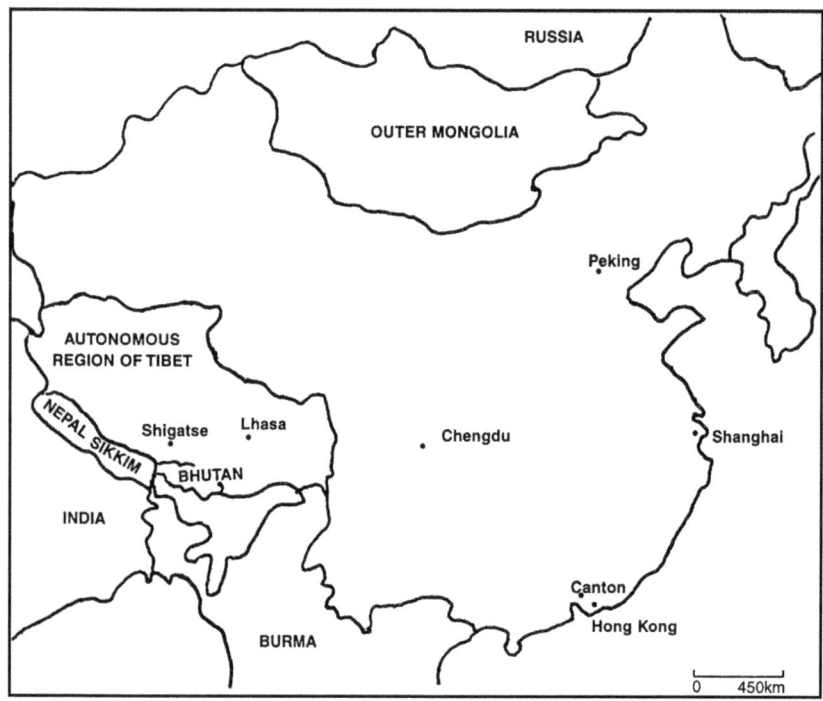

Tibet as the People's Republic viewed it.

It was stressed to the Dalai Lama that the Chinese intended to help Tibet in every way it could to progress and become modern and that they did not want to govern Tibet but wanted the Tibetans to govern themselves. The Dalai Lama was also told that the Chinese did not want to keep more than a few troops in Tibet, primarily for border defense purposes. Yet, even as this was being said, and contrary to what Mao had just told the Dalai Lama, more and more Chinese troops were being sent into Tibet over the extensive road network(s) that the Chinese had completed through the use of forced Tibetan labor.

Meanwhile, taking advantage of the Dalai Lama's absence, the Chinese were also busily trying to build up the position of the Panchen Lama. The Chinese even went so far as to rewrite Tibetan Buddhist history, claiming that the Panchen was ruler of Outer Tibet (Lhasa). The Dalai Lama they relegated to the disputed regions of Inner Tibet (Tsinghai Province). One version of this appeared in the Hong Kong Communist daily, *Ta Kung Pao*, in 1954. "The paper, misrepresenting historical fact, declared that after the death of Tsongkhapa, founder of the Buddhist sect that rules Tibet, two of his disciples ruled over Inner and Outer Tibet respectively in accordance with the will of Tsongkhapa. The elder disciple, the Dalai, became ruler of Inner Tibet, and the younger disciple, the Panchen, ruler of Outer Tibet. ...On January 19, 1955, an agreement was signed in Peking between the Tibetan Local Government and the Committee (the) Panchen Kanpo Lija *On Historical and Unsettled Problems*."[16] This deceitful charade attempted to establish on paper that the Dalai had ceded an unhistorical portion of his power in local Tibetan Affairs to the Panchen and his followers.

The whittling away of the previous powers of the Dalai Lama, both secular and religious, not only continued but increased with the passage of time.

On March 9, 1955, the State Council of the Chinese government passed a proposal, "Decisions Concerning Tibet," which included the "Preparatory Committee for the Autonomous Region of Tibet." This decision, as reported by NCNA on March 12, specified that "the Preparatory Committee shall be composed of 51 persons; 15 from the Tibetan Local Government, 10 from the Panchen Kanpo Lija Committee, 10 from the People's Liberation Committee of the Chang-tu (Chamdo) area [which was under the direct control of a Chinese General], 5 from the Chinese cadres of the Central People's Government working in the Tibet area, and 11 others, including representatives from the major monasteries, religious sects and public bodies. The Dalai Lama will be Director and Panchen (Lama) Ngoerhtehni and (Gen.) Chang Kuo-hua first and second vice-directors ... and Ngapo Ngawang Jigme, Secretary General. All three organizations (the Tibetan Local Government, the Panchen Kanpo Lija Committee, and People's Liberation Committee of the Chang-tu Area) will be directly responsible to the Chinese State Council concerning State administrative matters.... All the enterprises under the State Council which

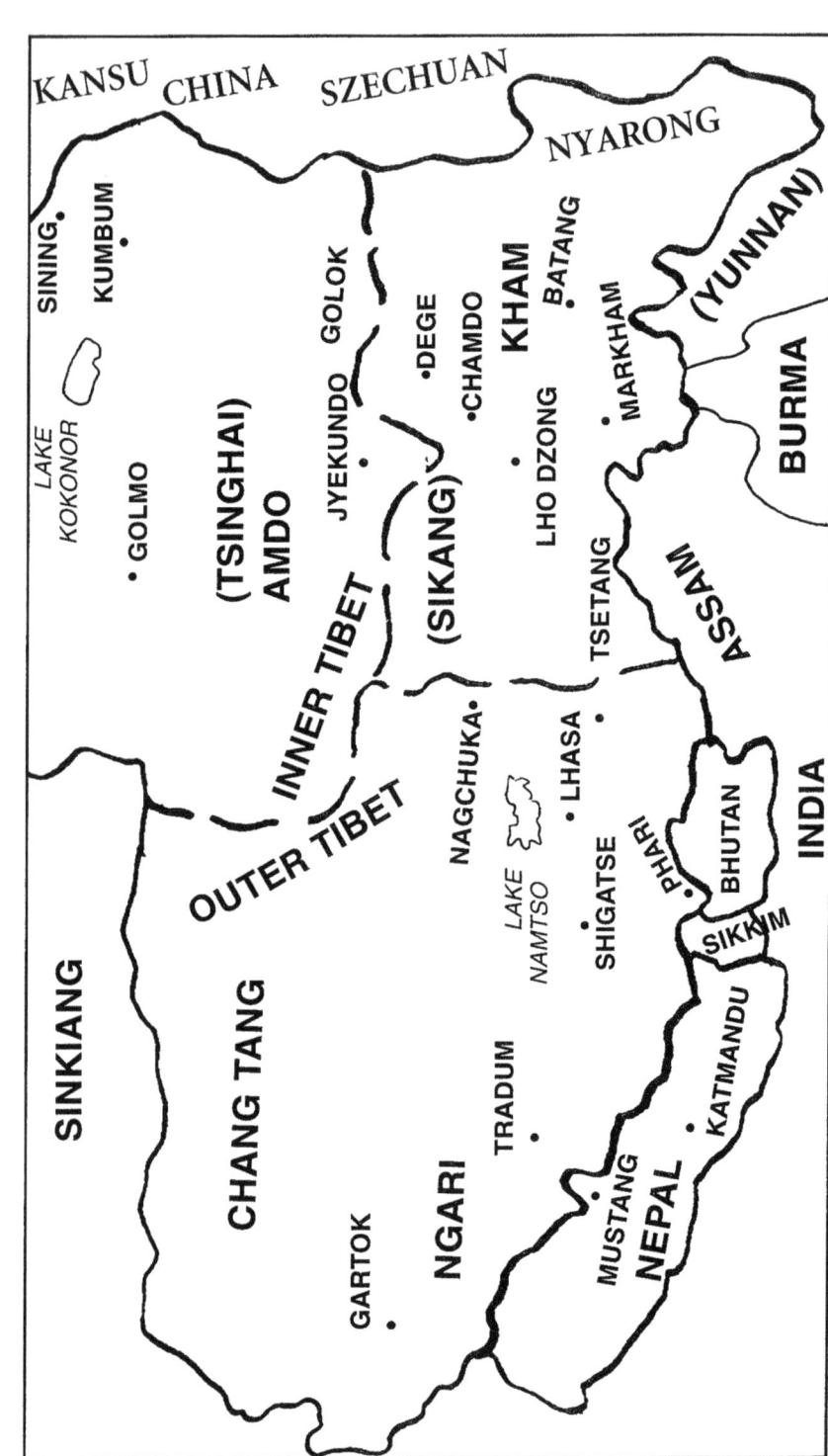

operate in Tibet will still be led by the various responsible departments of the State Council.... Matters approved by the State Council to be undertaken by the Preparatory Committee should also be observed and carried out by the PLA Tibetan Military District Command."[17] And all members had to be approved by the Chinese. Initially the Tibetan reaction to the idea of PCART as it had been described to them was generally favorable. They believed the glib explanations given them about PCART and thought that the Chinese had decided to grant them more autonomy; however, upon studying the details it was clear that the opposite was true.

It was also clear that under this new set-up the government of Tibet remained under the Tibet Military Command of the Communist Chinese Army, and that the nominal powers of Tibet's former sovereign, the Dalai Lama, were drastically reduced. The Tibetan Local Government had only 15 out of 51 seats on the new Committee and the Chinese had at least 25 members who would support the Chinese position, whatever it was. The Tibetan Assembly soon became a forum of constant conflicts of will and largely ineffective. Compounding the travesty was that when the PCART met, it was given an agenda prepared by the Party Work Group of the Chinese Communist Party in Tibet, which it was expected to rubber-stamp. It was obvious that the real power in Tibet was this Party Work Group, which was not elected and which consisted almost entirely of Chinese and which was but an extension of the Party apparat in Peking. The Preparatory Committee had been set up merely as a front in order to provide a semblance of legality and continuity for whatever the Chinese intended to do.

Following the State Council's announcement on March 12, 1955, relative to PCART, both the Dalai and the Panchen Lama departed Peking for Tibet, with each taking a different route. They returned to Lhasa in June. And on July 18, 1955, NCNA announced the abolition of Sikang Province and the incorporation of its territory into Tibet and Szechuan Province. The new boundary between the Tibet Military Area and Szechuan Province was now along the former de facto Sino-Tibetan boundary. Again, China had broken another point of her own 17 Point Agreement.

"For the first time in the centuries of Tibet's existence, the daily life of lamas and laymen was being dictated by a foreign government — ironically, one which subscribes to a philosophy thoroughly alien to Buddhism, of atheistic materialism and expansion by force. The initial moves to force the Communist economic and social system on Tibet, in defiance of the treaty agreement of 1951, were made in February 1956 on the country's eastern borders. Later, at the inaugural meeting of the 'Preparatory Committee for the Autonomous Region of Tibet' in Lhasa on April 22, 1956, Communist China's Vice Premier, Chen Yi, and Chang Kuo-hua, commander of the Tibet Military

Opposite: Inner and Outer Tibet.

District, told Tibetans that 'a new stage of work,' the complete exploitation of the Tibetan economy through collectivization, was about to begin. They proclaimed that 'necessary reforms would be introduced to rid Tibet of its backward situation and to bring Tibetans up to the level of the advanced Han nationality.'[18] The Chinese had already attempted to make many changes during the year-long absence of the Dalai Lama, including the first efforts of collectivization and other Communist reforms in eastern Tibet such as taxes on lamaseries, farms — even yaks and cattle. And "land reform" experiments were also being tested by the Chinese in the rural areas. With few exceptions, all these attempts had been met with increasing resistance by the Tibetans.

To add further to Tibet's problems, during 1954 India signed an agreement with China labeled the "Five Principles of Peaceful Coexistence" in which India renounced all historical and neighborly ties with, and rights in, Tibet. Nepal was also required by China to sign a similar treaty, surrendering all concessions she previously had with Tibet, including an agreement between Tibet and Nepal going back nearly a hundred years. China thus completed the severing of Tibet's many traditional links to India and Nepal. India also signed over to China all communications rights that Britain and India had maintained in Tibet for many decades, along with realigning respective trade offices to meet China's wishes. India's only remaining official link inside Tibet to the Tibetan government was via the wireless in the Indian Consulate in Lhasa, one which the Chinese took care to insure was largely a one-way arrangement.

The reactions in India to all these developments were, as to be expected, varied and interesting. As reflected in the debates in the Indian Parliament, there was a distinct lack of unity of opinion, as the following clearly reflects.

Prime Minister Nehru, in summing up his presentation to Parliament on May 15, 1954, regarding the Sino-Indian Agreement on Tibet, said, "Recent events made some other changes, factual changes, because a strong Chinese State gave practical evidence of exercising that sovereignty over Tibet. So that what we have done in this agreement is not to recognize any new thing, but merely to repeat what we have said previously, and, in fact, inevitably follows from the circumstances, both historical and practical, today. The real importance, I repeat, of this agreement is because of its wider implications in regard to non-aggression, recognition of each other's territorial integrity and sovereignty and non-interference with each other, external, internal or any other like interference."[19]

Responding to this, Mr. Acharya Kripalani said, "The plea is that China had the ancient right of suzerainty. This right was out of date, old and antiquated. It was theoretical; it was never exercised and then theoretically. It had lapsed by the flux of time. Even if it had lapsed it is not right in these days of democracy by which our Communist friends swear, by which the Chinese swear, to talk of ancient suzerainty and exercise it in a new shape in a country which has and had nothing to do with China. Tibet is culturally more akin to India than it is to China, at least Communist China, which has repudiated all its old culture. I consider this as much a colonial aggression on the part of China as any colonial aggression indulged in by Western nations. The definition of colonialism is this, that one nation by force of arms or fraud occupies the territory of another nation. In this age of democracy when we hold that all people should be free and equal, I say China's occupation of Tibet is a deliberate act of aggression. Whether certain nations commit aggression or are peaceful does not always concern us. But I say this, in (the) case of China and Tibet we are intimately concerned, because China has demolished what is called a buffer state. In international politics, when a buffer state is abolished by a powerful nation, that nation is considered to have aggressive designs on its neighbors."[20]

Mr. Brajeshwar Prasad followed Mr. Kripalani and said, "At the outset, let me congratulate the Prime Minister on the conclusion of the pact with China. The preamble, as he has said — and I agree with him — is far more important that the articles. I regard this pact as a non-aggression pact in embryo.... The Prime Minister has said that collective security is not possible unless it is transformed into collective peace. May I venture to suggest that collective peace can be achieved only by changing the status quo? The central problem of the age is how to change the status quo without resorting to war. This can be done in Asia by coming together with China and Russia. A mutual Defence Pact with China and Russia is the urgent need of the hour."[21]

It is interesting to note that in Mr. Prasad's view, Tibet did not deserve even a nod in discussing the Agreement. He failed to mention her at all.

In his presentation that same day, Mr. Joachim Alva, from Bombay and editor of the weekly Indian journal, *Fortune*, said, "We are only acting on the moral forces and we cannot wage a conflict with our nearest neighbor, China. I have constantly pointed out on the floor of this House that we cannot afford to have a quarrel with China and that the historic conflict between China and Japan cannot be repeated on this sub-continent. The day that is repeated will denote the downfall of the East. We ourselves will be enmeshed in a kind of international strife. We drove away the British with all the forces at our command under Mahatma Gandhi's able guidance and our freedom should not be frittered away by any strife with China.... Let not our friends lend their ears to foreign propaganda.... Tibet belonged to China."[22]

During a continuation of the debate in Parliament on May 18, 1954, Prime Minister Nehru said,

> In my opinion, we have done no better thing than this since we became independent [agreeing that Tibet belongs to China]. I have no doubt about this.... I do not want to go into the historical details as to the relations of Tibet with China in the past. It is not clear-cut; there is a long history. As to the treaties and maps which Dr. Satya Narayan Sinha has presented [showing conflicting

boundary markers between Chinese and Indian interpretations], let me tell him, after all, these treaties and maps were all prepared by British imperialists. These treaties and maps are intended to show that we must act as they did. Now, we must realise that this revolution that came in China is the biggest thing that has taken place in the world at present, whether you like it or not. It is entirely up to your own mind and heart, and you may make your own decisions, but this is the biggest thing that has taken place since the war. In a period of only a few years a country the size of China has moved and arisen from slumber, and for the first time in several hundred years of history China now has a strong central government. This fact is a very important fact for Asia and the world.... Now what is the significance of all these arrangements? Well, in the beginning of the agreement there is a preamble. The preamble contains a few things that are very significant, because if these few things are accepted, not only with respect to India and China but also the other countries of Asia, then this atmosphere of fear which is haunting us will gradually go away. Fear will gradually diminish, because we must realize that in the world of today there are several things that you don't like, there are several things that I don't like, but the world does not move simply according to your or my likes or dislikes.... Therefore, it must be an agreed principle that both should co-exist: live and let live. No one should invade the other, no one should fight the other. As a matter of fact, both sides are afraid of each other, as if the other would eat them up. It is a strange situation. If there were more trust, then they must live as they like. This is what India wants; in Russia, there is the Communist system; let her continue with her system; let America carry on with her own system. But they should not fight each other, because if they fight, then both of them will be finished, neither of them would win. This is the basic principle which we have put in our treaty with China. You see, these are the words which we have used: "recognition of territorial integrity and sovereignty, non-aggression, non-interference" and then we consider other things like "mutuality." Now territorial integrity and sovereignty mean that there should be no invasion. "Non-aggression" also means the same thing; and "non-interference" means that there should be no interference in domestic affairs, because some people are in the habit of interfering in other people's affairs. Now if these basic principles were accepted by every country and if every country were left free to progress as she likes, to follow any national or foreign policy she likes, no one else interfered, then gradually an atmosphere, a climate of peace would be established in the world. This is our policy and we try to act according to this policy.[23]

The question prompted by the above is: was Nehru speaking as an Indian or Asian statesman, or was this a man so afraid of Mao's dictatorial and expansionist ambitions that he was willing to adopt an extreme conciliatory attitude towards China in the hope or expectation that Mao would choose to leave India alone? A practicing and accomplished Brahmin, certainly Nehru knew the dangers and evils that existed around the world at the time, including those in China and the Soviet Union. And he had to know that rhetoric alone would not save India, or Asia, or the West, yet he seemed to be mesmerized by Mao and what Mao had done to centralize power in Peking unlike anything that had happened in China's previous history. Nehru had to recognize that it was the choke-hold that the People's Army exercised on the people, and Mao's heartless political faithful, and the extensive practice of dragooned informants, and the stringent control by the police, all under the large umbrella of fear, that kept Mao secure on his self-appointed throne. That Mao had adopted the practices of Lenin and Stalin in establishing his so-called Marxist state had to be obvious to Nehru, yet he virtually groveled in defending Mao to his government colleagues.

And if the Dalai Lama had thought that Nehru might be of some help to Tibet because of previous decades of close ties, then this hope was obviously without basis. Clearly, Tibet was alone, and history records that no one did anything to help at this point in time.

But Nehru's trying to rationalize a policy of naked abandonment was not well accepted. In a debate in the Lok Sabha in late September 1954, speakers continued to take their Prime Minister to task. For example, Mr. Asoka Mehta, a Socialist Party leader and a "Socialist intellectual," said, "Our Prime Minister has been emphasizing the five principles of the Sino-Tibetan Treaty on Tibet. These principles are undoubtedly welcome, but when it is realized that Tibet, whose people are alien to the Chinese in race, language, culture and religion, and who have received their Buddhism from India, whose script was devised by Indian Pandits and whose culture contacts with India spread over centuries, is described in that very Treaty as 'the Tibet region of China,' the valuable principles lose much of their motive power."[24]

Mr. N. C. Chatterjee, described as representing the Hindu Mahasabha and a distinguished jurist, followed Mr. Mehta: "Then there is the melancholy chapter to which reference has already been made in one of his speeches by Shri Purushottam Das Tandon and by Acharya Kripalani. I refer to the betrayal of Tibet. That is a melancholy episode in Indian history. The Tibetan Delegation was invited to Delhi. While the Delegation was going back (to Lhasa) via Calcutta the Chinese Army invaded Tibet and finally annexed it. Pandit Nehru was initially shocked and even sarcastically remarked: 'What is this liberation? Liberation from whom?' In the end, India has not the courage even to support a resolution sponsored in the United Nations on Chinese aggression against Tibet. If I remember aright, the Leader of the Indian Delegation announced that India would support that resolution condemning Chinese aggression on Tibet. But, later on, he backed out and did not give any support to that resolution. I call this appeasement of aggression. This is really not an effort towards peace. The Sino-Indian Treaty marks another episode. Our government has made a free gift of the telecommunications, even though China was prepared to pay for it. The Sino-Russian bloc is making today North Korea, Manchuria, Sinkiang and Tibet a strong military base and is thereby threatening the security of Asia and the world. Sir, I am raising this Tibetan question because I feel that this betrayal of Tibet and the surrender to the aggression of China has led to disastrous results in Nepal. There is a feeling that our foreign policy is neither independent nor really dynamic. There is a feeling that India is steadily, slowly drifting towards the totalitarian bloc. There is a feeling that India's Prime Minister is a fellow-traveller. A definite bias in favor of the Communist groups would be barren. Our foreign policy has succeeded in making America greatly anti–Indian."[25]

Then Mr. Joachim Alva, a Congress party member from Bombay and an editor, remarked, "I find that my friend, Mr. Chatterjee made a reference to Nepal and Tibet. I am surprised that he is still flogging a dead horse. The joining of Tibet with China is a historic fact. No one can undo it. If the British government in India was not capable of holding Tibet in the manner they wanted to it is not anybody's fault. If we want to be perfectly good neighbors with China, we must realise this and not raise any voice of protest in regard to Tibet.... When Mr. Chatterjee referred to the Prime Minister of India as a fellow-traveller, I felt we were all fellow-travellers. Who is not a fellow-traveller, if he thinks of the economic improvement of his own country? If we have an inner urge for the economic development of India, if we have an impatience with what is happening elsewhere and want to do those similar good things in our own land, then everybody is a fellow-traveller, and I do not think he can find fault with the Prime Minister of India by dubbing him as a fellow-traveller."[26]

And then Mr. Acharya Kripalani, one time Congress President, responded, "We have failed in arresting the march of Communist China to our borders. A small buffer state there was deprived of its freedom and that state was swallowed up. When we made a feeble protest, we were told — not very politely — to shut up. Not only that, we were told we were stooges of the Western powers."[27]

The ease with which Nehru and others in the Indian Parliament blamed the British for the troubles in Tibet and India's border problems is particularly interesting. It seemed to act as a relief valve of sorts for their various diplomatic pressures. And it was obviously worrisome to the Indians that India no longer had a meaningful buffer to the north. Where there had been none before, now there were thousands and thousands of Chinese soldiers in Tibet, and the extensive road-building efforts in Tibet included roads southward to the border areas of India, Nepal, NEFA, Sikkim and Bhutan. There were also new airfields that had been built in Tibet, where none had existed before. India had to read all of these factors as a potential threat. There is no way to know what Prime Minister Nehru really believed, but we have to conclude that his motives and actions were clearly what he judged best for India at the time. Whether he was correct is another matter.

The Dalai Lama and those officials that had traveled with him on visits to various communes and locations in China were able to see firsthand what the Chinese had done, and they received lectures by the Chinese covering what they intended to do further in China. But none of the Tibetans were allowed to converse with the people, only with their guides and designated Chinese contacts. It was obvious, however, that the Chinese intended to do much the same in Tibet, including the forced introduction of communes and extensive "agrarian reform," throughout Tibet, without regard to their previous promises. That China intended only to exploit Tibet, not to assist or to advance her, became increasingly evident to the Tibetan officials. And that Tibet was to become a heavily occupied part of Han China was also abundantly clear.

The Dalai Lama returned to Lhasa at the end of June 1955. Increased numbers of Chinese troops and an array of Soviet-made army trucks and vehicles were everywhere. Two new roads, one to the north and one to the east, had been completed and were heavily traveled by Chinese military vehicles. An airfield north of Lhasa had been built. Many new buildings had been constructed, including housing for the Chinese soldiers. A bank, a hospital, a school and a newspaper were new additions in Lhasa, as were women's leagues, and a new office for the Tibetan Communist Party. But most of these were only for the Chinese officials and a few invited Tibetan officials, not the general public. The Chinese had hoped to win more support from Tibetan officials by granting them use of these facilities, but this did not meet with the great success the Chinese had expected. Many Tibetan officials were simply afraid of what the reaction of other Tibetans might be, for the anti-Chinese feelings were increasingly strong and widespread. But there were a few Tibetan officials who chose not to resist the temptation. And we did not forget them.[28]

"The return of His Holiness brought great joy to the Tibetans. Everywhere along the way he was warmly welcomed and the people held receptions. In Lhasa there were huge gatherings and parades by the Tibetan army, with hundreds of monks in colorful robes carrying religious banners. His Holiness gave sermons, and all Tibetans gave thanks to the Lord Buddha for his safe return. However, there was also sadness in His Holiness, for as he traveled back to Lhasa, he had met with Tibetans from all walks of life. Collective farming was being forced everywhere. The Chinese knew nothing about how to farm in Tibet and wrong crops were resulting in many crop failures, which were then blamed on the Tibetans. The many reports of Chinese brutality were similar. Only the locations of the incidents differed, with the stories keeping pace with His Holiness as he traveled towards Lhasa. The beatings and robbing of the monks, farmers, and traders; the raping of Tibetan women; the looting and destruction of countless monasteries; the attacks on the religion by the Chinese; the destruction of religious items; the extensive theft by the Chinese of the gold and silver accumulated over scores of years from the monasteries; the forced and often unpaid-for labor of farmers and monks; the continued military attacks on the Khambas, Amdos and Goloks in remote areas — these were all stories that were repeated over and over again. The Chinese had simply taken advantage of the Dalai Lama's absence to do whatever they wanted to do, knowing that no Tibetan would officially complain. Chairman Mao's many promises proved to have been lies."[29]

The Dalai Lama said he was shocked by these reports, for no word of these things had reached him in China. "The Chinese had kept His Holiness well isolated from outsiders, including the Tibetan messengers that had been sent from Lhasa. Those messages were simply intercepted and not delivered. For example, the Dalai Lama did not learn until he was inside Tibet, well on his way back to Lhasa, that India had sent 1,000 tons of rice to help relieve the famine that had occurred in Lhasa during his stay in Peking. Nor had he heard anything about the Chinese forcing the introduction of so-called farm cooperatives in eastern Tibet during this same period ... or that many Tibetans had been executed by the Chinese soldiers when they refused to comply with the Chinese demands that the Tibetans give up their land as part of the farm cooperative program. Nor had he heard of the establishment of 'Thought Correction Centers,' where the Chinese demanded the Tibetans recite the extensive wonders of Chinese Communism and its programs, including the teachings and accomplishments of Chairman Mao, and to repeat back to the Communist Cadres their teachings that only Russia and China were great powers; that the Chinese Communists had won the war against the Japanese ... and had overcome the political struggle against the KMT Nationalists of Chiang Kai-shek; and that all other imperialist countries, especially the United States, were mere paper tigers. And the Thought Correction Centers were described as centers of learning, for in them the Tibetans learned slogans such as 'save grain, kill flies, destroy sparrows, resist imperialism'; along with other sayings of Mao Tse-tung."[30]

It is not particularly easy to understand how promises could be made by the two most powerful men in China to the theocratic leader of Tibet knowing that those promises had already been broken or soon would be. How could Mao blithely tell the Dalai Lama that the new governing administrative structure (PCART) for Tibet would give the Dalai Lama more powers, when just the opposite was true? And that there were to be no changes until the Tibetan government requested them? How did this equate with the unlimited powers for the Communist Party of Tibet? And the edict of death to all who opposed the land reforms and the collectivization process? What kind of political horror had Mao sired? And no one from the Free World to help or intercede on Tibet's behalf? How could this be in the twentieth century?

The Chinese civil and military administrators were, for the most part, nothing more than colonialists. In Peking, the Dalai Lama had seen that the Chinese retained at least some of the old, traditional courtesies, even if only a facade. In Tibet, all pretense was abandoned. "As one Chinese general told me, it did not matter what the Tibetan people wanted; the Chinese would draft in enough soldiers to make them do what they were told."[31]

The British believed the Indians to be ignorant natives, but the British recognized that the Indians had their own culture and way of life. "The Chinese did not care anything about the Tibetans and were determined to stamp out our freedom, our religion, our culture and to turn Tibetans into Chinese. When they set up schools, the teaching was in Chinese. The Buddhist religion and our monks were ridiculed and abused. Our way of life for centuries was ended."[32]

The Dalai Lama has said that he did not communicate his concerns to Mao because he thought it might result in only more harsh measures by the Chinese. There is little doubt that he readily recognized the inevitability that worse was to follow. He also had to recognize and reconcile that promises made by Mao and all other Chinese officials were intended only to deceive, mislead and pacify. And certainly he realized that it was only a matter of time before the Tibetans would decide that it served no purpose to remain passive, and that many would decide to engage in extensive armed resistance. It is less clear why he decided to simply let matters take their course while playing the Chinese game in Lhasa, rather than registering his concerns and objections forthrightly to Chairman Mao, or Prime Minister Nehru, or other statesmen and diplomats, either directly or by way of his two older brothers, or otherwise try to influence Tibetan history of the moment as it clearly continued its downward spiral. Sadly, he became part of that whirlpool until rescued by the Freedom Fighters in March 1959.

By the end of 1955 the Chinese had gone beyond what Tibetan patience would allow. Their freedom was threatened; their religion was threatened; the Chinese had taken away most of the powers of the Dalai Lama; their land had been taken; their taxes had been increased; the Chinese had used Tibetans as forced labor; famine and starvation had been experienced in Tibet for the first time; Tibetan children had been forcibly taken from their parents; Tibetan farmers and peasants had been treated brutally; the Chinese had ordered Tibetans to surrender their arms; a new Chinese style government had been imposed; many monasteries had been destroyed and many monks had been forced into hard labor, others simply killed. The Chinese promises had once again proven to be nothing but lies while the prophecies and warnings of the thirteenth Dalai Lama had proved accurate beyond belief. And a strong common bond of determination to challenge and resist the Chinese had begun, especially among those in eastern Tibet.

CHAPTER 5

Thunder in the East

As the Dalai Lama and his advisors had earlier concluded in Peking on completing their analysis of PCART and studying its detailed explanations of duties, responsibilities and authority, it was soon clear to the Tibetan officials and senior monks in Lhasa that the Dalai Lama's role had been reduced to being little more than a figurehead. Originally there had been five main administrative divisions under the Dalai Lama: U-Tsang, the Lhasa and Shigatse area; Gartok in West Tibet; Kham is East Tibet; Lhoka in South Tibet; and Chang in North Tibet. The Kashag was the Dalai Lama's six-man cabinet, and the Tsongdu was his 350-man Assembly, comprised of representatives from the five area divisions. This was revised by the Chinese to an organization wherein basically Tibet was divided into three sectors, the general Shigatse area under the Panchen Lama; Lhasa and central Tibet under the Dalai Lama and the Chinese military command in Lhasa; and eastern Tibet (Chamdo) under the Chinese military command there. PCART was a drastic change, raising the question of what could the Dalai Lama accomplish under its conditions. The answer? He was all but powerless. All important decisions were actually made by the committee of the Chinese Communist Party in Tibet, an extension of the Party committee in Peking. The Chinese like to use the term "government by committee," but there was no government by committee, except the Chinese Communist Party Committee. The Chinese recognized that they needed the Dalai Lama if only as a figurehead, for without him the chaos that loomed increasingly real on the horizon would have multiplied earlier and larger.

When the Chinese began to exercise the power PCART gave them, the Tibetans were told by Chang Kuo-hua that "a new stage of work, the complete exploitation of the Tibetan economy through collectivization, was about to begin." This prompted widespread protests in Lhasa and many public meetings and demonstrations. More petitions were sent to the Chinese officials in Lhasa, including demands that the Dalai Lama be consulted on all matters regarding the welfare of Tibetans and that the Chinese not meddle in Tibetan affairs. Other public demands included that the Dalai Lama simply not attend any meeting called by the Chinese. But the Chinese had no intention of changing anything or relenting. By use of threats of imposing further and more harsh restrictions, they pressured the Dalai Lama and the Kashag to issue proclamations banning public meetings, and proclamations prohibiting anyone from making any threats against the so-called good relations between China and Tibet, as well as other freedom-inhibiting proclamations. For example, posters protesting the Chinese in any way were prohibited, as were any conversations against the Chinese. Violators would be jailed, or worse.[1]

At the inaugural meeting of PCART in Lhasa on April 22, 1956, China's Vice Premier Chen Yi spoke of the many highways that had been constructed and how they had made it possible for China to "unify" Tibet, and that "a railway from Lanchow to Lhasa will be built in the future," which would cross the Tsinghai Province area of Inner Tibet where in the Tsaidam Basin the Chinese believed they had found oil fields as rich as the nearby Yumen fields. Then Gen. Chang Kuo-hua spoke, stating, "Appropriate reforms constitute a course which must be taken.... This is the road for transition to socialism.... According to instructions of the (Peking) government, the reforms in Tibet in the future must be carried out from the upper to the lower levels. Some people suspect that the present cooperation between the Chinese Communist Party and the upper sections of the (Tibetan) people is only an expediency for exploitation, and that after reform there will be no cooperation.... Some people worry over the possibility that after the reform, freedom of religious belief will no longer be protected, and may even be abolished. These fears are groundless. The Government intends to follow the example of the Soviet Union. As the Communists assert control in Tibet, counter-revolutionaries will become more active in sowing dissension and carrying out sabotage. Therefore, we must maintain vigilance against overt and covert enemies, and expose and administer firm and powerful blows in time. If the counter-revolutionaries and the imperialist elements should dare to create disturbances, we will crush them resolutely."[2]

Whether General Chang's speech was intended to reassure the Tibetans or to frighten them into submission and compliance, it failed totally. Certainly the reference to "following the example of the Soviet Union" was of no comfort to those Tibetans who understood the implication of the remark and Soviet control practices in their own domain. The attitude of the Soviet Union towards Tibet and its struggle against the Chinese had been made clear at the time the Tibetans had sought assistance from the United Nations in 1950. Obvious from General Chang's remarks was the intention of the Chinese to give no quarter. The Tibetans were not awed, and the tribals became only more resolute.

In another speech by Gen. Chang Kuo-hua in Lhasa on April 26, 1956, he quoted Mao as having said earlier, "Tibet is a huge area but it is too thinly populated. Efforts must be made to raise the population from the present level of two million ... to more than ten million. Besides, the economy and culture need development. Under the heading of culture, schools, newspapers, films and so on are included, and also religion."[3]

These remarks further angered all Tibetans and prompted a new round of protests and public demonstrations, which prompted the Chinese to order the Kashag to arrest three popular Tibetan officials who had joined those who had spoken out against the Chinese plans, charging that they had distributed anti–Chinese literature. Even though they had not broken any Tibetan law, the three were arrested and put in prison, where one of them died under less than clear circumstances. The other two were finally released after the abbots of the three main monasteries, Sera, Ganden and Drepung, appealed to the Kashag to release them, and in turn the Kashag appealed to the Chinese. Their release resulted more from embarrassment that one of the three had died in prison than for any humanitarian reason. Turmoil and confusion increased among all Tibetans throughout this period. In Lhasa despair and anguish rapidly replaced hope and trust. The future of Tibet under the Chinese looked extremely bleak for Tibet. And in the countryside the various Tibetan leaders knew that they would have to fight in order to survive at all, for the Chinese were obviously intent upon eliminating any who they thought might oppose them in any way.[4]

At the end of June 1956, "Peking made a tacit admission of serious revolts on the eastern Tibetan border. On June 27, NCNA reported that Hsi Jao Chiatso, Chairman of the Communist-controlled Chinese Buddhist Association, had told the National People's Congress that rebellion on the eastern Tibetan border was the result of local dissatisfaction with Communist policies (because) of some recent improper measures on land reform, and commercial taxes on lamaseries, farmland and cattle. These measures, he said, created worry on the part of the Lamas and the lamaseries and opened the door for enemies to sow dissension." He added the significant statement that the Chinese Communist army, "while collecting weapons from the people, even took away the weapons which had been placed as religious offerings. As a result, Buddhists doubted the sincerity of religious freedom."[5] The serious mistake by the Chinese had been the decision to collect the weapons from the tribals and from the rural monasteries. This act was resented far more by the Tibetans than the increased "taxes" and seizing of private property by the Chinese.

The many incidents of harsh and cruel treatment of Tibetans by the Chinese that had been related to the Dalai Lama as he traveled through eastern Tibet to Lhasa from China had since increased to the point that many Khambas had made the decision to retaliate. The mistreatment of Lamas, harassment of the people and monks by PLA soldiers and local Chinese officials, new taxes, brutality by the soldiers against both men and women, attempted confiscation of their weapons, the many incidents of outrageous behavior against the Amdos by the Chinese, etc., had combined to convince the Khambas that further patience, as still urged by the Dalai Lama, was not going to ease or solve the situation. Many of the Khambas and Goloks went on the offensive. Although not organized, and with only the mixture of rifles and various small arms that they had previously cached, the Khambas attacked a number of Chinese patrols, camps, storage areas, and convoys, destroying all they could. They captured a large number of weapons, destroyed many Chinese camps and killed many Chinese soldiers. Eventually, heavy Chinese reinforcements and aerial bombing forced the Khambas and Goloks to retreat, but not before many Chinese had felt the blade of the Khamba sword.[6]

Supporting the stories of resistance in eastern Tibet were NCNA releases. For example, on August 7, 1956, in a Peking dispatch, NCNA said that "the Communist Chinese Army had suppressed a rebellion on the eastern border of Tibet.... The rebellion started around the end of February, in western Szechuan, in the Kanze Autonomous Chou (province) on the border of Tibet. The rebellion, limited to the area of Bathang and Lithang in the southern part of the chou, has been mainly settled.... It was instigated by remnant Kuomintang agents and launched by a few feudal landlords hostile to the introduction of even the most elementary reforms. Military measures against the rebels were necessary." On July 23, 1956, NCNA had reported from Lhasa that "medals were awarded to 416 officers and men of the Chinese Army stationed in Tibet, who had fought in the Resist-Japanese War and in the liberation wars both to the north and south of the Yangtze, and in the peaceful liberation of Tibet." Further, "In late June a group of Tibetans, headed by a brother of the Dalai Lama, addressed a petition to Prime Minister Nehru charging that the Communist Chinese killed more than 4,000 Tibetans in the April bombing of the village of Lithang, on the Chinese side of the Sino-Tibetan de facto boundary." The petition, prepared at the birthplace of Buddha in India, as reported by news dispatch from Kalimpong (India), stated, "To us Tibetans the phrase 'liberation of Tibet' is a deadly mockery."[7]

The resistance effort by the Tibetans against the Chinese invader could be said to have begun with the events in eastern Tibet in 1956. However, there were earlier resistance efforts in Kham and Amdo, generated by the extreme and brutal treatment by the Chinese of the Tibetans in eastern Tibet. These actions were more spontaneous and tribal than well coordinated efforts, and more reactive rather than part of a widespread effort. As such, the Chinese obviously had an overwhelming advantage in countering the Tibetans. But that resistance was inevitable is likewise true. It began when the Chinese first invaded, just as Tibetans had resisted Chinese incursions for centuries. And it increased as the Chinese mistreatment of the Tibetans increased. As much as the Dalai Lama had hoped that there would not be resistance, he had to know that at some point the Tibetans, and especially the Khambas, Amdos, Goloks and Yi, would rise up if the Chinese continued to threaten their freedom and their religion, just as had happened throughout Tibet's history. The stealing and seizing by the Chinese of Tibetan lands, animals, weapons and belongings; the forced labor; the taking of Tibetan children; the mistreatment by the Chinese of the monks, including dragging them, and others, to death behind horses or vehicles; the pillaging of hundreds and hundreds of monasteries in eastern Tibet, including the stealing of the treasures and religious items from the monasteries; the Chinese molesting of Tibetan women; and all the other barbarous things they did in the name of Democratic reforms could not go endlessly unanswered or unchallenged. The demands for so-called confessions, the mock trials, the tortures, the summary executions — how could these be justified by the Chinese or tolerated by the Tibetans directly threatened by their actions? The Tibetans knew that terror and fear and slavery were not the tools of sane or just men. How could the Chinese expect that the Tibetans would not eventually resist?

More than likely the Chinese knew that resistance would result and for that reason had in five years hurriedly completed construction of thousands of kilometers of many new roads from China to and inside Tibet in order to insure rapid movement of and support to their troops. Too, the continued political demands by the Chinese on the Dalai Lama and their treatment and attempted humiliation of him were very deeply resented. Any threat to him in itself would be sufficient to cause a very strong reaction. To the Tibetans, it was all seen as a never-ending threat to their freedom, their religion and their precious way of life.

> Tibetans are normally very patient, and, despite the incredible abuses by the Chinese of them, not all patience had yet been exhausted ... primarily because the Dalai Lama had cautioned that there was need for continued calm, and that fighting the Chinese was not the right course. However, many leaders disagreed with their Dalai Lama and were ready and anxious to fight. Nor was it any wonder that nearly all outside of Lhasa urged an uprising, for in their view Tibet was rapidly becoming a land without hope. Starvation and deprivation are difficult to experience at best, and under the Chinese they were now commonplace. The never-ending demands by the Chinese and the land reform with its forced communization and forced public "confessions" were totally foreign to Tibetans. The false accusations and so-called confessions, the "struggle sessions" the Chinese called "thamzings" that had been put into effect in Eastern Tibet, and then more slyly in Central Tibet, had an indirect but significant impact on the decision to fight. Just the presence of thousands of Chinese soldiers, and the ever-increasing number of Chinese civilians, including officials and party cadres, settling in Tibet were reason enough for many Tibetans to decide to rebel.
>
> The haughty Chinese did not understand that Tibetans, especially the proud and independent and fiercely loyal tribal groups, were not going to become slaves of the invaders. The one calming effect throughout all this very difficult period was His Holiness, who continued to counsel that rebellion not be pursued. He repeatedly stated at the time that there were other solutions, although none of them had worked. He also instinctively knew what the terrible cost would be if the unequal armed struggle between the Chinese and Tibetans came to pass. The resistance that finally engulfed Tibet resulted from the never-ending pressures and demands by the Chinese, their constant deceptions and lies, and finally the realization by Tibetans that their choice was basically freedom or slavery. Their religion was obviously at risk, and the continued threats to His Holiness only increased the determination of the Tibetans to resist. The anger had

Early "thamzing" session: the Chinese are "addressing" assembled Tibetans.

been built up for an extended period because of the many terrible things the Chinese had done, and obviously intended to continue doing.

The resistance formed like gusts of wind slowly building in size and strength as they became a howling storm; it was like a gigantic storm one could see forming on the distant horizon in the east that would gradually come closer and closer until its full fury was felt. The fuse of resistance had been lighted for an extended time for many reasons ... but it was a long fuse that burned for quite some time before its detonation was felt throughout Tibet. There were many other shorter fuses and lesser explosions that preceded the large explosions that eventually came, but they too helped to protect His Holiness for they served to keep the Chinese off balance as well as off schedule, although that was not readily known or recognized at the time. And in the meantime, the tribal leaders were organizing and communicating.[8]

The Year of the Fire Monkey, 1956, was, just as the thirteenth Dalai Lama had predicted for this period, a year of constant political turmoil as well as the beginning of serious revolt against the extensive reforms the Chinese intended for all Tibet. "It was the year when most Tibetans finally understood that the promises made by the Chinese were not worth even the breath we used while talking or listening to them. Democratic reforms? Land reform?

Assistance? Progress? The translation of those terms was quite simple: violence, and threats, and starvation ... and death ... all in the name of socialism on the path to Chinese communism. It was clear that the Han intended to inhabit and totally control Tibet, and we Tibetans were to all but disappear. This was Mao Tse-tung's interpretation of welcoming Tibet to his so-called family. Very simple. I feel anger, but mostly only deep sadness about what happened to my country and my fellow Tibetans. But final judgement is based on the deed, not the word. I believe that both Mao Tse-tung and Chou En-lai, and the thousands of other Chinese who hurt our people and destroyed our way of life and took our freedom — wherever they are and whatever form they may have in their new life — now understand this clearly."[9]

In the early part of 1956 many hundreds, even thousands, of Khambas and Amdos in eastern Tibet, along with many Goloks, rebelled against the Democratic Reforms of the Chinese. In simple terms, they decided that they would take no more abuse from the Chinese. They took up arms and rode into the mountains to organize themselves as best they could into cavalry units and then began a series of fierce attacks against selected targets. Their quick and determined attacks on horseback resulted in many Chinese garrisons in the east being overrun and demolished. With swords and rifles the Tibetans attacked the Chinese posts in Lithang, Bathang, Kansu, Chamdo, Derge, Po and countless other places. Some parts of Kham and Amdo were described as being covered with smoke and fire for weeks from the fighting and the destruction of the Chinese camps. The Chinese infantry soldiers were no match for, nor were they able to resist, the swift surprise attacks of the determined and vengeful cavalry units. The wild charges on horseback by the Khambas, the Amdos and the Goloks, firing their rifles and wielding their swords, had not been experienced before by the Chinese and they fled in huge numbers. And they died in large numbers. And many of their installations were totally burned. The fighting continued for weeks and in some areas even for months.

Reacting to these attacks, the Chinese repeatedly tried to bomb the Tibetans nearly every day in some of the areas. At first they were not very accurate or successful because of the high and difficult terrain, but eventually they improved. Initially the Tibetans did not know what to do when the Chinese planes came, for they had never experienced this type of warfare and did not understand at first that the airplanes and bombs represented a serious threat to their lives. Casualties usually were not heavy but were higher than they should have been, for at first the Tibetans did not seek cover or hide when the airplanes came, but often remained in groups and watched the airplanes with fascination. These early lessons were hard, but quickly learned ones, and the Chinese successes with their bombings of resistance forces became less and less except on those rare occasions when large forces were caught in the open or massed together in one location.

"Eventually, the Chinese also brought more and more artillery and armored vehicles as well as heavy reinforcements of soldiers, leaving the Tibetans no alternative but to retreat back to the safety of the mountains. It was reported that at least 5,000 to 6,000 or more Tibetans had taken part in these early attacks. It was also said that just the Chinese dead from the many attacks throughout eastern Tibet just described were more than 40,000 in that same time period. Thanks to the Lord Buddha, there were few Tibetans killed, with most of the Tibetan casualties coming from the early bombings and artillery I mentioned. There were few, if any, prisoners taken by either the Chinese or the Tibetans. There were many reports that the Chinese killed nearly 4,000 Tibetans in Lithang by their bombing a large group of resistance fighters that had gathered in a large monastery there. They had successfully eliminated most of the Chinese forces in the area but had not thought about the possibility of being attacked by airplanes. The Chinese simply bombed and destroyed the monastery and everything near or in it. In retaliation, other Tibetan forces attacked and destroyed Chinese posts inside western China, again destroying hundreds of Chinese soldiers with few casualties to the Tibetans. The Chinese had not thought they would be hit inside China and were not prepared for the fierce cavalry attacks. Unfortunately, many Tibetans died in all these attacks from wounds that were not serious, simply because there was little or no medicine to treat the infections that often followed. Our medical treatment is very limited and there were no Tibetan doctors. Perhaps a few Tibetans knew how to use herbs and poultices, but that is all. There is a big difference between western medicine and that practiced by Tibetans ... and we had by our own standards only a few people who knew anything about medicine. Our resistance groups usually did not have this luxury."[10]

The Chinese established training schools both in China and Tibet where selected members of "minority" groups were sent for training, which consisted primarily of political indoctrination. One of these schools was located at Chengtu and was called the Southwest School for National Minorities. "There were about three thousand students, including about nine hundred Tibetans, a few Lolos, and other minorities from the Sino-Tibetan border areas. The rest, the majority, were Chinese, but no one questioned how or why they qualified as minority students. The Chinese instructors openly insulted the minority groups, referring to the Tibetans, the Lolos and the Turks as stupid and backward. The Chinese Constitution, all 106 points, was required study, as was the Chinese language and, of course, the writings of Chairman Mao. The instructors explained how the people were to travel on the road of democracy towards centralism, under the leadership of the Communist Party ... [and] that Democratic centralism is the only road to socialism. With that point made less than clear, the students were also repeatedly told that the Chinese are superior in the brotherhood of nationalities. Our superiority is not just a dogma we are imposing on you, it is a historical fact."

Not all the students agreed with these statements, and reportedly one

Lolo told the instructor, "Your conception of equality is a farce since you insist on the idea of one race being superior to the rest. I am a Lolo and proud of it. I do not think I am in any way inferior to a Chinese." This prompted other students to also disagree with the Chinese instructors, and many heated arguments with the instructors followed as did more harsh treatment of the minorities by the Chinese staff.

"The Lolos were tribal people living in the southern border area of China and Tibet. They were known as proud and independent people, and as very ferocious fighters. A Lolo judged a man by his strength, truth and courage. Racially, they were completely different from the Chinese, whom they despised. They first fought the Chinese Communists when elements of Mao's forces trespassed into Lolo country during the so-called Long March and again in 1955 when the Chinese suddenly invaded the Lolo country under the guise of putting down a nonexistent Lolo rebellion against the Chinese. For a brief time the Lolos were able to withstand the Chinese. They were reasonably well armed, but certainly far less so than the Chinese. They lived — and fought — in a terrain that was both jungle and steep mountains. Their hatred of the Chinese was well known, intense and traditional. The Lolos did not believe in surrendering and seldom took prisoners. Reportedly, many Chinese divisions were committed to the area, and thousands of Chinese soldiers died there in the subsequent fighting. Finally, through sheer weight of numbers and superior arms, the Lolo resistance was crushed. The Chinese reprisals were described as savage. Lolo men, women and children were bayonetted or shot in mass executions. The extent of these massacres will probably never be known. What is known is that the Lolos all but ceased to exist as a people."[11] Such is the road to Democratic Centralism and Socialism as interpreted and demanded by the Chinese.

Also in 1954, "...in Nyarong, in Kham, the Chinese had put their (reform) plans into action by increasing their personnel in the hsiangs, the local administrations. They had recruited layabouts and malcontents whom they used to denounce the traditional Khamba leaders, lamas, scholars and people of importance ... and they rewarded these collaborators handsomely. As was their practice the Chinese had kept precise records of all prominent men in Nyarong and they now proceeded to move against them. The collaborators who were to do the dirty work and be 'witnesses' were given the title of 'the diligent ones' and were granted special privileges and cash awards. But many of them, despite their proletarian backgrounds, refused to cooperate with the Chinese. Undaunted, the Chinese officials, backed by the army, began to implement their program of 'democratic reforms' by a startling display of Chinese brutality and ingenuity. Companies of Chinese soldiers accompanied by civil officials and 'diligent ones' proceeded from village to village, demanding the surrender of weapons. They then held 'thamzings,' the so-called 'struggle sessions.' Village headmen, lamas and prominent citizens were denounced, beaten, humiliated and sometimes executed. The whole area was rocked by these events, and any last illusion of compromise or peace was shattered when the Chinese turned against the tribal leaders whom they had previously honored and feted. For example, Gyurme of the Gyara Chipa family was one of the tribal chiefs and the Chinese-appointed administrator for the sub-district of Wulu Chue. He was away on some business at Dhartsedo when a number of Chinese soldiers and a Chinese official came to his house, which was just a two-hour journey from the Castle of the Female Dragon. Gyurme's mother, his wife, his young son, and an old family retainer were accosted by the Chinese who demanded that they surrender their weapons. The members of the family protested and the old lady declared they had none. Without a word, not even a single warning, the Chinese shot every one of them dead. This cruel and senseless murder enraged the people of Nyarong and the flames of the impending revolt now started to rage....

"The actual revolt began on the fourteenth day of the first moon in 1956, at Upper Nyarong. The Gyari Tsang family were traditionally the chief of that area. Gyari Nima, the chief, and his elder wife were away at Dhartsedo. Nima's younger wife, a beautiful and fearless woman, Dorje Yudon, was left at home to look after the family. As the course of events drew to that one unavoidable conclusion, she made the decision that the revolt was to be launched (then and) there. Dorje Yudon gathered her men and weapons and dispatched missives all over eastern Tibet, urging the people to rise against the Chinese. Dressed in a man's robe and with a pistol strapped to her side, she rode before her warriors to do battle with the enemy. She ferociously attacked Chinese columns and outposts everywhere in Nyarong. The remaining Chinese soldiers and officials retreated to the castle of the Female Dragon. The castle was stormed, with Dorje Yudon herself leading the many charges. But the great walls of that old castle were built to withstand such attacks, and without artillery — which the rebels did not have — they were virtually impregnable. Casualties mounted on both sides. Finally Dorje Yudon decided to lay siege to the castle....

"By now the whole countryside was in ferment and many other villages and tribes rose up to fight. Dorje Yudon's task at the castle was proving to be difficult. The Chinese garrison was well stocked with food and ammunition, and they also had a spring of clear water within the walls. After a month, six hundred Chinese troops from the 18th Division arrived from Kanze to relieve their beleaguered comrades in the castle. Dorje Yudon met them at Upper Nyarong and managed to defeat them. About four hundred Chinese soldiers were killed, but two hundred managed to break through the siege lines and enter the castle. Another column of about fifteen to twenty thousand Chinese soldiers soon poured in from Drango and Thau in the east. With this, Dorje Yudon was forced to give way and the siege was lifted. Yet the fighting accelerated and lasted for a month more, after which the superior numbers and arms of the Chinese began to tell....

"The Chinese suffered heavy losses, about two thousand dead and many more wounded. Two hundred Chinese officers were killed and in keeping with Chinese burial traditions, their bodies were buried with much ceremony outside the old castle. Finally, the Chinese regained some measure of control in the area, and the rebels had to take to the hills from where they initiated a relentless guerrilla campaign. Day by day their numbers swelled."[12]

Six months after the fighting in eastern Tibet broke out, in the summer of 1956, "General Wang Ji-mei, Chamdo's PLA commander, summoned 350 prominent Tibetans in the area to the city and asked for their endorsement of the Democratic Reforms. Forty voted in favor, and another forty voted for the reforms only if the Chinese would agree to introduce them gradually. 'No reforms' was the overwhelming vote. Four subsequent meetings and votes yielded much the same result. Finally, 210 leaders from Derge, the largest region in Kham, were forced to convene at the local fortress of Jomdha Dzong, known as the Female Dragon, forty miles east of Chamdo. When they were all inside, 5,000 Chinese troops surrounded the fort. For two weeks the Tibetans were held prisoner and were pressured daily to vote for reforms. On the fifteenth day of detention, they finally assented to the Chinese demands. After three more days, and actually the night before political indoctrination of the 210 was to begin, Jomdha Dzong's guard was relaxed — and that same night all 210 men escaped into the mountains. In this manner, Tibet's formal guerrilla resistance and leadership in that area were assured, the Chinese themselves having turned the Khamba establishment into 'outlaws' totally opposed to the invaders."[13]

In addressing the questions of "when, where, how and why did the resistance begin?," it is interesting to note that in two of the above examples of resistance activities in 1956, each of the narrators thought he was telling of the origin. That there were numerous serious encounters well before 1956 in many areas, especially involving the Khambas, the Amdos, the Goloks, and the Lolos in southeast Tibet, was not widely known except to the Chinese and, eventually, in Lhasa, thanks to the traders and travelers who brought countless stories to Lhasa with them. The "how and why" have been well chronicled in the foregoing, and are related in more detail in subsequent chapters, specifically in Chapters 7 and 8.

Communications between areas were difficult and slow, usually by a tribal messenger on horseback, much like the system used by our old Pony Express, only over much greater and more difficult distances. Following the Chinese invasion, all other forms of communications in Tibet — except for diplomatic radio links between Indian and Nepalese consulates to their respective governments — were controlled by the Chinese, an advantage that served them increasingly well as the resistance increased. Except for the occasional and scanty references in NCNA broadcasts, and an occasional story from Hong Kong, the outside world knew very little of what was transpiring inside Tibet.

The isolated Indian Consul in Lhasa could report to New Delhi only the gossip or leaked stories gleaned in Lhasa. And Kalimpong, a trading and transit center located near the Tibetan border, was a busy center of rumors and intrigue, but information on conflicts between the Chinese and the Tibetans reported from there was more often than not both sketchy and tardy and not always accurate. Because it was also a transit point for refugees escaping from Tibet, Kalimpong was often used by Indian and other reporters for stories on what was happening in Tibet, but interestingly, few reporters told of the atrocities and deceits of the Chinese, although there were countless such stories available from Tibetan refugees and from merchants who continued to trade in Tibet. Whether there was censorship of some kind by India is not clear, but the suspicion is extensive and strong.

Generally speaking, the resistance was a natural sequence to all that had preceded it, delayed for an extended period only because of the repeated requests by the Dalai Lama for patience while a way to accommodate the Chinese could be found but finally pursued when it was obvious to the various tribal leaders that no such accommodation was possible, just as had previously been the case in the decades and centuries past. "Most of these leaders had agreed for quite some time that armed resistance was inevitable, for it was clear to them that the Chinese intended to kill or enslave most if not all Tibetans and to destroy their religion. Many decided to ignore the Dalai Lama and to begin fighting the Chinese as best they could. Other leaders made preparations and tentative plans regarding where and how the resistance should be formed and identified areas where resistance could succeed. Some took pilgrimages to many areas throughout Tibet, not just for religious purposes but to make friends in the area and to establish contacts in monasteries and villages for future reference. Others took trade caravans to different areas and memorized or sketched the terrain and trails, establishing reliable friends in the areas visited. But unfortunately there was little communication or exchange of information between most of these leaders. Such planning and coordination was simply not the normal way of doing things, for each area in Tibet had historically been largely independent of others, and except for trade and religion, seldom were there close bonds. The difficult terrain between areas had historically made communications a slow and tedious process and discouraged close association between the various tribes. Over the years it had even increased the mistrust and animosity that existed between the provinces of Tibet and Lhasa. But slowly, bit by bit, many of the leaders began to exchange views and to share their thoughts about how best to survive the Chinese programs of Democratic Reform, including the strong probability of having to fight. These exchanges began largely one on one, or perhaps an exchange between three, resulting in each one becoming aware that much planning and preparations had to be completed if there was to be success in fighting the Chinese. But by increasing our direct contacts and exchanging ideas, and by

Gompo Tashi Andrugtsang (middle), Khamba leader, with two of his deputies.

communicating by messengers, we made considerable progress despite the close monitoring of us by the Chinese."[14]

One of these leaders, Gompo Tashi Andrugtsang, was born in Lithang, Kham, in 1905 into a prosperous family of merchants and farmers. He and one of his brothers further added to the family's good fortune as traders. As early as 1942 he made an extended pilgrimage to Nepal and India, visiting many holy places and establishing extensive contacts. Both as a successful trader and as a pilgrim he continued to travel extensively throughout Tibet and into Nepal and India over the years. In 1956 and 1957 he again visited many monasteries throughout different areas of eastern and southern Tibet, but this time the main purpose of his travels was to contact other leaders to discuss fighting the Chinese. Gompo also maintained contact with other leaders in Kham and Amdo by messenger and couriers. He made it his duty to expose the many lies and broken promises that the Chinese made throughout this period, either by talking to Lamas, laymen or leaders in eastern Tibet or in letters he sent to them. In late 1953 and early 1954, he had urged these same leaders to prepare to fight the Chinese, and in late 1955 and in 1956 he again urged them to complete preparations for what he had concluded as being inevitable: the extensive armed rebellion that would soon follow against the Chinese. In early 1956 Gompo also sent a number of his men and other leaders to various places in Kham such as Bathang, Lithang and Gyethang, urging them and other Khambas to attack the Chinese, noting that they "would have nothing to regret even if each of their bodies became a hundred pieces, for such deeds were truly worthy."[15]

An interesting example of the foregoing is that there was a Chinese collaborator by the name of Bapa Phuntsok Wangyal, a Khamba, who called for meetings with Khamba traders from northern and southern Kham visiting Lhasa, and in speeches told them that "The reason why there is a war in the Kham area is because the Khambas there don't know the Chinese policy. In actual fact, the Chinese treatment is very good. If you traders of Kham want to go to your native land or to China to trade, the Chinese Government will help you as much as it can." Bapa Phuntsok Wangyal also said these same things to many others, including the influential monks in the three big monasteries, Ganden, Drepung and Sera. Gompo learned of what Bapa Phuntsok Wangyal was saying and then talked to these same people, warning them about the lies they had been told. But it was also clear that the collaborator Bapa should not be allowed to continue to make such false statements. "A short while later Bapa was seen but not heard because he had suffered a fall from his horse which in turn caused his tongue to be cut sufficiently that he could no longer talk. It became a popular story that Bapa's horse had tired of his master's lies, so one day deliberately threw Bapa onto the ground, which caused his tongue to be severed, a fitting fate for a collaborator."[16]

Just as 1956 appeared to be well on the way to a year of near or total destruction of Tibet as the Chinese increasingly pushed their harsh practices under the guise of Democratic Reforms, the Dalai Lama was suddenly invited to India to attend the celebration of the 2,500th anniversary of the birth of Buddha. Even though the first invitation was delivered by the Prince of Sikkim, the Chinese initially denied permission for the Dalai Lama to attend. They obviously did not want him to have the opportunity to talk with Indian or other foreign officials. Fortunately, Prime Minister Nehru also invited the Dalai Lama to attend as his personal guest, and then sent a second invitation to include the Panchen Lama. This forced the Chinese to agree, for they dared not ignore the diplomatic protocols involved, or to say no to India in this obviously sensitive matter, for to do so would have been contradictory to the much publicized spirit of the Sino-Indian Agreement of 1954. Before he departed Lhasa, through General Chang Ching-wu, the commander in Lhasa, the Chinese tried to instruct the Dalai Lama on what he could and could not say, and with whom he could and could not converse.

In late November, His Holiness and his party left Lhasa for Sikkim. Traveling through Yatung to the south and then over the nearly 16,000-feet

Nathula pass, en route to Gangtok, the capital of Sikkim, he said his spirits were very high because of the absence of Chinese "escorts" for the first time in many years. Upon arrival by special plane in New Delhi from Gangtok, His Holiness was met at the airport by Prime Minister Nehru and most of the diplomatic corps, as well as thousands who cheered and cried as he emerged from the plane. As the diplomatic vehicles awaited their assigned passengers, the chauffeur of the Chinese Ambassador to India was observed by many as he furtively substituted the Chinese flag for the Tibetan flag on the vehicle to be used by the Dalai Lama. As you can imagine, this became a popular story in New Delhi, and one that angered most Tibetans. His Holiness had again thought he could possibly better serve Tibet by being in the free world, and in his first meeting alone with Prime Minister Nehru he told him this. The Prime Minister was very emphatic in disagreeing. He was obviously very concerned about what China's reactions might be if His Holiness remained in India and what that might do to his cherished peace and unity agreement, the Panch Sheel, between China and India. Too, he knew India was no match for the Chinese military forces, and Indian forces were already engaged with Pakistan. However, he did offer to speak to Chou En-lai, who was then in New Delhi en route to Europe, on behalf of Tibet. Mr. Nehru later told His Holiness that during his meeting with Chou En-lai he had been assured by him "that it was absurd for anyone to imagine that China was going to force Communism on Tibet."[17] And apparently Prime Minister Nehru believed him.

In his meeting in New Delhi with Chou En-lai, the Dalai Lama reportedly detailed to Chou En-lai many of the problems being experienced in Tibet because of Chinese behavior, including the extreme actions taken in Kham and Amdo against the Tibetans by the Chinese forces. "His Holiness got the impression that Chou En-lai did not know of the so-called Democratic reforms being forced on the people, although he seemed to know a good deal about the Tibetan resistance activities."[18] The meeting was described as proper and cordial, with Chou En-lai assuring the Dalai Lama that Chairman Mao would be advised of the problems in Tibet that had been described to him. Interestingly, Chou En-lai returned to New Delhi a short time later to again see His Holiness. He was obviously agitated and less friendly than he had been. Not only did he make it clear to His Holiness that the Chinese were prepared to use unlimited military force to eliminate any Tibetan resistance to Chinese rule, but he also demanded to know if the Dalai Lama was planning not to return to Tibet and made it clear that it was in Tibet's best interests if the Dalai Lama did return. The threat of armed reprisals was not very thinly veiled. "His Holiness described this conversation with Chou En-lai as one that had less than sincere exchanges. Chou En-lai told His Holiness that the Chinese had reports of Tibetan plans to mount very large revolts in Tibet, and said that the Dalai Lama should return to Tibet quickly to defuse the situation, for Tibetans were not to contest the Chinese military authority in Tibet. He also made it clear to His Holiness that the Chinese would not agree to Tibetan demands for self-determination, but (fatuously) assured him, as had Mao Tse-tung, that no reforms would be introduced against the will of the Tibetan people. He also advised His Holiness not to visit Kalimpong on his return trip to Tibet because of security concerns, but His Holiness ignored this advice."[19]

"Chou En-lai invited my brother (Gyalo Thondup) and I to the Chinese Embassy to discuss the situation in Tibet. We were very blunt in describing and protesting the mistreatment of Tibetans by the Chinese, including the many atrocities committed by the Chinese soldiers on our people, and the insulting creation of PCART. We noted the increasing number of violations by the Chinese of the so-called Agreement, and the record of their broken promises to date. He listened, and, as he had told His Holiness, said that it was possible that excesses had been committed and promised to look into this problem. And in turn, he made it clear that it was in Tibet's interest that His Holiness remain in Tibet, and warned that should there be Tibetan elements that resisted the Chinese that they would be harshly punished ... and that China would not tolerate any foreign interference in these matters. It was not a pleasant evening for any of us."[20]

Despite Chou En-Lai's "advice" to the Dalai Lama, Prime Minister Nehru readily assisted him to visit Kalimpong, which already was receiving an ever-increasing number of Tibetan refugees fleeing the cruelty of the Chinese. The Dalai Lama met with some of these refugees and others as he journeyed back to Lhasa. "The many stories of Chinese atrocities that were related to His Holiness as he visited Kalimpong and Gangtok en route back to Lhasa caused deep despair, not only for the great harm that had been done to the Tibetans, but also because of his concern about what was likely to happen if the Tibetan resistance increased. The many stories told by the refugees of the cruel and terrible treatment of Tibetans by the Chinese and the destruction of their monasteries were almost identical to those that had been told him by the Tibetans in eastern Tibet when he returned to Lhasa from China. Obviously, under the circumstances and the unwillingness of the Chinese to bend, there was no apparent solution."[21]

The Dalai Lama was also concerned about the successes that the Tibetan resistance forces had achieved against the Chinese soldiers in Ngapa and Gyalrong in Amdo and in Markham, Bathang, Tawu, Lingka, Shipa, Jupa, and Chaitaring in Kham, all of which had returned, temporarily, to Tibetan control after the Chinese garrisons were wiped out. "While these victories were tributes to the heroic and determined Tibetan tribes who had fought the Chinese and to all Tibet, the threat of harsh retaliations by the Chinese as promised by Chou En-lai was clearly of great concern to His Holiness. He did not support our view that there was no choice except to fight. But the resistance was still like the cat and mouse ... and Mao continued to steadily increase the number of soldiers in Tibet, including another 40,000 reinforcements having arrived in late 1956. This brought the number of Chinese soldiers to well over 150,000."[22]

"As expected, the Chinese continued to push ahead with their reforms despite the assurances of Chou En-lai to His Holiness — and to me and my brother — that they would not take place unless requested by the Tibetans. This obviously disappointed all of us, but it was no surprise."[23]

"Unbelievably insulting were the banners, huge red flags, and huge portraits of Mao Tse-tung dominating the prayer flags welcoming His Holiness back to Lhasa from India. How could the Chinese possibly believe that Tibetans would accept such insults? The welcome was for His Holiness, not for Chairman Mao! Even some of the Chinese officials and Chinese army officers expressed their embarrassment. But the Chinese message was clear — in the minds of the Chinese the position and power of His Holiness meant little if anything other than his serving as a symbol, much like the role they had created for the Panchen Lama. It was a most difficult situation for His Holiness as he continued to seek a peaceful solution with the invaders, and it made us all the more determined to fight. We had already lost far too much time."[24]

And unfortunately for the Tibetans, things would not get better, not only because of the hollow promises by the Chinese leadership in Lhasa and Peking — and those made in New Delhi by Chou En-lai — but also simply because few Chinese officials in Tibet paid much attention to the political oratory in Peking, and in turn Peking seldom bothered itself with how their officers and cadres carried out the party-approved programs. Seldom if ever were any Chinese punished for mistreating or abusing a Tibetan, no matter how serious the act. Despite the slogans such as "peaceful suppression of rebels," from 1951 on there was no such thing. The Chinese never hesitated to go back on their previous statements if it served their purpose. Thus Party communiqués and instructions from Peking were constantly changing, and even local officials were confused when a new order from Peking totally contradicted previous instructions. A good example of this was the change in party communiqués on the question of class struggle. Prior to 1956, the Chinese had declared that there would be no class struggle. The changes began from 1956. At first the Chinese proclaimed:

"... The unending class struggle between serfs and landlords must be a peaceful one." This then became:

"... The class struggle between serfs and landlords must be an open one, though it must be peaceful and only verbal." This then became:

"... The people must 'throw their tears of misery' on the landlords, and must begin an unending struggle until feudalism is wiped out." This then became:

"... All landlords are enemies of the people. They are like rotten meat. If we do not destroy the meat, it will always smell and collect flies."[25]

All those who did not support the Chinese were simply put in the same category as landlords and Freedom Fighters.

The charade was finally over. There were no more pretenses.

CHAPTER 6

Honey on a Knife

"To understand what the Chinese had in mind in regards to their 'Democratic Reforms' you first need to understand that their intent was total nationalization of all property, not just personal property but also that belonging to the monasteries and to the Tibetan government. The formation and implementation of communes was vital to achieving this goal. The other key point of their program was that nothing or no one was to be allowed to stand in the way of reaching their goal. Of course the Chinese did not proclaim their goals in these terms, but their inflexible attitude and actions soon made their true intentions all too obvious. Their public announcements constantly referred to their intention '… that necessary reforms would be introduced to rid Tibet of its backward situation.' As most Tibetans quickly learned, the arrogance of the Han Communist mentality was overwhelming and without compassion…. Tibet was to be a totally controlled Marxist state — or at least a Marxist state as interpreted by Chairman Mao. 'Democratic Reforms' brought a new and drastic approach. The goal was to totally destroy the previous way of life in Tibet and in the process insure that the will of the Tibetan people was broken, thereby making Tibet into a completely pliable colony of China."[1]

There are countless examples of the above. While the Dalai Lama made conciliatory speeches in Lhasa, the people of eastern Tibet experienced the real intentions of the Chinese Communists, and they became increasingly fearful and angry. Reform brought stark brutality. During and following the invasion the Chinese had made many promises in their early propaganda, then, by way of modest gifts, sought Tibetan support and cooperation. But next came the seizing of personal property, forced labor, and increasingly harsh treatment of all, including monks. The process by which the Chinese would enslave all of Tibet was underway.

The problem of nationality is given special consideration in Marxist-Leninist theory, including the fundamental right of secession and the right of self-determination of national minorities. Communist theory recognizes the right of self-determination of all nationalities, and the right to secede.

According to Article 11 of the Constitution of the People's Republic of China, "The State protects the right of citizens to own lawfully earned incomes, savings, houses and other means of life." But in Kham, in 1950, "a 33-year-old farmer witnesses the execution of his village chief, who was caught by the People's Liberation Army attempting to flee. His servants are shot and he is kept without food for several days and led like a dog with a chain around his neck. The Chinese accuse him of ill-treating the serfs, but the serfs deny this and plead for his life. He is not shot, but his property is confiscated and his four children, all under the age of 13, are taken to China." And in Amdo in 1956, "A list of people who have allegedly failed to surrender their assets is given to the Chinese by the new Tibetan 'People's Leaders', former beggars whom the Communists have 'reformed' by the simple expedient of giving them some coins. All on the list are arrested. Some are sent to work on construction. Others are shot in full view of the villagers. One man is shot in stages working up the body, there being nine stages in all. Another is asked whether he would prefer to die standing up or lying down. He prefers standing. A pit is dug and he is placed upright in it. Then it is filled with dirt and water and then compressed, a process which continues until his eyes protrude from his head and are severed by the Chinese. But he was already dead."

Article 89 of the Chinese constitution states: "The freedom of citizens of the People's Republic of China is inviolable." In Kham, 1955, the Chinese arrest a man, accusing him publicly of failing to turn in all his property to the "people." Tibetan beggars who had volunteered to become "soldiers" in the PLA beat him with sticks and pour boiling water on his head until he "confesses" that he has hidden lots of gold. He is tied and strung up by his thumbs over a fire and ordered to reveal the location of the gold. He is unable to answer because he has no gold. Finally, a red-hot copper nail is driven into his forehead. The Chinese search his place but no gold is found.

Article 96 of the Chinese constitution states: "The state protects marriage, the family and the mother and child." In Kham, 1954, fifty infants below the age of one are seized by Chinese and taken to China so their parents can do more work. Fifteen parents who protest this are thrown into the river by the Chinese and drown. In Kham in 1951, a 12-year-old girl is told by the Chinese that her father is an imperialist, and is ordered to shoot him.

Article 88 of the Chinese constitution states: "Citizens of the People's Republic of China enjoy freedom of religious belief." In Amdo, in 1955, the Chinese use the main room of a monastery to stable their horses, and bring in prostitutes. When the monks refuse to take the women, two monks are crucified by nails and die. Scriptures are used as mattresses, or for toilet paper. When a monk urges the Chinese to stop, they cut his arm off above the elbow. Buddha, they tell him, will give him back his arm. In Amdo, in 1957, three high Lamas are arrested and accused by the Chinese of being obstacles on the road to progress. The Chinese place them in a pit and order the people to beat them and urinate on them. Then the Chinese order the Lamas to demonstrate their religious powers by flying out of the pit or die. The Lamas are finally shot.[2]

In the book *A Strange Liberation: Tibetan Lives in Chinese Hands*, Ama Adhe relates that "... during thamzing, Chinese women made Lamas drink their urine ... and while in prison at Dartsedo, she was raped repeatedly. She ate grass, weeds, and insects to stay alive. And female Kuomintang prisoners were reduced to eating worms to survive, with some 12,000 of them starving in a three year period."

Similar stories were repeated again and again in all regions of Tibet but especially in the east where the Khambas and the Amdos were treated unbelievably bad from shortly after the invasion. Even the Dalai Lama cited specific examples of brutal treatment. "The Chinese dealt viciously with the Khamba resistance: not only were public beatings and executions carried out but often they were done by the victim's own child. Public self-criticism was also introduced. This is a method especially favored by the Chinese Communists. The 'offender' is trussed up with a rope in such way that the shoulders are dislocated. Then, when the person is utterly helpless and crying out in pain, members of the public — including women and children — are called forward to inflict further injury." The Dalai Lama also wrote that while he was in Jomdha Dzong, northeast of Chamdo, "... I was given a copy of a newspaper published by the Chinese at Karze in Kham. In disbelief, I saw that it contained a photograph of a row of severed heads. The caption said something to the effect that they had belonged to 'reactionary criminals.' This was the first concrete evidence of Chinese atrocities that I had seen."[3]

The Dalai Lama reportedly attempted to register protests about these atrocities with the Chinese commander in Lhasa, who disclaimed any knowledge of any such occurrences, and also with Mao, who apparently never answered his communiqués. Usually the reports of the Chinese acts in the rural areas were learned by the Tibetan officials in Lhasa only long after the incident, in which case usually no protest was made at all. Or if stories were lacking the many details demanded by the Chinese, such as names of all the Chinese involved, dates, times, location, details of the charges, names of witnesses, etc., no complaint was accepted. Many of the stories came to the Dalai Lama as he returned from India, and, as with the stories that he had been told during his return from Peking, he reportedly was reluctant at first to believe them. Finally, after countless stories had been given him, more objections were communicated to the Chinese, but for those thousands that had already been so badly mistreated, and for those that had been killed, it was far too late. Of course the Chinese officials in Lhasa claimed not to know or to have heard anything about any misdeeds by any of the Chinese cadres or soldiers in the provinces.

The earlier reluctance of the young Dalai Lama to believe the terrible stories that were told him is understandable. Chairman Mao, adopting something of a learned tutor's role, had told the impressionable Dalai Lama that the Chinese would pursue only a peaceful policy in reforming and modernizing Tibet.

And, while there had been a few problems in Lhasa and some stories about problems in the rural areas, the situation appeared to most of the high-ranking lamas and officials in Lhasa to be one that, while far from perfect, was not threatening and quite workable. Given his youth and lack of knowledge at the time of history or of other countries and other races, and because most of his "advisors" did not complain to him about the Chinese, the Dalai Lama very likely chose to believe that things were not unbearable and chose to think more about his religious responsibilities than things political or governmental. And it is also likely that he did not believe it possible in the middle of the twentieth century that the Chinese, ostensibly with thousands of years of culture, would indulge in such barbaric treatment as occasionally reported to him, in the name of Marx and Lenin, for Chairman Mao had assured him that China wanted only good things for Tibet.

However, Tibetans were regularly being crucified, dismembered, beheaded, burned or scalded to death, dragged to death by horses or vehicles, abused, and starved. Parents were being shot by their children; children were taken forcibly from their parents. Tibetans were sent to harsh labor camps or sentenced to prison death camps, forced into needless deprivations, even subjected to vivisection. Their monasteries and sacred images were desecrated, their personal and monastic property stolen. The atrocities go on and on. How does one justify people being brutalized or publicly flogged to death? How does one explain the rape of nuns, wives, daughters? All these things were done in the name of "Democratic Reforms," in the promise of "self-determination," and "self rule." But all of these things were being done away from Lhasa, beyond the sight and hearing of the Dalai Lama, so the reality and horror of the abuses were not real to him, despite the warnings of his brothers.

The Chinese officials had repeatedly stated that they had come to Tibet only to teach Tibetans how to rule themselves and that when this was done they would return to China. "Tibet must be ruled by Tibetans" was said repeatedly by the Chinese cadres, but when Tibetans tried to exercise this right they were usually executed.

The Chinese "advisors" had soon given more and more orders and less advice and did not listen to the Tibetans who spoke up with suggestions or asked questions.... And soon there were few Tibetans who dared to protest or even ask questions because those that had were usually severely punished or sent to a "Thought Reform" camp, or prison, or simply executed after public torturing. What had started first as the giving of small gifts and many promises by the smiling Chinese communist cadres to the Tibetans gradually became harsh orders and merciless punishment for those who did not satisfy the demands made for strict adherence to party dogma. The Chinese doctrine was based on the idea that under the principle of democratic centralism the people must progress on the road to socialism and then communism. The democracy part of this equation was to come ostensibly from the leaders of the workers and peasants and the centralism part from the central party, which dictated the principles and established the policies. Of course, the so-called leaders of the workers and peasants were either Chinese cadres or Tibetan dupes hand-picked by the local party cadre, which in turn took care of the democratic aspects.

The situation for Tibetans had quickly changed from guarded hope by some to that of someone accepting honey offered on the blade of a knife. In so doing there is real danger of being badly if not fatally cut. While the Dalai Lama continued to communicate diplomatically with his Chinese counterparts in Lhasa, the Chinese applied without mercy the realities of their reform programs in eastern Tibet, including the forced introduction of communes.

"First there were the collective farms, then came the 'progressive' transition to communes. The idea was that the communes, at least the so-called low level communes in Tibet, would be the next step of development from the collective farms ... but there was to be more control by the cadres, stricter rules and more controlled sharing of the productivity in the communes than had been the case in the collective farms. And after establishing the low level communes, there was to be advancement to high level communes, a process that the Chinese told the Tibetans would take about five years, possibly less. With the establishment of high level communes, the Tibetans were told that they then would have attained socialism. But one of the key questions we Tibetans asked ourselves regarding all this was how many Tibetans would be able to survive this obviously slow and very harsh process? The answer was, of course, not many. But there was no escaping the Chinese intent. Tibetans were told repeatedly, 'The culture and traditions belonging to your backward society must be reformed.'

"Of course Chairman Mao was credited as being the genius behind the commune system. The cadres explained that Mao saw this as a necessary step towards socialism on the road to true communism. What this translated into in Tibet was that individual ownership of property was no longer possible, including even the useless property that the Chinese had taken from the so-called landlords and given to the beggars, nor were the monasteries to continue to own any land. And remember, the Chinese had already taken nearly everything of value for themselves. Labor was to be performed by all, and to be paid for by the Chinese official in control of each commune in food and clothing, if there was any payment at all ... and according to a formula which was known only to the cadre in charge and naturally subject to change and whim. All of this was called Chairman Mao's new program of 'more production and less consumption.' For the Tibetans in the communes it simply meant that they were to eat less and work harder.

"Chairman Mao was quoted constantly by the Chinese cadres at all public meetings, including the saying, 'How wonderful it would be if every Chinese could save a grain of rice at every meal. Each individual would thus be able to save three gains of rice daily, and the nation would accumulate eighteen hundred million grains of rice each day.' And Tibetans were expected to accept these quotes and doctrines without question. There was some humor in all this for it became a popular joke among Tibetans to agree that all Chinese should save at least three grains a day ... and that to do so the Chinese in Tibet should return to China immediately to join in this worthy program to insure its success. The Chinese did not appreciate our humor, and many a beating was given in public to those who were charged with repeating the story. But that did not stop the telling. The program of 'Democratic Reforms' was really only an excuse for communes and stricter controls. Collectivization was simply an effort by the Communist party to move Tibetans into a very harsh and tightly controlled communal system."[4]

"After the brief period of false smiles and little presents from the Chinese in a few areas of Tibet, the smiles and presents disappeared completely as the farm collectives and indoctrination process increased. Then the Communist party cadres began their nightly 'thamzing' sessions to 'educate' the Tibetans. 'Thamzing' was designed to be dramatic and was used effectively as one of their tools of political and psychological control. Its setting was usually one where the Chinese officials sat at a table in front of the Tibetan people seated on the ground. A Chinese official would usually make a speech about the correctness of the Han ways, and then talk about the terrible old ways of Tibet and the need for extensive reforms under the guidance of Chairman Mao. The official would then summon the Tibetan or Tibetans that had been singled out for punishment and demand 'confessions,' including encouraging or demanding accusations by other Tibetans against the person being charged. Or the official might simply call for confessions of wrong thinking or wrongdoing from among the assembled Tibetans. And the meetings would go on until the Chinese were satisfied that enough confessions had been made for that day. Punishments were also given during these meetings, including flogging.

"The Tibetans were gradually worn down mentally and physically, for long days were spent working in the fields of the commune, followed by the compulsory meetings at night. Those who had been landowners, or village officials, or teachers, or merchants, were singled out and denounced by the cadres for various misdeeds such as reportedly having 'cheated' the people; or for having made too much money; or having too many personal belongings; or for not working hard enough; or for spending too much time in prayer and neglecting other duties; or for not learning the assignments given them, such as not knowing the Chinese constitution; or for wearing brightly colored clothing; or for not giving the proper or politically correct answers to questions posed during the nightly sessions ... in other words, for not readily reciting the 'party' line; not memorizing the sayings of Mao ... and all kinds of things like that.

"It made no difference if there was any truth in any of the charges, or even if those accused gave good answers to questions, for the cadres persisted in the public denunciations of their targets regardless, including threats, until some kind of a 'confession' was extracted from the accused, or enough accusations made that a sentence was passed without a confession.

"The confessions usually came after the individual had been beaten extensively by the cadre, or by the Tibetan 'diligent ones,' after which a sentence was passed. At first there was some leniency in the sentences, such as being sent to 'Thought Reform' classes rather than to prison. This was so that the people would not rebel against taking part in the meetings, but this all changed as rapidly as stricter controls could be imposed. And often the same individual was repeatedly charged and 'flogged' until he died from beatings, or he was sentenced to execution, or sent to a 'political' prison. The political prisons had very harsh living conditions, incredibly bad and totally inadequate food, no medical care, and hard labor. Most sent to these 'political' prisons usually died there.

"The cadres increasingly forced the thamzing procedure wherein Tibetans publicly accused other Tibetans. Those who did the Chinese bidding were rewarded for being 'diligent ones,' and those Tibetans who refused to accuse other Tibetans were in turn accused of being traitors to party doctrine, or some other ridiculous charge, and were themselves punished, and sent to political prisons, or simply executed.

"As I mentioned earlier, originally the Chinese had given many gifts to the Tibetan tribal leaders and officials, but with the introduction of Democratic Reforms, these same, and other lesser officials, then became the early targets of thamzings, and were treated severely in the public confession sessions. Some were wise enough to escape before they were accused, and many of those who fled made their way to one of the resistance groups. However, many had been lulled by the earlier gifts from the Chinese, and believed the Chinese promises. Thus thamzing caught these by surprise, unfortunately for them. And for many others it was simply difficult to make the decision to leave the area that had been home to them or their families for decades. Those without close ties to the land fared better than those that did. For example, most of those who had been nomads lost little time in escaping from any situation that remotely threatened them. Owners of farms were less fortunate.

"The Chinese were also determined to eliminate former officials and as many leaders as they could in order to reduce the chances of any organized opposition to their plans. The Chinese wanted to gain maximum control as quickly as possible of all individuals within the respective communes. In essence, total control soon became the essence of the communal structure, including the power of life or death over the members. And remember, very little of this same kind of treatment in the communes in China was known outside of China, so it is not surprising that little was known about these similar but worse conditions in Tibet."[5]

"Let me tell you a few examples that have been well recorded. Often the wives and daughters of the men being accused in the so-called trials (thamzings) were forced into being a part of the public confessions. They were stripped of their clothing in the presence of all, and if the man refused to 'confess' to the charges, the women were raped in front of the man. There were always enough Chinese soldiers present who had not been with a woman for a long time and who were more than willing to follow orders and participate. There were even cases of the man being forced to have intercourse with his wife in front of the others, after which he would be executed, and his daughters and wife then given to the Chinese soldiers. There were many cases where Tibetan monks were disrobed and forced to have intercourse with disrobed Tibetan nuns, with the Chinese cadre then disdainfully proclaiming that such is the religion of the Tibetans and the so-called vows of chastity. Then these monks would usually be executed and the nuns given to the Chinese soldiers. In many areas very few females escaped being raped, regardless of age, and often they were repeatedly raped before being killed. Forcing the accused to be flogged without clothes was common, be they male or female. Many were forced to stand in freezing water without clothes, while the accusers taunted them. The process was one intended to make the accused look very bad and for the accusers to look superior, and of course to attain total obedience of the Tibetans, whatever it took. And children were often induced with gifts to accuse their parents, and in some cases even to shoot their parents. It mattered not how outrageous the questions were…. That was not the point. Most questions concerned the old Tibetan practices and the new ones brought by the Chinese, with anything to do with the old obviously being very bad. The accused were expected to repeatedly swear that they now believed in Chairman Mao and the Communist party, and no longer had any allegiance to His Holiness. Many refused … and most of these died. And many welcomed death rather than agree with the Chinese. The strange words of the Communists were used extensively, such as 'proletariat' and 'bourgeois,' and few Tibetans had any idea about what the accusers were even talking about.

"The self-confession sessions were repeated many times each week. And after a period of time it became difficult for those attending to find things to confess that would satisfy the Chinese. But the sessions served another Chinese purpose also…. Friends and neighbors stopped trusting one another in fear of saying something that might be used against them in the public sessions. The Chinese encouraged the Tibetans to tell publicly anything about anyone in the commune that might disagree with the doctrine given by the cadre … anything at all, no matter how small. Those accusing others were given gifts by the Chinese as a reward. And Tibetans willing to flog accused Tibetans were also rewarded with money or gifts. These were usually from among 'the diligent ones,' the beggars and layabouts recruited by the Chinese. In this environment it sometimes did not take long for friend to accuse friend, neighbor to accuse neighbor, children to accuse parents. But these things probably should not be viewed as unusual practices by the Han Chinese, for remember ... the Chinese officials had tried to force the oldest brother of His Holiness to assassinate him ... and as we later learned, they did all these same things in their own communes and to their officials in China."[6]

A natural question is why didn't the Tibetans, particularly those in the eastern part of the country, try to escape from the communes? This question is best answered by another: "...how and where would they go? Those in the communes had no horses of their own anymore. They were weak from hunger, and the Chinese guards were many. And it is not easy to travel quickly with a family. Death was basically their only real alternative ... and many committed suicide rather than continue to live under the Chinese. Some did manage to escape and either joined a resistance group or eventually made it to the border, but many, including whole families, trying to make it to the borders were killed by Chinese soldiers who had been posted along roads to prevent escapes."[7]

Then suddenly and unexpectedly the Chinese announced the suspension of the Democratic Reforms they had pushed so hard to implement. "In late September, during the Eighth Congress of the Chinese Communist Party in Peking, it became evident that although the Tibetans had gained little else by their revolts, they had gained a little more time in which to enjoy their traditional way of life and to practice the Buddhist religion. Speeches by Communist leaders at the party congress contained clear indications that the regime had concluded that it must swallow Tibet a bit more slowly or suffer serious indigestion. Liu Shao-chi, Vice-Chairman of the Politburo and Party theoretician, stated on September 16 that in carrying out the 'socialist transformation' of national minorities such as the Tibetans, the regime must 'pursue a prudent policy.' Liu said, 'In regard to religious belief in the areas of national minorities, we must for some time adhere to the policy of freedom of religious belief and must never interfere in that connection during social reform.' The same theme was repeated in more detail by Gen. Chang Kuo-hua in his speech to the Congress on September 20, 1956. According to a summary of Chang's speech, reported by NCNA, Chang explained to the Congress that Communist 'reforms' cannot be undertaken immediately in Tibet because the working people do not want them and the Peking regime does not have the support of influential Tibetans ... (and) Lamaism had a deep rooted influence upon the people of all strata. (He) warned against premature reforms which, he said, would affect unity ... and could only create difficulties for peaceful reform. He outlined the necessary conditions for reform, unsupported by the people of the upper strata. He said, significantly, that these reforms would not begin for a comparatively long time."[8]

And why did the Chinese decide to halt the Democratic Reform program?

"The answer to that is quite simple. The communes were not meeting their goals. Crop failures were high, productivity was low, and the political goals that had been set by the party had not been met, not even close. Word of the many excesses of the Democratic Reforms; the increasing numbers of refugees; the mounting numbers of Tibetan suicides; the increasing attacks and many successes by the resistance forces; although smaller than before, the continuing demonstrations in Lhasa, which the Chinese had to assume were being reported to New Delhi by the Indian consulate; the increasing numbers of prisoners in 'political prisons'; the increasing numbers in the 'Thought Reform' camps and prisons; failures of the communes to meet even minimum crop growth goals; ... and the unanticipated high costs of all these failures to the Chinese, such as the need for more Chinese to handle the increased problems, more Chinese manpower required to administer solutions to the problems, more prison camps and more Chinese guards and cadres for the camps, more Chinese cadres to manage government offices, the need for more soldiers, transportation, equipment and food; all of these things finally came to the attention of high ranking Politburo members, and to Chairman Mao, who had pushed strongly for pursuing militant methods, and, significantly, to Premier Liu Shao-chi, who had urged that reforms in Tibet be done gradually and not harshly. The Politburo recognized that all these problems could no longer be ignored, and so the hardliner, Chairman Mao, and Premier Liu, agreed to simply announce in February, 1957, that ... 'because conditions are not yet ripe for Socialism, the "democratic reforms" would be suspended for six years.' And interestingly, this 'compromise' is said to have been one of the reasons that led to Liu Shao-chi eventually being purged, for Mao had not won the argument, and so had lost face. And Mao seldom forgot or forgave those who publicly disagreed with him."[9]

"His Holiness was still in India at the time of this announcement. He had earlier told Chou En-lai in some detail about the atrocities committed against the Tibetans, as had my brother (Gyalo Thondup) and I. The Chinese leaders had to assume that His Holiness had also told Prime Minister Nehru, and perhaps other diplomats, about what the Chinese were doing to the Tibetans. By announcing that reforms would be postponed for six years, Mao Tse-tung made himself appear to be benevolent in the eyes of the world, or at least in the eyes of Mr. Nehru, and so he scored an international propaganda victory for China, and effectively undercut what His Holiness and my brother and I had told Nehru about the Chinese practices in Tibet.

"The Chinese announcement to postpone further reforms was a lie, but nevertheless it was a very clever psychological and political move. It was also a move that was intended to deceive and calm the Tibetans, but such was not the case. Resistance and resentment had been steadily increasing both in numbers and fury. The number of refugees leaving Tibet had also continued to increase. This also embarrassed the Chinese, not only because so many hundreds had left Tibet but because of the stories of the terrible treatment by the Chinese being told by the refugees as they arrived in the neighboring countries. And not surprisingly, many of the Communist party cadres in Tibet were accused by the Communist party cadres in Peking of having caused embarrassment to the People's Republic of China. Naturally, those at the higher levels blamed those at lower levels for having failed to properly recognize and understand the problems and for not properly implementing the right programs.

"Mao had not changed his strong belief that '…political power comes out the barrels of guns' and continued to urge the PLA to 'exterminate the rebels' while reluctantly agreeing to the idea of slowing the pace of Democratic Reforms in Tibet. Chairman Mao (and many others) had insisted on achieving his version of socialism as quickly as possible, without regard to any consequences, and obviously without any regard to or concern for the Tibetans. The philosophical differences between Chairman Mao and Premier Liu were to continue for years until Liu was purged. It is interesting that it was said that the differences between those two leaders became very pronounced when the Politburo first discussed how best to solve the many problems that had surfaced at this time in Tibet, for some, including Mao, had reportedly suggested the use of massive attacks by the PLA against the Tibetans, while others said that this would only cause more problems and hurt China in the eyes of the rest of the world."[10]

Also embarrassing to the Chinese was that by Chinese Communist Party rankings of the stages of communes, Tibet had attained only the category of "feudal society" in 1956, which was just above "primitive" on the Chinese scale of things and far from the goal expected. Whatever the category, Chairman Mao and the Chinese Communist Party leaders were reportedly very angry because of these "party" failures, but not at all concerned that the Tibetan people were being destroyed in the process.

When it was announced that "Democratic Reforms" were to be postponed, there was very little reaction among the Tibetans in eastern Tibet, for few there believed the Chinese. Actually the reform program of "class struggle" was resumed before very long in most areas, particularly in the remote areas where the Chinese cadre had free reign.

"The Chinese sent delegations of party officials and special police to some areas on 'fact finding and condolence missions' for a month or so to attempt to soothe the Tibetans, but it was noted that very few, if any, Chinese officials or cadre were relieved of their positions in Tibet. The Chinese even resumed handing out gifts of food and blankets and clothing, along with their many explanations of the mistakes that the local cadres had made. They claimed again that the true policy of the Chinese was one of 'peaceful methods and the gentle path.' The political cadres also announced that there was to be a sizable reduction in the number of the Han Chinese posted to Tibet, that the

PCART staffs would be reduced by half, and repeated that there would be no reforms until the Tibetans asked for them. Again, few believed these empty promises; most of them had been heard before, and by now we knew that promises by Chinese officials were not kept. One bright aspect in all this was that even a brief period of relief afforded many Tibetans the opportunity to flee Tibet or to join the resistance.

"His Holiness was again openly optimistic that this time the Chinese would keep their word. As before, he continued to caution all those who sought his blessing not to engage in resistance but to be patient and exercise restraint. I suspect he knew in his heart that his trust in the Chinese would again be dashed ... and that wide-scale resistance would result. And as with all of us, he was aware what the price of armed resistance would likely be. Basically, His Holiness wanted so much to believe the promises of Chairman Mao, perhaps not completely, but in his thinking, even if only half of Mao's promises were true, he was optimistic that things would be better and that the Tibetans might eventually regain their country. He started his return from India in early April with much hope, but the stories that the refugees told him in Kalimpong and those that he heard in southern Tibet along the way of his journey to Lhasa dampened the earlier optimism he had expressed when he first heard the news in India.

"There was no real impact in the Lhasa or Shigatse areas because little had happened against the people in either city as yet. There were some political surprises in Lhasa, for the Chinese officials there acted more friendly and almost apologetically for a brief period, probably in fear that His Holiness might complain to Peking if reports of bad treatment of Tibetans continued, and they did not want to be accused in any way. Remember, what the Chinese had done and were doing by force in eastern Tibet they had been trying to accomplish simply by deceit in central and other parts of Tibet. But 'thamzing' and the other harsh public treatments had not yet taken place in Lhasa or Shigatse."[11]

However, the Chinese also used this short space of time before reforms and resistance resumed to send another 16 to 18 battalions into eastern Tibet. And the Khambas, Amdos and Goloks continued to keep themselves supplied by ambushing the Chinese arms convoys as they tried to keep their troops supplied over the long overland routes. There were stories of some 20,000 Golok horsemen having organized resistance groups, many of which joined the Khambas and Amdos in attacking the many Chinese positions in northern Kham and Amdo areas, even as far east as Lithang, Bathang, Derge, Chamdo and other locations east of the Yangtze. Even if the numbers are only half correct, a cavalry force of 10,000 Golok resistance fighters is impressive — and even if just a rumor, such a sizable force would cause fear and alarm within the soldiers of the PLA in Tibet.

"The Goloks maimed 2,000 PLA by cutting off their noses, and annihilated three Chinese regiments that were sent into the area to attack the Goloks. It was estimated that seven to eight thousand Chinese were killed. And the only road free of Tibetan interdiction was across the Aksi Chin desert from Khotan, then to Lhasa. The Chinese used their Ilyushin 28 bombers and MIG 15s (based in Chengtu, Szechuan) at Yaan and Jyekundo, as they had at Lithang, and artillery and armored vehicles"[12] to counter the Golok attacks, and the attacks in the east by other resistance forces.

The announced Chinese policy of "peaceful suppression of rebels," though widely propagated — but not believed — proved to be baseless and ineffective. For example, one incident that took place in 1956 tragically exposed the inherent treachery of Chinese promises and effectively destroyed any remaining illusions about their policy of "peaceful suppression." "Sanag Palden was the leader of a large guerrilla band, and although the Chinese had made many attempts to capture him, they had never succeeded. The Chinese learned that he was a faithful disciple of Lama Tsewang Gyurme, an old religious hermit, who lived in the mountains. The Chinese arrested the old man and then sent a message to Sanag Palden informing him that the life of his lama friend depended on his surrender. The Chinese also promised to abide by all the conditions in the policy of 'peaceful suppression of rebels.' His men pleaded with him not to believe the Chinese, but Sanag Palden left them in the mountains and gave himself up. He was arrested and summarily executed, as was the hermit. The Chinese then announced that Sanag Palden's surrender was not genuine. They claimed that he had given himself up in order to spy on the Chinese."[13]

This story was soon spread among the various resistance forces, underscoring that the promises of the Chinese were even less trustworthy than the parable of honey on a knife. The Chinese obviously did not care what the reactions were to any of their actions. In simple terms, Tibet was isolated, far from anyone important who might have objected or cared. The Chinese officials strongly believed that fear and terror and ruthlessness were very powerful tools. The Chinese also had an exceptional capability to repeatedly prove the truism that politics are of themselves not necessarily dishonorable or necessarily dirty, but officials can easily be, and more often than not are.

The following, written by a Tibetan who was at the time an interpreter for the Chinese, is an example of what the Chinese "peaceful suppression of rebels" campaigns intended. "The area of Thangkya in eastern Nyarong was in guerrilla hands. All the population of the three valleys that formed Thangkya and the nomads of neighboring Phisa were actively hostile to the Chinese, and they supported and supplied the guerrillas. No Chinese could pass through the area. The Chinese launched a 'peaceful suppression of rebels' campaign in that district, and two thousand crack troops of the 3899 regiment under General Shao were sent to implement this campaign. Word reached the Chinese forces that three nomad families had been sighted at the Thangkya pass. Most probably, the report ran, they were guerrillas. A detachment of two hundred soldiers under Colonel Len was dispatched to capture them. It was dusk when they rode out and returned the next day with the news that the guerrillas had already fled. 'When we got there, there was nobody and a good thing for them too—otherwise we would have wiped out every single one of them'. We asked Colonel Len whether it was Communist policy to execute innocent people, even women and children. 'No, of course not,' the Colonel replied. 'But these people are rebels. And as far as rebels are concerned, our instructions are very clear. We are to exterminate them all, even the women and children. I mean, who will feed the women and children anyway? It is better that they die. Little rebel children will grow up and make trouble in the future. If you squash the nits, there will be no more lice. These were the orders given to me by the General.'"[14]

The addition of more Chinese soldiers in late 1956 brought the total number of soldiers in Tibet to at least 200,000 or more. Sentences of death were obviously an integral part of the Chinese campaign of peaceful suppression of rebels, nor was that campaign affected by the so-called delay in implementing Chinese reforms.

Democratic reforms and public meetings were closely linked. In the public meetings the Chinese officials often boasted about the benefits to the Tibetans of the new programs they had introduced and how much better off all Tibetans now were under the Chinese. Then they would invite, or demand if necessary, a response from the Tibetans assembled. An interesting and widely told story about one of these mandatory public meetings in the Nyarong area in Kham relates that after a Chinese officer had made a rather long speech at one of the communes and had talked about the Tibetans now being fully liberated, and that the Chinese would now take care of the Tibetans, and that now that the Tibetans had freedom of speech, and were free of worry, the Tibetans should be very grateful to the Chinese for their help. He then asked if any of the Tibetans had anything to say. He was expecting that someone would dutifully say how much the Tibetans appreciated the Chinese but no one said a word. The sustained silence angered him and he finally demanded that the freedom of speech the Tibetans had be exercised and that someone speak, and that no one had anything to fear. Finally an old man stood, his patched robe and worn boots very noticeable. He spoke in a clear voice and proud manner, stating "My name is Shanam Ma. I am a poor man and an old one, as you all can see. There are a few things that have to be said here today and it is best that I say them. Since I am poor, I have nothing to lose; since I am old, death will come soon anyway. I have this to say to you Chinese. Ever since you entered our land, we have barely been able to tolerate your behavior. Now you try to force some strange new 'Democratic reforms' on us that we all think are ridiculous and nothing but a mule load of conceit. What do you mean you will give us land, when all the land you can see around you has been ours since the beginning of time? Our ancestors gave it to us, and you cannot give it to us again. If there is anyone oppressing us it is none other than you. Who has given you the right to force your way into our country and push your irrational ideas onto us? We are Tibetans and you are Chinese. Go back to your homes and to your people. We do not need you here." Another man named Apel Tsultrim arose and spoke in much the same way, telling the Chinese that they had not given the Tibetans anything but misery and that they, the Chinese, were not welcome in Tibet — and urged them to return to China so Tibetans could live peacefully.

All the Tibetans attending the meeting cheered, and the Chinese quickly terminated the meeting. However, General Shao and the Chinese officials met and decided to declare and charge that Shanam Ma and Apel Tsultrim were "serf owners and collaborators with the resistance." At the next public meeting, four Tibetan beggars that had been selected by the Chinese as "enlightened ones" were forced at rifle point to accuse the "serf owners." All four of the beggars had originally said that there was no evidence to be found that such a charge was true. The Chinese then threatened the four with death if they did not accuse Shanam Ma and Apel Tsultrim. After the four beggars finally repeated what the Chinese instructed them to say about them, the two Tibetans were then badly beaten by the Chinese and imprisoned. The four beggars were rewarded a hundred silver dollars each, given a rifle and ammunition each and praised as "model citizens" of the new China. Three days later two of the new "model citizens" escaped and joined the rebels, taking their new rifles and ammunition with them. The Chinese then quickly made the other two beggars surrender their rifles and ammunition.[15]

Incredibly, a short time after the Tibetans had been told repeatedly by the Chinese that all reforms were on hold and that their freedoms were not threatened, the Chinese issued an order to their cadres and military that all weapons belonging to Tibetans were to be confiscated. When the Dalai Lama heard this he knew that revolution was inevitable and remarked that, "I knew without being told that a Khamba would never surrender his rifle — he would use it first."[16]

Some weapons had been collected previously during the periods when the Chinese conducted their house-to-house census and when they chose to search for and seize private property, but only a few had been found. Most weapons, certainly the good ones, had been hidden from the Chinese. And those weapons that had been taken from the Tibetans had likely been replaced in most cases by newer weapons. Many Tibetan leaders, such as Gompo Tashi Andrugtsang, had quietly obtained more weapons over the months in anticipation of joining in the general fighting that most were certain would come.

"Word of this Chinese directive quickly spread and prompted the leaders in Kham and Amdo and U — from all parts of Tibet — to exchange ideas on what they should do. No Tibetans, and especially the fiercely independent tribes, would voluntarily surrender their weapons to the Chinese. If there was a single act by the Chinese that galvanized the resistance it was probably this plan to seize all weapons from the Tibetans. It could be interpreted by a Tibetan to mean but one thing: total loss of freedom. It was in effect the final insult. There would be no more broken promises."[17]

CHAPTER 7

The Gold Throne

It is difficult to believe that the decision by the Chinese to seize all weapons was not deliberately provocative. The Chinese army commanders, the Chinese political cadre, and other Chinese civilian officials, as well as those key Tibetan officials and high-ranking monks that had been collaborating with the Chinese, all had to know that the order would incite the Tibetan tribes just as had happened in Amdo when the Chinese tried to seize the weapons there in 1949 and 1950. The Dalai Lama's brother had described the reaction of the Amdos to the Dalai Lama and the Kashag and other officials upon his arrival in Lhasa, and now it was happening again throughout Tibet. That the Chinese reportedly did this without consulting the Dalai Lama as to possible reactions lends more substance to the thought that it was done deliberately to further stir the Tibetans to action, thereby justifying the harsh and heavy Chinese reactions to follow. The lofty thoughts and plans, posturing and lies regarding postponement of Democratic Reforms simply do not track with the order to all Tibetans to give up their weapons. At best it was incredibly careless as an order, and at worst it guaranteed general insurrection and armed insurgency as a reaction throughout Tibet.

In most countries, all the jargon attendant to Communism means very little except to those whose duties require them to be communist parrots, but to Tibetans, freedom and independence and their religion are precious and not to be tampered with. Now all the tribals finally concluded after some six years of barbaric treatment by the Chinese that no more time was to be wasted waiting for things to get better and that with or without the blessing of the Dalai Lama the Chinese were to feel the sword. To the majority of Tibetans, it was basically a choice of either trying to escape to another country or of fighting to defend their own.

"That our religion was at risk and that His Holiness was at risk and that our own lives were at risk were thoughts that were uppermost in the prayers of all of us. However, in the mind of His Holiness these risks had not yet extended beyond bearable levels of concern, and despite their many broken promises, he still thought it possible that the Chinese would change and keep their word. But the order to confiscate our weapons clearly impacted our customs, our personal freedom and personal independence as well. And when His

Holiness heard of the arms confiscation order he too had to recognize that widespread armed resistance was inevitable, knowing that Khambas and the other eastern tribes would not willingly surrender their weapons. In our minds was the question, 'How could the Dalai Lama be protected if we have no weapons to protect him with? And how could we protect ourselves and families?'

"For hundreds of years our weapons had been more precious than jewels. And now the Red Devils expected us to simply let them take our weapons away from us? We had no choice but to move forward with our plans to fight. But first we had to find a way for the resistance leaders to meet to complete and coordinate these plans if we were to be effective, for although the resistance in Kham was growing and had been successful it was not coordinated — and so the advantage remained with the Chinese. This had to be changed."[1]

"Early in 1957 the treasurer of the Lithang monastery and representatives of other monasteries met me with letters from many people in Kham. These letters urged that since the people were engaged in fighting against the Chinese, which they were determined to carry on at all costs, the Tibetan government should give them military aid. In responding to these letters, I thanked my fellow Khambas for what they were doing for the nation, and encouraged them to continue the struggle even if they did not get aid from the Tibetan government. Military aid seemed out of the question, but I nevertheless approached the monasteries and government officials to ask them to contribute their support to the Freedom Fighters in whatever way they could. About this same time, I received a letter from the Tibetan Trade Mission in Kalimpong, praising my work on behalf of the nation. I was deeply touched and thanked the Mission for their appreciation, asking them if they could not do something to further the Tibetan cause in India."[2]

"He (Gompo) approached His Holiness through Thupten Woyden Phala, the Lord Chamberlain (to the Dalai Lama); obviously, the contact had to be made in the strictest secrecy, or the Chinese retaliation would be terrible. Phala relayed the message to His Holiness ... who was torn in two directions. On the one hand, as a Buddhist and a man of peace, he was unwilling to condone the use of armed force against the Chinese, (and) he realized that such an uprising was hopeless.... On the other hand, he knew that for some people, at least, things could not get much worse. And as he said, he could not fail to be stirred by the courage and determination of the Tibetan Freedom Fighters ... but he resisted the requests for assistance. [He said] this was because he knew what the consequences of an uprising would be. He has since said that he believes that it is possible to fight, and indeed to kill, in a rightful cause. 'If you do choose such a course, you must do it with compassion and in full awareness of the consequences, which is not easy; but it may be the only course.'"[3]

The Dalai Lama has also since drawn the parallel with "smacking a naughty child: you do not do it in hate, but because you love the child." These lofty views are all admirable, but do not really explain his reasoning at the time. Was there no thought of his Amdo heritage and no consideration of how he and others in Lhasa might help? He might have recalled what the thirteenth Dalai Lama had done in times of peril, including seeking and taking refuge in India, which certainly would have gained him — and Tibet — support.

By simply staying in Lhasa as a willing hostage to the Chinese the Dalai Lama accomplished little if anything for his country and in fact made it more difficult for the resistance efforts then in progress and those that were soon to follow. His continued presence in Lhasa and cooperation with the Chinese made it much easier for the Chinese in every respect, including keeping what they had done and were doing in Tibet and to the Tibetans unknown to most of the world. Some of the advisers closest to him reportedly urged him to leave Tibet even then and to lend his support to the resistance. But others of these advisers obviously persuaded him otherwise. Looking at the names of those of his advisers who escaped to India with or separate from the Dalai Lama, but who then chose to leave him and India for other countries at an early opportunity, lends credence to the stories that certainly not all of his advisers agreed with his decisions and actions, just as there had been disagreements with his decision to return to Tibet from Yatung rather than accept the offer of asylum extended to him — and a large number (100 plus their families) of his entourage — in 1951. But such is now merely a historical footnote.

Even though Gompo was disappointed when he was advised by Phala that the Dalai Lama would not give any kind of support to or approval of the resistance, he said it was not unexpected. The decision to fight had been made, with or without the blessing of His Holiness; now it was a matter of coordinating the plans and fixing the time schedule. The return of His Holiness from India in April 1957 was widely celebrated in Tibet and especially in Lhasa, where thousands of pilgrims gathered. Gompo seized on "… the idea of requesting the approval of the Dalai Lama for a large and special celebration, Tensuk Shapten, an affirmation of faith in the Dalai Lama and special prayers for his long life and prosperity. This celebration would provide a very unique opportunity for Tibetans to affirm their faith and devotion to their Dalai Lama, and for the various Tibetan leaders and their people to join in these festivities in Lhasa, and for the leaders to complete plans for the resistance right under the watchful eyes of the Chinese. Joining in these ceremonies were the three leading monasteries, Sera, Ganden and Drepung, and the Tashilhunpo monastery as well. I contacted Pharo Chiso, a leading lama in the Drepung monastery, and asked him to supervise the offering. He was flattered and readily accepted. Abbots, monks, incarnate lamas, nuns, government officials, pilgrims — all would join in the celebration. For obvious reasons we maintained strict security and did not tell others, even His Holiness, about our planning. Preparations were involved and would take some weeks to complete, for we planned to present His Holiness with a gold throne complete with precious stones. This of course required that some of us travel to various places in Kham and Amdo, and others to travel to Shigatse and to the west and north to collect contributions from the businessmen and traders and people and from the monasteries, and for travel to Lhasa from all the areas. This served as excellent cover for our planning and lengthy consultations which otherwise would not have been possible. Fortunately, the Chinese chose to remain aloof and apart from all these preparations, so they did not interfere or even suspect us at all. Yes, it was a brazen idea, and totally foreign to the Chinese, which probably led them to decide to ignore us. A lesser gift or celebration would likely have had the Chinese demanding a role, which was the last thing we wanted. And remember, Chairman Mao had just announced that Democratic Reforms were being delayed, so we were able to move and meet more freely."[4]

As the Dalai Lama recalled in his autobiography, "However, as I later discovered, this [celebration] had another aspect. It also marked the formation of an alliance called Chushi Gangdrug, meaning 'Four Rivers, Six Ranges,' the traditional collective name for the two provinces of Kham and Amdo. This organization subsequently coordinated a widespread guerrilla resistance movement."[5]

The effort involved was obviously extensive, and the travel into and out of Lhasa was constant, just as travel and the activities in Lhasa itself remained extensive as the various work projects began and developed. The Chinese soon gave up trying to keep any semblance of records on the people and activities. "Forty-nine goldsmiths, five silversmiths, nineteen engravers, six painters, eight tailors, six carpenters, three blacksmiths and three welders, in addition to thirty general assistants, worked for several weeks on the construction of the throne. While the work was going on, the scriptures were read out, prayers conducted, prayer flags hoisted and incense burned. The whole throne contained 3,164 tolas of pure gold (well over 80 pounds), and in it were embedded precious stones such as diamonds, pearls, onyx, coral and turquoise. To paint some parts of the throne, eight tolas of liquid gold were used. A golden table was also constructed to go along with the throne weighing 203 tolas and it had many precious stones embedded in it.... Besides the throne and other items described, a number of gold and silver lamps and vessels were also prepared for the monasteries as part of the ceremony. These included a 720-tola gold lamp engraved with symbols of deities, three sets of golden bowls, weighing 112 tolas each, one 85-tola gold pitcher with turquoise, one 75-tola gold lamp, one set of silver cups and pitchers, one 50-tola gold lamp, four 100-tola silver lamps, and four sets of silver bowls weighing a total of 547 tolas. The dorje, the symbolic thunderbolt in the front of the throne, was made of 133 tolas and one anna of additional gold, and there were diamond and turquoise lions in the middle of the dorje.

"The completion of the throne was celebrated by religious offerings and cash presents, along with ceremonial white scarves that were distributed to the workers. The throne was offered to the Dalai Lama on July 4, 1957, which had been determined to be an auspicious day. Thousands of people watched this most important ceremony, which still lingers in the memories of those who witnessed it. There was dancing, and the Tibetan army marched; the monks blew their long trumpets; there were plays and so forth.

"The throne was placed in one of the balconies of the Norbulingka palace, and when the Dalai Lama sat upon it there was general rejoicing. A 75-tola golden wheel, with eight good-luck symbols, and many other gifts were offered to His Holiness, who recited prayers and blessed the people. The officials of the Dalai Lama decided that the throne should be kept in the Potala and the ceremony repeated every year, when the Dalai Lama would sit on the throne and receive the people in audiences. The reason why the people of Tibet had been able to construct such a fabulous throne for His Holiness was explained in a proverb: For those who have crossed the rosary of life, 'For those who are fortunate and exalted; There is no obstacle to the road of success, Even in deeds of great wonder and glory.'"[6]

Gompo spoke of the many meetings that the 23 principal leaders of the various Kham and Amdo and Golok tribes had managed to hold as work on the celebration continued. He said they agreed on the areas in the provinces where each would operate; they completed drafting their organizational plans, including designating the officers who would hold the key positions, and they listed the many things that needed to be done before the Chushi Gangdrug could become effective. These included obtaining weapons and ammunition, horses, pack animals, food for fighters and animals, training areas, and selecting likely targets to hit, such as storage areas used by the Chinese, and where smaller enemy units were located. They also exchanged information on escape routes that could be used in situations where it was necessary to avoid or escape from the Chinese.

"It had been an excellent beginning for the alliance. That the leaders were given to being tight-lipped and were increasingly security-conscious, including making sure that the Chinese did not learn of the meetings and plans, was to be expected, but it was interesting that others had also become more concerned as to whom to trust and whom not to. For example, during this same period, a petition from the Khambas fighting the Chinese in southern and northern Kham asking the Dalai Lama for blessing and guidance of their efforts was delivered to an influential monk, Ngawang Dakpa, in the Sera Monastery, for relay to His Holiness by way of one of the few government officials trusted by the Khambas. I mention this only as an example of the concern for security and secrecy that we had come to believe necessary involving even the highest levels in Lhasa. Phala, the Lord Chamberlain of His Holiness, our link to His Holiness, was trusted totally but we had to be very careful in communicating with him for he was in a difficult position not only because of the Chinese but because of Tibetan collaborators among the government officials and in the monasteries."[7]

"During this same period, the Chinese continued their attempts to locate and attack rebel units in eastern Tibet, and they also continued to try to further implement their Democratic Reforms. They tried to harass the Tibetans visiting Lhasa, but because it was a religious celebration that the Chinese officials had given their approval to, there was little they could do, so no really serious confrontations occurred in the city. The Chinese were very ill at ease with the large number of visitors that had come from many parts of Tibet for the religious celebration, and of course they heard rumors from their informants, but they had nothing specific, which further frustrated them. Had they known of the secret meetings of the resistance leaders they would have been furious, but the secrecy held. They cast about looking for something they could act upon against the Tibetans but could not find a thing.

"However, the Chinese officials were upset that many of the Chinese settlers who had come to Lhasa some ten or fifteen years earlier had volunteered to assist in the building of the gold throne, including some goldsmiths and silversmiths, and carpenters and tailors. And other Chinese residents of Lhasa had helped by providing food as well. Because of this, in late 1957 into early 1958, the Chinese communists began deporting the 1,500 or so of these Chinese settlers back to China from Lhasa. Their future was not very favorable, for the Chinese officials charged that those being deported had been passing information to the Tibetans and accused them of other so-called 'anticommunist activities.' Sadly, these Chinese had fled China to escape persecution and turmoil in China some years earlier, and now they were facing a far worse fate when they returned to China.

"Their deportation was also seen as being ominous by most Tibetans, for it was a clear sign that more reforms and controls were soon to be announced by the Chinese officials. The last of the Chinese settlers were deported in April 1958, and shortly after, the Chinese-controlled 'Office of National Policy Making' announced a seven-point program of 'new' reforms. Among them was the requirement that all Tibetans were to be required to have identification and travel documents and that only those living in Lhasa were to be allowed in the city without the permission of the Chinese. And a census was to be taken of all Tibetans, and identification cards issued ... and again an order that the Tibetans were to turn in their weapons. Then the Chinese officials demanded and pressured the Kashag to issue orders that the Tibetan army was to seek out and engage the Tibetan resistance forces, but the cabinet members refused to issue such an order. This infuriated the Chinese, but surprisingly the solidarity of the Kashag held firm. Perhaps they feared reprisals from the army, but the Tibetan army would have refused such an order in any event, and very likely there would have been fighting in Lhasa itself had the Kashag agreed with the Chinese. This prospect probably helped the Kashag to say 'no' because of the threat it posed to them as well."[8]

Like the orders to the Tibetans requiring that they turn in their weapons, surely the order requiring they have permission to travel, and to have travel documents, and that no one would be allowed into Lhasa without travel identification, was extremely inflammatory, for it directly impacted their historical freedom as well as their ceremonial access to the Dalai Lama. It created a tinder-box situation, like lighting a fuse and then waiting for the explosion. While the attempted order from the Chinese to the effect that the Tibetan army was to fight the Tibetan rebels had added fuel to this volatile situation, it had less of an impact than the one requiring travel approval. This too was essentially an order that would not be followed in any event and therefore served no purpose other than to again anger the Tribals. And, to be expected, many from the army soon joined the rebels, bringing their weapons with them.

It is certainly possible that these orders may also have been formulated to create a situation enabling or justifying, flimsy or not, the Chinese to forcefully retaliate to the extent they wished, even to the extreme wherein there would be few Tibetans left, except for those totally controlled in communes and those collaborators willing to readily renounce their Tibetan heritage in favor of China. In essence, possibly "Genocide" aided by administrative process was the intended plan, for then there would be only Chinese in Tibet — no Dalai Lama, no resistance, no Buddhism, the best of all worlds according to Mao, who by this time was becoming far less a visionary than an unstable autocrat. The Chinese had the military might readily at hand to accomplish this and had demonstrated elsewhere the will and ability to pursue such a course of action. While this speculation is perhaps incorrect, and although it did not happen as the Chinese may have scripted it, it easily could have, had not there not been strong resistance, had not the Dalai Lama escaped, and had not thousands of other Tibetans escaped assisted by or because of the resistance. Subsequent events in China and in the area tend to support this thought, as do most of the Tibetans with whom it has been discussed.

"When the Chinese finally heard that many of the resistance leaders had met in Lhasa and that wide-scale resistance was being planned, they summoned the Kashag, and the leaders of the three largest monasteries, Ganden, Sera and Drepung, and the Tibetan military commanders. They told them that anyone helping the reactionary resistance forces in any way would be summarily executed 'slowly and publicly.' The Kashag was pressured into issuing orders and proclamations that there was to be no resistance of any kind against the Chinese. The Chinese gave orders that no one was to join in opposing the Chinese and if this order was not obeyed it would be judged a criminal act, and anyone knowing of any such criminal act was to report it or be charged as a criminal for not having reported it. Many Chinese officials were also sent into the countryside to spread the same message. Strangely, most of the Chinese, especially their military officers and party cadres in Lhasa, did not seem to believe that the Tibetans would actually undertake armed resistance, or that if they did, they were certain the Tibetans could not combat the

Chinese might beyond a very few days at most. Some of the other Chinese civilian officials in Lhasa were less confident than their Chinese military counterparts, but were afraid to express their views. In the rural areas of Tibet it was reported that all of the Chinese, including the soldiers, were very ill at ease. That is quite understandable, especially given what the Tibetan resistance fighters had done to the Chinese soldiers in eastern Tibet for quite some time."[9]

These efforts by the Chinese had little impact on the Tibetans living outside of Lhasa. "It was one of the least effective things the Chinese could have done at that time, for Tibetans do not like to be threatened, especially by an enemy so intensely detested as the Han. It hardened the resolve of the Tibetans to commence armed resistance. Certainly it did not frighten many, if any, and there was almost an air of celebration in the rural parts of Tibet as more resistance forces organized to fight. His Holiness had not given his blessing or approval to the resistance, but neither had he spoken out in precise terms against it. He said in July 1958, 'The people of Tibet will stoutly resist any victimization, sacrilege, and plunder in the name of reforms, the policy which is now being enforced by representatives of the Chinese Government in Lhasa.'

"This was quickly interpreted by most of the resistance leaders to mean that the resistance should proceed, for they knew that under the circumstances His Holiness could not publicly support resistance. However, His Holiness was very concerned and despondent, for he knew the high costs that were to come to the Freedom Fighters, and the Chinese political demands and pressures on him also increased daily. It was a difficult time for His Holiness, and for all of Tibet, but as we know now, it was just the beginning."[10]

Earlier, in April 1958, many Tibetans had come to Lhasa to celebrate the New Year and to honor all of Tibet's Dalai Lamas. This had been a custom beginning with the seventh Dalai Lama, Kesang Gyatso. Gompo Tashi arrived with a party of some 300 from eastern Tibet. It was a brazen act on his part, for by this time the Chinese had become suspicious of him and would have arrested him if they had anything more than suspicions. But they were still not sure that he was a resistance leader or involved in it. After all, he was 53, thus in their mind too old to fight, and, to their knowledge, had so far only traveled extensively on religious pilgrimages and had continued his trade caravans. Again, under cover of the religious celebrations, Gompo Tashi completed plans with more than 20 other resistance leaders who had arrived in smaller groups.

"On April 7, the leaders signed a statement they had drawn confirming their willingness to risk everything to resist the Chinese. Two captains of the Khadang division of the Tibetan army and some others also volunteered to join the Chushi Gangdrug."[11] He also met with trusted monks and lamas in the area to arrange their support. And he again met with the Dalai Lama's Lord Chamberlain and briefed him on the plans, including that it was no longer possible for the Khambas and the Amdos to be passive. He did not ask for the

Dalai Lama's blessing but made it clear that the decision of the leaders of the Chushi Gangdrug was to fight.

"The fighting [in 1957 and 1958] throughout Kham and Amdo and now central Tibet continued to gain momentum. By early summer [1958] several tens of thousands of Freedom Fighters had joined forces and were pressing their raids closer and closer to Lhasa, despite being poorly supplied with small arms and ammunition. Some of what they had was captured from the Chinese, some of it had come from a raid on a Tibetan ammunition dump near Tashilhunpo, and a small amount of it had duly materialized courtesy of the CIA (Central Intelligence Agency) ... but they were still hopelessly ill-equipped."[12]

The statement by the Dalai Lama that some of the weapons and ammunition had materialized courtesy of the CIA is slightly askew. There were no airdrops of equipment in 1957 by the CIA to any of the resistance groups. However, in the fall of 1957 a pilot group of Khambas that had been selected in early 1957 by Tibetan leaders and exfiltrated for training by CIA officers was parachuted into Tibet in two groups. Both groups maintained contact with Tibetan leaders and the CIA via RS-1 radios, powered by hand-cranked generators. One team of two men, Athar and Lhotse, parachuted onto the banks of the Brahmaputra south of Lhasa, and eventually made contact with Gompo Tashi in Lhasa and via him with Phala, the Dalai Lama's Lord Chamberlain, and also with other resistance figures. Later, this team was part of the Khamba escort of the Dalai Lama from Lhasa to the Indian border in March 1959 and provided vital information on his location while serving as the communication link for the Dalai Lama's request to India for asylum.

Athar and Lhotse both survived their lengthy efforts with the resistance, but Lhotse died in India some years ago. Athar is still alive, and lives in India.

The other team, led by Gyato Wangdu, operated extensively in Kham. Wangdu eventually became head of the Mustang enclave in Nepal. Chapter 12 provides more on both of these and other teams.

Also impacting the deteriorating situation was the changed attitude of the Chinese regarding Buddhism in Tibet. "When the Chinese first came into Tibet they publicly said they supported freedom of religion. They were very friendly to the lamas and other religious figures and especially to His Holiness. They even described our Lord Buddha as a 'proletariat hero' for having given up his royalty and wealth. I don't think that many Tibetans understood that term, and most of us simply thought the Chinese to be very strange indeed to refer to the Lord Buddha in such a way. But this earlier attitude of theirs changed over the years, especially beginning with the Democratic reforms of 1956. Then came the restrictive edicts, such as 'All monks and priests must work. All monks performing prayers in households must be paid wages equal to that of a common laborer.' This was to discourage our people from seeking religious service in the home and to officially impose a cost on what had previously been a common practice. It also insulted the monks and our religion. Then came the Chinese claims that 'Religion is based on ignorance, and fed by blind faith,' and then in 1958, the Chinese proclaimed that 'Religion is the opium of the people. All monks and lamas are exploiters and enemies of the people. The clergy and the aristocracy officials are enemies and must be exterminated.' The Chinese had not yet taken action to carry through on the latter part of this, but it was clear that they were warning the lamas and monks of what was coming in the future and for them not to lend any support to the resistance under pain of death. And they demanded that the monasteries spread these proclamations, including the threat to those who might know of, or be inclined to assist, the resistance. What Chairman Mao had said earlier about religion and specifically about the Buddhist religion being of little use was very much like these proclamations."[13]

As noted earlier, the fighting in eastern Tibet was increasingly widespread. Whereas the budding resistance forces in central Tibet and the resistance leaders that met in Lhasa had exercised extra caution to be sure they were not detected, those in Kham and Amdo were not bothered by or did not concern themselves with such considerations. They were on a roll and enjoying increasing success. While activities there were not yet coordinated, it often happened that while things were calm in one part of the country there was often much violence and fighting in other areas. This unpredictable sequence helped keep the Chinese off balance, although the main area of resistance remained in Kham.

"The building and presentation of the Gold Throne had gone very smoothly, as had the later religious celebrations. And the resistance leaders had managed to meet often as they completed their general planning and coordination for the increased armed struggle that was soon to follow. All in code, assignments had been made, locations to be scouted had been assigned, decisions as to organization and responsibilities had been made, and the monasteries to contact for assistance had been identified. The locations of Chinese camps had been listed, their resupply routes identified, likely ambush sites plotted, escape routes noted, and a general timetable agreed upon. And the purchases of weapons, ammunition, animals, and supplies were in process. The construction of the Gold Throne had led to all this being possible. The various resistance leaders kept nothing on their person which would have given the plans away had the Chinese searched them. And very few Chinese knew our language, and none of them knew the codes we used. All in all, it had gone quite well."[14]

CHAPTER 8

The Volunteer Defense Force

The May 25 announcement by the Chinese that no one other than those living in Lhasa could enter the capital without a travel document signed by the Chinese authorities was further restricted by the accompanying edict that no one living outside U-Tsang province could visit anywhere in U-Tsang province without an approved travel document. This temporarily delayed the initiation of the resistance movement by Gompo Tashi Andrugtsang and the other resistance leaders while they reviewed this development, its impact and their options.

"The requirement included that the documents contain the person's name, age, birthplace, father's name and three copies of his or her photo. The Chinese believed this would afford them the control and safety that they wanted. They had become increasingly concerned about the rumors that the Tibetans had resolved to fight, and about the reports of increased fighting in all the remote areas. Gun shots had been heard in Lhasa for many weeks, and the Chinese believed that these came from resistance forces in the area. Some of the shots were from Tibetans attacking Chinese patrols ... and some were from nervous Chinese on guard duty outside of Lhasa shooting at just about anything they heard or that moved. But many of the shots that were heard during the night were fired by two or three Tibetans firing different weapons from different positions to upset the Chinese as part of the psychological warfare that had been devised by the resistance leaders. These nightly firings had the Chinese nerves very much on edge, and the previous tranquility of Lhasa was no more. These new restrictive orders by the Chinese served only to further anger we Tibetans from the provinces. The orders were futile, for it did not take long before 'travel' documents, even those requiring a signature by a Chinese, could be duplicated or, if necessary, obtained for a small amount of money. And there were many ways into Lhasa that the Chinese could not control.

"But the orders were bothersome, and of course served to warn us that stricter controls were likely to follow very soon throughout Tibet. Consequently, we [the resistance leaders] had difficulty in concluding all our discussions about going to war because of possible consequences to His Holiness, our religion and the people. We decided to approach the Shukden oracle to find out what we should do. He told us that the people of Tibet should no longer remain idle but should unite to defend their country. He also said the headquarters for the voluntary army should be established in Lhoka Trigu Thang. With that decided, there would be no further delay.

"I then devoted all my energy and efforts to promote the voluntary army. I used the wealth of the Andrugtsang family, accumulated through generations, for the good of the country. I did this for the benefit of all without the slightest hesitation or regret, for the welfare of one family could not and should not be compared with the welfare of our country or our religion. In addition to the arms and ammunition already accumulated, I bought more, including Russian-made guns of short and long range. There were German, Japanese, British, Canadian and Czechoslovakian rifles and pistols. Most of these came from India with the rest from Nepal, Sikkim, Bhutan, and even China and Pakistan. All the arms I provided to the volunteer army were the best available of their kind, without regard to price for the weapon or for the ammunition. Each rifle cost from 800 dortses to 1,300 dortses. Some other prices ranged from 300 dortses to 700 dortses per weapon. Each gun was furnished with 1,000 bullets packed in boxes at the cost of 15 to 75 sangs per bullet. (One dortse equals 50 sangs.) These arms and ammunition were taken secretly to the army formation camp at Lhokha Trigu. Furthermore, I furnished 46 men of my own, arming them to the teeth, and each was given a horse and charm boxes. In addition, over 100 horses and mules were provided as pack animals. I also provided large quantities of white canvas for making tents and khaki cloth for clothing. I provided men and money to fight the enemy, not for personal benefit but to recover our nation. Right from the start it was clear and known to all that the Chinese were the enemies of religion and freedom. My countrymen and I had held many conferences under the cloak of religious celebrations for years preparing for a revolt, and now was the time for the formation of the voluntary army headquarters in Lhoka Trigu Thang* as stated by the oracle and as sworn to by the resistance leaders on April 7, 1958."[1]

"In May, a Chinese Communist artillery commander in Lhasa named Chang Ho-ther deserted the Chinese and sought refuge in the Khadang Tashi division headquarters of the Tibetan army. He brought with him two rifles and two pistols with about 650 rounds and some interesting documents. The Tibetan commander of the division felt it was too risky and dangerous to grant him asylum and considered returning Chang Ho-ther to the Chinese. However, two captains of the Khadang division came to see me and asked my opinion. I told them that if Chang was earnestly defecting we should not return him to the Chinese. I asked them to hide Chang in the monastery of Tashi and said I would have him removed from there soon. Then I sent some of my men with Ngawang of Lithang to the Tashi Monastery for Chang. After they

---

*Lhoka Trigu Thang is southeast of Lhasa, south of the Brahmaputra River, in Kham province.

dressed Chang like a Khamba, my men escorted him to Tashi Rama Gang, and then another group of my men under Khache Chazo moved him to Lhoka Trigu Thang, our chosen base area. After satisfying ourselves that Chang was to be trusted, we accepted him. He proved to be very valuable to our resistance efforts and was an excellent fighter. He was the first of many other Chinese who chose to rebel and join us. All fought well. Some of them died in combat, but a number survived including Chang, who is still alive and, along with a few other former Chinese soldiers who decided to join the resistance, is now living in a Tibetan community in India."[2]

Before leaving for Lhoka Trigu Thang, Gompo sent a letter by courier to the Dalai Lama explaining that he could no longer delay joining the resistance. He wrote that not only had the Khambas and Amdos repeatedly asked him to join them, but the increasing Chinese oppression over the people could no longer be tolerated, for soon there would be nothing left for Tibetans.

"On June 1, 1958, the fifteenth day of the fourth Tibetan month of the Earth Dog year, I sent two of my servants and three horses to Dip. Then I left Lhasa and went to Dip via the Kuru Sampa bridge over the Kyi Chu River on my motorcycle. I had decided that this was the most secure way, for it was not likely that a bored, half-asleep Chinese guard would concern himself with a lone motorcyclist — nor could he have stopped or caught me even if he wished. The three of us then headed for Lhokha on horseback. On the way we were joined by hundreds of others who were on their way to join the volunteer army. When we arrived in Lhoka Dhama Dzong we explained to the officials of the area our objective and asked them to help us to obtain food. In response to our request, they provided 1,500 khells (1 khell equals 26 pounds) of barley grain. After making some barley flour, we went to a nice grassy area near the top of Digu Tashi Thongmon Dzong and Yamdog Yutso Chinmo lake on June 16. There all the people, including people from the Chushi Gangdrug area and other parts of Tibet who were risking their lives and properties for freedom, religion and the government of the Tibetan people, met together like a confluence [of rivers]. Then we all paraded proudly on our horses in four lines (abreast), each of us dressed in our traditional tribal clothing, and with rifle and sword, and celebrated the founding of the Volunteer Defenders of the religion of Tibet. We offered incense and carried a picture of His Holiness, the Dalai Lama into a tent. We put up the flag of the Volunteer Defenders for the first time. The flag was yellow and had an emblem of two swords, one representing Gyawa Riksum Gonpo (a deity) and the other a dorje, a symbolic thunderbolt with lotus flowers.

"After provincial officials and representatives of monasteries and the people of that area and the Volunteer Defenders gathered together and worshiped the photograph of the Dalai Lama, one of the representatives of the Volunteers made these announcements:

"'In 1950 the Red Chinese invaded Tibet from Kham in eastern Tibet.

Since then they have been increasing their oppression and deceitful activities. Since 1956 they have been burning, bombing and destroying thousands of monasteries in northern and southern Do-me (Kham). In addition, they have been destroying property and torturing and murdering monks and incarnate lamas, the upholders of Buddhism. They have also been murdering regional officials, well-to-do people, traders and others. They are still intending to exterminate the power and the government of Tibet by means of reforms. Therefore, the situation has become very dangerous. Due to this dangerous situation, we Chushi Gangdrug of Do-me and Amdo cannot bear the thought of our fellow countrymen, government and freedom being destroyed. Therefore, we are willing to risk our property and lives in order to resist the Chinese, the destroyers of religion. To do this, we established a garrison of the Volunteer Defenders of the Religion of Tibet. However, we cannot fight in or near Lhasa because of the many sacred places such as the Tuelpa Tsuglakhang [the Tsuglakhang Cathedral], and sacred people, such as His Holiness, the Dalai Lama, will be in danger. Therefore, just as incarnate lamas and oracles have advised us, we have established a garrison here in Trigu Thang. We are compelled to ask you to lend us grains, meat, butter, etc. as your war effort. We will pay you back in accordance with your receipts when Tibet becomes free and secure. There are almost 1,000 of us here and we are representatives of various places in Kham. The rest of our cavalrymen will join us later.'

"In order to boost the morale of the local people, we had to tell them a lie by saying that we were just representatives and that the rest of the cavalrymen would arrive later on, for we did not know then how many more would join us ... but soon hundreds more arrived.

"In reply to the speech by our representative, a representative of the provincial government, monasteries and the people of the area said:

"'As the representative of the Volunteer Defenders of the Religion of Tibet said, the Chinese have been trying to exterminate our country, government, religion and freedom. We all know this. Now we would like to thank you from the bottom of our hearts and not just from our lips for thinking about Tibet's government, religion and freedom, and for establishing the garrison of the Volunteer Defenders of Tibet. We cannot but help you to obtain foodstuffs since our religion and country are very important. We will collect foodstuffs from monasteries, estates, individuals and the 25 Dzongs [counties] of the Lhokha area. Moreover, we will collect men from the Lhokha area to join the Volunteer Defenders to resist the Chinese Communists. On your part, we know that you will abide by your rules and regulations and will not rob the people or cause any trouble. We also know that all of you will always be patriotic and united for the good of Tibet.' We then thanked them many times for their support and swore that we would keep faith with our pledges."[3]

As Gompo related these and subsequent steps and events, it was obvious that despite the many meetings and discussions among the resistance leaders over the past months, there was still a great deal that had not been done. Perhaps had one of the more senior officers in the Tibetan army been involved, especially one that had received some training from one of the British advisers or from a Tibetan army officer that had received training in India, the organization and planning would likely have been much further along. On the other hand, given the Tibetan way of normally doing things by consensus, especially among the tribes, it is probably singularly unique that there was as much coordination and progress as there was. The British, had they still been there, would probably not have been surprised that the Khambas and Amdos were not at all yet well prepared for organized resistance. Many important considerations had not been covered in detail, nor had an overall operational plan been prepared. On the other hand, a well thought out 27-point law governing the conduct of the Volunteers had been completed. And once they commenced, those in the Chushi Gangdrug rapidly became effective and fearsome fighting units ... until attrition and overwhelmingly superior enemy forces both in numbers and far superior weaponry finally prevailed years later, as related in ensuing chapters. The early periods of the resistance enjoyed extensive and impressive successes ... and throughout its existence the deeds of bravery, determination, and selflessness never ceased.

"Now that we had formed the voluntary army, we had to appoint people to lead the men into war. We needed to appoint men who were capable of controlling the army from mistreating the rank and file of the people; men who were sincere to the cause and willing to give up their lives if time and events demanded them; men who were capable of controlling and taking care of the army while creating a friendly relationship among all involved; men who were capable of solving personal differences or local problems. We did our best to appoint persons to lead the men that possessed leadership abilities and had a sense of duty and responsibility. We appointed four main leaders: Samphel Jama Tsang of Lithang, Jinpa Gyatso of Amdo, Thupten of Chatreng, and Chazo Tashi of Bapa. Five others were appointed to establish good relations and understanding between the army and the people and to create an atmosphere of unity and friendship. Another five were appointed to take care of the supplies. Four were placed in charge of the financial department, and four were appointed to the secretariat. We appointed four scout leaders, and 18 commanders were appointed to control the military movements and were responsible for the actions of the soldiers with the common people. With the confidence and hope that more and more men would join the army, an officer was appointed for every ten soldiers. Every soldier took an oath to destroy ten Chinese soldiers. (Even) cooks and stewards were appointed. A 27-point military law was sworn to, and many new clauses were added as necessary."[4]

As Michel Peissel noted in his book *The Secret War in Tibet*, a very rich and wealthy trading family, the Pangdatsangs, was also active during this time frame, although the three brothers were not in agreement about what was best for Kham and Tibet. Rapga, a controversial figure, strongly influenced by Sun Yat-sen and by extension, Karl Marx, had "resigned" as Governor of the Markham District in Kham in 1953 and fled to India. There he became politically active, as previously described, after concluding that Mao's plans for Tibet would not include supporting his earlier (1934) separatist aspirations for Kham. His brother, Topgye, attempted to negotiate with the Chinese in 1956 at Ngapo Ngawang Jigme's suggestion but was unsuccessful and so retreated to India where he made rewarding contacts with Chinese Nationalist representatives, including, reportedly, providing a few but ineffective recruits from the Po region of Tibet to the Chinese Nationalists on Taiwan. Yampel, the eldest brother, remained staunchly supportive of the Dalai Lama and the Khambas. Reportedly he spent large amounts of money to provide the resistance forces with thousands of rifles and ammunition and continued support to them via Assam and Bhutan. Yampel had earlier (1950) offered the Tibetan government the help of the Pangdatsangs in resisting the Chinese but unknown to the family, Ngapo—who had received the offer in Chamdo—had not relayed the offer to the Kashag or the Dalai Lama, which in turn caused serious misunderstandings in Kham, including undermining the Khambas uniting at the time to resist the Chinese. Yampel escaped to India in 1955 where he is said to be very supportive of the Dalai Lama and the refugees.

Wisely, one of the first things that the resistance leaders did was to address some of the local problems stemming from the activities by a number of renegade Khamba and Amdo bandits who had been harassing the local people. "Some people from Kham and Amdo had, like nomads, been wandering in different parts of the country, taking what they could from the people under the cloak of defending the religion and the country, pretending to be resistance fighters. Even in small matters of no importance these renegades had punished the people severely, taking their goods by force. There was almost nothing that we could do to prevent such action by the wandering bands, but we publicized these incidents to the people of the Lho Dzong area and encouraged them to capture such bands and to kill them if they refused to surrender. We also appealed to the people to report to us any such bands in any area ... and promised to send in troops to defend the people from these bands.

"Having made this point clear, we dispatched soldiers in groups of 50 to 100 men to those areas where these wandering bands were most likely to be. The soldiers were under strict orders to capture the members but to kill them if they resisted arrest. They were urged and ordered to carry out the 27-point military law of the voluntary to the fullest extent. This word spread and the people were appreciative of our defending them from robbers. The Chinese also learned of our efforts and about what we had told the people. They tried to make the people think that our volunteers were those that had plundered the rural areas, when actually it was the Chinese that were paying the renegades and bandits to cause problems. We solved this problem without much difficulty by simply eliminating those that were mistreating the people, especially those that had been paid by the Chinese to do so."[5]

"Some Chinese soldiers pretended to rebel and attempted to join us as spies at the direction of their officers. None of these efforts proved to be successful for very long. We tested them in various ways, and it was not difficult to determine those that were sincere and those who were not. We eliminated most of those that were not real but released a few of these pretenders alive, but without a stitch of clothes and with fewer fingers and ears than they had earlier, or with a brand on their face. They were released not far from Chinese camps so that they would be certain to find the camps and tell their Chinese commanders and comrades about our treatment of pretenders. Soon the Chinese stopped trying this silly effort, which is what our purpose had been in letting a few of them live to return to their comrades. The sincere Chinese who joined us even helped to uncover those trying to deceive us. It was a bothersome but interesting challenge, but each side eventually grew tired of the cat-and-mouse game, particularly as fewer and fewer Chinese were released by us.

"But a surprising number of Chinese rebelled and fought with the Tibetan resistance in different areas. The Chinese Communists never admitted that Chinese soldiers rallied to the Tibetan side, or that many others simply deserted and fled to China, or that many were shot by their Chinese officers when they refused to fight. Unless their forces were much larger than ours, the Chinese soldiers usually chose to run rather than fight, for they especially feared our swords and our marksmanship. It surprised us to often see some of the Chinese officers shoot their own men when they would run from us. The Chinese officers were usually in back of the soldiers, not leading them ... probably to make sure that the soldiers did not run away.

"I would guess that in most cases the Chinese soldiers who decided to join the resistance forces must have struggled in their minds, for it was a personal rebellion, not based on any religious reason or for freedom. They had been told that in Tibet there was no freedom and that if captured they would be killed by the barbaric Tibetans. Their joining us was a rejection of all the indoctrination they had previously received. Some joined us because of their own harsh treatment, while others no longer believed the Chinese propaganda, having seen or heard of the extensive mistreatment of the Tibetans by the Chinese cadres and soldiers as Chairman Mao's doctrine was applied. Obviously not all of them blindly believed their political cadres, and they enjoyed the acceptance we extended to those that joined and fought with us. They had not been treated as well by their officers nor by any of their cadres or police. And Chinese command appeared to be exercised more by use of fear than by leadership or loyalty. It is difficult to say ... but the Chinese that joined us fought very hard and bravely. They seemed to be very thankful for their new life ... perhaps experiencing camaraderie that they had not had before is a better term, even though the life of the resistance fighter was very hard and demanding. Many of the Chinese who joined us were killed in the fighting, but in turn each of them killed scores more of their former comrades."[6]

In discussing the early days of the Chushi Gangdrug with Gompo Tashi Andrugtsang, and the questions that were asked of him by those that were undecided about joining the resistance, or questions that the people in the provinces asked him about the resistance, he said "... there were many questions asked of me, such as: what are the facilities for fighting the war? what are the means and sources of military supply? what if the plan to drive away the Chinese Communists fails? why has the Dalai Lama not spoken out in support of the resistance? who is behind the resistance operation? how will it be supported? These questions were asked by the volunteer soldiers from both the Chushi Gangdrug and Amdo, and the people, and the province officials and the monks. Some of these questions were very difficult to answer, while some were very easy. For example, obviously His Holiness, the Dalai Lama, could not publicize his support of the resistance, nor could the Kashag, nor could any of the few leading lamas who supported us. The Chinese orders and threats had made that clear. And if the resistance fails? ... then Tibet will likely disappear except in name, and our religion and personal freedoms will die, just as we may die fighting the Red Devils. Who is supporting us? The people of Tibet are supporting us; most of the monasteries are supporting us; our religion is supporting us. If they asked if the resistance had outside help, such as from other countries in the free world, what could I say? Will the free world send soldiers to help us? No, that is not possible. Maybe the truth discouraged those who asked these questions, but I could not lie to those who asked honestly and who likely faced death if they joined the volunteer fighters.

"Also, I did not know if these questions came from some who were simply concerned about joining the volunteer army or from frightened or collaborating members of the government planted by the Chinese. I did not know—but many rumors spread. In succession, beginning in early May 1958, seven or eight different messengers came to me from the Kashag. Each of the messages stated basically the same. 'The religious rites that you have performed for His Holiness in the sacred places of Lhasa and the three great monasteries are unprecedented. These noble acts certainly deserve the highest respect and esteem. Sometime in the second month of our calendar, some Blue Chinese (the Chinese who had been living in Lhasa for years) were arrested and deported back to the places from which they originally came. However, later on, there was a rumor saying that Khambas and Amdowas must also return to their home areas. This matter was taken up with the Chinese authorities by our government. It has been settled and publicized by the three great monasteries, the Tibetan army, and Provincial leaders of the people. The people, both high and low, are living in peace and free from anxieties. However, recently in the fourth month, you, the people from Kham, without cause or reason or even informing our government, suddenly have taken up arms against the Chinese Communists and moved into areas of Lhokha and Chang (in Kham). Such an unlawful move should never have started at this peaceful time. This move has not only created worries and anxieties both among the Chinese and Tibetans but has created uneasiness and disturbances for the Tibetans. However, living in peace, if you have food problems, etc., in the future, the government of Tibet will be happy to consider the matter if reports on the situation are made to the government.'

"Then on July 12, four representatives of our government arrived with a large escort: Zasak Monling Pa; the governor of Lhokha, Shenen Tenzing; Khensur Thupten Samten of Serra Jay Pa (Monastery); and Khensur Losang Choden of Ganden (Monastery); carrying special messages from the government. It was said that these representatives came not of their own choice, nor were they sent by our government. The Chinese had sent them because the Khambas had 'violated the laws of the land' by suddenly taking to arms and above all by ignoring the orders issued by the government of Tibet. The representatives said, '... it is the ultimate result that we must be concerned with. Therefore, to prevent any disastrous consequences, we must put an end to the congregating of people which is not only unlawful but also unwise.' The representatives also said that '... to discuss the matter in detail, Gompo Tashi must present himself in person before the Dzong [the Provincial government].' I thought about this. If I presented myself before the Dzong, difficulties and problems were apt to arise with regards to our plans and purposes. I could not spare any time. I sent a number of leaders of the volunteer army to represent me, but even after three or four days the government representatives refused to discuss matters with them and demanded that I see them. So I sent 12 more leaders with an escort of 50 cavalry soldiers, but they too were refused. Then my representatives told them that if the government representatives did not care to leave orders with them or to tell them what they wanted to discuss, then they should leave the area and return to Lhasa because more and more soldiers were coming into the area and the responsibility for their safety was growing heavier. Simultaneously, another 150 of our soldiers were spread out in the area of the government representatives in a way to be certain that they would be seen. In the end the government representatives gave in and left the orders. They also repeated that the present peaceful relationship between the Chinese and the Tibetan people must never be disturbed. They also asked why I, Gompo Tashi, and Jago Namgyal Dorje, and the people of Kham had left their homes and taken up arms. They demanded explicit answers and reasons for our actions and the movement, then left. We sent the demanded report. We stated that our movement did not generate out of disrespect for our government nor was it ever conceived as a means to raid the people, a story that had been started by the Chinese. We said the Chinese Communists, the enemy of religion, are oppressing the people of Tibet. Under a cloak of 'reforms,' they are confiscating property, arresting people, and imprisoning them without cause or reason. The situation is that the religion, holy people and sacred relics are being uprooted from the land and destroyed. There is nothing left to look for or live for. With our religion destroyed and property confiscated, the invaders barbarously enforce Chinese Communist doctrine on all. Freedom of any kind is unheard of and unknown since the invasion of the Chinese. People are being constantly arrested, imprisoned, and killed. There is no limit to their inhuman conduct and persecution. Consequently, we rebel not out of choice but because we are compelled to do so because of the Chinese.

"We stated all these facts in the report to the Kashag, and copies were sent to the three great monasteries, to the important courts and to other places. We requested that these facts be publicized, including that since the situation was so risky and fragile, we did not have the opportunity to clarify the conditions of the people and the situation. We had no choice but to act."[7]

In answer to the suggestion that possibly the intent of these delegations, especially the last one, was to keep the volunteer force stationary while Chinese forces surrounded it, and perhaps even capture him and the other main leaders, such as Jago Namgyal Dorje, there in Lhoka, Gompo Tashi said that he had been concerned about that possibility, but he had sent his scouts to watch for any Chinese forces. He said he had not wanted to move until after the delegation had left, for he wanted to show them the volunteers were not afraid and to impress the delegation with the numbers he had shown them. He said he was sure that in their reports each of the delegations had exaggerated the numbers of volunteers they had seen, especially the last one, and so by bluffing them at their own game, including having been able to defy them, and to openly explain the reasons for the resistance, the Tibetans had won a great psychological victory. "Some of the important officials sent by the Tibetan government to dissuade us from our activities even joined us. For example, Tekhang Khenchung Thupten Samchok and Tsepon Namseling, both fourth ranking government officers of the government delegations, chose to join the resistance rather than to return to Lhasa."[8]

Obviously, the volunteer force had gambled and won handily. But the victory had negatives as well, for by staying so long in one area the Volunteers had made it possible for the Chinese to move sizable numbers of troops into the Lhoka area undetected. The Volunteers were soon to suffer accordingly.

"Because our large military base had quickly become quite well known, we decided to subdivide into three separate groups and move. Now that the government delegations had departed, we were mindful of the threat of being bombed by the Chinese, and also of being attacked by a large Chinese force.... We knew we could not stay in any one place too long. The new headquarters was set up in Tsona. And in mid-August, one of our three divisions was ordered to move to Shang Dadhen Chokhor to scout the area. There was a store of weapons and ammunition in a depot there that we wanted, along with supplies of grain and hay. Another group of 150 men went to Chu Shur near Nasop, where Chinese patrols had been reported. As it moved, this group cut Chinese telecommunication lines they found throughout the area, and also ambushed a Chinese patrol near the Zachu River. There were no Chinese survivors, and the bodies of the Chinese were thrown in the river, which was running quite high. Our men were warmly received by the people, and the government representatives there told our men of the terrible treatment and many atrocities that the Chinese had committed in the area. They promised their full support to the resistance, and assisted our men as they traveled through the area. Some of the mule and horse herders there told us they had encountered a small Chinese patrol and had killed them and their leader just before our men arrived. Asked if they had found any papers on the Chinese, the herders said they had taken the weapons and ammunition and one pair of field glasses, but had not searched the bodies, … which we asked them to do in the future because there might be information useful to us. They said they understood and apologized for their mistake.

"About this time we also had our first violation of the rules we had laid down. Three of our men had taken about 100 mules and horses from pasture grounds and driven them back to camp. I told them it was a disgrace to rob animals and they must be returned. One of the commanders from Lithang said that we must also return those animals pasturing in Yangpa Chen belonging to some of the families of members of the Chushi Gangdrug and to some traders in that area. I agreed and ordered 100 of our men to drive the 500 horses and mules we had there to the upper part of the Drechu [Yangtze] river to a place where the Chinese Communists had not been so the people and traders could sort out their animals from ours. The sorting out did not take long and the families and traders thanked us for our good deeds. Most of the 300 horses and mules remaining in the herd that belonged to the resistance were then hidden and pastured in the lower part of the Drechu river as replacements that we knew we would eventually need."[9]

Gompo Tashi said that he reprimanded those in the Volunteer Force that had made the mistake of mixing the animals belonging to others with those of the Chushi Gangdrug, but not harshly, for the mistake had given the Volunteers the opportunity to demonstrate to the people in the area the keeping of promises made earlier. He said that he and the other leaders knew that they had to have the support of the people, for without it there was no hope of success. And shortly after this, the Volunteers learned another hard lesson.

"In all the activity of moving from our base camp and returning the horses, a Chinese collaborator that we had captured by the name of Phewu Tang Tenpa escaped. He had been one of the 'enlightened ones' [beggars] the Chinese recruited, and he had quickly chosen the Chinese side. After escaping from us, he told the Chinese of our location and likely travel routes, so when our scouting party of 150 men arrived in Nemo Lhokhar August 26, the Chinese were waiting for them. Our men had earlier met two women on the road and asked them if they knew of any Chinese in the area. The women answered that there was a large number of Chinese soldiers not far from there busy digging trenches and preparing to make an attack. Then an hour later the group had met two beggars who told them there were no Chinese in the area. Although suspicious because of these conflicting stories, our men decided to take a chance and proceed because they had previously heard that the Chinese soldiers did not bother the casual passersby, and the advance scouts were dressed as traders. Our men foolishly proceeded on that belief without checking the area thoroughly, and after passing by two road construction projects they found the road blocked. They had fallen into the Chinese trap. Mortars, hand grenades, automatic weapons, and rifles opened up from two sides. Our men fought fiercely from the positions of cover they could find. I heard the sounds of weapons as I crossed the river some distance away with 50 men and then shortly could see the fighting with my binoculars. We rode towards them, dispersed and took positions in the hills. I sent another 50 men to the other side of the river to take positions in the hills there. Another 100 were sent in groups of ten to take good positions in the valley and other nearby hills. By noon we occupied the hills and for two days we fought. Finally we were nearly out of ammunition, so we drew our swords and charged the Chinese positions. We killed countless Chinese soldiers and captured many weapons, lots of ammunition and grenades. We lost 21 men, including seven officers: Yaphel Tsultrim of Chatring; Gelek Phuntsok Gaba; Ahsong of Khojo; Chophel; Ahpho of Lithang; Peldhen of Kauze, Lesang Chozen of Gelthang. And 34 horses and mules were killed. Most all of these losses happened when the Chinese first opened fire. We had 17 wounded. And some of the men had been shot many times, but because of their Tso Sung [religious charm boxes] none were badly injured. We recovered and withdrew about ten o'clock at night along the road. Later, however, before we could cross the river near Ma Chang La, the Chinese were again waiting for us. The battle was short and fierce, but we did not suffer any serious casualties. Some of our men who had been separated during the battle and were following us skirmished with the Chinese again in the early morning for nearly three hours but suffered no casualties. Then the Chinese withdrew.*

"We did not pursue them for we were again very low on ammunition and also needed a brief rest, after which we moved north rapidly. Again we had captured some weapons and ammunition, but not as much as from the earlier fight, and we badly needed more ammunition. By rough count, we had

---

In his book Four Rivers, Six Ranges, *Gompo Tashi Andrugtsang cites Tibetan losses at 40 dead, 68 wounded and a loss of 50 horses and mules, and does not mention any of the Tibetan losses by name. Whichever the correct numbers, the Tibetans obviously gave a good account of themselves, despite having been ambushed.*

left at least 200 Chinese dead, including ten or so of their officers. There were many Chinese wounded that had been left behind by their comrades, but we did not have time to dispatch them to their ancestors, so left them to the Chinese to find.

"We made our way north to Shang Gyatso Dzong where I knew the Tibetan army had weapons and ammunition stored. Upon arrival we learned that the Kashag had ordered the weapons and ammunition to be given to the Shang Gadhen Choling Monastery there, leaving only 25 guns and a little ammunition in the fort. Our situation was desperate, for if we were attacked now we had very little ammunition for our weapons. We pleaded with the monks to listen to us, and finally after nearly three days, the gates of the monastery opened and the Rinpoche and the acting governor came to talk to us. We told them of the Chinese deceits, and the threat to our religion and to the freedom of all Tibetans, and why the Volunteer army had been formed. They finally agreed with us but said that the Kashag had ordered them not to give any weapons and ammunition to the Khambas for any reason. We explained that this was like having much medicine on hand but not using it when it was badly needed by the sick. The government had placed the arms and ammunition in the monastery for a reason, and obviously it was to defend Tibet's religion and freedom ... and that is why the resistance needed it so badly and that there would never be a greater need or better use than now. To our great relief, after three days of debate, they gave us four small cannons with many shells, two 60 mm mortars, two 80 mm mortars, 18 Bren guns, 385 Lee Enfield .303 rifles, 378 bayonets, and large amounts of ammunition for the weapons. We signed for these things in the name of the Volunteer army, thanked them warmly and quickly departed.

"Again we sent 50 scouts ahead to the Wuyuk and Takdru Kha areas to scout the Chinese. Another 100 were also sent to follow and reenforce the advance scouts in case of trouble. These two units spotted a Chinese convoy and ambushed it, destroying or disabling 16 trucks. Two of the trucks unfortunately belonged to Tibetans and were loaded with a total of eight horses, seven of which our men captured. The other horse was injured and had to be destroyed. We suffered no casualties, and there were no Chinese survivors among the 18 men and officers in the convoy. After stripping the bodies and taking the documents found for later study, and after loading the weapons and ammunition we had captured on our horses and mules, the force headed south to rejoin the main group.

"Again 50 men were sent in advance to Wuyuk Zomthang and Takdru Kha to scout for the Chinese. Another 50 scouts were sent later to check out the banks of the Nemo River. As they approached Nemo Shung, they suddenly came face to face with a large force of Chinese soldiers that probably was coming to the aid of the group our men had just annihilated. A firefight erupted, and one of our men was killed and another wounded. Our scouts quickly withdrew, but encountered other Chinese forces in two of the valleys near the river. During this retreat, two more of our men were killed and three wounded. We had sent out some additional 20-man units into the area, but they too encountered large numbers of Chinese and were overwhelmed. To make matters worse, some of the old Bren guns we had received from the monastery jammed, and another three men were lost and one wounded because their weapons did not fire. We sent additional reenforcements to different points on the battlefield and fought for 24 hours. We could see many, many Chinese dead, but the riverbank and the whole area were still swarming with Chinese soldiers. They were in the fields, in houses and in defensive positions on the ground. They even used the dead bodies to hide behind. They had all kinds of weapons and they showered us with gunfire and mortars until it became impossible to remain any longer. The Chinese were massing to flood us, and to remain in our position was to invite death. With 70 men, I decided to try to hack through the Chinese using our swords. Praying aloud and yelling and swearing loudly, we charged at full gallop into the enemy, and as we reached the edge of the river our two buglers gave the signal for the others to attack. The men leaped from their defensive positions like wild animals. We all fearlessly charged into the Chinese, fighting hand to hand, wielding our swords and knives and firing our weapons. Much to our surprise, most of the Chinese ran and hid in the nearby villages, and soon the rest of the Chinese also quit fighting and ran. They did not like to face us [hand-to-hand] and our swords. At first we did not chase them, for we were nearly exhausted ... and our men were scattered, resting and searching the battlefield. We rested briefly, had some tea, reorganized and began to search for the escaped Chinese soldiers. Unfortunately for them, rather than retreating they had remained in the villages. We fought in and around the villages until finally we saw a Chinese commander and a number of his soldiers retreat into two large buildings containing offices and telegraph equipment. We shot out every door and window in the houses and buildings, and when the Chinese did not come out we burned the buildings down. We were deeply saddened when we learned that only four Tibetans were able to escape from the buildings. We did not know how many Chinese were killed, but even some horses, cows and chickens were burned to death with the Chinese. It is believed that all told at least 700 Chinese soldiers were destroyed and many more gravely wounded.

"Almost miraculously, our casualties were 12 men killed and about 20 wounded. And we captured many automatic rifles, lots of ammunition and grenades. Around noon I took about 10 men with me and went to a hilltop, and through my binoculars I could see in the far distance more Chinese marching into the area. I immediately returned to the camp area and told the men that because we had been fighting almost constantly over a period of days it was wiser if we now retreated. After a very short rest, everything was secured, briefings were completed and the line of march was set. Our advance scout force of 50 left at 7:00 P.M.; the main body of troops and pack animals left at 8:00, followed at 9:00 by a rear guard of 100 men. We moved eastward via Jang Yangpa Chen, riding day and night with brief stops toward Nemo Junpa. It was our intention to put considerable distance between our force and the Chinese.

"We later learned that when the Chinese soldiers hid in the houses in the villages, they simply shot the Tibetans and the animals they found in them at the order of their officers ... men, women, children. It was a wonder that even four Tibetans had been able to escape.

"We had just reached Nemo Junpa near the complex of the government's office buildings there in the late afternoon when about six o'clock we saw through our binoculars more than 1,000 Chinese soldiers arriving in the area of the office buildings. We sent our scouts to the nearby hills, but they were spotted and shelled. We knew we could not stop now to fight, for we had fought and traveled for days without proper rest and care. There was no doubt in our minds that victory could have been ours, but the cost might have been very high under the circumstances. We decided to withdraw, reenforcing our 50 scouts with 100 more men to be sure that they too could escape. I again sent 50 scouts ahead and took the lead of the main body, and another 100 men were to follow. The main body moved straight on. Suddenly we came face to face with a large number of Chinese soldiers approaching from the opposite direction on a huge plain not far from Nemo Junpa. Our advance group of 50 fought bravely while I divided my force into two groups which attacked from the right and left. The fight continued until dark. When we withdrew, we had lost one officer, and two other men were wounded. The Chinese had lost nearly 200, with many more wounded. We had also captured more Chinese weapons and ammunition but did not have time to strip the bodies of anything but a few propaganda documents which did not prove valuable.

"I sent the main group toward Jang Yangpa Chen and our scout group joined them there. After we had rested and eaten, two officers and 50 men scouted ahead. We were in nomad land and were told by some of them that there were 10,000 Chinese encamped in the lower part of the area. The nomads said that the Chinese soldiers had dug trenches, built strong points and had completed all preparations for an attack. The nomads begged our men not to advance any further. They took some of our scouts to a hill from which they could see the large Chinese force. Then the scouts returned to report what they had seen. I ordered that the nomads be given two rifles as a reward for their help and trusted that they would not tell the Chinese about us.

There were over 200 Chinese trucks in Yangpa Chen apparently ready to move, but our scouts did not see large numbers of soldiers. It was clear that if we remained in our present camp overnight we might be crushed between the two Chinese forces. We did not know how many Chinese soldiers were with the trucks, but concluded that there were fewer there than the 10,000 camped not far from us that the nomads had warned us about. We also decided that probably their defenses were not as good either. There was no other choice than to move forward, so mounting our horses we charged, shouting and shooting through what suddenly seemed to be countless Chinese soldiers. The Chinese were totally shocked and surprised by our charge; they ran from us like a large herd of sheep and fired only a few shots at us. We killed a large number of them and then destroyed a number of their vehicles with grenades and by setting them on fire. We did not have time to count or search the dead because we were concerned that the other Chinese force would soon arrive. But we captured a large number of their weapons, lots of ammunition and some food.

"After leaving that area, we destroyed two Chinese jeeps we encountered traveling between Shigatse and Lhasa, killing one Chinese officer, and two soldiers who we discovered were women, and two other Chinese in civilian clothing. The Chinese officer was carrying a brief case with some documents which we took with us. And we also found documents being carried by the Chinese civilians. We learned from them that the Communist party was experiencing difficulties with its communes and reform program in China and that a program was being implemented in China called 'Great Leap Forward.' Other documents indicated that there were some Communist party differences within the leadership of the Chinese Communist Party. Another of the documents stated that more Chinese troops were to be assigned to Tibet. We had only two or three Volunteers who were well versed in Chinese so we were not certain about all the contents, especially regarding the Communist terminology which remained strange to us. However, these documents were recognized as having intelligence value and we sent them by couriers for passage to the Dalai Lama's brother in India. We also made a separate report summarizing what the documents said and sent them to Lhasa by a courier disguised as a monk for passage to certain government officials.

"We rested at Jang Namtso for several days. Then Phurpa Trinley of Derge and his five scouts that we had left behind at Yangpa Chen to watch the Chinese arrived and reported that the Chinese were massing all around, digging trenches and making fortifications, and that 1,000 Chinese were following us. We also saw airplanes looking for us again, but we were well hidden. We disguised as traders a few of our older fighters familiar with the area and sent them to find a safe passage. If the Chinese questioned them they would not suspect they were Volunteers, for they believed that all the resistance fighters were young, except for myself and a couple of my deputies that they knew about. They did not think those that were older could endure the hardships of being guerrillas. Our 'traders' found some difficult but safe trails, so we moved in groups of 100 with about eight to ten miles between groups to Thanghsiung, near where the Chinese had an airfield and supply storage. We were in need of supplies so attacked the storage area, killing all the Chinese there. We took rice and other needed items and burned down the storage site. Later we destroyed two other Chinese supply trucks that were en route to Shigatse from Lhasa and took those supplies as well. We then rode quickly to Nakchukha and then to the south, knowing that the Chinese would soon follow us.

"Our scouts managed to ambush another three Chinese trucks loaded with soldiers that were headed towards us, and when we reached the Dre Gung Drakhe bridge we ambushed a small Chinese force that had been trailing us. The few survivors fled. We did not chase them but collected the weapons and ammunition the Chinese had left behind. We continued south but had little luck in finding more food. The steward at the Dre Gung Monastery charged us 49 dortse for a small bagful of barley flour, an outrageous amount, but this was the only food the scouts could find, so they bought it.

"Then one of our scout forces of 100 was ambushed by the Chinese. Because of the terrain our scouts could not charge and hack through the Chinese soldiers, so they withdrew looking for alternate routes. They sent messengers about 8 P.M. telling us what had happened and then they sent two more messengers at 10 o'clock and again at 1 A.M. stating they were pinned down and asking for help against the larger Chinese force. A meeting of the leaders was called immediately and we decided to send 100 men on either side of the valley, while the main force cavalry rode straight ahead along the main route. The infantry moved out at 4 A.M. and the cavalry one hour later. We left the pack animals under the care of another 100 men so we could move quickly. At dawn we joined in the battle from three different points. In the initial attack our men killed a Chinese officer and 18 soldiers and wounded many more. Then suddenly the Chinese fled. We suspected that after their commanding officer was killed the Chinese soldiers decided to quit fighting and to retreat. We captured a Bren gun, a submachine gun, 13 rifles, field glasses, a set of medical equipment and eight horses. We lost one man. Our main force then moved through the area safely, including the pack animals.

"After we were rested, we again prepared to move out, sending 50 scouts ahead. Just as the main body was ready to move, we met two nomads who reported that the entire area was full of Chinese soldiers and trucks. Not knowing what to believe, I sent another 100 men ahead of the main force as a precaution, and to reenforce the 50 sent earlier.

"Our main force had advanced less than a mile when I saw my personal guard Tadrin Tsewang galloping his horse at full speed down a hill toward us. He said that the place was swarming with Chinese making preparations for an attack, including digging trenches and making positions for heavy weapons. He said the scouts had counted about 400 trucks and estimated that there were close to 10,000 Chinese soldiers before them. All the leaders quickly met on the huge plateau that we occupied to decide what to do, when suddenly there was a tremendous barrage of over 500 rounds of mortar fire and machine gun fire all over the plateau. The explosions raised so much dust that we could hardly see the men next to us, much less see the Chinese. The heavy dust may have saved us, for we were immediately hidden from view by it and the Chinese could not see where to concentrate their fire. I was wounded immediately by shrapnel and bullets, as were 21 others with me. Six of our men were killed instantly, along with 20 horses and mules. Our men returned fire fiercely and did not scatter, nor did they lose our supplies or the pack animals. When the firing was less, my wounds were examined briefly and 12 places were found, but by the grace of the Three Precious Jewels, none of them were fatal, and I could still ride. My clothing, and that of many of the men, was again torn and shredded where bullets and shrapnel had passed through, but only a few men had actually been hit despite the heavy barrages the Chinese had fired at us. We quickly decided to move out as fast as possible, but as the dust settled the Chinese must have recognized the horse I was riding, for as we left many more shells poured in near me and my horse. One of my men noticed this and gave me his horse to ride, and he wisely chose to ride one of the mules, rather than my horse. The dust from this last barrage in late afternoon was again like a protective screen and we rode out at full gallop, just escaping the Chinese soldiers approaching on foot attempting to surround us on the hilltop. Their attempt to encircle us was fortunate for us, for not only were we able to ride through the gaps in the ring, the Chinese fired very little because they would likely hit other Chinese troops foolishly deployed immediately across from them. Even after dark we could see and hear in the distance the Chinese still trying to find us with flares and cannon fire. Their trucks could not follow us on the trails we were on, and their infantry could not hope to keep up with our horses. Stupidly, the Chinese tried to pursue us with some of their vehicles on our trails, but soon lost at least three or four loaded with soldiers when they rolled off the narrow paths.

"The next morning Chinese aircraft tried to find us, but low clouds obscured their vision. We continued on with only very brief pauses for two more days and nights until we reached the trijunction at Kong Tse La where we rested for a few days and treated our wounds. All of us were very tired, including our horses and mules, but our determination remained high. But we were again getting low on ammunition and food, so we sent scouting parties out to hunt for food and to locate the Chinese we knew would be looking for us in the area.

"After resting, 50 more men were sent in search of food, while 50 others were sent in different directions to scout. Others were also sent to hunt animals, leaving only three security positions on perimeter guard duty to protect the rest of us. One of them soon spotted a large number of Chinese soldiers closing in. They opened fire, getting off about 30 shots which alerted the rest of us. Some of our men quickly occupied the surrounding hillsides, while others saddled the horses, ready to move out. The Chinese force behind the patrol was large and well armed. They showered our camp site with cannons, machine guns, and other automatic weapons, but we had already moved from that position. We fought back until dusk, then withdrew by a route which was almost an impossible trail, but there was no other way out. We traveled the night through. The sure-footed animals saved us. We had lost 15 men and three others were wounded from the skirmish, and all of us were very tired. We had killed at least 170 Chinese soldiers and six officers, and wounded many more Chinese ... but because they had run out of ammunition, nearly 100 of our men had been captured in an ambush the Chinese had set up. This caused us great sadness and concern, for such a heavy loss was very hard to accept. We had weapons and some ammunition, but all other supplies such as food were very low, which increased the danger to all of us.

"We traveled for days and nights to escape from the Chinese in the area, but eventually we had to rest and treat the wounded. We also decided not to let the Chinese chase us any further, for this had led to many ambushes and hardships. Instead, we set up a very elaborate ambush against the Chinese we knew would come soon. We waited for some time, but the Chinese traveled by another route; we missed them, which made us frustrated and angry, but decided to move on to Japho Jakey near Ahtsar Lake, where two rivers meet. Here we split our force into three groups and camped for two days, again sending out our 50 scouts. Another 150 men prepared an ambush site. Then some of the scouts returned and reported they had found no food but that a force of 3,000 Chinese were at Ahtsar Lake. We prepared to attack, but our scouts then reported that even more Chinese soldiers had arrived and that the Chinese were massing their forces and also sending out patrols. Our fighters then raced to take positions at the ambush site and arrived there ahead of the Chinese. Soon 18 Chinese soldiers arrived and our men killed them all. At the sound of the rifles and machine guns more Chinese poured into the scene. Our men fought back hard and bravely until late dusk. By that time we were at a great disadvantage in weapons, ammunition and numbers. The Chinese fired more than a hundred mortar rounds, but no one was hurt. And at great risk some of our men crawled along the ground and took some grenades and ammunition from the Chinese that had been killed earlier. Others of our force had also heard of the firing and, flanking the Chinese, they joined in the fight to help us, but it became obvious that we could not stay there. We all withdrew silently under cover of darkness. From a distance we could hear the Chinese shooting, thinking we were still there. Fortunately, we had suffered only two wounded, thanks again to the excellent cover of the ambush site and our charm boxes. We had killed many Chinese and wounded many, for there were Chinese bodies piled up at the site, but we never did learn the exact figures.

"And, fortunately, some of our men had earlier found and prepared a yak and some game, so we all had something to eat as we rode.

"A nomad we met told us that over 5,000 Chinese soldiers were waiting for us near Jang Lhari, so we moved to Jang Methikha. We also located a Chinese spy there that we had learned of, and after interrogating him, we killed him and took his rifle and pistol. We were soon traveling in snow but pushed on to Naksho, where we met friendly herdsmen called Chunggyu Woma. We bought grain and five sheep from the nomads and paid for them with two rifles, 300 bullets, two mules and 160 dortse. We also left a note promising to pay them more when our government was again free.

"To our surprise and joy, Captain Ahzin also rejoined us, having escaped from the Chinese shortly after he had been captured at the ambush where we had lost 100 men. Captain Ahzin understood Chinese and reported that the Chinese had talked about completely destroying all Khambas. He said that while a prisoner he had heard Chinese radio broadcasts mentioning that reenforcements were vitally needed in Chamdo and Nakchuka to destroy all the Khambas, and describing the Khambas as 'bourgeois saboteurs of peace.'"[10]

In answer to a number of questions I asked in discussing these engagements, Gompo Tashi stated that obviously the Chinese were often able to locate the Chushi Gangdrug forces by the use of aircraft. While the difficult terrain or the weather nearly always prevented the Chinese from bombing them, the planes could spot and report groups that looked suspicious, such as the large scouting patrols that were used so often. It was then simply a matter of the Chinese sending scouting parties of their own after the suspected sightings and then pinpointing the main body of the resistance forces. The Chinese troops had extensive air-to-ground and ground-to-ground radio communications, which made it relatively easy for Chinese units to coordinate with other nearby Chinese units in tracking and locating the Volunteers.

Supplementing these methods was the extensive network of informants the Chinese established in Tibet, for if the serfs or monks did not answer the questions asked by the Chinese, they were usually beaten, executed or jailed. And with the increasing numbers of Chinese and the increased use of military vehicles the Chinese could often move rather quickly into position to intercept or ambush the Volunteers. Without radio communications of their own, the Volunteers were at a distinct disadvantage.

Gompo Tashi also noted that the mobility and firepower of the Chinese steadily improved, especially artillery, which the Chinese used increasingly. Serious problems experienced by the Volunteers were attrition, for there was little time for resistance forces to recruit and train new Volunteers; food, which was in short supply throughout Tibet; lack of rapid (radio) communications between resistance groups; and unequal firepower. Shortages of ammunition and medicines were also a constant problem for the Volunteers.

Gompo Tashi agreed that there was no doubt that the Chinese wanted to eliminate all the Volunteers, for they represented the symbol of unified resistance, not only from the time of the formation of the Volunteer Freedom Fighters on June 16, 1958, in Trigu Thang but the resistance that had begun well

THE VOLUNTEER DEFENSE FORCE

before then as well. There were other excellent resistance groups engaged in heavy fighting in other areas of Kham and Amdo, as well as in most other areas of Tibet, but the Chinese were especially determined to totally eliminate the symbol of unified resistance and defiance, the Freedom Fighters of Gompo Tashi Andrugtsang, after which they would concentrate on eliminating the others.

The following are brief examples of some of the activities of other resistance groups:

> ... During the previous year (1957), there had been a considerable guerrilla force, over 10,000 people, in Tromtha, a day's ride from Zamdo where we were. But due to Chinese pressure and the problems of supplying such a large force, they had split up. One of the biggest bands, under Gyari Nima, had headed for the Lhasa area in the fifth moon. Another group, under Ghaba Dorje Gompo, had also headed westward around the same time. But such travel was difficult and hard, and one had to fight through many Chinese patrols to get there. Some groups had too many women, children and old people; they could not possibly accomplish the journey and had to stay behind. Yet guerrillas were still operating in western Nyarong and constantly raiding Chinese out-posts and patrols. There were many other such guerrilla bands scattered all over Nyarong. Too many of them were encumbered with women and children and did not have sufficient weapons and ammunition. Yet they persevered and refused to surrender.
>
> [Another example] ... We traveled past Derge Yhilung, and towards nightfall encountered another company of Chinese troops. We began firing at each other and finally the Chinese disengaged. Two of our men were killed. The Chinese suffered about twenty casualties. That same night we crossed the Zachu river.... East of Zachu are the grasslands of Zachukha, the home of a fierce nomad tribe of about three to four thousand families. At this time there were no Chinese in Zachukha. They were operating west of the river where they had built roads, and had many strong garrisons.... We decided to raid a nearby Chinese base at Zamey Naghdo, as our spies had reported that it had large supplies of food and equipment. We joined forces with the local guerrilla bands who were from the tribes of Bachu, Yadi and Thargyen. There was also a group of nomads from Zapa-Liru in Nyarong. In all we had a force of 300 men for our raid. We expected the raid to be a pushover as our scouts reported that there were only 20 to 30 Chinese soldiers guarding the camp. But somehow news of our proposed raid must have leaked out, because when we got there we found about 200 Chinese soldiers waiting for us. These soldiers were normally stationed at the Zokchen Monastery, a few days ride away ... The Chinese wisely disengaged early and barricaded themselves in their camp. We managed to take about 200 horses and about 800 dres (cows) and yaks. Although it wasn't really a victory as we hadn't wiped out the garrison, the local people insisted on calling this incident the "victory of the five tribes." ... That day we lost one of our best fighters, a strapping young lad from Nyarong called Nolo. A Chinese bullet got him right in the middle of the forehead.
>
> [Another example] There were two famous monasteries about a day's ride from Zakchukha, the Zokchen Gompa and the Shichen Gompa, both of the Nyingma order. There were some 1,000 monks at the two monasteries, and both,

especially Zokchen, were famous throughout Tibet for the many saintly and learned lamas and ascetics they had produced. The Chinese had come to the Zokchen monastery and demanded that the monks of the Zokchen and Shichen monasteries attend a special meeting. The Chinese then proceeded to occupy the best quarters in the monastery, which was the residence of the chief Lama, Zokchen Rinpoche. They kept the Zokchen Rinpoche and the other prominent Lamas as hostages with them. At the meeting the Chinese informed the monks that henceforth all monks were to disrobe and marry. They also made the monks work, chopping trees in the forests, and held constant criticism sessions and meetings for about two months. The sacred images of the Buddhas and other deities were torn down; the sacred books were thrown onto the ground and the monks forced at gunpoint to walk on them. On the 25th day of the eighth moon in 1958, the Chinese announced that the monks would have to criticize their Abbots and Lamas in a "struggle" session.

The monks of Zokchen met secretly to discuss what they should do. One monk called Nyarong Gyulo spoke out his intentions. "We have witnessed terrible acts and blasphemy with much forbearance — some would say, with much cowardice. Now the Chinese want to denounce our Lamas, our very teachers who taught us the Dharma and passed the sacred teachings of Buddhism to us. I know not what you all wish to do, but as for me, I will never denounce them. Let me die a thousand deaths and roast in a thousand hells before I ever contemplate such a terrible deed."

All the monks agreed ... and decided that their only option was to fight. Before a senior monk, all of them gave up their monkhood to free themselves of their vow not to kill.

There were 300 Chinese soldiers at the monastery and they were all armed. The monks had nothing but swords, knives and the axes the Chinese had given them to cut trees. The monks decided to attack when the soldiers were having lunch, since at that time they could be expected to be off guard. A smaller contingent of monks would hack their way through the building to where the Lamas were held and rescue them. The monks chose Nyarong Gyulo to lead them. The Chinese somehow stumbled upon what was happening, for the night before the attack they made ready to arrest Gyulo ... but Gyulo in turn discovered what the Chinese were up to, and without wasting a moment summoned all the monks and attacked. They stormed the residence building, cutting down the guards, and getting inside, began to hack away with their axes at anything that moved. It was dark in the building and there was a great deal of shouting and confusion. The Chinese soldiers panicked and started to shoot indiscriminately. It was a bloody and chaotic massacre.

But one aspect of the monks' original plan was still working. The picked contingent of monks, ignoring the melee, rushed to the top of the building and, cutting down the guards, rescued the Lamas. The Chinese Commander and a few of his officers were with the Lamas, and they were hacked to pieces. In the fighting Zokchen Rinpoche was wounded by a flying axe. The monks quickly rushed their Lamas out of the building and called off the attack. As soon as all the monks managed to come out, they piled dry faggot, hay and other flammable substances against the side of the building. Ignoring the firing of the Chinese within, the monks set fire to the place. The Chinese that had survived the axes and swords were all burned to death. There were no survivors. About 50 monks were killed and many more wounded, but except for Zokchen Rinpoche, all the other Lamas were unhurt. The monks also captured 80 rifles and other small arms in good condition. Some 700 or so monks, trailing their wounded and with the old, feeble monks made their way to Zachukha where the local people and guerrillas provided for them. The Zokchen Rinpoche and his entourage were housed at the small monastery of Wongpo Gon. The great Lama died of his wounds after three days. Most of the monks then joined the guerrillas.[11]

"By the end of 1958, the revolt against the Chinese was in full flow. The battles were tremendous, but despite enormous Chinese superiority in numbers and equipment, the Chushi Gangdrug inflicted terrible damage.... The Freedom Fighters were using everything they could lay their hands on, from captured Chinese (mortars) and machine guns to swords, and their utter fearlessness terrified the Chinese. They also had to act as police, because the Chinese had armed and supported bands of robbers in order to blacken the name of the Freedom Fighters; after a few robbers had been caught, tried in the field, sentenced to death, and shot, there was a marked reduction in the number of bandits."[12]

All the tribes in Kham were united against the Chinese, including the ten clans of Nangchen; the Nakchu and Rakshi Gumpa; the Horpas of Kandze; the Changthang herders in the south; and the dozen or more tribes in the Markham area. The Amdos were also resisting the Chinese, as were the 20,000 Goloks of Khangsar, Tsangkor, Khangring, and Butsang. Unfortunately, few knew how to wage effective guerrilla warfare, nor did they have the weapons and ammunition needed to do so. There was little coordination of effort; there were no means of communications between or among these tribes except by messengers on horseback, nor were any of the remote tribes in radio communication with Tibetan leaders or outside support. The Chinese steadily increased their margin of power, with the outside world knowing precious little of what was transpiring throughout the land of the Lotus.

"It is quite amazing that virtually no news of this massive uprising appeared in the Western press, so effective was Chinese censorship. A lone voice was that of George Patterson, a brave and strange combination of missionary and journalist, but his reports were often accorded less space than Chinese denials."[13]

India allowed little in print, even though there were countless reports that came from the hundreds of refugees that crossed into Nepal and India from Tibet, as well as the official communiqués from the Indian and Nepalese consulates in Lhasa. These reports were kept not only from the press but from other members of the respective governments. Oddly, the Chinese refusing Prime Minister Nehru's request to visit Lhasa in 1958 received little press attention or speculation, nor did the demand of the Dalai Lama by Gen. Tan Kuan-san in the fall of 1958 that the citizenship of Taktser Rinpoche (Thubten Jigme Norbu) and Gyalo Thondup, the elder brothers of the Dalai Lama, be revoked. As the Dalai Lama said later in explaining his action, "The revocation of their citizenship was in retaliation for the siege by resistance forces in the fall of 1958 of a large Chinese garrison at Tsethang, two days ride from Lhasa."[14]

The attack on and siege of Tsethang had involved 2,000 resistance fighters attacking a garrison of 3,000 Chinese soldiers only some 35 miles from Lhasa. The Tibetans had captured scores of weapons, a large amount of supplies and caused the Chinese hundreds of casualties. Only when the Chinese sent heavy reenforcements to the area did the Tibetans withdraw into the mountains, having suffered only a few casualties. It had, by any measure, been a serious embarrassment to the Chinese.

In early 1958, at the insistence of certain U.S. government officials, a radio message was again sent to the resistance leaders requesting them to again solicit the Dalai Lama for his approval and support of the resistance. This was done through Phala, the Lord Chamberlain. Not unexpectedly, His Holiness again refused, choosing to ignore the large-scale atrocities and many broken promises of the Chinese.

As was the case in and since 1950, the world was largely ignorant of what savagery the Chinese had brought to Tibet and knew little if anything of the efforts by the Freedom Fighters to rid Tibet of its hated invader. The United Nations remained steadfastly uninterested, its members intimidated by the long shadow cast by Mao Tse-tung's supposed military might. The Chinese and Indian censorship practices had succeeded — the one because of extensive and effective controls, the other largely because of Nehru's naked fear of China. Other than the efforts by the older brothers of the Dalai Lama, Thubten Jigme Norbu and Gyalo Thondup, Tibet had no voice, and there was little or no interest by the international press, beyond an occasional story out of Hong Kong. It was not until after the Dalai Lama escaped that the media took a belated interest. China had played the role of bully in Tibet and India effectively throughout the nine-year period (1950–1959), both internally and externally — just as she has since, including across the board of international politics and economics. Interestingly, few have chosen to seriously question or write about the horrors of her practices behind her own bamboo curtain, just as the United Nations still remains aloof to Tibet's plight. But this is ahead of the story of the rapidly changing situation then evolving in Tibet.

CHAPTER 9

The Pendulum Swings

In discussing the extended period of fighting that the Chushi Gangdrug forces had experienced in 1958, Gompo Tashi Andrugtsang said that with few exceptions there was no diminution in the spirit and determination of the volunteers to continue their attacks on the Chinese, despite the many actions. The Chinese broadcasts that they occasionally heard continued to refer to the intention of the Chinese to eliminate all armed resistance and to annihilate the Khambas, but also referred to Chinese reinforcements being sent to Tibet to destroy the rebels. This latter admission told the Chushi Gangdrug that their successes — and the successes of the other resistance groups — against the Chinese were taking a toll on the Chinese. However, Gompo Tashi also said that there were some among the volunteers who became frightened and fled to India with their families, and a few others who deserted for reasons without honor.

"Victims of fear, not being able to overcome it, three of our leaders abruptly left the voluntary army to travel separately, taking 80 men with them. For them, life was more precious than our cause and goal. They left the volunteer army to follow their own destiny. Some went to west Tibet and others to Lhoka in south Tibet. Fear does strange things to men. And when one becomes a victim of fear and cannot control or overcome it, that person is lost. I had no strong reaction to their departures beyond disappointment. They left without discussing their decision or plans with me, which led me to believe they were ashamed. I would not have tried to force them to stay but would have urged them to reconsider. I would also have suggested safe routes to them for their escape to India and cautioned them not to do anything on their journey that would reflect badly on the Volunteer Freedom Fighters. I also tried to think back to see if I should have noticed anything about the three leaders indicating that they were wavering, but nothing measurable came to mind. It was frustrating and puzzled many of the Volunteers, but the return of Captain Ahzin (who had escaped after having been captured by the Chinese) and his determination and confidence also made the men more resolute. A week or so later we learned that after Zenang Ahker and Relpa Bhuchung, two of the leaders who had deserted with 40 men, left, they had moved south towards Shota Lhosum and soon started robbing the people of horses, mules, gold, silver, and food. Reportedly they had thought to move from Powo Tamo south to Lhoka, but the Chinese were already there, so they returned to the Shota Lhosum area, not very far from our force, in order to enrich themselves at the expense of the helpless people. These deeds doomed them.

"We also heard that the other group that had deserted us was headed westward and intended to go to Nepal. Then later we learned that after some skirmishes with the Chinese along the way, they had arrived safely. They should not be judged too harshly.

"At the end of October, our force arrived at Gyasho Pengyal, where we were given a very warm welcome by the monastery and the local people. They gave us large amounts of grain, butter and yaks for our meat supply. We camped there for four days, resting ourselves and our animals. Then we went to Dramthang and camped there for three days. Again the people greeted us and gave us food, hay and firewood. Here the people and the monastery told us that Zenang Ahker and Relpa Bhuchung were robbing the people in the area and said that if these things happened again there would be no help from them for the resistance. We apologized and promised we would take care of the problem.

"We then left for Sarteng. Again the people were very helpful and cooperative, and they gave us good information. We learned from them the location where many weapons were stored that the Chinese had seized from the people in the area. We also learned from them that Shiwa Lha Rinpoche and the Abbots of Chamdo Monastery had been thrown into prison by the Chinese, and even though they were very high-ranking monks the Chinese tortured them and forced them to do hard labor. We also learned of many other mistreatments and robbings of the people in the area by the Chinese, and the destruction of their monasteries, raping of women, including nuns, and many public executions and beatings of the farmers and traders. And again we heard that Zenang Ahkar and Relpa Bhuchung and their men were badly mistreating the people in the area, including forcing themselves onto the women.

"Before searching them out we decided to act first on some information that we received. Not far from Sarteng Gyalton, the Chinese had a large storage area, and at the moment it was lightly guarded. We attacked, quickly dispatching the 40 or so Chinese soldiers guarding the area and seized a great supply of grain and many weapons with ammunition. From there we moved quickly to Chulthun. We then sent four very strong leaders with 100 men each with instructions to enforce the laws we as Volunteer Freedom Fighters had established.

"In a place called Chukhor our men found and arrested Zenang Ahker and Relpa Bhuchung. They were then brought before the public and told that their actions had brought disgrace and shame on the Freedom Fighters and resentment from the people against the Volunteers. The two were then given a brief trial, found guilty, sentenced to death, and quickly executed. Their men were given a choice of paying a large fine or receiving 50 lashes. A few who did not recognize that they had brought dishonor to our Volunteers received both the fines and the lashes, and some donated either a finger or two or an ear for the problems they had caused. All their weapons and animals were seized, and the animals and other things they had taken were returned to those they had robbed. They were then driven from the area in disgrace, after physically being branded as traitors and bandits."[1]

In expanding on the punishments noted in the telling of the story about Zenang Ahker and Relpa Bhuchung, Gompo Tashi related that while lashing and branding may seem cruel to the westerner, such punishments, including mutilation, had long been a way of life in China, India, Pakistan, Nepal, Sikkim, Bhutan, Tibet, etc., and most other Eastern and Mid-Eastern countries, and were not seen as unusual. Those that broke the laws or the codes knew what the consequences would be, and especially in cases impacting the Freedom Fighters there could be no exceptions if the respect and needed support of the people was to continue. He also contrasted what the Chinese had done and were doing to Tibetans without justification with the actions of the Volunteers. He also noted that the punishments given by the resistance were considerably less than the punishments given by the Chinese — and some Tibetans — in previous decades.*

As explained by Gompo Tashi, "... those that were not executed were often branded or their fingers or ears cut off to identify them as less than worthy persons. The resistance did not hesitate to track down and punish the deserters who broke the resistance code, or the traitors or the bandits. And often it happened that the people would travel to the camps of the Volunteers to pass the name of a known collaborator or spy, and teams from the Volunteers would then investigate the stories ... and return the accused to the camp for trial if the stories were judged accurate. Or, if necessary, and the evidence was great enough, the guilty would simply be publicly executed after a public hearing. In particular, Chinese collaborators and spies were seldom safe in areas away from Lhasa. And bandits did not fare well either, for their acts, like the acts of traitors, were not forgivable. In the Tibetan mind all these people had already soiled their lives and abandoned their souls, and so the act of killing them was, under the circumstances, an act of goodness. And remember, the Chinese often supported these brigands in the hopes that the people would not support the volunteer forces. But this attempt served only to add to the hatred that the people held for the Chinese. I think I mentioned that the Chinese even tried disguising their own soldiers as tribals and sent them to plunder areas so that the people would think the resistance forces were nothing but bandits. They were seldom successful."[2]

This latter point is well substantiated in the punishments described in A History of Modern Tibet, 1913–1915, *by Melvyn C. Goldstein.*

Gompo Tashi said that it was about this same time the resistance leaders realized that some adjustments needed to be made in the way they had been operating against the Chinese. It had become increasingly difficult to avoid detection by the Chinese, and in order to maintain their mobility and effectiveness it was necessary to reduce the numbers operating in an area and to rely more on ambushes than on attacks by larger groups.

"On December 6, the 25th day of the 10th Tibetan month, 1958, we left Sarteng and reached Chakra Pelkhar. The monastery and the local people gave us a very warm welcome and many supplies. On December 8, a meeting of the leaders from Jungpo Karnak, Sersum, Derge, Podhopa, Ribochen, Shota Lhosum, Rongpo, and Gyelton was called. The meeting lasted a week. Agreement was reached that:

"1. Jago Namgyal Dorje, Sadu Tsang Lhonedrak, Jama Samphel of Lithang and Sengye-long of Chatreng were to command the main force of 500 cavalry in the Lhoka area.

"2. Thirty men were assigned to Tsethang and thirty men were assigned to Dre to conduct guerrilla activities in those two areas.

"3. The remaining soldiers were to be combined and divided into two general divisions, operating in forces of about 100 men each. Plans were then made to attack Kongpo Ningtri on January 14, 1959, from two different directions.

"4. The Volunteers in Jang were to leave on December 18 and attack Potamo Chunpo Tengchen Rongpo Rapten on December 25. The four commanders, Gyado Dhondrup of Lithang; Dawa of Chatreng; Pema Yeshe of Kanze; and Namgyal of Bapa were to attack Potamo with 200 of our Freedom Fighters and with 200 local Volunteers at the same time.

"The men attacked on the date set and fought the Chinese for 15 days, destroying more than 500 Chinese quarters and many vehicles. Unfortunately, the force from Lhokha could not reach and attack on the given date, which made it possible for Chinese reinforcements from Lhasa, Chamdo and Kongpo to pour into Potamo, forcing our men there to retreat. The Chinese communist newspaper in Chamdo carried news of the fighting and reported that more than 550 Chinese soldiers had been killed 'heroically' in this battle. We lost 20 men and nine others were wounded. Two of our leaders, Naduk of Thargya Gonpa and Ludup of Chatreng, with 29 Volunteers and helped by more than 400 local people, also attacked another Chinese camp in the area. That battle lasted for 10 days and nights. They inflicted heavy casualties on the Chinese and destroyed a large number of trucks and burned some of the Chinese barracks and storage buildings. Later some Chinese armored vehicles and tanks escorted some Chinese trucks and soldiers from Nakchu and carried back to Sokkhul all that was left of their supplies, along with many wounded Chinese soldiers. Our losses were 7 dead and 2 wounded. The Chinese burned what was left of the supplies that they could not get on the trucks to make certain that the Tibetans did not recover anything.

"Another of our Volunteer forces of 130 men, led by Tramo of Amdo and Samdeng Chazo, attacked the Chinese in Tengchen of January 24, 1959, the 15th day of the 12th month of our calendar. They overpowered the Chinese and seized the fortresses in Teng Dzong. The people were overjoyed and more than 4,000 people from the local area volunteered to join us. Surrounding the Chinese outposts, the Volunteers tried to cut off their water supply and laid siege until February 23. The destruction of the Chinese was systematic and about completed when unfortunately the skies cleared and the Chinese began bombing and machine-gunning us from their airplanes. Our men had inflicted very heavy casualties on the Chinese soldiers but were stopped by the repeated bombing and firing from the airplanes. We had no choice but to pull back. We lost 21 men with several others wounded from the bombing. We had not killed all the Chinese but would have if we had had better communications between our forces and if the weather had not cleared. But this was the last of our big attacks.

"Shortly before this, on December 29, 1958, a number of scouting forces were sent into the Naksho Tsogu area, to Lho Dzong area and to Tsawa Pesho to recruit Volunteers, to scout and to obtain as much arms and ammunition as possible. Our supplies were again running low. On January 22, 1959, I took 150 soldiers to Tsawa Pesho, having first sent 60 men ahead with 10 older men familiar with the area to act as scouts and spies to gather information from the people in the area of Shota Lhosum. The rest of the men were to make camp at Pala. After I arrived I made an appointment with the governor of the area, a friend of my family. He said he would help us with supplies, but he would not help us recruit more Volunteers from his area because it was too risky. He gave us 100 rifles, a great amount of ammunition, 200 loads of Chinese rice, candles, soap, newspaper printing equipment and medicines. After three days we returned to Lho Dzong for our New Year, the Year of the Earth Hog. We made chang (barley beer) and feasted on yak meat and hundreds of dry cakes. It was the first that we had celebrated in a long time.

"On January 29 we set the throne of His Holiness, the Dalai Lama, in its palace in Kirong, and on the 30th our soldiers and the monks of Shitam Monastery held a ceremonial parade carrying pictures of His Holiness and religious banners and the flag of Tibet. The flag of the Volunteer Freedom Fighters was also carried proudly. On February 1 we all offered prayers and received the blessing of the monks. On the 2nd the people gave us a great feast. On the 3rd we had horse races and archery contests with the local people, and we sang and danced late into the night. On the 5th we left Lho Dzong for Shodor where the people of Poshokar and the Volunteers already operating in that area gave us a warm welcome, including a ceremonial parade. Many messengers from the nearby areas, including Markham, Drakyab and Derge arrived to report on resistance activities in those areas. We sent letters back with the messengers asking them to recruit more Volunteers, and urged them to destroy all Chinese communist land lines and road communications in their areas. Each area was asked to form its own resistance force and we promised to send whatever arms and ammunition we could afford. We also sent representatives with a few weapons and ammunition to many other areas to organize small resistance units. Grain, tsampa, tea, butter, meat and flags of the Volunteer Freedom Fighters were also sent to each area. More than 60 veteran Volunteers were selected and sent to some 12 places with supplies and instructions to recruit more Volunteers, train them and then to commence guerrilla operations. The intent was to expand the resistance effort, while operating in smaller groups."[3]

In discussing this development, Gompo Tashi confirmed that the Freedom Fighters realized that in the areas where the Chinese had established sizable forces it was no longer feasible for large resistance units to operate successfully. Travel by horseback for units was increasingly difficult and dangerous. The Chinese had increased their air and ground capabilities, and the price for a small piece of land or an attack on a sizable Chinese location was simply too high. It was decided therefore that the resistance needed to operate only in smaller numbers using guerrilla tactics and no longer attack the Chinese in force. It was hoped that by ambushing and attacking vulnerable Chinese targets in many areas, it would be difficult for the Chinese to know how many and where the guerrillas were located.

"After assigning responsibilities to those with qualities of leadership, our further stay in the area was unwise and unsafe. As we had suffered no major and disastrous blow from the Chinese attacks and counterattacks, I looked into the possibilities of our Volunteer forces moving to join the main guerrilla force in Lhokha before it was too late.

"Mindful of the losses we would suffer if ambushed during such a long ride, we decided to consult the soldiers and leaders alike. On February 21, 1959, our 13th day of the 1st month, we called a meeting to discuss the plan as well as the best ways and means to move again. It was unanimously agreed that the army should move cautiously towards Lhokha to join the main force there. Commander Namgyal of Bapa and 50 soldiers were sent to the Lhari hilltop to learn of any Chinese buildups and concentrations between Lhari, Makkul and Kongpo Gyatha. Captain Ngatruk of Thargye and 50 soldiers were assigned to locate Chinese locations in the upper and lower part of Kongpo and Ahlachak. With these scouts protecting our movement, our supply trains loaded with arms, ammunition, food and other vital supplies set out in varying sized convoys to insure against discovery and loss. We traveled mostly at night and had scouts ahead and on our flanks. Eventually more than 500 of our main-force soldiers arrived safely, with no loss of Volunteers or loss of any of our supplies, thanks to the tactics that we had employed. Commander Pema Yeshi of Kanze and Lotse of Markham, along with 30 others, were supposed to have stayed in Shodor as a permanent guard post, but because of Chinese in the area, they had decided to move carefully via Wakho towards Chamdo, Ribochen Chamdha, upper and lower parts of Sok, Gyasho Bonkhar and via Naksho to Nakchukha, thereby providing us with good information on those areas. I and 250 soldiers set out to reenforce the leader of Chungpo Karu and also met with representatives of Rongpo Rapgon to discuss the possibilities of more actions. Later, Commander Gyado Dhondrup of Lithang, Dawa of Chatreng and 150 cavalry soldiers moved to the plains of Rongpo Gyelten and Sek. At the same time, I and 100 soldiers went to Chakra Pelbar, scouting the rear for any Chinese in the area. From all reports, our force was secure."[4]

Before continuing with his story, Gompo Tashi said that he had omitted an incident that had happened before leaving the Shota Lhosum area that he thought I should hear. He told it as follows.

"Before heading for Lhokha, we had a report of a marauding band in the area of about 100 men posing as a Volunteer force that had killed and beaten and robbed many farmers and nomads. Reportedly there were some Chinese soldiers, including two officers, as well as Tibetan bandits and a few nomad collaborators in this force. I decided to make an example of them and to restore honor in the area to the Volunteer Freedom Fighters. After picking 65 men, including two Chinese soldiers who had joined us some time ago, our small force set out, traveling mostly at night. The third night we spotted the bonfires of the outlaw group from a distance and carefully rode into position on the hill above and downwind from them. The only sound came from the muffled creaking of the saddles as some of the men moved restlessly, and the occasional pawing of the ground by the horses. The camp fires some 300 feet below us illuminated the outline of the sleeping forms near the fires, and their rifles neatly stacked nearby. I studied them through field glasses to make sure our plan of attack was correct and to be sure that none of the four guards had an automatic weapon. Even the guards were huddled near the fires, obviously confident that no Volunteer force was in the area or dared to attack them. I checked to be sure that our three attacking groups were ready, then drew my sword and with it signaled for the attack to begin. We charged down the hill, swords raised, loudly shouting insults about the ancestry of the Chinese, and sliced through them quickly with but two or three shots being fired by the startled guards. Most of the Chinese died before their souls had a chance to escape, and most of them did not even escape from their blankets before feeling the blade. Fittingly, many were beheaded. We took no prisoners, but as planned, we let two of the surviving Chinese soldiers and two of the Tibetan nomads 'escape' on foot and without clothes, and appropriately branded, so that they would report the attack. We had only one man slightly injured when he fell with his horse as it stumbled over a couple of the Chinese that were struggling to get to their feet. We knew that the report of those that had 'escaped' would be retold many times, and certainly the size of the force that had attacked them would be exaggerated in the telling, for they would not admit that a smaller force had successfully wiped them out. We also knew that few who heard their story would willingly join in another similar effort by the Chinese in the future. We gathered all their horses, weapons and ammunition and searched the bodies for documents but this time found little of value other than the names and ranks of the Chinese officers and soldiers we had dispatched. The Chinese that had fought with us were as jubilant as ourselves, and asked to administer the 'branding' of the four men to be set free, which they did in neatly carved Chinese meaning 'devil' on the foreheads of the four. The two nomads also lost an ear each to some of our men who knew them from before as willing collaborators. The four of them that were set free without clothes were so frightened that they were barely able to walk, and each had soiled himself repeatedly before we bid them goodbye. After resting briefly, and retelling the success of the attack among ourselves, we left the fires burning so the site and our message to them could be found by the Chinese and other nomads. Then we rode from the area quickly and rejoined the Volunteers, after which we all prepared to move to Lhokha."[5]

Gompo Tashi said that he had been told that this story was circulated widely among the Chinese and that was the last time the Chinese were able to get the nomads to pose as Khamba Volunteers. As he said, "... even the lawless have a fear of beheading ... and of our type of branding."

"On March 22, the 13th day of the 2nd month, we learned of the uprising in Lhasa through an All-India radio broadcast on the battery-powered radio we carried with us. We were very excited and also very concerned with the safety of the Dalai Lama. With this news, we again split our forces and agreed to meet at Jang Lhari. We sent scout groups of 50 and 100 throughout the area to watch for Chinese and to ambush them wherever and whenever possible to keep them from trying to intercept the Dalai Lama. Most of our Volunteers then moved to Ahzar Lake, and then to Chaksam Chupo. As my force approached Benta hilltop, messengers met me carrying a letter from His Holiness, the Dalai Lama, announcing his safe escape from Lhasa and his presence in Lhuntse Dzong with many of his senior officials. The messengers said that the Dalai Lama had announced that he and the members of the Kashag with him hoped to establish a temporary government there.

"Just a few days earlier, I had received a message via couriers from His Holiness which read, 'You have led the Chushi Gangdrug with unshakable determination, resisting the Chinese occupation army in the national cause of defending the freedom of Tibet. I confer on you the rank of Dzasak (General) in recognition of your services to our country. The present situation calls for a continuance of your brave struggle with determination and courage.' It had been a wonderful honor to receive such a message and high appointment from His Holiness, the Dalai Lama ... but now I feared that if he chose to stay in Lhuntse Dzong he would be seized by the pursuing Chinese. I immediately made plans for the Volunteers with me to move towards Lhuntse Dzong to provide further protection. I knew from the messengers that hundreds of our Volunteers had guarded His Holiness throughout his escape and were with him. Other messengers provided scouting reports of the extensive search the Chinese were conducting to locate the Dalai Lama. The aircraft that we had seen in recent days crisscrossing the skies gave us lots of evidence of that. Then on April 3, as we arrived at Ahzar Lake, messengers brought the wonderful news that His Holiness, the Dalai Lama, had entered India. This brought great relief and cheer to all of our Volunteers, including the Chinese soldiers that had joined us and fought alongside of us for so long. We could not help but wonder how he had escaped from the very center of the Chinese in Lhasa.... [I]t was like a bird flying from his prison cage into the sky, escaping from his many captors and countless hunters. It was truly a miracle! And it was very gratifying to think that the Chinese in Lhasa and Peking could do nothing but stare into space, wrapped in regrets, wondering how it had all happened!

"We regrouped and arrived in Kongpo Gyatha on April 4 and then moved on at midnight, having received reports that there were Chinese in the area. The next morning we watched the Chinese airplanes that were looking for any resistance forces in the Kongpo area. They did not spot us in our hillside positions, but obviously the Chinese were intent upon finding and attacking any group of Freedom Fighters, having lost their prize catch, His Holiness, the Dalai Lama. After the airplanes left, we headed for a valley called Drephur, reaching there the next day. We had not seen any Chinese trucks or soldiers on the way. We were to meet another volunteer group there that was bringing supplies from Tsomo Rak. However, a large Chinese force arrived in the area on more than 300 trucks from Lhasa, forcing our Volunteers en route from Tsomo to retreat, leaving their supplies behind after fighting a fierce battle against the Chinese. Our men were far outnumbered, and when they began to run short on ammunition, they had no choice but to ride out. They cut the pack animals loose, but the supplies they had been carrying were lost to us.

"Soon, messengers arrived with reports of many Chinese forces in the area, obviously still trying to find His Holiness, the Dalai Lama, and any Volunteer units. Apparently the Chinese did not want or choose to believe the many radio broadcasts from India that His Holiness was already safe in India or that India had welcomed him. The Chinese soldiers continued to flood the area with heavy concentrations of troops supported by their airplanes. Our small groups could not stop them from seizing Tsethang and Tsona,where we had planned to move our base of operations. Only Trigu remained viable in our plans, but the Chinese forces were between us and that area. The Tibetan soldiers of the Khadang and Tashi Divisions that had joined us months ago again fought bravely but had to withdraw along with our own Volunteers. The numbers of Chinese and their firepower were just too much for our forces.

"On April 12, when we arrived at Lhuntse, reports of defeat and the loss of Yarto Thargye and Lhodrak were received. We sent out messengers asking the Volunteers to do whatever possible to stop the Chinese advances. On our arrival at Nel monastery, the urgent need for reinforcements in the upper and lower parts of Lhodrak, Trigu and Chunggyu was reported by messenger. Commander Gen Yeshi of Bapa and Ngawang of Lithang personally came to report the increase in Chinese forces and the difficulties of retaining the Nel area. On April 13 they expressed hope and determination to retain and defend Tsona and urged me not to stay where we were any longer. I sent ahead the leaders and arrived at Jora Gen (Monastery) on April 14. On April 15, as we were about to leave, we learned that the day before, the Chinese had occupied Tsona. The commander of the Khadang Division (Tibetan army), Tashi Pelrel, and his men and many incarnate lamas and the local people had been forced to withdraw. I could not give up the idea of retaking and defending Tsona, where the Voluntary Army had first been established. We had fought the enemy hard for so long; I could not bear to see our volunteer forces disband.

"I called a meeting to discuss and make plans to attack Tsona and recapture it. However, the idea now seemed to carry very little weight at all, for most of the soldiers and leaders said that it was time to become refugees. The odds to them were just too great. I could not persuade them, and I could do nothing but follow suit.... I sent the soldiers of the Tashi Division ahead the next morning. We followed.

"The morale of our Volunteers was mixed — joyous that His Holiness had escaped the hated Chinese but frustrated by the futility of fighting against the massed forces of Chinese that were already present and constantly increasing in the area. We were all but boxed in and very low on ammunition.

"Two of my most trusted friends, Jinpa Gyatso of Amdo and Commander Tramo of Kham, said to me as we rode towards the Khardag Monastery, 'What if something happens to you if you remain here? All that the Chushi Gangdrug and all that the Volunteer Freedom Fighters stood for and fought for would become something of the past and forgotten, with no successor. This cannot happen. You are needed in India, and we have hired a guide to take you. This is also the wish and order of His Holiness, the Dalai Lama.'

"There was nothing for me to do but to follow those instructions. Before going, I tried once again to get the other leaders of the Chushi Gangdrug to make a final attack the next morning against the Chinese with the 2,000 Volunteers we had with us. At first the leaders agreed but then soon said that 'It would be only a regrettable memory if most or all of these men were killed. And we have to consider Indian reaction as well, for the fighting could spill

Opposite: The Dalai Lama (light-colored robe, third horse back) en route to India in 1959 escorted by Khambas.

onto Indian soil which could only hurt the Tibetan refugees that are there and the many others that will follow.' I had no choice but to agree. There was nothing else I could do.

"That there were still many Volunteer groups fighting from bases in Kham and Amdo was a consolation that I clung to as we crossed into India near Mhar-Go-La on April 21. There the Indian border guards greeted us warmly, but it was difficult for all of us when the Indian guards took our weapons. We realized by this act that we were surrendering, but at least it was not to the hated Chinese. Tears flowed freely down our cheeks as we turned our backs on the border of our beloved land and began the trail that would take us into India as refugees."[6]

The Chinese had finally succeeded in herding and driving Gompo Tashi's force from Tibet. They would now turn their increasing resources to trying to eliminate the thousands of other Freedom Fighters that continued to beleaguer the Chinese patrols and the Chinese storage areas and the Chinese supply routes into and in Tibet. An additional 100,000 Chinese troops were committed into Tibet in April and May, along with more artillery, motorized transport and air support. The odds had been and were being tilted severely.

Gompo Tashi also spoke at length of the countless Chinese atrocities and their broken promises and the terrible sufferings of the Tibetan people at the hands of the Chinese. He told of meeting with Prime Minister Nehru and of having given him a very frank briefing on what the Chinese had done and were doing to Tibet — and of thanking him for granting asylum to the Dalai Lama and the Freedom Fighters and the refugees — and of his impression that Nehru had not really believed the many stories he told him about the Chinese atrocities, or the successes and victories the rag-tag Volunteers had achieved over the Chinese.

Gompo Tashi continued to be active in assisting the refugees and supporting the Mustang guerrilla effort until his many old wounds finally brought him poor health and eventually death in a nursing home in Darjeeling, India, despite months of medical treatment in England, in late September, 1964. His funeral procession was five miles long and attended by thousands as befitting him and what he had done for Tibet. As Gompo Tashi Andrugtsang expressed in prayer, "May the tragedy of Tibet be a warning and a lesson to all mankind and impel people everywhere to resist tyranny and suppression of human rights. May Lord Buddha bless my country and raise a new Tibet. And may his noblest representative on earth, His Holiness, the Dalai Lama, lead our people once again to freedom, peace and happiness."[7]

The many and extraordinary deeds, as well as the devotion and patriotism of this extraordinary man are, deservedly, still talked about by those that joined and experienced the noble effort against the Chinese invader.

CHAPTER 10

The Red Devils Unmasked

There are photographs of the ruins of many of the 6,000 monasteries in Tibet that the Chinese destroyed, including Ganden, which had been the third largest monastery in the world, and Yambulakang, a monastery that had been built in 127 B.C. These structures had withstood all the perils of man and nature until the Chinese chose to destroy them.

Reportedly there are also photographs of the death and destruction that the Chinese let loose on Lhasa beginning early on the morning of March 20, 1959, including the hundreds of Tibetan bodies stacked in the streets, sprawled in the square and before the Tsuglakhang Cathedral, which itself was shown on fire. But apparently few Chinese or Indians have seen these photographs and fewer, if any, westerners. The extensive and vicious destruction and executions in Lhasa by the Chinese were efficient and without regard to history or religion or human life. Many of the streets were blocked by rubble from the buildings destroyed by Chinese weapons. Some buildings that were centuries old simply disappeared or were severely damaged. Reportedly Tibetan bodies were piled like cordwood.

"The shelling began at two in the morning on March 20th, just over forty-eight hours after His Holiness had left. The first target had been the Norbulingka, but after that they (the Chinese) had turned their fire on the Potala, the Jokhang, the neighboring monasteries, the Chakpori medical school, and then the city of Lhasa and the (nearby) village of Shol. Literally thousands were killed; the exact number will never be known, but the streets were littered with dead bodies. Many were women and children. After the carnage, the Chinese apparently inspected all the bodies, turning them over to see if they had killed the Dalai Lama. It was obvious that they did not care who else they had killed."[1]

The events preceding this slaughter of more than 10,000, and the Dalai Lama's escape were as follows.

Shortly after the Dalai Lama had taken his examinations for the degree of Geshe,* the Chinese sent a curt invitation to him to attend a Chinese opera to be presented in the Chinese military compound in Lhasa. As asked, the

---

**Tradition requires that the examination for Geshe — a very high monastic order — be a public affair, wherein thirty examiners ask questions in rapid-fire manner of the candidates on any* (continued)

Dalai Lama provided convenient dates. The Chinese then issued the Dalai Lama a command "invitation" to attend the opera on the 8th. The Dalai Lama replied that he could not attend on the 8th, but would attend on the 10th. This exchange transpired following the public announcement by the Chinese that the Dalai Lama would attend the upcoming congress of the Chinese National Assembly in Peking in April, despite the Dalai Lama having so far avoided accepting the invitation. This simply added credence to the suspicions of the Tibetans in Lhasa that he was to be kidnapped. That three Chinese aircraft had arrived and were parked at Damshang airport outside of Lhasa served only to add to these concerns.

"The commander of the 25 man strong ceremonial bodyguard of the Dalai Lama had been told curtly by the Chinese that the Dalai Lama was to come to the Chinese Military Headquarters unaccompanied by any of his ministers or his personal bodyguards. Instead, the Chinese would post their own soldiers on the bridge and along the way. That His Holiness should appear unescorted was not only irreverent and against all Tibetan protocol, it was quickly perceived to be a ruse by the Chinese to make it easy for them to snatch him away from his people. Among the first to hear the news was the Great Mother, Gyeyum Chemmo, whose distressful wailing infected the milling crowds which had filled the street."[2]

In addition to stipulating that he should not be accompanied by his personal 25-man armed bodyguard, the Chinese ordered that the Dalai Lama's armed guards not be posted anywhere along the route His Holiness would take to the Chinese compound. This only fueled more suspicions. The Chinese further instructed that on the day of the performance the bridge between the military encampment and Lhasa would be closed to all except the Chinese and those Tibetans having a special permit. Adding further insult, the Dalai Lama was told to keep his visit to the Chinese camp a secret.

It was estimated that there were at least 100,000 Tibetans in Lhasa at the time, most of them pilgrims that had not yet left Lhasa after celebrating the recent Losar and Monlam religious celebrations. Given the very strong anti–Chinese emotions of these Tibetans, it was impossible that the Dalai Lama could have met these Chinese demands, for the crowd would have blocked him from going to the Chinese camp or the Chinese from coming for him. It was also unthinkable that the Dalai Lama would move about Lhasa without his honor guard.

After learning of the Chinese demands, members of the Cabinet and the

subject for a full day. Most of the questions examine the candidate's knowledge and interpretation of Tibet's religious history and the lives and achievements — and mistakes — of previous Dalai Lamas. In turn, the candidate is required to ask penetrating questions of the examiners in an attempt to stump them. Trick questions are considered fair, and the watchful public readily expresses its appreciation for both good questions and good answers and its dismay for poor answers. Most candidates are in their thirties when they submit themselves for examination as Master of Metaphysics; the Dalai Lama was not yet 24.

National Assembly met and, after nearly a week in extensive debate, issued a Proclamation of Independence. Following the unprecedented firing by the Chinese of two mortar rounds towards the Potala, "they [Cabinet and National Assembly members] also came to a unanimous decision in the afternoon of March 17th that His Holiness should leave Lhasa and seek safety beyond the reach of the Chinese. The decision was conveyed to His Holiness with pleadings to leave immediately."[3]

Although initially inclined to find a way to accept the invitation in order to calm the tense situation, the Dalai Lama recognized on March 10 that the matter was out of his hands. The Norbulingka was surrounded by a crowd of thousands of Tibetans who had obviously decided that they were not going to allow their precious leader to fall into the hands of the Chinese. There was no way possible under the circumstances that he would be allowed by the Tibetans to make his way to the Chinese compound.

With the increased unrest there were widespread anti–Chinese demonstrations in Lhasa, including demands that the Chinese leave Tibet and that all authority be returned to the Dalai Lama. For example, "… a monastic collaborator named Phakpa-la Kenchung was spotted on the street and stoned to death by the crowd. He was widely known and despised for his pro–Chinese sympathies … and for some unknown reason he had foolishly risked his life by defiantly wearing Chinese clothing and openly carrying a Chinese pistol. By so doing he had signed his own death warrant."[4]

The massed Tibetans had sent a clear message to the Chinese: if seen, the Dalai Lama would be followed, and he would be protected according to custom. He would not be controlled by the Chinese.

Since the demonstrations of March 10, the Dalai Lama and the Chinese commander, Gen. Tan Kuan-san, had exchanged brief letters addressing the tense situation and the inability under the circumstances of the Dalai Lama to visit the Chinese military compound. In a long and stormy meeting in his compound with close advisers of the Dalai Lama on March 10, Gen. Tan Kuan-san, making extensive use of obscenities, had made it clear that the Chinese intended to use military force against the "reactionary" Tibetans demonstrating in Lhasa and that the patience of the Chinese in the face of rebellion was exhausted. The situation was at an impasse.

Fortuitously, and without involving the Dalai Lama, contingency plans had been completed in early 1959 addressing the possibility that it might be necessary for the Dalai Lama, his family and certain others to escape to India from Lhasa. "Ratuk Ngawang of the resistance forces; Tashi Para, commander of the 2nd regiment of the Tibetan Army; Phala, the Dalai Lama's Lord Chamberlain; and certain others had planned a tentative escape route from Lhasa through Kham to Sikkim and the Indian border."[5] The plans included the use of two other groups to serve as diversionary units leaving Lhasa in the same general time frame for other border areas to confuse and prevent the Chinese from knowing which group was actually the one escorting the Dalai Lama. These units were to consist of Tibetan army and resistance personnel, each approximating the size of the Dalai Lama's group, one traveling south and the other southwest. Both groups were to be well armed and able to defend themselves against any pursuers, just as the Dalai Lama's group traveling eastward through Kham would be protected by hundreds of the Freedom Fighters along the route to the border.

Little did the planners know at the time that these plans would be implemented on March 17. Fortunately there had been just enough time to put the integral pieces of the puzzle together.

Meanwhile, the Tibetans massed outside the government buildings in Lhasa demanded that the Chinese leave Tibet. Led by Khamba and Amdo representatives, and others, "A Freedom Committee" was formed that in turn quickly announced the repudiation of the 17 Point Agreement. "Before the approximately 30,000 gathered at the Potala, the Committee also declared war against the Chinese and burned a copy of the 17 Point Agreement ... then repeated both actions again at the Jokhang, the main cathedral in Lhasa. Some 70 government officials, the Kusang Regiment [the bodyguard of His Holiness], and other Tibetan soldiers declared their full support of the Freedom Committee. The Freedom Committee also arrested four senior Tibetan government officials — including Prime Minister Surkhang, whose strongly pro–Chinese actions had belied his claims to being pro–Khamba — for their having collaborated with the Chinese. These were placed under house arrest, much to the dismay of those arrested but to the great delight of the rebel crowd."[6]

Throughout the week the Dalai Lama had continued to urge restraint. He told the rebel leaders that it was their duty to try to calm the crowds rather than to inflame them, hoping that the high tensions would relax, and that the crowds would disperse. Both of these hopes were futile. In replying to a letter from the Chinese generals inviting him into the Chinese camp "for his own protection," he unwittingly set the stage for later trouble for himself by his conciliatory tone. This reply, and two subsequent letters that he wrote to the Chinese commander, were later pointed to by the Chinese as evidence that he had been prepared to accede to Chinese rule, and that he had been abducted against his will by "reactionaries and imperialists."*

The impasse that began on March 10 continued until March 16, when Chinese surveyors were seen aligning their instruments on the Norbulingka. It was soon suspected that the Chinese were preparing to fire on Tibetan government offices and the crowds of Tibetans assembled outside of them. This was confirmed when a letter from Ngapo Ngawang Jigme, the former governor of East Tibet who had earlier "negotiated" with the Chinese and who had since openly made it clear that he had cast his lot with the Chinese, advised

---

*These letters are quoted in Chapter 11.

the Dalai Lama and the Kashag to take shelter in an inner part of the palace, where, he wrote, the Chinese would take good care that he and those with him were not injured.

In an attempt to avoid what seemed inevitable, the Kashag had also sent a conciliatory letter addressed to Ngapo advising that the Cabinet recognized that the Tibetan crowd was behaving badly, but that there was still some chance of convincing the crowd to disperse and a peaceful compromise found. The Chinese reply to the first note basically repeated what had been said before. Their reply to the second one was the firing of two mortar shells, both of which landed harmlessly in a pond (near the Norbulingka) at four o'clock in the afternoon of March 17. The Chinese had made their intentions clear to the Dalai Lama and the thousands of Tibetans assembled in Lhasa.[7] There was no longer any hope of a peaceful solution.

Thus began — and ended — the real Chinese play in Lhasa to which the Dalai Lama had been "invited," but without the posturing, the false faces and the costumes of a standard Chinese opera.

Obviously, there was no choice but to try to escape. The Dalai Lama reportedly spoke of giving himself up to the Chinese, but this was not acceptable to the other government and religious leaders, nor was it possible, for there were still thousands of Tibetans around the Norbulingka. The only logical course of action was to escape, taking with him his mother, his youngest brother, his older sister, and some 18 key religious and government figures plus their escorts. Time was running out, so it was impossible for anyone to return to the Potala to recover, or destroy, important state records or to pick up even a small fraction of the treasure housed there. Secrecy was vital, and there was very little time to make last minute adjustments to the contingency plans that had been made earlier.

Their escape from Lhasa required that they not only avoid the Chinese patrols but also that they not be detected by the Tibetans surrounding the Norbulingka, for such a discovery could in turn lead to alerting the Chinese because of the commotion that was certain to follow by the large Tibetan crowd. The plan called for the Dalai Lama's escape party to be divided into three groups, with each of their departures staggered a half hour apart. In the first group were the mother, sister and brother, with their small escort, all dressed as Khambas. They left shortly after 9:00 at night. The second group consisted of the Dalai Lama, his Chamberlain, the Lord Chancellor, the Commander of his bodyguard and two Tibetan soldiers. All in this group were dressed as Tibetan soldiers, with their story of making a brief inspection going unchallenged by other unsuspecting guards. The third group was composed of advisers, tutors and ministers, all hidden under the tarpaulin of a truck. Tibetan soldiers riding on the truck made it appear to be routine travel by a military vehicle. At the rendezvous point outside of Lhasa, the entire group crossed the river in coracles, the boats made of yak skin. There they mounted

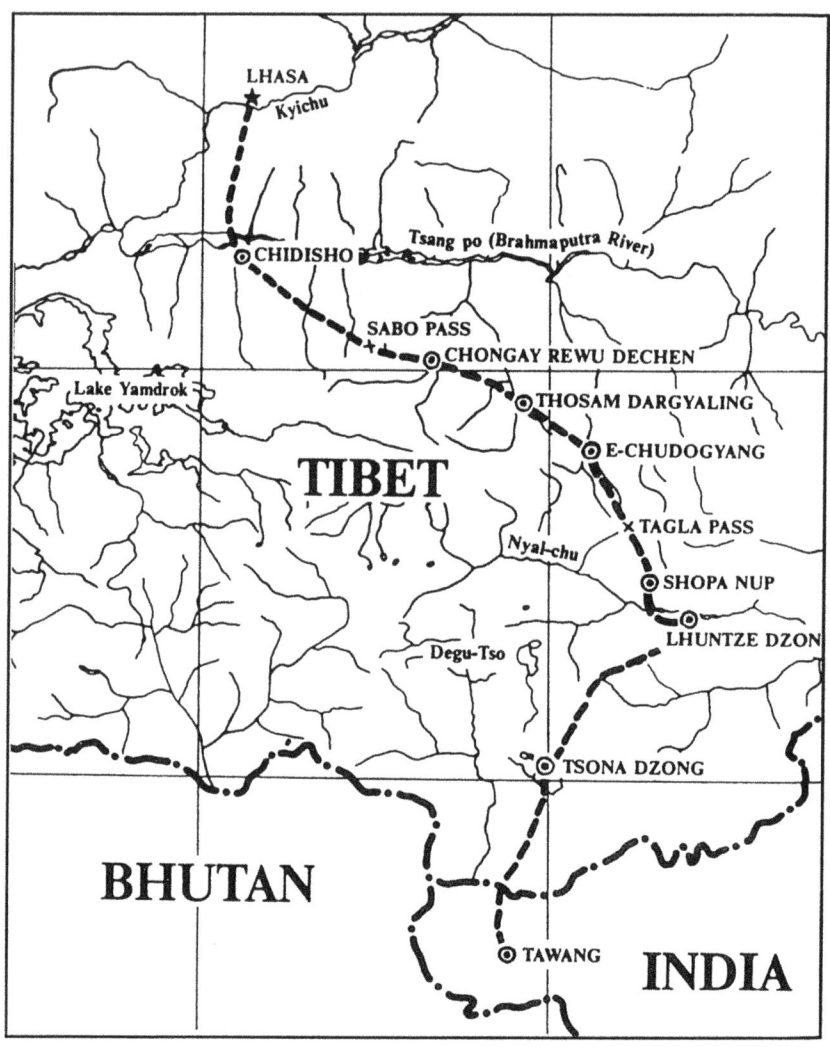

Escape route taken by His Holiness's Party in March 1959.

on ponies provided by a nearby monastery and began their journey, escorted by well armed Khamba resistance fighters, and by the Tibetan soldiers who had left with them. Riding apart from the main party were many other Khamba resistance fighters acting as guides, as well as insuring protection against any Chinese patrols or pursuit. The wind had helped provide cover, for it was blowing from the northwest. The sound of the hoofbeats had not been heard by the Chinese guards posted about the city, and blowing dust and dirt had served well to obscure movement.

Two other groups also departed the area that night, each taking a different direction from Lhasa towards the border. Each was disguised as a party of traders, pilgrims and monks traveling together. "This was part of the plan to confuse the Chinese when they finally discovered that His Holiness was no longer in Lhasa. Hopefully, they would not know in which group the Dalai Lama was located ... making their efforts to identify and intercept the right group that much more difficult."[8]

The Dalai Lama's party stopped at 3:00 in the morning to rest briefly at a peasant's house after having ridden nearly five hours straight with but little pause. Travel was not easy and occasionally one or more of the party strayed from the path in the dark and had to be found and returned to the group by the escorting Khambas. After taking tea and some tsampa, the group continued, leaving the host clutching the scarf that the Dalai Lama had given him. Later in the morning, an old man, a Khamba by the name of Tashi Norbu, suddenly arrived out of the mist. He said he had noticed that the pony being ridden by the Dalai Lama was nearly worn out, and so he wanted to give the Dalai Lama his pure white horse as a gift in exchange for the tired pony. He said he was worried that the Dalai Lama might not escape if his tired mount faltered. And then as suddenly as he had appeared, Tashi Norbu left. This was spoken of many times during our journey, for it was mystical, but all agreed it was a good sign. The group was also constantly alert for Chinese aircraft patrols searching for the escapees, but fortunately the skies remained clouded for the most part. All knew that the escape of His Holiness would soon be realized and that an extensive and frantic search would follow.

For the first few days of the march, His Holiness and his advisers were still formulating plans. What they hoped to do was to get to Lhuntse Dzong, a large fortress not far from the Indian border, and from that location reopen negotiations with the Chinese. Their intention was that if negotiations failed, the Indian border was near; if they succeeded, Tibet might be saved. However, on March 24, a Khamba messenger named Tsepon Namseling arrived with news that made it clear there was no hope of a peaceful settlement. He reported that Lhasa had been heavily bombarded beginning early the morning of March 20th by the Chinese, destroying many buildings and killing many Tibetans.

Ironically, some seven months earlier Tsepon Namseling had been sent by the Kashag to persuade Gompo Tashi Andrugtsang and the Volunteer Freedom Fighters to stop fighting, but after discussions he agreed with the cause and joined it. He had been one of the Khambas guarding the Dalai Lama's group as it left Lhasa and had stayed in the outskirts of the city as part of a rear guard. He did not have many details about the fighting but enough that it was clear there would be no further negotiations with the Chinese.

The next day two more messengers arrived from Lhasa providing details. They said the Chinese began shelling on March 20 early in the morning. First

One of the Tibetan trainees drew this depiction of the Chinese attack on the Potala in March 1959.

they fired on the Norbulingka, then on the Potala, then on Jokhang, then on the nearby monasteries, then on the Chakpori medical school and other places in Lhasa, and the adjacent village of Shol. The estimate was that more than 15,000 were dead or wounded, for there were bodies of men, women and children strewn everywhere. After the barrages of heavy fire by artillery, mortars and machine guns were finished, the Chinese then inspected each body, looking for the Dalai Lama. The wounded were simply killed or left to die as the Chinese continued their search.

At first, the Tibetans had given strong resistance on the Iron Hill located behind the medical college, but the only weapons they had were their rifles and swords. They even tried to use the old cannons located there to return fire against the Chinese. They made Molotov cocktails and fired mortars and other weapons captured from the Chinese. They attacked and took out the Chinese garrison at Shukti Lingka, mostly in hand-to-hand fighting, where the Tibetan swords were used very effectively. And with Molotov cocktails the Khambas destroyed one of three tanks that the Chinese had brought into Lhasa.

But eventually the overwhelming numbers of Chinese with their extensive and superior firepower prevailed. On March 22, Ngapo Ngwang Jigme used the public address system to order all Tibetans to put down their arms and surrender, warning that death or prison were the only alternatives, citing that death had already come to 10,000 and that another 10,000 were in prison. Those that could not escape had no choice, but many of these chose suicide.[9]

And in the Potala, the ancient treaty displayed there between Tibet and China still read "All shall live in peace and share the blessing of happiness for ten thousand years."

"Other messengers arrived and reported there had been several pockets of lightly armed resistance that had fought back, but the Chinese simply used their far superior firepower to destroy most of them. The Chinese claimed 4,000 Tibetans were taken prisoners and jailed, but later reports were that the Chinese arrested and put in prison almost every adult Tibetan they found in the city. So it was that the Tibetans from all parts of Tibet, including Kham and Amdo and other tribal areas that had remained in Lhasa to celebrate the religious holidays and Tibetan New Years, were jailed or slaughtered. The messengers reported it took days to bury all the bodies that had been collected and piled near the summer palace, and that the stench from the dead permeated the entire area. It was also reported that Chinese soldiers had surrounded the nearby monasteries and held more than 25,000 monks from the Norbulingka, and the monasteries of Sera, Drepung and Ganden under house arrest. And there was nothing we could do. His Holiness offered many prayers honoring those who had been killed and imprisoned, but the hearts of all were heavy at this terrible news. At Chongay, His Holiness met more of the Khamba guerrilla leaders. He knew what the resistance fighters had given up and what they faced. He later said that he could not honestly advise them to avoid violence."[10]

"The travel was difficult, for there was snow and ice in the mountain passes; the paths up and down the mountains were slippery with water and mud from the melting snow and rain, and the low lands were like mud bogs. The messengers that arrived daily brought only more bad news, which made our travel all the more difficult. His Holiness remained determined to take the necessary time to announce the formation of a temporary government in Lhuntse Dzong despite the increasing dangers of the Chinese locating his whereabouts. Just before we arrived there we heard on a battery-powered radio one of the officials had brought the Chinese announce that the old PCART had been reorganized under the leadership of the Panchen Lama, Ngapo Ngawang Jigme, and the three ranking Chinese army generals in Lhasa; that the old Tibetan government under the leadership of the Dalai Lama and the Kashag had been dissolved; that the Seventeen Point Agreement had been dissolved; that Kham and Amdo had been formally severed from Tibet and divided into other Chinese provinces; and that the Panchen Lama was now the leader of Tibet, assisted by Ngapo Ngawang Jigme as the next highest Tibetan official. Messengers also soon brought this same news. The Khambas were furious about Ngapo and the realignment of Kham and Amdo into Chinese provinces. Many wanted to send a small group back to Lhasa to assassinate Ngapo but finally agreed not to when they were reminded by the Lamas that by his own terrible deeds Ngapo had doomed himself, so it was not necessary for any Khamba to risk his own life while seeking some kind of revenge. From that point on when Ngapo's name was mentioned, the resistance members used the past tense, underscoring that in the minds of most Tibetans Ngapo no longer existed."[11]

The Dalai Lama "now fully recognized that his only choice was exile in India, but before doing so he formally declared for all living Tibetans and history that Tibet was fully free and independent and that the Tibetan government would from that day forward function under his leadership. He made this speech on Tibetan soil to reflect that he would return and to reaffirm the importance of Tibet as a nation. He knew that there was no hope of a peaceful settlement with China anytime in the near future once he made these formal declarations. He named Lhuntse Dzong as the site of the temporary government and announced that he intended to reform the Tibetan government and that he would complete a new Tibetan Constitution. This proclamation was dutifully affixed with his seal and witnessed by the government officials and high monks traveling with him. Then copies of it were carried by Khamba messengers to all neighboring dzongs and to the remaining resistance groups. The news that His Holiness had escaped from Lhasa and had proclaimed a new Tibetan government was received by Tibetans throughout Tibet with joy and pride."[12]

Athar and Lhotse then sent a coded message on their RS-1 radio, which was powered by a hand-cranked generator, relaying the request from His Holiness to Prime Minister Nehru for asylum in India. Although the route of this particular communication was of necessity to Washington, D.C., decoded, then re-encoded to the U.S. Embassy in New Delhi, decoded and delivered to Mr. Nehru, and his response then sent via reverse route, the answer granting asylum was received back by Athar and Lhotse to His Holiness less than 24 hours later. Also added to the permission was the C.I.A.'s strong urging that the party not delay any longer in reaching and crossing the border to safety.

"Messengers reported that the Chinese commanders in Lhasa, and particularly Chairman Mao and his Politburo, were like exploding bombs when they learned that His Holiness had escaped Lhasa and could not be found. Chairman Mao was said to have personally demanded that His Holiness be located and not allowed to reach the border. We all understood what was meant by that.

"The remainder of the trip to the Indian border became extremely difficult. The ice and snow and sleet in the passes nearly caused frostbite for all of us. Our animals were exhausted, for it was difficult for them to forage, and they had little rest from carrying their burdens. The pace was very slow, and the Khamba escort—and the other resistance forces in the area—were increasingly concerned that Chinese search parties would locate the Dalai Lama."[13]

The Dalai Lama later acknowledged that the Khambas had served far more than as escorts and that without their guidance and capable protection, many in the group would have become lost or not made it to India safely.

"On the few days that the skies were partially clear we could see Chinese planes in the distance searching for us. One day a plane flew low directly over us, but apparently did not see us. We remained motionless, somewhat hidden in the difficult landscape. Perhaps the pilot chose not to see us, for there was little at that point that he could have done to stop us. The terrible weather had provided good protection, so we did not mind the clouds and rain, for the Chinese had to cope with these same difficulties ... but the health of His Holiness was getting worse. Finally we reached Mangmang, the last Tibetan village before the border. We rested a day there, for His Holiness was exhausted and too ill to travel safely, and we feared that he could not stay on his horse. It was decided to have him ride a dzo (a large animal that is a cross between a yak and a cow) for it is very sure footed, wide of back and a gentle animal. The white horse he had been riding did not seem to like this change, acting almost as though he was the protector of His Holiness. This was interpreted as a good sign, and our spirits lifted. We could delay no longer, so most of the party crossed the border on March 31, with His Holiness on the amiable dzo, where a detachment of India's Assam rifles greeted him along with some Indian officials. His Holiness was now safe from the Chinese."[14]

More than three weeks had passed since the Chinese had demanded the presence of the Dalai Lama in their camp outside of Lhasa to attend the opera. And it was two weeks since he had left Lhasa on the nearly 300-mile journey to the border. To the travelers it very likely seemed an eternity. "Like the winds that had covered his departure from Lhasa, nature helped His Holiness as he crossed into India. The skies cleared, and the sun shone, enabling the Chinese planes to see clearly that he was no longer in Tibet, but was safe across the border from the pursuing Chinese ground forces. And the other two parties that had left Lhasa to confuse the Chinese had also crossed the border to safety."[15]

The reaction in New Delhi was quite mixed. Prime Minister Nehru was nervous—perhaps fearful would be a more accurate term—about the Dalai Lama's arrival onto Indian soil. Asylum had been granted quickly, but Mr. Nehru was clearly very much concerned about the reaction of the Chinese to the Dalai Lama being in India. There is little doubt that the press was very much controlled in the days immediately following the arrival, and "for security reasons," as Nehru explained, access to the Dalai Lama was tightly held. A statement by the Dalai Lama, written in the third person for some reason unknown to the press, was read in Tezpur on April 18 which reviewed the

From left: Athar, Wangdu, Lhotse and Dumdrup. Athar and Lhotse were a team, and Wangdu with Dumdrup were leaders of the team that parachuted into Kham in 1957.

events that led up to his flight, including the complete disregard by the Chinese of the Seventeen Point Agreement, but the press got little else. "The obvious inference is that Nehru was very frightened of the Chinese reaction, and that he was doing everything in his power to avoid offending them short of actually refusing asylum."[16]

The Chinese continued to claim that the Dalai Lama had been kidnapped by the resistance and forcibly taken to India, and attacked the Dalai Lama's "so-called statement as full of lies and loopholes,"[17] stating repeatedly that it had not been the work of the Dalai Lama. Predictably, the Chinese blamed "spies and collaborators," and suggested that the Dalai Lama was being held against his will. Few outside of China believed such nonsense.

Nehru asked the Dalai Lama not to speak of the sufferings the Tibetans had endured and forbade him to make political statements while on Indian soil. Belatedly, Nehru had finally come to realize that Chairman Mao's communism had not benefited the people of either China or Tibet, as he had naively believed it would. However, he remained very much afraid of China's military intentions and so did all that he could to pacify Chairman Mao.

In the Lok Sabha, Nehru reported that the Dalai Lama would not be permitted to carry out any political activities. In response, Jaya Prakash Narayan, one of the more outspoken leaders opposing this stance, noted that this could only be read as an act of self-interest bordering upon cowardice but he did not prevail against Nehru. Indeed, far from allowing the Dalai Lama freedom of access to the media, the Indian government continued to block any semblance of a give-and-take press conference.

The so-called official press conferences were very controlled. Questions were required to be submitted in writing beforehand, and no question-answer periods were allowed following the "press" statements. For example, on June 10 it was announced that the Dalai Lama would hold a press conference on June 20, but only written questions would be answered, and that these would have to be submitted by June 15 at the latest. There were 130 correspondents present, but of the close to a hundred questions that had been submitted only a dozen innocuous ones were asked. By using such control methods, Nehru insured that the rape of Tibet by the Chinese would remain out of the public eye for some time to come, thereby permitting India to continue her accommodating relations with China.

The blame for such actions, if blame is to be given, and for not allowing the revelations of what China had done in Tibet for nearly a decade, has to be placed on Mr. Nehru and those in his government that shared his deep fear of China. The Dalai Lama heeded Mr. Nehru's instructions, perhaps more than he should have, but it must be remembered that he was 24 years of age at the time, and knew next to nothing about the world nor the politics of same, and that he was the guest of a prime minister in his seventies. Unlike his older brothers, the Dalai Lama's foreign travel and government contacts had consisted almost exclusively of India and Nehru, and China and Mao. That he listened to Nehru, a man three times his own age is not surprising, nor is what Nehru told the Dalai Lama surprising, for Chairman Mao and Chou En-lai and the Chinese ambassador to India did not let up in their condemnations of the Indian government for having granted the Dalai Lama asylum and for accepting thousands of Tibetan refugees. Nehru obviously felt very uncomfortable in his new role of landlord for the Tibetans.

However, there were many in the Lok Sabha who were openly critical of China and also of Nehru. They did not hesitate to express themselves clearly. As indicated above, the voice of Jaya Prakash Narayan was particularly supportive of Tibet, but there were many others equally strong in their views, and critical of the Chinese — and of the Indian policy under Nehru towards China. That there had been very little news released in India on what had transpired in Tibet infuriated many of those in both houses of government, for it was also found that the Indian consul in Lhasa, Major Chuba, had reported on what had transpired during the uprisings in Lhasa, and that these reports had been kept from the newspapers. And incredibly, it was on March 17 that Nehru had told Parliament that the stories of alleged unrest in Tibet were merely bizarre rumors, and blamed the British reporter George Patterson for the "unfounded" stories that had been written about unrest and bloodshed. Nehru had earlier described the Tibetan-Chinese problems as more of a clash of minds than a clash of arms. In the Asian sense, Nehru had now lost considerable face and credibility but the Tibetans had lost their country.

CHAPTER 11

Four Sides of the Story

News of the early March demonstrations and uprisings in Lhasa first appeared in the Indian and world press late the third week of March, mostly citing Tibetan sources outside of Tibet and primarily those in Kalimpong who had heard from Khamba messengers. On March 28, the Chinese government by a proclamation signed by Prime Minister Chou En-lai made the first official admission of the uprising, declaring "... that the Dalai Lama had left Lhasa 'under duress.'"[1] On the same day, the New China News Agency in a news communiqué gave the Chinese version of the Tibetan revolt, which the Chinese labeled as imperialist inspired.

The escape of the Dalai Lama ignited a firestorm of harsh rhetoric from Peking, as well as considerable invective in the Indian press and Parliament against Prime Minister Nehru for his continued weak posture in response to the harsh and shrill attitude of the Chinese. That Nehru continued to give negative responses to the Dalai Lama's request for support at the United Nations and to block any Indian initiatives to raise the question of Tibet at the United Nations brought his attackers to their feet to debate the Tibet question in both houses of the Indian parliament. That Nehru expressed little concern for the many reports of Chinese violations of the McMahon boundary lines between India and Tibet (China) and gave the impression that he was willing to give up relatively large amounts of Indian territory to China, especially in remote areas where Chinese incursions had taken place, brought verbiage to the floor in discussions that was unusually abrupt. His assurances that India would not tolerate Chinese incursions into Bhutan, Sikkim and Nepal mollified most in both houses, just as the undiplomatic pronouncements from Peking against India and Nehru also brought support to him from all in the collective sense of their shared sense of nationalism. A few examples of these points follow.

On March 28, 1959, Chou En-lai made the following proclamation:

> Most of the Kaloons (cabinet members) of the Tibet Local Government and the upper strata reactionary clique colluded with imperialism, assembled rebellious bandits, carried out rebellion, ravaged the people, put the Dalai Lama under duress, tore up the 17-Article Agreement on measures for the peaceful liberation of Tibet and, on the night of March 19, directed the Tibetan local army and rebellious elements to launch a general offensive against the People's Liberation Army garrison in Lhasa.

Such acts which betray the motherland and disrupt unification are not allowed by law. In order to safeguard the unification of the country and national unity, in addition to enjoining the Tibet Military Area Command of the Chinese People's Liberation Army to put down the rebellion thoroughly, the decision is that from that day the Tibet Local Government is dissolved and the Preparatory Committee for the Tibet Autonomous Region shall exercise the functions and powers of the Tibet Local Government.

During the time when the Dalai Lama Dantzen-Jaliso, Chairman of the Preparatory Committee for the Tibet Autonomous Region, is under duress by the rebels, Panchen Erdeni Ghuji-Geltseng, Vice-Chairman of the Preparatory Committee, will act as the Chairman.

Pebala Choliehnamje, member of the Standing Committee of the Preparatory Committee for the Tibet Autonomous Region, is appointed Vice-Chairman of the Preparatory Committee; Ngapo Ngawang Jigme, member of the Standing Committee and Secretary-General of the Preparatory Committee, is appointed Vice-Chairman and Secretary General of the Preparatory Committee.

... It is to be hoped that the Preparatory Committee for the Tibet Autonomous Region will lead all the people of Tibet, ecclesiastical and secular, to unite as one and make common efforts to assist the People's Liberation Army to put down the rebellion quickly, consolidate national defence (sic), protect the interests of the people of all nationalities, secure social order and strive for the building of a new democratic and socialist Tibet.[2]

Chou En-lai's proclamation listed the 18 Tibetans who had been arrested that had been members of the Preparatory Committee, identifying them as traitors, and noted they were to be "punished individually under the law." It also named five Chinese and eleven Tibetan replacements for those arrested. The news communiqué released in Peking on March 28 read:

Violating the will of the Tibetan people and betraying the motherland, the Tibetan Local Government and the upper strata reactionary clique colluded with imperialism, assembled rebellious bandits and launched armed attacks against the People's Liberation Army garrison in Lhasa during the night of March 19.

Acting on orders to put the rebellion down, the valiant units of the People's Liberation Army stationed in Tibet completely smashed the rebellious bandits in the city of Lhasa on the 22nd. Now the units of the People's Liberation Army assisted by patriotic people of all sections, both ecclesiastic and temporal, are mopping up the rebellious bandits in some other places in Tibet.

The armed rebellion of the Tibetan Local Government and the reactionary clique of the upper strata in Lhasa began on March 10. The Dalai Lama was originally scheduled to attend a theatrical performance in the auditorium of the Tibetan Military Area Command of the People's Liberation Army on March 10. The proposal was put forth by the Dalai Lama personally more than one month earlier and the date of March 10 was fixed by the Dalai Lama himself.

On that day, however, the rebellious Tibetan cliques spread wild rumours (sic) alleging that the army units of the Tibetan Military Area Command would detain the Dalai Lama, and by using this rumour (sic) as a pretext, staged armed rebellion, put the Dalai Lama under duress, raised such reactionary slogans as "Drive Away the Han People" and "Independence for Tibet," and, at the same time, killed Kanchung Soanamchiatso, a Tibetan official of the Preparatory Committee for the Tibet Autonomous Region, who opposed the rebellion, and wounded Sampo Tsewong-rentzen, the Tibetan Vice-Commander of the Tibetan Military Area, and others. The armed rebels at the same time surrounded the Headquarters of the Tibetan Military Area Command of the People's Liberation Army and the offices of the Central Government Agencies in Lhasa.

The rebellious activities of the Tibetan traitors have been of fairly long duration. These rebels represent imperialism and the most reactionary big serf-owners. Since the Chinese People's Liberation Army entered Tibet and the Central People's Government and the Tibetan Local Government concluded the Agreement of Measures for the Peaceful Liberation of Tibet (the 17 Article Agreement) in 1951, they have been plotting to tear up this agreement and preparing for armed rebellion.

But as the motherland is thriving and prospering day by day, the policy of the Central People's Government toward Tibet is correct and the garrison units of the People's Liberation Army in Tibet observe strict discipline, all of which enjoy the warm support and love of the people of all sections in Tibet, the rebellious conspiracy of this handful of reactionaries had no support from the Tibetan people. In accordance with the stipulations of the Constitution, the Central People's Government has always insisted on the solidarity of all the nationalities in the country and solidarity among the Tibetan people, and has carried out regional national autonomy in Tibet.

This is warmly welcomed by the Tibetan people. The Preparatory Committee for the Tibet Autonomous Region was established as early as April 1956. Yet, owing to obstruction by the reactionaries in the Local Government of Tibet, the preparatory work for the Autonomous Region has made little progress.

The Local Government of Tibet is called Kasha (sic) in Tibetan and its six members are called Kaloons. Of the six Kaloons, two are patriots: Ngapo Ngawang Jigme and Sampo Tsewong-rentzen who was wounded by the rebels on March 10. One of the other four, Yuto Chahsidongchu, had already turned traitor in 1957 and fled to Kalimpong — the centre (sic) of the rebellious elements' activities abroad. The three others, Surkong Wongching-Galei, Neusha Thubten-Tarpa and Hsinka Jigme-dorje came out into the open as traitors in the present rebellion.... Their rebellion was engineered by the imperialists, the Chiang Kai-shek bands and foreign reactionaries; the commanding center of the rebellion was in Kalimpong; and their leader is the dismissed Silum Lokongwa Tsewon-grouten. Many of their arms were brought in from abroad. The base of the rebellion to the south of Tsangpo River received air-dropped supplies from the Chiang Kai-shek bands on a number of occasions, and radio stations were set up there by agents sent by the imperialists and the Chiang Kai-shek clique to further their intrigues.

Between May and June of last year, on the instructions of the Tibetan Local Government and the upper strata reactionary clique, the rebel bandits intruded into Chamdo, Dinching, Nagchuka and Lokha, destroyed communications, ravaged the people by plunder, rape, arson and murder; and attacked agencies and army units of the Central People's Government there.

... At 10 A.M. on March 20, the troops of the Tibetan Military Area Command of the Chinese People's Liberation Army were ordered to take punitive action against the clique of traitors who had committed monstrous crimes. With the aid of the patriotic Tibetan monks and laymen, the People's Liberation Army completely crushed the rebellion in the city of Lhasa after more than two days of fighting. A rough count shows that by the 23rd, more than four thousand rebel forces were taken prisoners, and eight thousand small arms of different kinds, eighty-one-millimeter calibre (sic) mortars, six mountain guns and ten million bullets were captured. Encircled by our troops, many of the rebel troops surrendered in groups.

The rapid putting down of the rebellion in Lhasa showed that the Tibetan traitorous clique is certainly doomed and that the future of the Tibetan people is bright. Primarily this is because the Tibetan people are patriotic, support the Central People's Government, ardently love the People's Liberation Army and oppose the imperialists and traitors.

In order to wipe out the rebel bandits thoroughly, the State Council has ordered the units of the Chinese People's Liberation Army stationed in Tibet to assume military control in various places in Tibet. The tasks of the military control committees are: to suppress rebellion; to protect the people and the foreign nationals who observe the laws of China; with the authorisation (sic) from the Preparatory Committee for the Autonomous Region of Tibet and the Tibet Military Command of the Chinese People's Liberation Army, to set up administrative bodies at various levels of the Autonomous Region of Tibet, and organise (sic) self-defence armed forces of patriotic Tibetans to replace the old Tibetan army of only a little more than three thousand men who are rotten to the core, utterly useless in fighting and turned rebel.[3]

(The rest of the release continues much the same, including how much the Chinese had done for the Tibetans, about the further reorganization of government structures in Tibet and the Chinese claim that the Dalai Lama had been abducted by rebel forces.)

In the May 5, 1959, "Special Tibet Number" issue of the weekly magazine, *Peking Review*, the lead editorial contained the following statements: "During recent weeks, much has been said and written abroad about Tibet. Imperialist interventionists and Indian expansionists, taking advantage of the rebellion in Tibet, have launched an all-out campaign of slander against People's China. Their favourite but long discredited weapons include name-calling, mud-slinging, deliberate distortions and outright lies. All these tricks, however, will be of no avail once the cold, hard facts become fully known. The motley band of slanderers and liars will stand exposed to the entire world in all their nakedness.

"The first fact that has to be faced is that Tibet is an inalienable part of China. A complete record of Tibet's relationship to China dating back to early days is given elsewhere in this issue. It proves beyond doubt that the Tibetans, like the Mongolians, the Uighurs, the Huis, the Chuangs and other minority nationalities in China, constitute an integral part of China's multi-national population. The Tibet question, therefore, is China's internal affair, pure and simple. No self-respecting, independent country, least of all, People's China, will tolerate outside interference in its domestic politics.... As a matter of fact, all talk about 'independence' for Tibet is nothing but a smokescreen for the imperialists and interventionists' evil designs on Tibet.... In fact, they are butting into China's internal affairs under the cloak of 'sympathy.'"[4]

In the same May 5, 1959, issue of the *Peking Review* appears an article labeled "Eyewitness in Tibet" and titled "Sunshine After Rain." The article is written in diary form by Shan Chao and covers Tuesday March 10, Thursday March 12, Sunday March 15 and then daily until March 23. The diary reads that shortly after eleven o'clock on Tuesday morning the Chinese learned the Dalai Lama would not be attending the song and dance (opera) program the Chinese had scheduled. The scene Shan Chao portrays follows: "... the radio mechanic came rushing in. All of a sweat and panting, he stammered out: 'What a disaster! The reactionaries are holding the Dalai Lama in the Norbulingka. They are killing progressives. People living near the Lingka are in a panic, they are trying to find a place to hide.'... I returned to my room but was in no mood to sit quietly. From my window, with the help of binoculars I had a clear view of the Potala and the Yo Wang Hill. The window sills of the innumerable windows of the Potala are usually a favourite playground of doves; now rifle barrels glinted from them. Halfway up Yo Wang Hill rebel troops had taken up positions; at its summit there were signs of artillery activity. Many men were hauling up ammunition and supplies."

Tuesday, March 12 reads in part, "Members of the Tibetan cadres' families have been asking for permission to move for safety into our office buildings. In less than a day, all the rooms were packed. They said: 'If the houses are full, we won't mind staying in the courtyards. As long as we are with the Communists, nobody will suffer even if the sky falls down.'"

Monday, March 16: "We decided to take a look around the Norbulingka. The rebels were building fortifications there.... We set out in a big armoured car with two accompanying smaller ones, one in front and one behind us.... We drove to the back of the Potala and thus got a clearer view of things. At the Yabzhi Lingka to the east and the Dragon King Pond to the north of the Potala, two of the loveliest summertime beauty spots, the rebels were busily digging in.... No one moved on the roads to the west of the Potala. The rebels were also busily digging in at the northern entrance of the Norbulingka."

Tuesday, March 17: "The rebels have been busy day and night deploying troops and bringing up munitions.... We have also been working day and night building defensive fortifications.... The families of the Tibetan cadres insisted on joining us at our work. They asked: 'Don't we have a share to do in fighting the scum of our own people? The reactionaries want to kill us.'"

Wednesday, March 18: "The Dalai Lama is 'missing.' The reactionaries abducted him from Lhasa last night.... Many ordinary residents of Lhasa came to the Working Committee to complain that the rebel bandits were everywhere pressganging (sic) people to join them as 'volunteers.' Many people have been beaten to death on the spot for refusing to go with them."

Thursday, March 19: "On the approach of evening, messengers of the militia corps came racing to our place in a jeep and then sped away in a cloud of dust. You didn't need to ask what was going to happen. Those who had their ears and eyes open once more began polishing their rifles and bullets.... Word came round that the rebels would start a large-scale attack against us either tonight or tomorrow night!"

Friday, March 20: "It was already long after midnight.... Just as I stepped out, bursts of fire came from the Norbulingka, the Yo Wang Hill and the Potala Palace. Instantly the whole city resounded with rifle and artillery shots. I looked at my watch. The time was exactly forty minutes past three.... Everyone was up and listening to the guns.... Nobody went to bed; we sat up till daybreak.... At ten o'clock sharp, our troops launched their counter-offensive. Our artillery thundered. It was a stirring moment for the people of the whole of Lhasa.... From our watch tower we could see the whole city. The rebel positions were in utter confusion.... The Tibetan and Hui cadres of our office kept asking for permission to join the attacking forces.... Actually there was no need to be over-anxious. Some time after three o'clock in the afternoon, our national flag was hoisted high atop Yo Wang Hill."

Saturday, March 21: "A number of comrades went to the Norbu Lingka. When they came back, they said: 'All our shells fell right on the fortifications in front of the walls. What shooting! Our men didn't destroy a thing in Norbulingka.' But the rebel bandits, when they were cornered and put up a desperate fight, knocked out corners of houses and broke down walls; they dug out holes in the wall to fire their rifles through.... Our artillery fire now turned to the Potala. However, we saw shells exploding only on the concealed pillboxes at the foot of the palace.... We found out later that the artillerymen had been given orders that no shell should fall either on the Potala or the Jokhang Temple. They could fire only on places of secondary importance so that no building would be destroyed. The Tibetan and Hui cadres at our office were amazed. They said, 'What a humane and polite way of fighting a battle!'"

Sunday, March 22: "Just about the time for breakfast the call went around for us all to fall in.... It turned out that we were to go out and help take prisoners. The rebels remaining in the Potala and Jokhang Monastery had been captured. They filed past us. We found in their ranks oldsters, including one man aged 68, as well as children in their teens. One 14 year old youngster, named Pintso and a resident of the city, had been kidnapped by the rebels three days before the outbreak of fighting. He had been tending a herd of sheep. The bandits drove away his sheep and forced him to join their ranks. He was crying as he told us his story. We wiped away his tears and thrust a handful of steamed bread into his pocket. His face broke into a smile and he scampered off home.... By the afternoon no more gunfire was heard in Lhasa. But a few rebel bandits were still hidden in private homes and firing pot shots at our men.... Among a group of captured upper-class reactionaries, I saw a Tibetan regimental commander whom I knew. In 1950 when the People's Liberation units marched to Chamdo, it was this man who had personally directed a machine-gun ambush against our cavalrymen near the Kingsha River and caused us quite a few casualties.... Now for the second time he has been taken prisoner."

Monday, March 23: "I went out into the street in the morning. The Jokhang Monastery was the first place I visited. The monastery, with its golden-roofed buildings, remains intact.... People were once again walking freely on the streets. Everywhere you could see faces bright with smiles. When people met us on the streets, they held up their hata (white scarf) and spoke the Tibetan greeting: 'Chuhsidelai!' (sic) It means 'good luck and good fortune.'"[5]

Thus ended the article written by the Chinese "eyewitness," Shan Chao.

The Chinese seized on the letters that the Dalai Lama had written to Gen. Tan Kuan-san between March 10 and 16, citing them as proof that the Dalai Lama had been abducted and forced to flee by the rebels. In and by themselves the letters could be viewed and interpreted in many ways, such as disarming or even coquettish, but the Chinese blatantly overlooked or ignored all other possibilities, including even the declarations and statements made by the Dalai Lama while he was still in Tibet en route to the border, and those he made after crossing into India. The letters in question follow:

(The letter to the Dalai Lama on March 10 from General Tan)

> Respected Dalai Lama, it is very good indeed that you wanted to come to the Military Area Command. You are heartily welcome. Since you have been put into very great difficulties due to the intrigues and provocations of the reactionaries, it may be advisable that you do not come for the time being.
> Salutations and best regards
>
> Tan Kuan-san

(Dalai Lama's letter of March 11)

> Dear Comrade Political Commissar Tan,
> I intended to go [to] the Military Command to see the theatrical performance yesterday, but I was unable to do [so], owing to obstruction by people, ecclesiastical and secular, who were instigated by a few bad elements and who did not know the facts. This has put me to indescribable shame. I am greatly upset and worried and at a loss what to do. When your letter (of the 10th) appeared before me, I immediately became overjoyed, you do not mind at all.
> Reactionary evil elements are carrying out activities and endangering me under the pretext of protecting my safety. I am taking measures to calm things down. In a few days when the situation becomes stable, I will certainly meet you. If you have any internal directives, please tell me frankly through this messenger [refers to Ngapo Ngawang Jigme].
>
> Dalai Lama

(General Tan's letter of March 11)

> Respected Dalai Lama,
> The reactionaries are now so audacious as to have openly and arrogantly carried out military provocations. They have erected fortifications and posted large numbers of machine-guns and armed reactionaries along the national defence (sic) highway (north of Norbulingka) thereby seriously disturbing the security of the national defence (sic) communications.
> Many times in the past, we told Kasha (the Kashag) that the People's Liberation Army is duty-bound to defend the country and to protect the security of

communication lines related to national defence, and, therefore it certainly cannot remain indifferent to this serious act of military provocations. Therefore, the Tibet Military Area Command has sent [a] letter to Surkong, Neusha, Shasu and Pala asking them to tell the reactionaries to remove all the fortifications they established and to withdraw from the highway immediately. Otherwise, they will bear responsibility themselves for all the serious consequences. I want to inform you of this. Please let me know what your views are at your earliest convenience.

Salutations and best regards

Tan

(Dalai Lama's letter of March 12)

Dear Comrade Political Commissar Tan,

I suppose you have received my letter of yesterday forwarded to you by Ngapo. I have had the letter you sent me this morning. The unlawful actions of the reactionary cliques break my heart. Yesterday I told Kasha to order the immediate dissolution [of] the illegal People's Conference and the immediate withdrawal of the reactionaries who arrogantly move into the Norbulingka under the pretext of protecting me. As to the incidents of yesterday and the day before, which were created under the pretext of protecting my safety and have seriously estranged the relations between the Central Government and the Local Government, I am making every possible effort to deal with them. At 8.30 Peking time this morning a few Tibetan army men suddenly fired several shots near the Chinghai-Tibet highway. Fortunately no serious disturbances occurred. As to the questions mentioned in your letter, I am planning to persuade my few subordinates and give them instructions. Tell me frankly any instruction you have for me.

Dalai

(To Dalai Lama from General Tan)

Respected Dalai Lama,

I have the honour to acknowledge receipt of your two letters dated March 11 and 12. The traitorous activities of the reactionary clique of the upper strata in Tibet have grown into intolerable proportions. These individuals, in collusion with foreigners, have engaged in reactionary, traitorous activities for quite some time. The Central People's Government has long adopted an attitude of magnanimity and enjoined the Local Government of Tibet to deal with them seriously, but the Local Government of Tibet has all along adopted an attitude of feigning compliance while actually helping them with their activities with the result that things now have come to such a grave pass. The Central People's Government still hopes that the Local Government will change its erroneous attitude and immediately assume responsibility for the traitors. Otherwise the Central People's Government will have to act itself to safeguard the solidarity and unification [of] the motherland.

In your letter, you said: "As to the incidents which were created under the pretext of protecting my safety and have seriously estranged relations between the Central Government and the Local Government, I am making every possible effort to deal with them." We warmly welcome this correct attitude on your part.

We are very much concerned about your present position and safety. If you think it necessary and possible to extricate yourself from the present dangerous position of being abducted by the traitors, we cordially welcome you and your entourage to come and stay for a brief period in the Military Area Command. We are willing to assume full responsibility for your safety. As to what is the best course to follow, it is entirely up to you to decide.

In addition, I have much pleasure in informing you that the Second National People's Congress has decided to open its first session on April 17.

Salutations and my best wishes

Tan Kuan-san

(Dalai Lama's letter dated March 16)

Dear Comrade Political Commissar Tan,

Your letter dated the 15th has just been received at three o'clock. I am very glad that you are so concerned about my safety and hereby express my thanks.

The day before yesterday, the fifth day of the second month according to the Tibetan calendar [March 14, 1959] I made a speech to more than seventy representatives of the government officials, instructing them from various angles, calling on them to consider seriously present and long-term interests and to calm down, or my life would be in danger. After these severe reproaches, conditions took a slight turn for the better. Though the conditions in here and outside are still very difficult to deal with at present, I am trying skillfully to make a demarcation line between the progressive people and those opposing the revolution within the government officials. A few days from now, when there are enough forces that I can trust, I shall make my way to the Military Area Command secretly. When that time comes, I shall first send you a letter. I request you to adopt reliable measures. What are your views? Please write to me often.

Dalai[6]

The Dalai Lama, in his statement that was read at Tezpur to newspapermen on April 18, 1959, referred to openly strained relations between Tibet and China beginning in the early part of February and the continuation of these strained relations until: "On March 17, two or three mortar shells were fired in the direction of the Norbulingka palace. Fortunately the shells fell in a nearby pond.

"After this the advisers became alive to the danger to the person of the Dalai Lama and in those difficult circumstances it became imperative for the Dalai Lama, the members of his family and his high officials to leave Lhasa.

"The Dalai Lama would like to state categorically that he left Lhasa in Tibet and came to India of his own free will and not under duress.

"It was due to the loyalty and affectionate support of his people that the Dalai Lama was able to find his way through a route which is quite arduous. The route which the Dalai Lama took involved crossing the Kyi Chu and Tsangpo rivers and making his way through Lhoka area, Yarlung Valley and Tsona Dzong before reaching the Indian frontier at Kanzeymane near to Chuhangmu."[7]

And on April 19, Radio Peking broadcast a reply to the Dalai Lama's Tezpur statement, and then circulated it by the New China News Agency. It read, "The so-called Dalai Lama statement issue by Indian diplomatic officials on April 18 in Tezpur is a poorly composed document which contains constrained arguments and is fraught with lies and loopholes. Disregarding the fact that China is a unified country formed by the Han, Mongolian and dozens of other nationalities, the statement begins by clamoring about the so-called independence of the Tibetan people.

"As a matter of fact the political and religious systems in Tibet were all instituted successively by the Central Government in Peking in the course of several hundred years from the 13th to the 18th century. Even the title, status and functions and powers of the Dalai Lama were not instituted by the Tibetans themselves. The so-called Tibetan independence in modern history has all along been the scheme of British imperialism for aggression against China and first of all against Tibet."[8]

It continued: "... Since entering Tibet, the People's liberation Army has adhered to the 17 Articles of the Agreement with complete faithfulness. No changes have been made in the existing political system in Tibet, nor in the original status and functions and powers of the Dalai Lama. Officials at all levels, both ecclesiastic and secular, performed their duties as usual. Religious activities and the customs and habits of the local people have been respected and the Tibetan currency has continued to circulate. The stipulations in the agreement that the Tibet Local Government should carry out reforms on their own initiative and the Tibet army should be incorporated step by step into the People's Liberation Army were not carried out by the Tibetan Local Government.... In short, during the past eight years the political, social and religious systems in the Tibet region have remained the same as before its peaceful liberation. Almost all the affairs within Tibet were handled by the former Tibet local government."[9]

The rest of the commentary continued to seriously distort what had happened to Tibet since the Chinese invasion, as its writer staunchly parroted the party's cemented position, disregarding, as it had in its earlier portions, any semblance of accuracy. Not likely, but perhaps Marx, Engels and Lenin blushed a bit, although certainly not Stalin or Mao.

Reflecting on the above examples of Chinese propaganda, it is impressive, yet also repulsive, that the socialist/communist apparat must depend on and has sustained the ability to locate those willing and able to twist to the desired political interpretation thousands and thousands of words on just about any subject without regard to facts, propagandists with the ability to take a tiny shred of fact and then surround it by countless statements of party pap and distortions. Where do they find these party hacks so adept and glib in distorting the truth? It remains equally remarkable that the socialists and communists are still able to sell their obviously flawed and transparent products. This is accomplished largely through constantly repeated distortions and statements in which much is misrepresented by party functionaries who know their presentations to be empty and false. Their collective goal is to destroy all under the veil of wonderful things "their" form of government is going to do for the "people" and the world. The party dogma is incessant, all packaged by varying semantics designed to conceal the hard truths. And when achieved, Communism and Socialism — even so-called liberalism — can only be maintained by more stringent laws, big government, less freedom and increased force. Their level playing fields do not exist. For those that have succumbed, it is too late to recognize that freedom is reduced and that Socialist and Communist ideologies are like a movie set, where nothing of substance exists behind the cosmetic facade. Sadly, few seem to learn from the many lessons history offers about fatally flawed political options. Certainly Stalin and Mao, and others since, recognized that Lenin's iron-fist policies required strong military and police support, both being absolutely essential to the communist political dogma and its longevity. Many millions in China and the Soviet Union — and at least a million in Tibet — died in the terrible process involved.

But the Chinese had to try to make the world believe their story, for prior to the escape of the Dalai Lama the world had known very little of the suffering of the Tibetan people at the hands of the Chinese and how the Tibetans had chosen to fight the People's Liberation Army despite the overwhelming odds rather than lose their freedom. The Chinese and Indian censorship and controls had been very effective. And now that the Dalai Lama had escaped, the Chinese Communist Party had to try to persuade the world that his story was without foundation and that their story was correct, including the far-fetched story that the Dalai Lama had been abducted by the Freedom Fighters. On April 19, 1959, Radio Peking noted, "The present gang of Tibetan rebels has been completely fostered by the British. Indian expansionist elements have inherited this inglorious legacy from Britain."[10] And just days earlier Peking had publicly blamed Chiang Kai-shek for supporting the Tibetan resistance.

At his press conference at Mussoorie on June 20, 1959, the Dalai Lama made quite clear what had really happened and how the People's Republic of China had badly misrepresented things. He first noted that he had received reports daily of continued inhuman treatment of his people, of their agonies and harassment and persecution, and of the terrible deportations (to prisons) and executions of innocent men and women. He said that he was speaking out to the world in order to save Tibetans from the danger of near-annihilation. He also pointed out that "... the very structure, terms and conditions of the so-called agreement of 1951 conclusively show that it was an agreement between two independent and sovereign States. It follows, therefore, that when the Chinese armies violated the territorial integrity of Tibet they were committing a flagrant act of aggression. The agreement which followed the invasion of Tibet was also thrust upon its people and government by the threat of arms. It was never accepted by them of their own free will. The consent of the government was secured under duress and at the point of the bayonet."[11]

And then later in the statement he said, "Far from carrying out the agreement, they [the Chinese] began deliberately to pursue a course of policy which was diametrically opposed to the terms and conditions which they themselves laid down.[12] Thus commenced a reign of terror which finds few parallels in history. Forced labor and compulsory exactions, a systematic persecution of the people, plunder and confiscation of property belonging to individuals and monasteries, and execution of those that dared to disagree — such are the glorious achievements of the Chinese rule in Tibet.

"At this point I wish to emphasize that I and my government have never been opposed to the reforms which are necessary in the social, economic and political systems prevailing in Tibet. We have no desire to disguise the fact that ours is an ancient society and that we must introduce immediate changes in the interests of the people of Tibet. In fact, during the last nine years several reforms were proposed by me and my government, but every time these measures were strenuously opposed by the Chinese in spite of popular demand for them, with the result that nothing was done for the betterment of the social and economic conditions of the People. In particular, it was my earnest desire that the system of land tenure should be radically changed without further delay and the large landed estates acquired by the State on payment of compensation for distribution amongst the tillers of the soil. But the Chinese authorities deliberately put every obstacle in the way of carrying out this just and reasonable reform."[13]

The Dalai Lama included in this statement that five million Chinese were already in Tibet and that the Chinese planned to send another four or five million, thereby far eclipsing the number of Tibetans in Tibet. He also noted the broken promises of Prime Minister Chou En-lai to Prime Minister Nehru and the many deceptions of Chairman Mao Tse-tung and Chou En-lai in their representations to Mr. Nehru and the Government of India concerning Tibet. The Dalai Lama also asked for an independent investigation of the situation in Tibet (preferably by the United Nations) and repeated that Tibetans only wanted peace and a peaceful settlement but with the status and rights of both the State and the people. The Indian and most other papers prominently featured the press conference, although Prime Minister Nehru was reportedly upset by the charges against the Chinese made by the Dalai Lama. And unfortunately, but not surprising, the United Nations remained moribund.

There was also much posturing and some finger pointing in the Indian Parliament, as one would expect. The speeches were largely along party lines, including the Indian communists who were staunch in their defense of the People's Republic of China. There were many demonstrations against the Chinese Embassy in New Delhi and an incident in Bombay that upset the Chinese and the Indian communists to the extreme. Reportedly an anti–Chinese demonstrator had taken some fresh cow dung and thrown it onto a large portrait of Chairman Mao, much to the delight of the other demonstrators. The story was carried widely in the papers, and of course the Chinese formally protested, as did the Indian Communist Party. It was also mentioned in Parliament. Reportedly one paper in India suggested that Chairman Mao should not be too upset for the dung had come from a sacred cow, but the paper was admonished by Nehru for expressing such sentiments.[14] And Kalimpong was again discussed at length because the Chinese kept insisting that it was the headquarters for the Tibetan resistance, despite Prime Minister Nehru's repeated statements that extensive investigations stemming from such charges had proven it was not. A few of the more interesting exchanges in both houses of the Indian Parliament follow.

On May 4, 1959, Mr. Shiva Rao, a distinguished journalist and a delegate to the U.N., pointed out that in discussions between Premier Chou En-lai and Prime Minister Nehru in 1956, Chou En-lai had reiterated that "... the people of Tibet were different, and that the regional autonomy of Tibet would be respected. Sir, in making that statement to our Prime Minister in 1956, Premier Chou En-lai was only underlining the assurances which were given abundantly in the agreement which was entered into in 1951 between China and Tibet ... but I shall read out some of the relevant articles from that agreement to point out in what mood the Tibetan delegation was persuaded to sign that agreement. These articles are — in the language of the agreement —

"'All national minorities are fully enjoying the right of national equality and have established or are establishing national regional autonomy.
Freedom is guaranteed to all nationalities to develop their political, economic, cultural and educational work.

"The Central authorities of China will not alter the existing political system in Tibet nor will they alter the established status, functions and powers of the Dalai Lama.

"The religious beliefs, customs and habits of the Tibetan people shall be respected and Lama Monasteries shall be protected.'

"Sir, those are some of the articles of the Sino-Tibetan Agreement of 1951."[15]

Mr. Shiva Rao had been a member of the Indian delegation to the United Nations in 1950 and was well aware of what had happened there. Referring to November 1950, when it was first proposed that Tibet be put on the Agenda of the General Assembly, he said, "The leader of the Indian Delegation under instructions from the External Affairs Ministry here presumably on the basis of reports received from our Ambassador in Peking at that time — Sardar Panikkar — gave the assurance to the Steering Committee that the Chinese forces had halted at Chamdo, some three hundred miles from Lhasa, and that they had no intention of going further. And, Sir, it was on that assurance given by the Leader of the Indian Delegation to the Steering Committee that the proposal to discuss Tibet in that session was dropped. What happened subsequently? Only a few months later, in the spring of 1951, the Chinese forces resumed their advance towards Lhasa. A Tibetan Delegation was summoned to Peking.... When the Delegation reached Peking, it was asked to sign an agreement which already had been drawn up. The Tibetan Delegation was reminded that there was already established in Lhasa Chinese Military Headquarters and the Delegation was asked to sign on the dotted line. After that, Sir, who are the people who keep other people under duress and make them sign statements?"[16]

On May 8, during a debate in the Lok Sabha, Acharya Kripalani said, "It is nothing unusual for countries to criticize each other in their internal and external policy. Nobody takes this criticism to be interference in the internal affairs of the country. If it were so, the hard criticism that is being leveled by China itself against Yugoslavia would be considered internal interference with that country. But in the Communist world there are two standards of judgement — one for themselves and the other for others with whom they think they are in opposition.

"Recently, China has become supersensitive to any criticism. When a person is supersensitive, I am afraid he has a bad conscience. Even the mildest remarks of the Congress President were denounced. Why? Because she said that Tibet was a country. In 1954, I said in this House (that) 'Recently we have entered into a treaty with China.' I feel that China, after it had gone Communist, committed an act of aggression against Tibet. The plea is that China had the ancient right of suzerainty. This right was out of date, old and antiquated. It was never exercised, in fact. It had lapsed by the flux of time. Even if it had not lapsed, it is not right in these days of democracy, by which our Communist friends swear, by which the Chinese swear, to talk of this ancient suzerainty and exercise it in a new form in a country which had and has nothing to do with China.... I consider this as much colonial aggression on the part of China as any indulged in by the Western nations.... In the same year I said: 'A small buffer state on our borders was deprived of its freedom.' When we made a feeble protest we were told that we were stooges of the western powers. If I remember aright we were called the 'running dogs of imperialism.' Again, Sir, in 1958, talking about Panch Sheel I said: 'This great doctrine was born in sin, because it was enunciated to put the seal of our approval upon the destruction of an ancient nation which was associated with us spiritually and culturally.' Sir, at that time, some hon. Member intervened and asked: 'Is that nation suffering?' My reply was: 'Whether it is suffering or not is not the question. It was a nation which wanted to live its own life and it ought to have been allowed to live its own life.' A good government is no substitute for self-government."[17]

The arguments continued to and fro but with few, if any, results. There were also many discussions outside of Parliament. At an All-India Convention on Tibet held in Calcutta on May 30, 1959, Mr. Jaya Prakash Narayan made a lengthy speech that contained many telling points that stirred debate in India and China.

In a dramatic and brilliant presentation, Mr. Narayan said,

> Tibet is being gobbled up by the Chinese dragon. A country of less than ten million being crushed to death by a country of six hundred and fifty million people. Patriotism, courage, faith can perform miracles. The Tibetans love their country; they are brave; they are devoted to their religion and their Dalai Lama. Yet, one to sixty-five is an odd that even a nation of Herculeses will find it difficult to overcome.... Is world peace possible if the strong are free to oppress the weak with impunity? Such a world would be dominated by a few powerful nations and peace would consist in an uneasy balance of power between them and the small nations would be at their mercy.... Tibet is not a region of China. It is a country by itself which has sometimes passed under Chinese suzerainty by virtue of conquest and never by free choice. Chinese suzerainty has always been of the most nominal kind and meant hardly more than some tribute paid to Peking by Lhasa. At other times Tibet was an independent sovereign country. For some time in the 8th century Peking paid a yearly tribute of fifty thousand yards of Chinese brocade to Tibet.... India's acceptance of the suzerainty formula gave to the Chinese action a moral and legal sanction and prevented the formulation of Afro-Asian opinion on the question. It thus prevented the true aggressive character of Chinese communism from being realised by the backward people of Asia, aggravating the danger of their being enslaved in the name of liberation.... There are some who say that facts of history must be taken into account and if Tibet has sometimes been under China, it is irrelevant to raise the question of Tibetan independence now. This is an amazing argument. Any one who believes in human freedom, and the right of all nations to independence, should be ashamed to talk in this fashion. According to the logic of this viewpoint, Hungary, for example, having long been a part of the Austro-Hungarian Empire, should never be entitled to independence. Would any sensible person agree with this view? ... For years an illusion was in the making. It was said that China was different. It had an ancient civilization. Therefore, Chinese communism was different from Russian. And so on and on. That illusion has been shattered — to the great good fortune of the peoples of Asia, who have been warned in time. China rants incessantly about imperialists and expansionists. But China herself has been revealed as a cruel imperial power. If communism had been a truly liberating and anti-imperialist force, the Chinese communists, on assumption of power, should themselves have proclaimed the independence of Tibet and foresworn the old imperialist notion of suzerainty and made a treaty with Tibet of equality and friendship. But communism under Russian and Chinese guidance has become expansionist and aggressive, just as nineteenth century capitalism under the leadership of Britain, France, Germany had become aggressive and expansionist. Somewhere or other Marxism had gone wrong. Lenin wrote a famous thesis on imperialism as the last phase of capitalism. Some one should write another thesis on communism as the first phase of a new imperialism.
>
> The Chinese interfered in everything, in the matter of religion as well as administration. Revered Lamas were purposely ill-treated, humiliated, imprisoned, tortured. The sanctity of shrines and images was violated. Monasteries were demolished and their properties confiscated. A new system of administration was imposed in which Chinese were posted to all key points.... A vast scheme of colonization by China was set on foot, so that large parts of Tibet should cease to be Tibetan and become Chinese.... Resistance to such

a state of affairs was natural. Soon it took the form of a national resistance movement.

The Marxism of Karl Marx was meant to be an objective science of society. But present-day communism is nothing if not a complete travesty of objectivity.... Had it not been so, the Tibetan upsurge could not have been represented by the Chinese as only a minor disturbance caused by a handful of reactionary Lamas and landlords. It is not [that] the Communists do not know the truth. It is only that communism cannot bear the truth. Truth is communism's deadly enemy.

There is one thing of which I am absolutely clear: the need to create a powerful opinion on this question. The Tibet situation should be presented to the world in all its naked reality. No attempt should be made for reasons of diplomacy to play down, cover up, belittle or misrepresent what is happening in Tibet. Diplomacy has a vast deal to answer for in history, and I do fervently hope that diplomacy, like the cold war, is kept out of the issue.

Then is Tibet lost forever? No. A thousand times No. Tibet will not die because there is no death for the human spirit. Communism will not succeed because man will not be slave forever. Tyrannies have come and gone, and Caesars and Czars and dictators. But the spirit of man goes on. Tibet will be resurrected.[18]

There was extensive discussion in various newspapers throughout the Far East about the Dalai Lama's statements and the All India Convention on Tibet. There was also an incessant stream of official statements and news releases from Peking talking about interference in China's internal affairs; how the Dalai Lama had been abducted; statements by the Panchen Lama against India and the Tibetan exiles; statements by Ngapo Ngawang Jigme against the Dalai Lama and the resistance; anti–Indian statements by Chou En-Lai; official statements in Peking charging India with a desire to make Tibet a colony; articles about how India was slandering China; thinly veiled Chinese threats against India; and the announcement of the Panchen Lama's rejection of Mr. Nehru's invitation to him to visit India to see the Dalai Lama—which the Chinese would not have allowed anyway under any circumstances; and stories of thousands attending "spontaneous" rallies in Peking protesting against India for its intervention in China's internal affairs.

In sum, these exchanges were more self-serving than meaningful except to the real victims, the Tibetans. But at least the world was finally learning of what the People's Republic of China and her Liberation Army had done in and to Tibet. And the division between the countries of the Free World and the countries of the Socialist World became more pronounced as a natural extension of these arguments. However, Prime Minister Nehru was all but an apologist for China as he continued to rationalize China's role in Tibet while stressing the necessity of preserving Panch Sheel and its message of peaceful co-existence above all other considerations. He was not pleased with the reactions of leaders in other parts of Asia who spoke in support of Tibet, such as South Korea, Pakistan, Singapore, the Philippines, South Vietnam, Japan and Thailand. (Taiwan expressed dismay but maintained that Tibet was a part of

Chiang Kai-shek's Republic of China.) Nehru expressed the view in Parliament that he thought that these expressions of support for Tibet did little but further complicate and harden the respective "Cold War" philosophies. There were also expressions of support and sympathy for Tibet in other Free World papers as well, but Nehru quietly, perhaps stubbornly, stayed his course.

In contrast, Nehru had earlier let his vexation show clearly, after Prince Peter of Greece made a statement to the press that while staying in Kalimpong he had discovered that truck convoys to Tibet from India were full of military supplies for the Chinese. Nehru said of Prince Peter's story, "... a more fantastic and despicable lie I have never heard" and reaffirmed to members of Parliament that the supplies consisted only of a thousand tons of rice being sent to Lhasa because of the famine there in 1954–1955. "And it was a terrible job to send this. It took seven or eight months for these mule caravans to carry this rice over the Nathula (pass).... This is physically impossible apart from the fact that it is inconceivable that we should send military supplies of all things to the Chinese authorities — by mules — who had far more military supplies than we possessed."[19]

Since Greece posed no threat to India, Nehru had no need to hesitate expressing anger. But for good reason, he was very sensitive about the border areas. When asked occasionally in both houses of Parliament about the truth in the oft-recurring stories that India had allowed Chinese troops to pass through Indian territories in the border areas in order to avoid or outflank Tibetan resistance forces, he would bridle but denials were generally weak, as were the accusations, because of the lack of details. "The stories continued to persist among the resistance forces as well as among the people living in the border areas. They were believed because in the more remote areas there were fewer officials (all underpaid), and bribery was simply a way of life with the Indian civil servants and border police."[20]

While very sensitive to what Peking had to say, to his credit Nehru did not waiver from his position of granting the Dalai Lama and all Tibetan refugees asylum. He remained fully supportive of the philosophy of hinging nonalignment with freedom. He was confident that this policy was in India's best interests, and he readily recognized that her military ability was very limited.

Throughout the spring and summer of 1959, the Chinese continued to repeat the same things over and over, and the Indian responses were similarly repetitive. Yet little was asked directly of the Tibetan refugees, or the Lamas, or of the Dalai Lama in India. Nehru and Mao talked about Tibet as though the Dalai Lama and thousand of Tibetans were not in India. And the Dalai Lama was still prohibited from saying anything political against the Chinese. He was simply kept isolated from newsmen. Except for rare instances, neither was he allowed to receive or visit members of the Diplomatic Corps in New Delhi or key figures from the United Nations. There were thousands of Tibetan refugees in India, and more arriving daily, yet there was little assistance provided by the U.N. Whether this was because of Chinese pressures, direct or indirect, or because Nehru preferred to keep the story of Tibet quiet remains a mystery, but such was the situation for years. India preferred to handle these problems by herself.

Despite Nehru's efforts, the "war of words" continued at a heated pace in China and India and was well monitored and reported in other Asian papers. For example:

> Tokyo, April 26. (1959) Indian Official Blamed.
> A high Chinese official yesterday charged that "British imperialists and Indian expansionists" instigated the Tibetan rebellion. The charge was levelled at the second National People's Congress by Mr. Ulanfu, Vice-Premier of Inner Mongolia. A Chinese newspaper accused Mr. P. N. Menon of acting "outright as a spokesman for the Tibetan rebels in India." The *Kwanming Daily* said: "It seems that the mission of this envoy was not to greet the Dalai Lama but act outright as spokesman for the Tibetan rebels in India. As a matter of fact he has made more utterances than Tibetan rebels."

And another story:

> Hong Kong, April 27. Chinese Deputies Warn India.
> Deputies of China's National People's Congress, now meeting in Peking, today continued their criticism of "Indian expansionist interference" in China's internal affairs, the New China News Agency reported. One, an international law expert, said: "The backing and encouragement given by certain Indian politicians to the rebellious cliques in Tibet and the issuing of the so-called statement which was imposed on the Dalai Lama constitute a barbarous act of interference.... The Chinese people who value Sino-Indian friendship cannot keep silent over it." Mr. Shao Li-tzu, member of the Standing Committee of the Revolutionary Committee, warned India: "You have made wrong calculations. Though they love peace and cherish friendship, over 600 million Chinese people are not at all weak. They will never allow foolish hogs to poke their snouts into our beautiful garden." Another deputy alleged that so-called independence for Tibet was a British imperialist plot and another name for colonialism. "Now the Indian expansionists are playing the old tune of the British imperialists," he said.

While there was a great deal of civility between Nehru and Mao on the surface, underneath this facade the Chinese were clearly showing their teeth with their ears back — a warning in the canine world of anger and intent. This was the first time that the two leaders of Asia were publicly in strong disagreement, and the bully, Chairman Mao, was making it very clear who was the stronger. This was seen by Asians as a key point for, in reality, Tibet had been brutally subjugated by China and the question for the bystander countries became "who, or where, is next?"

In the various incessant editorials and broadcasts that China made during this period many were seen as clear warnings, if not threats, to the other Asian countries as well. For example, in the *People's Daily* of May 6, 1959, there was a 10,000-word-long editorial which attempted to justify China's policies and conduct in Tibet. Some of the more interesting points presented were, "The Tibetans are different than the Hans. That is perfectly true. And that is not all: the Mongolians, the Uighurs, the Chuangs, the Huis, the Miaos, the Koreans and many other minority nationalities of China are all different from the Hans. The Chinese Communists and the Chinese Government face the question of minority nationalities in the country. We have approached this question with extreme caution.... For nearly ten years we have trained up indigenous cadres among the various national minorities.... The Inner Mongolian Autonomous Region, the Kwangsi Chuang National Autonomous Region, the Ningsia Hui National Autonomous Region and the autonomous chou and autonomous counties were established in this way. In Tibet, we displayed especially great patience in order to win the cooperation of Tibetan upper strata elements.... The People's Liberation Army had the strength to quickly put down the rebellion in the Lhasa area.... It could have surrounded the Norbulingka in good time and prevented the rebel bandits from abducting the Dalai Lama. Any sensible person need only think for a moment and he will understand this and will pay no attention to the fairy tales about two or three mortar shells fired in the direction of the palace.... The Communists have always dealt very carefully with the question of nationalities and in particular have exerted the maximum efforts to win over the upper strata elements in Tibet. Such a policy can only be carried out in earnest by the revolutionary proletariat. The bourgeois or other exploiting classes could never carry it out, even if they wanted to.... Only the revolutionary proletariat can find a thorough and correct solution to historical national problems.... Nor is it possible to make (humanitarians) believe that the People's Liberation Army men warm-heartedly and amiably help Tibetans in their labors and treat their diseases, and do not take from them so much as a needle or a piece of thread.... There lies the fundamental reason why the rebellion was entirely without support from the Tibetan people and was utterly routed in the twinkling of an eye, in spite of the national and religious sign-boards held up by the rebels, the difficult terrain with high mountains and precipitous valleys and the many different kinds of foreign aid they got.... Once the Indian side stops its words and deeds of interference in Tibet, the present argument will end. China has never interfered and never will interfere in India."[21]

It is impressive that the Chinese devoted 10,000 words to a single article in trying to persuade India, and presumably other Asian countries, and possibly themselves, of the rightness of their version of what had transpired in Tibet. As one of the Indian writers commented at the time, "Even the peacock does not take that long to preen itself." The points that the Chinese made were usually more subtle, intentionally so, for they seldom want to let others know their true intentions. The naming of the many tribal groups and nationalities that China claims as hers, especially Korea and the Miaos, should have served as alarm bells for all foreign diplomats, especially those of the Free World. Both

Koreas belong to China? And the Miaos, who are located in many Asian countries, all belong to China? Think of the empire that results if China were to have all that she claims. And does China claim all Moslems? How did the brilliant statesmen of the free world miss these points — or perhaps they did notice and simply became more afraid of China. And do the Mongolians now think of themselves as belonging to the Chinese? And have the Tibetans accepted China?

The statement in the article about the revolutionary proletariat being the only group that can effect change should also have served as a red flag to all. That the Chinese believe that the communist doctrine is not for the bourgeois is interesting — or do the Chinese really mean that only the party (communist) aristocracy can effect change? That certainly has been their practice. While the old Soviet Union is no more, the Communist China of today is not politically unlike the Communist China of yesterday, and certainly things have not changed for the better for Tibetans living under the massive Chinese presence in Tibet. Strict party and political conformity is strict party and political conformity, regardless of the packaging.

Usually there were a number of questions asked about the Panchen Lama during press interviews of the Dalai Lama. In responding, the Dalai Lama simply noted that the Panchen Lama had been under Chinese influence since boyhood and had never had the opportunity to enjoy freedom. He was never critical of the Panchen Lama and always expressed sympathy for his situation. Nor did the Dalai Lama single out for ridicule the Tibetan officials who had chosen to support the Chinese.

In the June 20 press conference, the Dalai Lama remarked that "... the revolt was still going on (and) the leaders of the rebellion were drawn from various sections of the people, and that they would welcome support from all countries in the world for the Tibetan cause. He said that more than 1,000 monasteries had been destroyed by the Chinese; that countless lamas and monks had been killed or imprisoned; and that from 1959 onwards a full-scale campaign was conducted [by the Chinese] in two provinces [Kham and Amdo] for the final extermination of the religion." He described the recent division into three groups of Tibetans in Lhasa as reported to him by arriving refugees. He said that the first group was "... deported to China where their fate is not known; the second group was imprisoned, interrogated and punished without limit in the various Chinese military headquarters in Lhasa. The third group was given the meanest food and driven to forced labor." This had considerable impact on those attending the press conference. He also told the press corps that by Chinese order, in the streets of Lhasa, two Tibetans could not converse with each other, and that "all the places of worship are closed."[22]

On August 30, the Dalai Lama released a statement announcing that he was appealing to the U.N. for support. "On the 20th of June last, I was impelled by the steadily deteriorating conditions in Tibet to break my silence and to give to the world a glimpse of the dark and dismal tragedy of people. I also made it clear at the same time that I and my government were fully prepared to accept a just and peaceful solution of the entire problem.

"Since then the picture of Tibet has become immeasurably darker and gloomier, and the sufferings of my people are beyond description. On the other hand, there has been no response to my appeal for peace and justice.

"In these circumstances I have no other alternative than to appeal to the UN for the verdict of the peace-loving and conscientious nations of the world. I also take the opportunity to make a personal appeal to all civilized countries of the world to lend their fullest support to our cause of freedom and justice."[23]

In the telegram that the Dalai Lama sent to the U.N. on September 9, 1959, he outlined Tibet's status as a sovereign State at the time the Chinese violated Tibet's territorial integrity, and listed six categories of Chinese "offenses committed against the universally accepted laws of international conduct.

"(1) They have dispossessed thousands of Tibetans of their properties and deprived them of every source of livelihood and thus driven them to death and desperation;

"(2) Men, women and children have been forced into labor gangs and made to work on military construction without payment or only nominal payment;

"(3) They have adopted cruel and inhuman measures for the purpose of sterilizing Tibetan men and women with a view to the total extermination of the Tibetan race;

"(4) Thousands of innocent people of Tibet have been brutally massacred;

"(5) There have been many cases of murder of leading citizens of Tibet without any cause or justification;

"(6) Every attempt has been made to destroy our religion and culture. Thousands of monasteries have been razed to the ground and sacred images and articles of religion completely destroyed. Life and property are no longer safe and Lhasa, the capital of the State, is now a dead city.

"The sufferings, which my people are undergoing, are beyond description, and it is imperatively necessary that this wanton and ruthless murder of my people should be immediately brought to an end."[24]

On October 21, the U.N. General Assembly adopted a joint Malay-Irish resolution on Tibet:

> Recalling the principles regarding fundamental human rights and freedoms set out in the Charter of the United Nations and in the Universal Declaration of Human Rights and adopted by the General Assembly on December 10th, 1948,
> Considering that the fundamental human rights and freedoms to which the Tibetan people, like all others, are entitled include the right to civil and religious liberty for all without distinction,

Mindful also of the distinctive cultural and religious heritage of the people of Tibet and of the autonomy which they have traditionally enjoyed,

Gravely concerned at reports, including the official statement of His Holiness the Dalai Lama to the effect that the fundamental rights and freedoms of the people of Tibet have been forcibly denied them,

Deploring the effect of these events in increasing international tensions and in embittering the relations between peoples at a time when earned and positive efforts are being made by responsible leaders to reduce tension and improve international relations,

1. Affirms its belief that respect for the principles of the Charter of the United Nations is essential for the evolution of a peaceful world order based on the Rule of Law;

2. Calls for the respect of the fundamental human rights of the Tibetan people and for their distinctive cultural and religious life.[25]

It was a mild resolution. Diplomatic intrigue and pressures resulted in China not being named as the violator. Forty-five nations supported the resolution. Nine opposed it (the Soviet Bloc countries). Twenty-six abstained, including Afghanistan, Belgium, Britain, Burma, Cambodia, Ceylon, Dominican Republic, Ethiopia, Finland, France, Ghana, India, Indonesia, Iraq, Lebanon, Lybia, Morocco, Nepal, Portugal, Saudi Arabia, Spain, South Africa, Sudan, the United Arab Republic, Yemen and Yugoslavia. Guinea and Costa Rica were absent. Shortly before he died, Nehru, in a letter to a friend in 1964, explained India's position. He said that "United Nations resolutions are useless anyway.... We are not indifferent to what has happened in Tibet. But we were unable to do anything EFFECTIVE about it."[26]

The International Commission of Jurists had earlier issued a statement in Geneva on June 5, concluding that there had been "a deliberate violation of fundamental human rights" and that, "There is also a prima facie case that on the part of the Chinese, there has been an attempt to destroy the national, ethnical, racial and religious group of Tibetans by killing members of the group and causing serious bodily harm to the members of the group.... These acts constitute the crime of genocide under the Genocide Convention of the United Nations of 1948."[27]

Mr. Purshottam Trikamdas, Indian member of the Commission, in summarizing the report, noted that "From 1912 to 1950 there was no Chinese law, no Chinese judge, no Chinese policeman on the street corner; there was no Chinese newspaper, no Chinese soldier, and no representative of the Chinese government in Tibet.... Soon after 1951 the first impact of Chinese control was felt in the feverish construction of roads and highways. The labor for this work was Tibetan men, women and children, laymen and monks, many of them forcibly drafted into labor projects and about one-fourth of them are said to have died from the cold, weather, hunger and fatigue.... The financial and physical losses sustained goes into thousands of acres of agricultural land. The Chinese destroyed agricultural lands, irrigation systems and ancient consolidated holdings by indiscriminately using the tracts in the name of highway priority. Numerous religious monuments, shrines, Maniwalls and even houses of poor peasants that were in the path of the highway or road were destroyed.... According to reliable sources, about five million Chinese have already been settled. The present population of Tibet is estimated at 3,000,000 people [Tibetans]."[28]

After studying the evidence, the International Commission "... reached the following conclusions:

"1. From 1950 onwards, a practically independent country has been turned by force into a Chinese province.

"2. The terms of the 17 Point Agreement of 1951 guaranteeing broad autonomy to Tibet have been consistently disregarded.

"3. There has been arbitrary confiscation of property belonging to monasteries, private individuals and the Tibetan Government.

"4. Freedom of religion has been denied to the Tibetans and the Chinese have been trying to destroy the Buddhist religion in Tibet.

"5. The Tibetans have been denied the freedom of information.

"6. There has also been a systematic policy of killing, imprisonment and deportation of those opposed to the regime."

The report further stated "... Since the rebel area is mountainous and difficult terrain for the army to operate in, large-scale aerial bombing has been resorted to. In the accessible parts veritable terror has been let loose on the population. Reliable estimates of the persons killed come to about 65,000. The number of persons deported is stated to be about 20,000. These figures include the recent massacres in and around Lhasa. It is reliably reported that after the suppression of the rising in Lhasa all males between the ages of 15 and 60 have been removed from the city to some unknown destination."[29]

The Tibetans had hoped — and expected — that at least some of the Free World countries, such as the United States, Britain, Japan, Malaya and Thailand or Singapore, would officially support Tibet, or at least extend an invitation to the Dalai Lama to visit, but international politics made this a false hope. "We were told unofficially that the U.S. State Department was preoccupied with concern for the military strength of China and what China might do next. Britain was very concerned about (their interests in) Hong Kong and was afraid of alienating China. And both were concerned with the reaction of the Soviet Union, so without the U.S. taking a lead role, others were hesitant. And we learned that a number of State Department officers in the Embassy in New Delhi, including those senior, referred to Tibetans simply as 'unhygienic, rag-tag remnants of a feudal system.'"[30]

John Kenneth Galbraith, the Canadian-born liberal Keynesian economist, served as Ambassador to India from 1961 to 1963. He referred to the Volunteers as "... deeply unhygienic men who had once roamed over the neighboring Tibetan countryside." He also noted "I was especially disturbed by one particularly insane enterprise. Long flights were being made by the CIA from the neighborhood of Bangkok over India to the northern border of Nepal. There the planes dropped weapons, ammunition and other supplies...." He also noted that he had managed to use his influence with the Kennedys in Washington to get support to the Volunteers canceled. He claimed, "Aborting these activities was perhaps my most useful service that spring." His further boast was that in doing so, "I was not troubled by an open mind."[31]

Galbraith obviously had not been interested enough to know that Prime Minister Nehru had long known of the many flights made to support the Tibetan Freedom Fighters and had not objected to them. And interestingly, when the Chinese invaded the NEFA area of India in the fall of 1962, Nehru instantly turned to the United States, and specifically the CIA, for support, which was promptly provided, Ambassador Galbraith's concerns notwithstanding.

Galbraith's boorish remarks and acts hurt all Tibetans and insulted many Indians, but obviously they delighted the Chinese. Many Tibetans and Indians also wondered what the reaction of these "diplomats" would have been to Nehru's predecessor, for Mahatma Gandhi had long shunned western dress and western affectations. Gandhi's dress and manners were quite different than that of normal diplomatic protocol, yet he had the respect of most, if not all. But that was before the days of political illusionists forming, if not dictating, U.S. policy.

It was not until the fall of 1967 that His Holiness left India for a visit to Japan and Thailand. In September 1973 the Pope invited him to visit Rome, after which the Dalai Lama visited most of the European countries, except for France which finally invited him to visit in 1982. In September 1979, His Holiness made his first visit to the United States, but was not given an official reception in America until April 16, 1991, when he was invited by President Bush to visit Washington, including a courtesy call at the White House. A day later, Congressional leaders honored him at the Capitol, after which the Chinese protested the U.S. official reception of the Dalai Lama. On April 28, 1993, President Clinton met His Holiness privately and briefly in Washington, then again in September 1995.*

The travels to Europe, North America and Asia by the Dalai Lama are now commonplace and are met with ever-increasing popular support, yet no official government support for Tibet's plight or cause has surfaced beyond meaningless "resolutions" primarily addressing the issue of Human Rights. The Free World simply continues to do business with China as usual.

*Appendix D is a copy of a letter dated September 7, 1995, delivered to President Clinton by a spokesperson for the Dalai Lama, protesting the gratuitous announcement on Voice of America on August 24, 1995, that, "Like many other countries, the U.S. recognizes that Tibet is part of China." At the unpublicized September meeting in the White House with the Dalai Lama, President and Mrs. Clinton reportedly expressed considerable sympathy for the Tibetans and condemned the violation of Human Rights suffered at the hands of the Chinese but did not explain the difference between U.S. announced policy and their privately expressed views.

"It is disturbing that nothing meaningful has really happened at the United Nations on Tibet's behalf. Some food and health help has been provided to the refugees by the United Nations, but other than the impressive support given to our exile government and refugees by the government of India and private Indian citizens, help has come mostly from generous private and religious sources in other countries. We deeply appreciate this assistance, for it has meant the difference between success and failure for our refugees, and sometimes the difference between life and death for them, especially the children.

"His Holiness focused first on trying to solve the countless problems which needed to be addressed on behalf of the Tibetan refugees, and also began work on a new constitution for Tibet as he had promised to do. Schools, orphanages, dispensaries, hospitals, housing, monasteries, libraries, cottage industries, trade schools, farming efforts, a new government, etc. were begun and still continue. The gold and silver of the treasury that His Holiness had sent to Sikkim many years before provided a financial basis for many of these projects, but private Indians and the government of India have also contributed greatly. Much help has come from many countries since those early days, and many Tibetans have been resettled in countries around the world. Before, few Tibetans ever traveled outside of Tibet, but now there are Tibetans living and studying in many countries of the world.

"Clearly the Chinese did not succeed in destroying Tibet or our religion. And His Holiness is now a successful diplomat welcome in many countries in the world. But our work to regain freedom and independence for Tibet must continue. As long as China occupies our country we cannot rest. And we need the help of many countries in all these things, including political matters, but no country has offered to take the lead to help us. The United Nations has chosen to ignore even our basic pleas regarding the issues of Human Rights violations in Tibet.... Prime Minister Nehru was right about the United Nations ... [not being 'effective.']"[32]

CHAPTER 12

The Blood of Patriots

"During the evening of March 23 or 24, some 35 Volunteers individually and in pairs made their way under cover of darkness into the Chinese military compound just outside of Lhasa using many different routes, bypassing the Chinese guard posts. Fifteen of them went to the Happy Light Cinema, where inside about 80 or 90 Chinese were watching a film. The Volunteers quietly took up positions along the back and sides of the theater and on signal opened fire on the Chinese soldiers. Others of the Volunteers had taken good ambush positions in the camp, including some near the theater, and they killed or wounded most of the Chinese soldiers who rushed toward the theater to see what all the firing was about. They also shot the Chinese trying to escape from the theater. And before withdrawing, the Volunteers used Thermit grenades to set fire to some warehouses and some of the military vehicles that were inside the compound.

"A few days earlier, from well concealed positions outside of Lhasa, the Volunteers had used their binoculars to watch many Chinese soldiers leaving their camp and the city hurriedly in trucks after the search throughout the city for His Holiness had proven fruitless. They quickly concluded that the Chinese intended to intercept His Holiness before he and his party made it to the border, and believed he was headed south. Given the large number of Chinese that had left Lhasa in a hurry, and given the slaughter of Tibetans in Lhasa by the Chinese just days before, the Volunteers were quite sure that the Chinese had left only a small force behind, believing that no Tibetans would or could do anything. Two of the older Volunteers disguised as beggars made their way into the city and scouted the area of the camp, confirming that most of the Chinese soldiers were gone. This information was relayed to the Volunteers waiting in a safe area outside of Lhasa. The idea was to seize the opportunity to let the Chinese know that retribution was always nearby and that the flame of resistance would never be extinguished. In the attack there was only one Volunteer killed — when a grenade that he had picked up that a Chinese had thrown at him exploded as he was trying to throw it back towards the fleeing Chinese. The Chinese soldiers ran in every direction in their confusion trying to find a place to hide, and so there was really little opposition to the Volunteers. The Volunteers didn't take time to count or search the

Chinese casualties, but they reported that there were bodies of Chinese soldiers on the ground all over the camp. Once initiated, the whole action in the camp took about ten minutes, maybe less, and the Volunteers quickly departed and headed back to their safe area north of the city. All of the Volunteers considered it not only a very well done action, but a big psychological victory as well. However, nothing could make up for the extensive killings and destruction by the Chinese of Tibetans in Lhasa that had just happened."[1]

What had originally been thought of as a probable suicide mission by the resistance fighters planning the raid on the Chinese compound turned out to be incredibly successful. Those that had planned and volunteered for it were determined to revenge the slaughter by the Chinese of their countrymen regardless of personal cost. This was not uncommon, for many times in the past similar raids had been made against Chinese units that had chosen to slaughter or brutalize Tibetans who had no chance to resist and had been taken prisoner. It had become a way of life as well as honor for the Volunteers to revenge themselves this way. As Gompo Tashi, Wangdu, Athar, Lhotse and other Tibetan Freedom Fighters readily explained, the Tibetans wanted the Chinese Devils to know that they could not stay in Tibet without the Tibetan Lord of Death, Shinje Choegyal, watching and stalking them very closely.[2]

The Chinese reportedly were very upset by the attack, but surprisingly there were few reprisals, probably because of the Chinese having massacred so many Tibetans in Lhasa following the Dalai Lama's escape and not wanting any publicity about that, and certainly they did not want any embarrassing publicity about a successful attack by the Freedom Fighters against their central command military camp in Lhasa. Some Tibetans and Indians speculated that the Chinese officials in Lhasa may not have fully or accurately reported the "attack" to Peking for fear of incurring more wrath from their leaders, who were already extremely upset that the Dalai Lama had escaped. It would not have been the first time that the Chinese commanders in Tibet covered up or reported defeats and failures less than accurately, just as they had not reported factually the extent of their many problems in the rural areas.

In a lengthy article in the May 5, 1959, issue of the *Peking Review* titled "The Rebirth of the Tibetan People Cannot Be Halted," by Chang Lu, reprinted after it first appeared in the May 1st "Red Flag" publication of the Central Committee of the Chinese Communist Party, the opening paragraph stated, "The armed rebellion in Tibet [referring to the March 10 demonstrations in Lhasa] met with ignominious defeat. Aimed at selling out the motherland and striking at the unification of China, this rebellion was launched by the reactionary clique of the upper social strata in Tibet and the former local government there which they controlled, and at the instigation of imperialism and the expansionist elements in India." On the second page of the same article the author described the resistance efforts of the Volunteers as follows: "They (had) held up and attacked motor convoys, wrecked highways, murdered cadres, killed and maimed people, and sniped at the People's Liberation Army. Their activities culminated in the all-out rebellion launched in Lhasa on March 10 this year, when they openly raised the slogan of 'Independence for Tibet!' and 'The Han People Must Get Out!' and abducted the Dalai Lama in their flight to India." In the last paragraph of the same article, page 4, we learn, "Contrary to the wishes of the imperialists, the expansionists in India and the rebel clique in Tibet, the rebellion of the reactionary elements in Tibet and its suppression have helped the unification of the motherland and brought a new life to the Tibetan people. They attempted, through armed rebellion, to block the way to social reforms in Tibet and to realization of democratic regional autonomy there.... The suppression of the rebellion, and the dissolution of the former reactionary local government of Tibet have also cleared the way for introducing democratic reforms in Tibet; this will lead to an early realization of democratic reforms in Tibet so that the mass of the Tibetan people may become the masters in their own house and really bring about democratic regional autonomy. Future democratic reforms in Tibet will be carried out step by step, in accordance with the will of the Tibetan people, with regard for the specific conditions there, and by appropriate means.... There is no doubt that once the Tibetan people are rid of their many shackles, they will succeed in creating an earthly paradise on the Tibetan plateau."

The question might be asked as to when the Chinese intend to rid the Tibetan people of their shackles.

"Hundreds of guerrilla bands remained active in Tibet long after the suppression of the Lhasa revolt. While the number of large battles decreased as the guerrillas were isolated from the villages they used for support, ambushes of PLA convoys continued intermittently. Besides Lhoka, another main theater of combat lay in a zone above Lhasa where southern Amdo, northwestern Kham and the Changthang met. Here, large groups, cut off from escape routes through Central Tibet, fought major battles for a full three years following the revolt. The Goloks, a nomadic warrior tribe from Amdo numbering 100,000, were particularly stubborn. Their names meant 'Backwards Heads,' or 'rebel'—which they had always been, mainly against the central government in Lhasa. They had fought fiercely from as early as 1952, waging guerrilla campaigns in which large numbers of Chinese had died. By the time the revolt erupted in Central Tibet, they still had not been crushed. Though both they and the other 'wild men' of Tibet, the Khambas, were hampered by limited supplies, catching them in the rugged and trackless countryside was not so simple. Once a guerrilla band was located, the Chinese, equipped with machine guns, mortars and field artillery, would attack its camp in the middle of the night, or at dawn, and the massacres that resulted were characteristic of the fighting all across Tibet ... no quarters given or asked. But despite the Tibetans' heavy losses, combat continued. For example, in December 1964, almost five years after the uprising's official suppression, Gen. Chang Kuo-hua noted publicly that 'the feudal lords have not been eliminated; they are resentful of their defeat and attempt to regain power by all means.' Almost a year later, he again referred to internal turmoil by stating: 'The people can thoroughly smash the reactionary administration of the feudal lords only by carrying out resolute struggle, especially armed struggle.'"[3]

Throughout 1959 the Chinese continued to blame the "upper strata reactionary serf owners" and "the elite aristocracy" as the source of their problems and for their failures, even though it was the privileged Tibetan officials, both government and religious, especially in Lhasa, that had not and did not resist the Chinese. Very few of them evidenced any support for the rebels. The Tibetan officials recognized that the tribals still strongly resented them and their politics of appeasement — which was prompted largely by selfishness — and that the tribals thought of them as cowards. The Chinese thought to drive this division further by simply labeling all freedom fighters as "serf owners." While laughable in Tibet, unfortunately this Chinese propaganda was believed in many other countries — even after the International Commission of Jurists publicly documented and accused the Chinese in January 1960 of having committed the most abominable of crimes, genocide.

Anna Louise Strong, author and strong apologist for Chairman Mao, described in her book *When Serfs Stood Up* (Peking, 1965) how the People's Liberation Army, following the March 1959 uprising, "... now moved from Lhasa out into Tibet, and put down the rebels in the name, not only of the Government of China, but also in the name of Tibet's new local government, which, under the Panchen Lama, had declared for reforms. Wherever the troops now went, they confiscated the great whips and torture instruments from the monasteries and manor houses and turned them in to the county governments under military control." This dutifully echoed the Chinese propaganda about the Tibetans and the accusations of the "serfs" having been mistreated by the land owners. And the NCNA noted that in Lhoka, the People's Liberation Army fought 47 engagements in two weeks and disposed of two thousand rebels. By May the Chinese were proclaiming that the "rebellion was utterly routed in the twinkling of an eye."[4]

One has to admire the track record of the Chinese in seldom missing an opportunity to push their propaganda themes, wherever and however, and without concern for letting facts get in the way, using their own outlets (NCNA, *Peking Review*, etc.) or willing apologists such as Ms. Strong and other vocal Maoist supporters.

However, there were indicators that the zenith of the resistance efforts had been reached and that the slow decline in the success rate of the Volunteers had begun. "In April the Chinese did succeed in retaking Tsethang in Kham which the Tibetans had seized and held for nearly six months. Given the constantly increasing numbers of PLA committed by the Chinese to Tibet, holding towns or other fixed positions was no longer practical. And most of the resistance forces that had been operating in the Lhoka area moved from there because of it being flooded by Chinese troops. The Trigu Lake and Yamdro areas became the main areas in Kham for operations against the Chinese by the Khambas. And again there were stories of PLA units using Indian and Sikkim border areas to move into positions from which they could attack Tibetan resistance forces, but none of these stories could be proven."[5]

Occasionally there was a story about Volunteers using a captured vehicle to move captured supplies or to serve some other purpose to the disadvantage of the Chinese. One such story involving a Russian made vehicle, an ambush of a Chinese convoy and typifying the Khamba spirit follows:

After an ambush of a small Chinese convoy near Shigatse, one of the Volunteers dressed as a Chinese soldier and decided to drive one of the small vehicles that was still running into a nearby Chinese outpost. Although with little driving experience, he managed to get the vehicle turned around and headed down a trail towards the outpost, followed some distance by other Khambas on their mounts. He drove past the startled Chinese sentry into the camp and right through two of the tents in his way. The vehicle killed two Chinese officers who had been sitting in one of the tents, and then, sliding wildly while dragging the tents, the vehicle virtually destroyed the rest of the campsite, including smashing a Chinese military radio located in another tent. The Volunteer could see very little for the vehicle was now covered by tent canvas. The few other Chinese in the camp simply ran about, fearful of the vehicle, watching the carnage and not knowing what to do. The vehicle eventually turned onto its side, but the Tibetan driver crawled out, and quickly mounted a horse tethered nearby belonging to one of the Chinese. He then escaped with the rest of the Tibetan patrol, which by then had ridden up during the confusion and killed the remaining — and startled — Chinese.

Unfortunately, not all stories of Tibetans attempting to drive enemy vehicles ended in success, for some failed to keep the vehicle on the road. Fortunately, seldom were there serious injuries or damage, except to the vehicles and perhaps to individual pride.

Some Khamba resistance forces moved into the more remote areas of northern Kham and into Amdo, while others moved to northern, and north central areas, ambushing and cutting the Sinkiang supply routes. Other resistance units moved into the Tingri Tsang area north of Shigatse. In the Chamdo and Markham areas other Freedom Fighters conducted a series of ambushes resulting in heavy casualties to the PLA. "Truck loads of dead Chinese were also reported in the vicinity of Yatung. The Chinese armed some of the Panchen Lama's monks from the Tashilunpo monastery in Shigatse, but most of those that received arms soon joined resistance forces in the area. Resistance units also closed the Shekar-Lhasa road and the Shekar-Trigu road. Special teams also again infiltrated Lhasa and assassinated some half dozen party officials, and anti–Chinese Communist posters again appeared in both Lhasa and Shigatse."[6]

So much for the "rebels being eliminated in the twinkling of an eye," as earlier reported by the Chinese, and echoed by Anna Louise Strong. But it was true that the tide was changing in favor of the Chinese against the Volunteers.

The sharply increased numbers of Chinese troops in Tibet with improved armament and mobility and increased air coverage reflected Mao's desire to eliminate the resistance before the outside world learned from the Dalai Lama of all that had transpired in Tibet at the hands of the Chinese communists, and to present the picture of an untroubled China to the National Assembly meeting in April in Peking. He and the PLA had been embarrassed by the escape of the Dalai Lama and the successes of the resistance, and the political moderates who had called for a less militant approach to the Tibet situation had not lost the opportunity to point out that the hardliners had been wrong. That there were also many reports of rebel activities in the other autonomous regions in China in this same period added to Mao's problems and concerns. However, with the army fully behind him, Mao's position was not seriously threatened.

There was even speculation, particularly in the councils of many of the Asian countries, that the Chinese leadership, while chagrined and embarrassed that the Dalai Lama had been able to escape, was also relieved that he had, for it cleared the way for the Chinese to do now whatever they wanted to without concerning themselves with having to go through any motions of consulting with the Dalai Lama.

In June 1959, Mao wrote, "Cold eyed, I surveyed the world beyond the seas…and reminisced about the Great Leap Forward; the backyard steel mills; the drive to put all peasants [referred to by Mao as 'Blue Ants' because of their mandated blue attire] into communes; the split with Nikita Khrushchev [over atom bombs and assistance to China]; the Hundred Flowers drive for 'free expression'; and the wave of executions in China of intellectuals that followed when they surfaced to seek free expression; the demise (murder) of Peng Te-Huai some 16 years after his being removed from office; the critical attitude of some of his comrades; and the question of Lin Biao's reliability."

At Mao's direction, hundreds of leaders from the so-called Long March had been removed from various offices, charged with a variety of crimes and then imprisoned, or killed. "To think that once we all ate out of the same rice bowl," Gen. Chu Teh ruefully remarked. Mao firmly believed in Stalin's policy and practice of periodically (every seven or eight years) eliminating or at least transferring those around him that held key positions.

As Mao had written, "Destruction is the elemental method of social change."[7] Mao's studies of Buddhist philosophy in 1920 had obviously long been forgotten.

Although Mao had wanted maximum retribution immediately — before the situation in Tibet could be fully exposed by the Dalai Lama — this was not acceptable to the less strident forces in the Chinese Government, including China's President, Liu Shao-chi. Because Chairman Mao's "Great Leap Forward," which had begun in 1958 and proven to be a failure, and because there had been serious famines in China largely due to his incredibly illogical decisions regarding agricultural practices, Mao's power at that point was less than absolute. In addition to Tibet, there were also serious problems of unrest in other non–Han populated areas of China, especially in Honan and Sinkiang. These problems served the policies of the so-called "moderates" aligned (loosely) against Chairman Mao, with the result that Tibetans and the other minorities in China were spared for a time the full wrath that Mao Tse-tung wanted to inflict, although the respite was rather brief.

Following the People's Congress in Peking in April 1959, the Panchen Lama and the Chinese developed and announced two stages of reforms for Tibet, the first of which was to be the "Three Antis and Two Reductions." The first and strongest of these was "anti-rebellion," which in essence made it a crime punishable by death for any Tibetan to assist or participate in any way in the resistance. This served to make it extremely risky for anyone to assist the Freedom Fighters in any way, such as providing food or fodder or information, or a place to rest. The Chinese hoped to cut off all food supplies, thereby forcing the Volunteers to leave Tibet or be run to ground and killed.[9]

There were also proclamations issued about anti-unpaid labor, anti-slavery and anti-tax measures that were used as a guise by the Chinese simply to seize more properties from the Tibetan government and from the monasteries and from independent land-owners. This authorized the official "seizing" (looting) of not only the gold and silver from the Tibetan treasury, but also the taking of countless Buddhist scriptures and images that were priceless, some being a thousand years old or more, some of solid gold, many of them inlaid with jade, coral and other precious and semi-precious jewels, and solid gold lamps and images of the many-armed patron god Chenrezi, and the gold leaf which had been placed on the tombs of the former Dalai Lamas by pilgrims for centuries. Some of the tombs were up to sixty feet high and each with its own gold-leaf-covered roof. Monasteries, temples, chortens, and monuments were ransacked and destroyed. And every private household was again visited and more personal properties seized by the Chinese. As before, the items of high value were taken to China. The remainder was divided among the Chinese officials and officers in Lhasa. This pillaging process even included livestock, farming tools, horses, sheep, clothing, virtually everything that was useable. It was reported and confirmed by many that countless convoys of trucks taking valuables, including the treasuries of the Tibetan Government and those belonging to the monasteries, continued into 1962 and later. These years of concentrated looting remain beyond estimate or measure.

Chiang Kai-shek had used a scorched earth policy against the Japanese, as had Stalin against the Germans; perhaps the total pillaging of Tibet was Chairman Mao's version of that practice. The looting was of considerable financial benefit to the PRC, thanks to its selling of many of the precious artifacts in various foreign markets, including Hong Kong.

In July 1959 the Chinese also brought the practice of thamzing to Lhasa, under the guise of political education meetings. It was basically the same script as before but new to Lhasa. Again the assembled Tibetans sat on the ground before the Chinese officials who were seated at a table. One of the Chinese would make an opening speech as to the need for political cleansing and usually explain that thamzing, or public confession, was but a process in this cleansing, not just a single event. The "process" was, of course, repeated until the Chinese eventually gained a full confession from the accused. As before, the accused would be brought forward and a list of "crimes" read, after which one or more of the Tibetan "diligent ones" (collaborators) would denounce the accused. Then the beatings would begin.

This time a few new and even more brutal types of public torture and execution were introduced, such as smashing the heads of those accused with rifle butts; the gouging out of eyes; wrapping the accused in blankets and then setting the blanket on fire; public castration; trussing and roasting the accused over a bonfire; or the accused being shot or stabbed by their own and other children. The practices of stripping women naked, and of forced intercourse in public, and gang rape by soldiers soon became as common in Lhasa as it had in rural areas.[10]

There is no accurate record of how many Tibetans died from the "confession" sessions, or how many died during the thamzing, or in the prisons where most survivors of the thamzings were sentenced. It is probable that the Chinese do not know either, for often the Tibetans that were not executed just disappeared as far as their families knew. Those that were executed immediately after the thamzing were simply left for their families or friends to remove, and no Tibetan dared to keep such records. The vast majority of those that were sent to Chinese prisons died there from systematic starvation, exposure, or untreated sickness. The International Commission of Jurists recorded many hundreds of such cases from witnesses, and from their records it is estimated that multiple thousands died in 1959 and 1960 from thamzing alone.

Among those that were subjected to this extreme punishment was Lhalu Tsewang Dorje, the official that had organized the defenses in Chamdo in Kham before Ngapo Ngawang Jigme replaced him in 1950, shortly before the Chinese invaded. Lhalu was repeatedly brought before the officials in thamzing sessions in Lhasa and beaten but kept alive only so that he could be punished in public again and again to impress upon the Tibetans the completeness of the Chinese military and political control. It was a cruel fate for an extraordinary man, and for so many others like him.[11]

Throughout Tibet, lamas, monks and nuns were forced out of their monasteries. Most of the nuns were physically brutalized and publicly gang raped again and again, and when of no further use they were usually killed. Many lamas and monks were forcibly taken from their monasteries and simply bludgeoned to death without the thamzing process. "The Chinese took special delight during thamzing in publicly challenging high ranking lamas and monks to perform miracles, such as to escape by flying away, or to assume a different form, or make gold or food to appear, and then beat them to death when the miracles were not produced, all the while telling the Tibetan audience that the Buddhist religion was obviously false and useless."[12]

The Chinese seemed intent on eliminating all who failed to swear obedience to and love for Chairman Mao and Communist China and to totally destroy the Buddhist religion. Not content to simply steal and destroy all religious items, they physically defiled the monasteries in every way imaginable, including with excrement. They drew obscene cartoons on the walls, and defaced the religious tonkas, and eventually totally destroyed all but a few of the more than 6,000 monasteries in Tibet. If they could not destroy them by cannon fire, they used dynamite to reduce them to rubble. "The monks were accused of being possessed by devils, or of being insane, especially those with the unique ability while chanting to intone a chord of three notes at the same time. This very difficult accomplishment was seen as something evil by the Chinese, and many of these monks were executed, but usually only after public thamzing and beatings."[13]

The Chinese established museums devoted to displaying items of torture the Chinese claimed that Buddhist monks had used against the Tibetan people. They took the foreign diplomats that the Chinese invited to visit Lhasa to this sham to try to convince them of their propaganda. Even President Bush visited such a museum, but no Tibetans were allowed to talk to him, nor did he talk with the Dalai Lama in India. He reportedly chose to believe the Chinese, whether because of personal or political and economic persuasions of the time is not known.

"Many political prisons were established and the prisoners became slave labor ... and most died from exhaustion, starvation or sickness, for medical attention was not provided by the Chinese. Imprisoned Tibetans provided the labor force used in constructing the hydroelectric plant at Nachen Thang, a few miles outside of Lhasa on the Kyi Chu River. More than 8,000 prisoners were housed there in some ten compounds."[14]

Hundreds and hundreds of Tibetan prisoners were simply worked to death, while hundreds of others starved to death. And when replacement workers were needed by these camps the Chinese simply conscripted more Tibetans. "There were two camps that were particularly bad and soon earned the title of 'death camps.' These were Golmo and Tsalo Karpo. Golmo was a prison camp established in northern Amdo province by the Chinese to hold the thousands of Tibetans they used as forced labor to build part of the railroad linking northern Tibet with Han China. The prisoners were worked 12 or more hours a day, and were given very meager rations, no proper clothing to protect them from the cold and winds of the more than 10,000 foot altitude, and no medical attention. At Tsalo Karpo, a dry lake bed northwest of Lhasa, the Chinese forced the Tibetans to work from first to last light digging for borax. The food for the prisoners consisted of the poorest grade of barley. On Sundays, the prisoners were sent to gather fire wood outside of the camp, which, after a short while, resulted in the prisoners having to go increasing distances from the camp to find wood. While many died there, the wood gathering requirement afforded some of the prisoners an opportunity to escape, after which many of the escapees found one of the resistance forces still active in nearby areas ... while others attempted the long trek to safety across the border."[15]

The food provided by the Chinese in such camps was hardly enough to keep one alive, much less able to work twelve or more hours a day at hard labor. "Most prisoners resorted to eating roots, or insects or grubs, or anything edible they could find, even going through animal dung heaps looking for undigested grain — anything to ease their starvation. There were other prison camps in the remote areas of the northwest, in the Amdo and Kiansu areas, where the treatment was such that it was clear that the prisoners were not expected to survive. It was as though the Chinese knew that they could do anything to the Tibetans they wanted without any fear of any punishment or adverse publicity. Fortunately for the few who were sent there, the Chinese also had established two prison camps in southern Tibet where the lower altitudes made living less difficult. These camps also held Chinese accused of political deviances and other 'crimes,' as well as some Tibetan officials who had been accused by the Chinese of less than total devotion."[16]

It did not take long before the thamzing process had sufficiently cowed the Tibetans to the point that they realized they could no longer confide in or fully trust one another for fear of being reported for a slight or even an imagined indiscretion. The Lhasans soon became so fearful of the Chinese that they would say or do anything to keep from being "interrogated" and sent to prison. This inspired the Chinese to become even more brutal to the Tibetans, treating them more and more as total slaves. With the Dalai Lama gone, there was no element left in Lhasa that spoke for, or could protect, the Tibetans. Only the Freedom Fighters in the provinces continued to resist the Chinese. And, as the Chinese had planned, it became increasingly difficult for the Volunteers to find food as the Chinese slowly strangled and eliminated the support of the people in the rural areas that the Volunteers needed so desperately and that they had previously had.[17]

Initially, the Panchen Lama continued to parrot the party line of the Chinese, but to his credit, he also strongly insisted that the portions of the Potala, the Norbulingka, and the Tsuglakhang and Ramoche cathedrals that had been badly damaged by the Chinese in their March shellings be repaired. The Chinese army had begun using the undamaged portions of these buildings to house some of their soldiers and for storage, but reluctantly the Chinese agreed to repair the damage. Then rumors surfaced that the Chinese generals in Lhasa and the Panchen Lama were arguing about the harsh reforms that the Chinese intended to implement. Stories were also circulating that the father of the Panchen Lama had assisted the resistance groups in the Shigatse area, and that he had also helped the diversion group that had traveled south and west through the Shigatse area at the same time the Dalai Lama was making his way towards the Indian border. The diversion group passing near Shigatse had changed horses there, but whether or not the father of the Panchen Lama had actually provided fresh mounts to the group from the many horses that he and the Panchen Lama owned was not proven. It is possible, for the father reportedly had little or no regard for the Chinese and at times was openly critical of them.[18]

In late 1960, while the Panchen Lama was in Peking, the Chinese surrounded his monastery in Shigatse and seized all 4,000 of its monks. Some of these were among those publicly executed in March 1961, after being accused of having assisted the resistance and the Dalai Lama's escape in 1959. Most of the rest were sent to prison, and the monastery was all but destroyed by the Chinese. Despite this, in his sermons the Panchen Lama continued to refer to the Dalai Lama as Tibet's leader and to note that, as Chairman Mao had repeatedly said, "the Chinese are in Tibet to help, and that Tibetans must lead the way." By this time, the Chinese had dropped most, if not all, pretenses of any such thing, but by quoting Chairman Mao, the Panchen Lama was able to mention the Dalai Lama. The Panchen Lama did not attack the Dalai Lama but often referred to him publicly in a manner that made it clear the Dalai Lama was still the religious figure the Panchen Lama honored. Then, in 1962, after having finally decided that they could no longer use the charge that the Dalai Lama had been abducted, the Chinese instructed the Panchen Lama to denounce the Dalai Lama as a deserter and traitor, promising him that after doing so he would be rewarded by being named by the Chinese as the theocratic head of Tibet. This the Panchen Lama refused to do. The Chinese were furious, but also fearful of taking action that might further discredit them in the outside world, reflecting that China was continuing to experience serious internal problems, the news of which had begun to make some of the newspapers in Hong Kong. The People's Republic did not want Tibet added to such publicity.

In 1964 the Chinese again ordered the Panchen Lama to publicly denounce the Dalai Lama during a Great Prayer Festival in Lhasa during which he was to address the gathered crowd. Instead, the Panchen Lama said to the some ten thousand Tibetans that had come to the religious festival, "I must tell you of my firm belief that Tibet will regain her independence and that the Dalai Lama will return." He then concluded his speech by saying "Long live His Holiness, the Dalai Lama!" The Panchen Lama was then quickly but quietly placed under house arrest that same day by the furious Chinese officials.

When they heard of what had happened, Chairman Mao and Chou En-lai ordered that the followers of the Panchen Lama were to be arrested and that the Panchen Lama was to be publicly denounced, imprisoned and put on trial as a traitor. Thus the Panchen Lama was subjected to thamzing, complete with elaborate staging and the most far-fetched of accusations. Many Tibetan officials (who had been willing collaborators), including Ngapo Ngawang Jigme, and Dorje Phagmo and Phakpa-la Gelek, and others, willingly participated in this publicly staged "trial." After some three days of repeated charges, the Panchen Lama was physically attacked and beaten. Most Tibetans could not believe that such terrible treatment would be given to this high level religious figure, a reincarnation, especially since he had been "chosen" by the Chinese. They were totally shocked at the behavior of the Chinese against the Panchen Lama. Obviously, the Chinese were intent on destroying the remaining vestiges of the Buddhist religion, and by removing the Panchen Lama they believed they had accomplished this.

The Panchen Lama was charged publicly with stealing, murder, womanizing, including having seduced his brother's wife, with having aided the resistance, and having planned to attack the Chinese with a force of his own, and of planning to escape to India. The charade continued as the Chinese then staged a lengthy so-called public debate as to a suitable punishment for the Panchen Lama. Some of the collaborators demanded his death, others urged a long prison sentence and a few of the brave recommended a lenient sentence for him. This well scripted Chinese opera ended when he and his parents and members of his immediate entourage were chained, forced onto closed trucks and driven out of Lhasa under heavy Chinese guard. He was branded a traitor at the 151st Plenary Session of the State Council in Peking in December 1964, and at the Third National People's Congress four days later, Chou En-lai announced that the Panchen Lama was a traitor for having "led the reactionaries against the people, against our country, and against socialism."[19]

Following the arrest and disappearance of the Panchen Lama, Ngapo Ngawang Jigme, the ultimate collaborator, eventually became the Chairman of the People's Council, the highest Tibetan office in Tibet's so-called self rule.

Many thought the Panchen Lama had been executed or died in prison, but in 1978 he unexpectedly appeared in public in Peking, having been released by Deng Xiaoping from a political prison located not far from Peking. For fourteen years he had been held without mention by the Chinese. He remained without stature in the PRC until his death in January 1989.

To return to the resistance in Tibet: despite the extensive superiority of military firepower and the constantly increasing numbers of Chinese soldiers sent to Tibet, the Chinese continued to suffer heavy losses, reportedly more than the number that fell by the wayside during Mao's so-called "Long March." But many hundreds of Tibetans were also killed as they tried to flee Tibet, and many hundreds continued to be executed, and even hundreds more died in prison. The Volunteers also suffered increasing casualties. Unlike the Chinese with their unlimited manpower and little regard for their own casualties, each loss of a Volunteer was devastating, for replacements were in ever increasingly short supply, especially in the category of trained and experienced.

As previously noted, long before the escape of the Dalai Lama most of the resistance groups had recognized and agreed that if they were to survive and be successful in their efforts, it was necessary that they operate in small groups. The earlier days of sizable numbers of Volunteers capturing and holding areas, or of mounting up and charging Chinese forces or positions were long over. The larger groups were too easily seen by the many Chinese airplanes that were increasingly on the search whenever the skies were clear. The increased mobility, improved firepower and extensive use of artillery by the Chinese soldiers also added to the problems of the Volunteers, as did the increasing numbers of PLA armored vehicles. Even ambushes and travel by small groups of Volunteers during the day became very difficult, especially along or near the main roads, and the Chinese seldom traveled at night, even in convoys. Unfortunately for the Tibetans, the ability of the Chinese to react quickly and effectively was becoming unrelenting. By mid–1959, the operating advantage had changed to the Chinese.

For reasons only known to them, some of the resistance forces chose not to, or did not want to, recognize the necessity for operational changes, which in turn led to the death of many. And tragically, because of many interlocking circumstances, it had become the practice that when the decision was made by a Tibetan to join one of the resistance forces, he usually brought along his family, and perhaps relatives, or friends and their families, etc. Prompting this development was that it was increasingly difficult to escape from Tibet, so families understandably, but wrongly, concluded that it would be safer and better if all were together with a resistance group. This proved to be a fatal decision for most of those who made it. But how could the families of these resistance fighters have been turned away? Many tears were to mix with much blood in the terrible events that followed.

With their increased numbers the Chinese were able to establish military positions along the traditional trade routes and the main roads southward to the border areas, thereby making it extremely difficult for groups of Tibetans to escape. Those caught were usually summarily executed, the many fears of the Tibetan families about their fate being well justified. But insufficient thought was given to what bringing the families would do to increasing the danger to the resistance units, or how these dependents reduced the vitally needed mobility and effectiveness of the Volunteers. Not only were there many more mouths to feed, but also more animals to feed, and food for all was increasingly in small supply and an increasingly serious problem. Movement was slowed by the presence of dependents at a time when it badly needed to be increased. Shelter and sickness also became serious problems, for the rigors of living off the land were very demanding even for the experienced Volunteer, and all but impossible for the wives and children and the elderly. And when attacked or forced to move by the Chinese, the fighters would understandably be concerned more for the safety of members of their family than for anything else.

In some places this resulted in terrible disasters. For example, in the Pembar area in Kham there were reports of some 40,000 to 50,000 Tibetans gathered and anxious to fight the Chinese. Had they all been Freedom Fighters and able to disperse into small fighting units this would have been ideal to their cause. However, at least seventy five per cent of this number included women and children of all ages and many elderly. Most of those gathered there did not believe the Chinese would attack the large force, for the resistance fighters had for many months enjoyed repeated successes against the Chinese throughout the area, inflicting extensive damage and heavy casualties on the hated invaders. But most did not recognize that this was all the more reason why the Chinese would attack in force as soon as they were prepared and ready to do so.

"First, Chinese aircraft came to the Pembar area and located the large encampments. Then the planes returned and bombed and machine gunned the camps repeatedly for many days. The Tibetans had no weapons capable of countering attacks from the air, and many died or were wounded from the bombings. Then the Chinese soldiers came in convoys of trucks and armored vehicles, well supported by artillery and with mounted cavalry. The arriving Chinese forces were described by the surviving Tibetans as like a flood. It was soon obvious that the Chinese intended to eliminate not only the Volunteers assembled there, but all Tibetans, including women, children and the elderly."[20]

It is difficult to understand why the Volunteer units, especially the Tibetans who had earlier received training and were experienced in guerrilla warfare, permitted such a large group to assemble, for they knew better. When the large numbers were first reported by radio message, the information was received in Washington with considerable skepticism, including the possibility that the reported numbers were simply in error. However, subsequent exchanges of messages confirmed the growing numbers. The Tibetans at Pembar were instructed to form into smaller units and to disperse to other locations from which they were to continue to ambush Chinese supply convoys and patrols. Most, but not all, of the former trainees did so, taking a large number of Freedom Fighters with them as instructed, but thousands of other

Volunteers and their dependents remained in the area, including many who had been fighting the Chinese for years. Without doubt, those that chose to remain did so in order to protect their families, knowing that the families could not survive on the run, but also knowing that it was likely that most, if not all, that remained could not escape and would soon die at the hands of the Chinese.

The Chinese brought with them superior firepower, including heavy mortars, howitzers and heavy machine guns — and air support. Their bombings and bombardments were constant, and the resistance force had nothing with which to counter them. It was soon overwhelmingly evident that the only recourse for the Tibetans was to try to break out of Pembar as best they could, for slaughter in place was the only other choice.

A leader named Tulku and another named Jongdung Bhu Dhudul had arranged a defensive position there where large boulders and other natural cover provided some protection from the Chinese firepower. This compelled Chinese ground forces to advance closer in order to complete the attack, since there was no sign the Tibetans would surrender. As the Chinese drew near, the two Tibetan leaders mounted their horses and, followed by many other Volunteers, rode headlong into the advancing Chinese infantry, yelling and firing their weapons, forcing the Chinese to break ranks. Other Volunteers even managed to seize a Chinese machine gun position, from which they turned the weapon against the Chinese. The clothes of the two leaders were said to have been shredded by bullets, but their actual wounds were few and slight, nor had their horses been wounded seriously. Many of the charging Tibetans were able to ride through the broken Chinese lines and escape, largely because the disrupted formation of Chinese were hesitant to fire on the Tibetans for fear of hitting their own soldiers as the Tibetans charged through them. But as Tulku and Jongdung continued through the Chinese infantry, their horses were finally hit and fell, throwing their riders almost at the feet of the Chinese. The Tibetans that escaped were certain that the two leaders had been killed, but surprisingly, both Tulku and Jongdung, and some others from the Pembar fight, were released from prison in 1979, some 19 years after the 1960 attacks by the Chinese on Pembar. The number of Tibetans and Chinese that were killed in the Pembar action is not known, but conservative estimates put the figure into many thousands, for the area was described as red with blood, the majority of it Tibetan. Death was the fate for most that had stayed there, including the many that chose to commit suicide rather than surrender to the Chinese.[21]

Those that had decided earlier to leave the Pembar area and form into smaller groups in other areas fared far better. Most of them encountered Chinese forces, some almost daily, and had to fight many skirmishes as they fled westward or northward from the Chinese. They also quickly found that travel was best at night and away from the roads over which the Chinese used to move their soldiers and supplies in convoys almost daily. These smaller Volunteer units were still able to set ambushes along the supply routes, but to prevent pursuit by other Chinese units responding to calls for help from those being ambushed, the Volunteers often had to rely on using a series of ambushes to escape pursuing Chinese, and to use escape routes that were impassable to the Chinese vehicles. This they did, but the Chinese eventually introduced non–Han cavalry units which they used to pursue the Volunteers on trails as the latter rode from point to point. Knowledge of the terrain often became the difference between escape and death, and there were many stories of the Volunteers taking their pursuers into well laid traps from which there was no escape other than to join their ancestors. But there were also stories of members of resistance groups being run to ground and killed by the non–Han cavalry units when the Volunteers and their mounts became totally exhausted or simply collapsed from lack of water and food.

Quite often throughout the years of resistance, Chinese officers and PRC Party officials that were killed in ambushes of Chinese army convoys were found to be carrying documents that provided valuable information. For example, captured documents made clear that Chairman Mao was experiencing political difficulties with others within the party in China. Later documents noted that the so called "moderates" were losing strength and being purged. Other documents reported that the Chinese were experiencing difficulties in their provinces where other "minorities" had chosen to rebel, underscoring the need for the People's Liberation Army to quickly eliminate all resistance in Tibet. Documents also noted there was famine and starvation in some areas of China and ordered that food be taken from Tibetan storehouses and trucked from Tibet to China. That the Great Leap Forward was in reality far less than a great leap was also noted in captured documents, as was that Mao planned to send large numbers of Chinese civilians to Tibet as soon as the resistance was exterminated to settle the land, while others engaged in technical development projects important to China. Documents also contained orders that the Chinese were to eliminate all Tibetan resistance, and their families, using whatever means necessary. The early concepts of the Cultural Revolution were also intercepted, as was information on PLA forces and order of battle data relative to Tibet, including China's plans to use portions of Tibet militarily as part of their missile development plans.

The increasing numbers of mobile Chinese soldiers eventually reached the point that the Volunteers were more on the run than on the offense, pursued by soldiers in armored vehicles, or, as noted previously, by non–Han cavalry units, usually well supported by Russian-made aircraft with little or no let up. Some of the chases by Chinese units provided considerable satisfaction to the Tibetans, for it was not unusual for the pursuing Chinese to drive their vehicles over cliffs or off steep trails because they did not know the terrain; or when they suddenly found rock slides descending on them; or when the trail ended and there was no way out, the Tibetans having simply lured their pursuers into a heavy ambush. But the Volunteer units often found themselves being ambushed after they had set an ambush, thanks to the Chinese having good communications — while the resistance had little or none. Yet for nearly three years after the Dalai Lama had escaped, the Freedom Fighters continued to ambush and seriously harass the Chinese in most areas of Tibet, as best they could wherever they could, and successfully destroyed many Chinese convoys. The smaller groups continued to be effective, while the larger ones were soon recognized by even the more stubborn resistance leaders as increasingly ineffective and costly.

Resistance efforts continued largely in the south and east but also extended into some areas in the north and west. For instance, in the east the Freedom Fighters operated in the areas of Nakchuka, Choporgya, Lithang, Posul, Markham, and Gonja. In the north there were units in the areas of Koko Nor, Pema, Dzado, Jyekundo and Naksho, and in the west there were units in Sakya, Jongka and Namling. In the south there were units in Trigu, Nang, Tsethang and Sakya. The Chinese usually avoided the more distant or remote areas because of the difficulties they faced there such as altitude, cold and snow, extended supply lines, lack of suitable vehicles, little or no effective artillery support, no reinforcements readily available, lack of motorable roads, lack of shelter, and because of their deep fear of the Volunteers in any situation except where all the odds favored the PRC.

The resistance units that located into the remote areas in the north and west were able to get some rest, for they did not constantly encounter Chinese soldiers — but food and forage was scarce for them. The snow and cold in the north also made day-to-day living very difficult for both the Volunteers and their horses. In the east and south there were far more Chinese soldiers, but these areas were very well known by the Khambas, their terrain knowledge helping to offset the numerical advantages to the Chinese. However, the situation was becoming similar to the lengthening shadow of the setting afternoon sun, for bit by bit there were fewer and fewer safe places for the resistance fighters. Food was increasingly a problem, and the many days and weeks and months of constant fighting and riding were also taking a heavy physical toll on the Volunteers and their mounts.

The daily life of the Volunteers was extremely hard. Seldom was there anything other than the cold ground on which to sleep, and only a very limited amount of food and water to keep them going. It was also hard on their horses and mules, for often they were ridden hard in order that their rider could escape the Chinese, and forage was not always readily available. There were usually armed encounters of some kind with the Chinese at least three or more times a week. With fewer and fewer viable base camps from which to operate, survival and resupply became a serious problem, not just one of attacking the invader. And getting food from the people or monasteries was no longer

Tibetan nomads

a sure thing, for food was in short supply everywhere. The emotional pressure was heavy, but the Freedom Fighters continued to live day by day, still hopeful of driving the Chinese from Tibet. They also risked their lives guiding many hundreds of Tibetan families safely through the Chinese-infested areas to the border, making escape possible for those who otherwise would likely have been killed.

The Chinese, recognizing the opportunity to further hurt the resistance, resumed sending some of their soldiers into areas disguised as Tibetan Volunteers. Their intent was to maraud and mistreat the Tibetans living in the rural areas, thereby giving the resistance forces a bad name. Another purpose was to see if anyone tried to join what they thought was a resistance group, and then to arrest or kill those that did, or to identify any who evidenced any kind of support for the resistance, or anyone even talking favorably about the resistance. The Chinese also used Tibetan collaborators in these efforts, especially among the bandit bands and in a few nomad groups. Although the Chinese rewarded the turncoats well, these efforts were marginally successful at best.

After the Chinese found that they still were not very successful in trying to imitate Volunteers themselves, they offered rewards to the nomad and bandit groups to bring in resistance fighters, dead or alive, and offered rewards for weapons taken from resistance fighters. Quite often small groups of Volunteers on patrol were killed and their weapons taken by bandits in order to gain the offered rewards or simply because the bandits envied and wanted for themselves the American-made weapons of the Volunteers. The incidents of the killing by bandits of some of the Tibetans that had been trained by the CIA were especially upsetting to the resistance — and to the CIA — for these men were uniquely valuable to the Tibetan effort. And obviously, they were not easily replaced. The Volunteers learned to avoid the bandits or to simply kill them, for they were a threat to the Freedom Fighters and of no use to Tibet.

"The nomads were generally considered trustworthy, for nomads had been a part of the Tibetan landscape since time began. Most were supportive, and many fought against the Chinese ... but a few were deceitful, pretending to be friends of the Volunteers, offering them the customary hospitality of food and warmth from the fire, then, as with the bandit groups, killing them for their weapons and other belongings as they slept. There were instances when members of the Volunteer units recognized some of the weapons in the hands of the bandits and nomads they met as having belonged to Volunteers who had disappeared. If outnumbered, the Volunteers would ride off after having tea with their hosts, for they knew a similar fate awaited them if they stayed overnight. If the Volunteers were equal in number or if the opportunity presented itself, the Volunteers would not hesitate to kill. It was difficult enough to fight the Chinese, but to have to worry about the bandits and traitors was something the Volunteers did not appreciate. There were many times that these collaborators or spies were caught by the Freedom Fighters, and while the sentence was usually death, there were many times that a loss of fingers or ears or hands was judged as punishment enough, with the disfigurement serving as a warning to others. The Khamba swords were always handy for carrying out such sentences."[22]

The increasingly heavy concentration of Chinese soldiers in eastern Tibet caused the resistance leaders to decide it was time to move their main base of operations to the Mustang area in the northwestern part of Nepal near the Tibet border. This area had traditionally been Tibetan, having served Tibetan traders for decades. The Maharajah of Mustang was sympathetic to the Tibetans and had for years graciously permitted them to come and go freely. Here the resistance fighters established their enclave. The multiple passes and routes into Tibet from Mustang made it a natural choice as a base for resistance operations into western and central Tibet. From it, ambush efforts were carried out against Chinese convoys throughout the general Shigatse area as well as into areas to the west, eastward and into southern Tibet.

One of the ambushes of a small military convoy in the Shigatse area in 1961 resulted in a number of documents being recovered from the dead Chinese officers that provided detailed order-of-battle information on Chinese forces; Communist party doctrine directives, including additional reform and control measures Mao intended to implement; references to party personnel

Tibetans in Mustang area in western Nepal.

changes; numerous Chinese army journals; orders regarding the movement of many more troops into all areas of Tibet, including the western area; and instructions requiring the total elimination of the resistance and all those supporting it. Recognizing these documents to be of intelligence value, the resistance group passed them complete with the bullet holes and dried blood, by couriers who then forwarded them to others for eventual passage to the CIA in Langley, Virginia. There the contents were studied and disseminated to other interested parties, including the Indian intelligence service. Similar ambushes by Mustang-based Tibetans in subsequent periods resulted in additional captures of valuable information on Chinese political and military plans, intentions, capabilities, and party matters, such as the formation of the Red Guards, reforms, etc. In addition to the Volunteers capturing such documents, the radio teams and the trained resistance cadres reported unique and insightful information that was in turn made available to the intelligence community.

Initially there were many in Washington who were highly skeptical of the information being reported by the trained Tibetan radio teams, especially since little other or collateral data was available to corroborate it. Internal problems of and political developments in the PRC, party matters and military-related information, such as plans, intentions and strength, was a scarce commodity in the intelligence community at the time. Often the reports and documents provided by the Tibetan resistance proved to be uniquely valuable, once confidence in their reporting had been established. In one particular case involving documents captured from Chinese officers following an ambush, the analysts described the take as the best intelligence coup since the Korean War.

Many have written about the support, or lack of support, given to the Tibetan resistance by the Central Intelligence Agency, but few have been accurate in their statements. The range of these writings is from completely erroneous to very nearly correct. The following are provided as examples of the wide range of portrayals.

Michael Harris Goodman, in his book *The Last Dalai Lama*, wrote,
> A group of six Khambas were selected by Gompo Tashi to be trained by the Americans in guerrilla warfare and then to be parachuted back into Tibet. One of them was Gompo Tashi's nephew, Gyato Wangdu.
>
> The six Tibetans were taken to an unidentified island somewhere in the North Pacific — most likely Okinawa, Saipan, or Guam — and trained for four months in map reading and radio transmission. During the last month they were flown to another island which they believed was in the Philippines for cursory parachute training. Then in late 1957 they were loaded into a "small black four-engined airplane" probably belonging to C.A.T., a commercial airline and CIA proprietary based on Taiwan, and parachuted back into Tibet. Each man carried with him a pistol, a small machine gun, an old Japanese radio, $132 in Tibetan currency, and a bracelet containing vials of poison in the event of capture. Two men were dropped in southern Tibet and made their way to Lhasa, where they contacted Gompo Tashi. The others were dropped into Lithang. Of the four men who went into the heartland of Kham, only one came out again — Gompo Tashi's nephew Wangdu.
>
> In January (1958) of that fateful year Gompo Tashi Andrugtsang had arranged a meeting between the two Khambas who had been parachuted into southern Tibet and the Dalai Lama's Lord Chamberlain, Thupten Woyden Phala.... Despite his legendary sense of humor, Phala was not at all amused by the request of the two men for the help of the Tibetan government in overt resistance of the Chinese. He explained to them that this would be out of the question for a number or reasons ... [and] the Dalai Lama was still firmly opposed to armed opposition to the occupation forces ... [and] on the practical side he viewed the Chinese atrocities in Kham and Amdo "as a dreadful example of what the Chinese could do so easily all over Tibet if we fought them," and so could not give his consent to the request of the freedom fighters.
>
> Having been apprised of Phala's response, Gompo Tashi sent a message to the CIA through the two radio operators asking if the Chushi Gangdrug could count on American support if fighting broke out. The reply was disheartening: help would be given only if requested directly by the Tibetan government.
>
> It was about this time (February 1959) that the CIA decided to deliver its first consignment of weapons to the guerrilla forces. Furious that Gompo Tashi and two radio operators had left Lhasa the previous summer, they (the CIA) had adamantly refused to act unless requested to do so by the Tibetan government itself. As the year drew to a close it began to dawn on them that ... no such request would be forthcoming. With the situation in Lhasa deteriorating every day, they reluctantly decided to deal instead with the Chushi Gangdrug, and announced somewhat precipitately that the first arms drop would take place on

THE BLOOD OF PATRIOTS   237

a Lhoka plateau. When it was pointed out that this was directly over a nomad encampment, they refused to alter the arrangement. Moreover, they sent word that the guerrillas should assign a single man with thirty mules to await the shipment; the fact that it was impossible for one man to control so many of these obstreperous animals had not apparently occurred to them. The arms themselves — a hundred rifles of British manufacture, twenty submachine guns, sixty hand grenades, a pair of fifty-five millimeter mortars, and three hundred rounds of ammunition per gun — fell far short of what the freedom fighters had been led to expect. They did not realize it at the time, but it was the last shipment they should receive.[23]

This portrayal is wholly inaccurate.

In *Freedom in Exile: The Autobiography of the Dalai Lama*, the Dalai Lama is quoted as having said: "Although there was no talk at this time of an armed struggle against the Chinese, my brothers, unbeknown to me, had already made contact with the American Central Intelligence Agency. Apparently the Americans felt that it was worthwhile to provide limited assistance to the Tibetan freedom fighters, not because they cared about Tibetan independence, but as part of their worldwide efforts to deestablish all Communist governments. To this end they undertook to supply a limited amount of simple weaponry to the freedom fighters by airdrop. They also made plans for the CIA to train some of them in techniques of guerrilla warfare and then parachute them back into Tibet. Naturally, my brothers judged it wise to keep this information from me. They knew what my reaction would have been.

"... When I went into exile, I heard stories of how weapons and money were dropped into Tibet by aircraft. However, these missions caused almost more harm to the Tibetans than to the Chinese forces. Because the Americans did not want their assistance to be attributable, they took care not to supply U.S.-manufactured equipment. Instead they dropped only a few badly made bazookas and some ancient British rifles which had once been in general service throughout India and Pakistan and thus could not be traced to their source in the event of capture. But the mishandling they received whilst being air-dropped rendered them almost useless.

"... By early summer (1958) several tens of thousands of freedom fighters had joined forces and were pressing home their raids closer and closer to Lhasa, despite being poorly supplied with small arms and ammunition. Some of what they had was captured from the Chinese, some of it had come from a raid on a Tibetan ammunition dump near Tashilhunpo, and a small amount of it had duly materialised courtesy of the CIA, but they were still hopelessly ill-equipped."[24] This account is also inaccurate.*

In his book, *In Exile from the Land of Snows*, John Avedon relates: "In the aftermath of the Khambas' first victories, (the) Chushi Gangdrug had been

---

*There are extensive errors in both of the above works. See pages 336–341 for details of the CIA support.

formed: 'Four Rivers, Six Ranges'—a traditional epithet for Kham and Amdo, now used by the newly allied Tibetan chieftains as the name of their joint guerrilla organization. Gompo Tashi Andrugtsang, an important trader from Lithang, took charge in the field, while Gyalo Thondup, the Dalai Lama's second-eldest brother, who lived in Darjeeling, upgraded an intelligence-gathering operation he had established with the CIA in 1951. A small number of guerrillas were smuggled to Guam via India and Thailand, where they were introduced to modern weaponry and commando techniques. Parachuting back into Tibet at night, they took up the task of organizing the resistance on a more efficient course, aided by periodic airdrops of light arms. By then, however, the fighting had escalated, the PLA having counterattacked with a full fourteen divisions—over 150,000 troops.

"By mid-1957, a ruthless pattern of attack and reprisal developed, turning much of Kham into wasteland. The guerrillas, clad in shirts of parachute silk, wearing heavy charm boxes to protect against bullets and living on dried meat and tsampa or parched barley, operated on horseback from mountain strongholds, ambushing ... small PLA outposts and convoys coursing between the large, heavily garrisoned towns....

"To the Tibetans' great amusement, they were (at the outset of their training) forthwith dubbed Doug, Bob, Willy, Jack, Rocky, Martin and Lee, etc., confirming what many of them had already surmised, to wit, that the Communists' worst enemy had finally seen fit to become the Tibetans' best friend — a distant country called America.

"Stepping from the trucks, the Tibetans were astonished to see towering, snow-covered peaks under a brilliant starry sky. The mountains looked so familiar that for a moment some thought that they had returned to Tibet.

"Camp Hale's curriculum covered a wide variety of topics. The Tibetans were taught weaponry, survival techniques, coding, radio operations, how to organize an underground network, make letter drops and chart contact points ... parachuting, rock climbing ... and the more refined arts of espionage."[25] This is a more nearly reliable account.

On October 20, 1962, some 25,000 Chinese troops invaded over the Thagla Ridge into NEFA. At the same time some 1,500 miles to the west, a similar-sized Chinese force attacked Indian army forces in Ladakh. The PLA pushed all the way to Bomdila in the east, with the Indians fearing that the Chinese would then continue southward into the plains area of India. In the west, the Chinese seized some 14,500 square miles of the Aksai Chin. The PLA withdrew to the original McMahon Line separating India and Tibet in NEFA in late November but remained in force in most of Ladakh. New Delhi's humiliating defeat finally prompted Nehru to admit: "We have been living in a fool's paradise of our own making." Prompted by these Chinese actions, Nehru's critical attitude towards the United States changed abruptly, and he quickly requested and promptly received military equipment from the United States.

Two of the first six trainees inside Tibet in 1957.

Other than to flex some military muscle and to further intimidate India, especially in regards to Chinese claims of border areas belonging to India, the reason or reasons for the Chinese incursion into India are still the subject of debate and conjecture. But for whatever reason, it opened Indian eyes and most of those in the rest of Asia, and provided new hope to the Tibetan Freedom Fighters.

The cornerstone of India's decision to arm and protect its northern border lay in the formation, with covert CIA support in close coordination with the Indian Intelligence Service, of a new 10,000-man commando group, known as the Special Frontier Force. Formed in November 1962, under the command of the Research and Analysis Wing of Indian Intelligence, the Special Frontier Force was to be a Tibetan force (trained and commanded by Indian army officers) charged with the mission of guarding India's highest borders. Most Tibetans were delighted with this development, for it was seen by them as the Tibetan Volunteers being maintained more formally as a multipurpose entity, and potentially being the basis for a well-trained force that might be of great use to Tibet in the future. There was some opposition from many of the clergy and officials in the Dalai Lama's exile group in Dharamsala, but that was to be expected.

In order to establish historical reference, the following is a factual and chronological highlight of the CIA's support of the Tibetan resistance from 1957 to 1962:

In 1957, a pilot group of six Khambas was exfiltrated from India and flown from East Pakistan (now Bangladesh) to Saipan, where they were trained by a few selected CIA officers for four and a half months. They had been selected by Gyalo Thondup, the elder brother of the Dalai Lama and Gompo Tashi Andrugtsang, assisted by Lhamo Tsering, a close colleague of Gyalo's. The names assigned the trainees were Walt, Dan, Tom, Lou, Sam and Dick. Training included Morse code, cut numbers, radio signal plans, the U.S. made RS 1 crystal operated radio transmitter and receiver (powered by a hand cranked generator), encoding and decoding using one-time pads, use of telecodes (a Tibetan telecode was developed during the training), map and compass reading, small arms up to and including 60 mm mortar and 57 mm recoilless rifles, fragmentation and incendiary grenades, fire and movement tactics (using the basic concept of five-man fire teams), offensive and defensive ambushes, an array of simple sabotage techniques, use of demolitions, Molotov cocktails, booby traps, unarmed and hand-to-hand combat, cross-country and night movement, observation, casing, authentication, elicitation, information collection, reports writing, tradecraft techniques, resistance organizations, sketching, preparation of drop zones, parachute ground training, simple psychological warfare techniques, first aid, simple disguise techniques, and physical fitness. The six men were divided into two teams and, after three familiarization jumps at Okinawa from the infiltration aircraft, a B-17, using a modified T-10 parachute (but without a reserve parachute), and wearing forest service smoke jumper suits, the two teams were flown to a staging area to await infiltration. The two-man team of Athar and Lhotse were dropped well south of Lhasa onto a large sand bar along the banks of the Brahmaputra during a full moon in October. They cached most of their equipment for later recovery and made their way to Lhasa where they contacted Gompo Tashi Andrugtsang.

Due to heavy cloud coverage over eastern Tibet in the October full moon phase, the other team, led by Gyato Wangdu, was not infiltrated in October but was parachuted from the same B-17 over eastern Kham into an area familiar to and selected by the team during the full moon phase in November. By chance they landed near a resistance force not long after it had been in a brief firefight with a PLA unit. Ironically, the team was initially suspected of being paratroopers dropped by the Chinese. However, members of the resistance force soon recognized some of the team members and the team was warmly welcomed. After clearing the drop zone and arriving in a safe area, the team reported by radio its successful landing and contact with one of the Khamba resistance forces.

Each of the infiltrated teams carried two sets of radio equipment, back-up signal plans, Tibetan boots, hat and clothing, tsampa, dried beef, Tibetan and Indian currency, a pamphlet message of encouragement from the Dalai Lama, waterproof maps, compasses, small cooking pots, binoculars, entrenching tools, Tibetan knives, shielded flashlights with extra batteries, signal mirrors, first aid kit, flares, matches in waterproof containers, writing materials, ponchos, and a Lee-Enfield .303 rifle for each member with considerable ammunition. Each member also jumped with a folding stock Sten submachine gun with extra magazines, some canned rations, and the primary radio operator for each team also carried the primary signal plans for the team's radio. Most of this equipment, except for the submachine gun and ammo, some food, and the signal plans for the radios that were carried in a small bag attached by D-rings to the individuals, was put into a single bundle that was suspended over the "joe-hole" (where the belly gunner position was formerly located) in the B-17. This bundle was released over the drop zone and followed immediately by the jumpers, with a deployable line from the bundle attached to the first jumper to insure recovery.

Athar and Lhotse had been instructed to proceed to Lhasa to contact Gompo Tashi Andrugtsang and to assist him in organizing resistance groups, after passing word to Phala (and, assumedly, thence to the Dalai Lama) that the first group of trainees had returned to Tibet. Wangdu and his team were to make contact with resistance groups in Kham, assess their capabilities, radio their findings, and help organize and train resistance groups.

These two teams were considered a pilot group upon whose success would depend the decision of whether there would be further assistance and training. Both teams radioed their safe arrival shortly after their respective jumps and maintained contact regularly via their radios, providing information on the locations and data on the expanding resistance groups, order of battle data on the Chinese forces in their respective area, and the increasingly successful ambushing of Chinese supply convoys by the Freedom Fighters in their assigned areas of operations.

It was not long before each team requested that arms and other material be air-dropped to resistance groups, and each provided information on selected safe and suitable drop zones. However, before final approval was given to the CIA to proceed with the initial supply drops, there was a requirement levied on the Agency that the Tibetan government, i.e., the Dalai Lama, first needed to request U.S. assistance.* The State Department had earlier wanted a request from "The Tibetan Government" for assistance to the resistance, and again asked for it in 1958. This was relayed on two different occasions in radio messages to Athar and Lhotse, and was in addition to the request that

---

*This was similar to the requirement previously levied on the Dalai Lama in 1951 by the U.S. government at the time he was considering the offer of asylum for himself and other key personnel in his government.

had been made by Gompo Tashi in 1957 to Phala prior to the return of the trained teams into Tibet. When it became obvious that no such request would be forthcoming from the "Tibetan government," just as it had not come in the 1951 period, despite Tibet's provinces having suffered for years from brutal Chinese atrocities and despite the mounting resistance against the Chinese in eastern Tibet, the Eisenhower administration approved the CIA providing the support requested by the Freedom Fighters, including resupply drops as well as additional training of Tibetans by the CIA.

The first resupply drops to reception teams in Kham were made by a C-118 and restricted to some 12,000 pounds each, consisting largely of weapons (Lee Enfield .303 rifles, 60 mm mortars, 57 mm recoilless rifles, 2.36 bazookas, grenades and .30 caliber light machine guns) and ammunition. The load factor was determined by the round-trip distance to be flown and the altitude requirements. (The C-118 did not have the lift capability to fly above the mountains in Tibet but at times had to make its way through passes illuminated by the full moon, much to the particular discomfort of the navigators.)

After the initial "blind" drops in 1957 by B-17s of the teams, all subsequent drops were made to drop zones picked by teams on the ground, using the clandestine techniques they had learned in training. Following each drop, the teams radioed the amounts of equipment received and any damage incurred, which was very seldom and usually limited to one or two of the ammunition boxes in one of the bundles having a broken corner.

The teams also reported on any related problems, such as occasionally some of the fired mortar rounds (World War II vintage) failing to detonate on impact. This information enabled the CIA logisticians to change to different lot numbers to be dropped, for the last thing needed by the Volunteers was to experience faulty ordnance.

The reception teams were always advised well in advance of the total weight and the total number of bundles that were to be dropped in order to be certain that they would have enough pack animals and slings available to carry the supplies from the drop zones. In most of the drops, the contents of the bundles were configured and prepacked to enable loading directly and quickly onto the pack animals, a maximum of 80 to 85 pounds to each side of the animal, thereby reducing the time and effort required by the reception party to sanitize and depart the drop zone.

The teams provided detailed descriptions of the drop zones, identified the location of the nearest Chinese units, confirmed the authentication signals to be used, and gave timely local weather information, such as prevailing winds and the amount of cloud coverage, including the four-to-six hour periods immediately preceding the scheduled drop. Because most weather in that area of the world originates in Tibet, this was of particular use to other sources that were also providing weather data for the missions.

To improve measurably the safety of flights and increase the pay loads over that of the earlier resupply drops, C-130s with long-range tanks were used beginning in late 1958. Depending on the location of and distance to the drop zones, drops of between 15,000 to 24,000 pounds became common. Three to five drops were often made during a single full moon phase to two or more groups in order to begin to meet the supply requests from the teams on the ground. Two or three drops to the same drop zone during a single night by a lead and trailing C-130s were not uncommon. Some of these flights included parachuting into their chosen areas the Freedom Fighters that had completed their training in Colorado, along with the supplies requested by the ground teams in place.

Beginning in late 1958, U.S. M-1 rifles replaced the British .303 rifles; 80mm mortars were added to the 60mm mortars; and the 75mm recoilless rifles were added to the 57mm recoilless rifles. More 30 caliber light machine guns were provided, as were other shoulder-fired weapons, e.g., 3.5 bazookas, shot guns, sniper rifles, plus other upgraded items that the trainees had learned to use, such as demolitions, field printing presses, cameras, medical supplies and other items. The Colorado training was expanded to include a variety of psychological warfare techniques, survival courses, extensive field exercises, driver training (jeep, trucks, tank) use of snow shoes, field expedients, making and firing of simple, short range incendiary rockets, multiple ambushes, diversionary tactics, etc., all in addition to the basic curriculum given to the first trainees on Saipan.

Arrangements were also made for one of the training groups to be given a week-long special and intensive course at Quantico by the Marines, following which approval was sought and given for two Marines to be assigned on detached duty to the instructor staff at the camp in Colorado. That the Tibetans were impressed with the demonstrations at Quantico of live fire and movement and uses of firepower is an understatement. It was also difficult to explain to the Tibetans that unlike what their own situation would be in Tibet, the Marines were not equally concerned in demonstrations with having to conserve ammunition, especially not during their very impressive "mad minute" of night firing of multiple weapons that the Tibetans particularly enjoyed.

Estimates of the number of airdrops into Tibet range from 35 to 40, the great majority of which were from C-130s. (Exact records were not located.) This calculates into a minimum of 550,000 to nearly 800,000 pounds of material being parachuted to the Volunteers plus the trainees that were parachuted into Tibet after training. This is not an insignificant accomplishment, especially under the difficult operational circumstances attendant to the clandestine and highly sensitive undertaking involved. A small number of brave American air crews repeatedly risked their lives to fly into Tibet's unchartered high country to make these drops, and each crew competed, and took great pride, in putting the drops "on the money," i.e., in the middle of the drop zones. The strong attachment of the air crews to the Tibetans was evident, and many of the crews sought to be assigned the missions despite the hazards involved.

Unfortunately and in retrospect, the effort to support the Tibetans began far too late, and that none of it had been requested by the "Tibetan Government" in Lhasa hindered widespread political support for Tibet in the U.S. government. That only those who were committed to fighting to save their country from an invader were asking for help, while the government of the country at serious, if not fatal, risk would not ask for assistance was not easily understood by either those who were fighting to save their country or by the government bureaucrats in Washington from whom approval was needed to provide the help. Fortunately, President Eisenhower was very supportive, as was, at least initially, President Kennedy. However, the downing of a U-2 on May 1, 1960, and the capture in Russia of the pilot Gary Powers led President Eisenhower to suspend the C-130 resupply flights into Tibet.

Other miscellaneous points of information needing emphasis and clarification include: as with the first six trainees, no American was involved in the selection process of those chosen to be trained. The selection continued to be a function performed primarily by Gyalo Thondup, Lhamo Tsering and Gompo Tashi Andrugtsang. Because of this, and as to be expected, the majority of the trainees were Khambas from southeastern Kham and a few from adjoining areas in Kham. Only a few Amdos and but two or three Goloks were trained, despite requests by the CIA officers for trainees from all areas. The difficulty of selecting trainees from the more remote areas as opposed to being able to locate eager Khambas in areas not far from the borders is the obvious answer as to why few non–Khambas received training and subsequent support from the CIA. A companion problem to this situation was that all but a small fraction of the many resistance groups and leaders that had been impressively successful against the Chinese in 1955, 1956, and 1957 — long before Gompo Tashi Andrugtsang organized his resistance efforts — were not able to receive airdrops because there was no radio communications with them.

Also serious was the difficulty in arranging the exfiltration of trainees and the locating of English-speaking interpreters. Locating volunteers for the program was not a problem for the Tibetans involved in the process, but there were not many qualified English speakers among the Tibetans; still, trainers and trainees quickly adapted to one another.

The bureaucratic delays in getting policy approval to assist the Tibetan resistance also seriously impacted the program. Not until years later was it recognized just how extensive and serious the impact was. Had there been a much earlier decision to assist the Tibetans, including training of and aerial resupply available to more Tribal groups, there is no doubt that the Tibetans would have, at a minimum, very severely tested the Chinese. As stated above, but unknown at the time, when the first six arrived at Saipan in 1957 for training, it was already too little and too late. That they and subsequent groups accomplished as much as they did for as long as they did and under the circumstances existing is only all the more impressive.

As for other operational data worth noting, only one Tibetan was reported injured among all those scores that parachuted into Tibet. He received a concussion resulting from jarring his head while landing (all but a couple of the drop zones used in Tibet were between 12,000 and 15,000 feet above sea level), but he recovered after a day or two of rest. No doubt the quality football helmet all Tibetans wore in jumping saved his life. No one was hurt while making parachute jumps during training, with most of the training classes making three familiarization jumps in one day.

All air dropped supplies were recovered and receipted for by radio by the receiving teams. No crewmen or planes were lost or damaged. No Americans were ever with any of the Tibetan resistance groups on the ground in Tibet. There was never any involvement of any kind by the Chinese Nationalists in any phase or part of this program. There was never an incident of a trainee causing a serious problem of any kind at any point. One trainee had an emergency appendectomy (Saipan); one accidentally wounded himself slightly during training; and one other suffered a serious head laceration (Colorado), but all quickly recovered. During driver training (jeep, truck and tank) in Colorado, there were some close calls — as to be expected — but no injuries to drivers, passengers or instructors, although some of the terrain and vehicles took a beating. And to the delight of the Tibetans, they were far more successful than the Americans in handling the very large mules that were obtained for use as pack animals for field training exercises in Colorado.

The training curriculum was constantly reviewed and modified to meet the needs of the resistance. And some of the English-speaking Tibetans were given the opportunity to see other parts of the U.S., including Washington and New York — and the U.N. — and to observe and experience academia and government in action.

Athar and Lhotse, after escorting and reporting the progress and location of the Dalai Lama during his escape, and performing as the communications relay link to obtain India's approval of refuge for the Dalai Lama, became assistant instructors in 1960 in Colorado for trainees that followed the pioneering efforts of the first six. They returned to India with the last group of trainees.

Wangdu, one of the original six trainees and leader of the team infiltrated into Kham in November 1957, survived years of fighting in Tibet and relocated to the Mustang base in northwestern Nepal as one of the key leaders there when operations in eastern Tibet were no longer feasible. In 1969 he became the commanding officer of the Mustang base when Baba Yeshe, one of the top leaders and former heroes in the Chushi Gangdrug, was relieved of command there.

In 1973 Baba Yeshe, apparently seeking revenge because of having been relieved, along with a few of his followers, offered his services to the Nepalese in return for asylum. He provided the Nepalese full details of the Tibetans' Mustang base and its complete modus operandi. The Chinese had begun to pressure King Birendra in 1973 to force the closure of the Mustang base, which prompted the ordering by the King of some 10,000 Nepalese soldiers and Gurkhas into the Mustang area in early 1974. Much to the dismay of the Freedom Fighters, the Dalai Lama also sent a taped message to the Mustang forces telling them to lay down their arms and to surrender peacefully. With much anguish, most did so, but some chose to commit suicide rather than give up the fight against the Chinese invader. Then the Nepalese reneged on their earlier promises to assist the Tibetans to relocate and launched an abusive arrest operation against all those who surrendered, seizing all the land and property of the large base.

Wangdu, upon learning of the duplicity of the Nepalese, quickly gathered some of the vital operational records and with a small cadre began the 200-mile ride to the Indian border. Unfortunately, Bapa Gen Yishi had provided the Nepalese, and thence the Chinese, with information on the route that Wangdu would likely take. Pursued and escaping a number of ambushes set for him and his men along the way, Wangdu and the others became a victim of the treachery when they were intercepted by a large Chinese patrol near Tinker pass, a border location at an altitude of nearly 18,000 feet. Their magnificent effort came to an end 20 miles from safety when Wangdu, in advance with four others of the rest of his small group, realizing there was no escape, charged head-on into the Chinese. He and the four with him died in a hail of bullets. Most of the others in his party managed to escape under cover of darkness following a long firefight by scaling the cliffs along the border, then reaching the safety of an awaiting Indian army patrol.[26]

From the extensive information provided by Bapa Gen Yishi and the documents that the Nepalese and Chinese recovered from Mustang and Wangdu — and shared with the Chinese by the Nepalese — the clandestine informant nets and assets that had been carefully established and nurtured in nearly all areas of Tibet for nearly 20 years were identified and subsequently arrested or neutralized. This was all but an impossible setback to the resistance effort and ended resistance operations from the Mustang base.[27]

Many have asked why the Tibetans usually enjoyed the impressive success rates — more often than not 10 or more to 1— over the Chinese that they did. There were a number of factors that gave the Tibetans distinct advantages, none of them mysterious nor difficult to understand. First, Tibetans, especially the tribals such as the Khambas, Amdos, and Goloks, learned to shoot and ride at a very early age. They quickly became excellent marksmen, for

Opposite: **Tibetan trainees at Camp Hale, Colorado, 1961.**

being a good rider and a good shot were very important to a Tibetan. Often life depended on such abilities, such as eluding or fending off Tibetan bandits or bagging game. And they learned to shoot many weapons, for there have always been many different kinds in Tibet because of the extensive trading by the tribals with India, Nepal, Sikkim and China. And when hunting they needed to be good shots, for ammunition was expensive and precious, and game was not always plentiful. Equally important, the Tibetans had lived their lives as independent, proud, free spirits, as had their ancestors.

In contrast, the Han Chinese were generally very poor marksmen. Most had not learned to shoot until they were in the army, and even there they shot only a few rounds during training, for the Chinese did not "waste" money on such things as ammunition and firing ranges. The Chinese army depended more on heavy fire from artillery pieces and massive numbers of ground troops and less on individual accuracy. Further, the Chinese soldier was usually not well led, nor was he usually mentally prepared for combat and thus was easily frightened. The Chinese have historically been quite good with artillery, reflecting the many years that China's armies were trained and indoctrinated by the German military that historically believed strongly in the use and effectiveness of artillery to command the battlefield. But the military role of the individual Chinese soldier has largely been ignored in favor of simple blind obedience and strict political demands.

However, the single major advantage of the People's Liberation Army in Tibet over the Freedom Fighters was their ability to communicate quickly with all echelons. They had extensive radio equipment enabling voice communications between units, including air-ground, whereas the Tibetans had no such rapid interunit communications capabilities. This posed countless problems for the Freedom Fighters, who usually had to rely on couriers on horseback or signal mirrors to communicate with other units. This remained an overwhelming disadvantage that did not improve until the Mustang base became fully operational in the mid–1960s. Two other distinct advantages the Chinese employed effectively were the use of air power and the extensive use of indirect fire, most of it long-range. Finally, the above factors, combined with the increasing and endless supply of manpower employed by the Chinese, made the final result inevitable.

Despite their numerical advantages, the Chinese soldier was seldom prepared to improvise or to survive in difficult situations. The Tibetan, however, is strong willed and mentally well prepared to meet most if not all challenges. The Tibetan had to survive in difficult circumstances from an early age and was taught to be self-sufficient, including being able to face and overcome the threat from bandits or marauding nomads. The Chinese soldier does not share such a background and is more comfortable and used to being told what to do than having to make a decision on his own.

Like his Mongolian brothers of yesteryear, from an early age the Tibetan learned to be an excellent rider, whereas most of the so-called Chinese cavalry was largely for parades, not for combat. The Chinese cavalry improved over time but only when the non–Han minorities were brought in as cavalry. The Han horseman was usually less than good under fire and was described by the Tibetans as being far better riding away from a fight than riding towards one.

The Tibetans also learned at an early age how to wield a sword. On the other hand, the Chinese were afraid of the blade and totally intimidated by Tibetans riding at them with drawn swords. The sight and sound of hard-riding and shouting Volunteers with drawn swords charging a position would likely frighten most, and far more often than not the Chinese chose to flee in disarray.

The Tibetans were instinctive fighters and knew how to use the terrain to their advantage, which could not be said of the Chinese in the hostile geographical environment of Tibet.

The hard terrain and high altitudes proved to be very difficult to the Chinese soldiers, and their endurance proved to be very limited. These were distinct advantages to the Tibetans, and many Tibetans, and others, argue strongly that if necessary support (training, better weapons, voice communications, and ready resupply) had been available in the early 1950s, the Chinese would not have succeeded or would have paid a terrible cost even for the Han mentality, for they would have died by the thousands in the easily defended passes and high altitude between Tibet and China.

The biggest advantage to the Tibetans was motivation. The Tibetans were fighting for His Holiness, the Dalai Lama, and his and their freedom. The Chinese soldiers were in Tibet because they had been ordered there and were fighting only because their officers had ordered them to do so. The nonmilitary Chinese assigned to Tibet, such as the political cadre and the police, were not there by choice either, nor did they like it. To the contrary, they found Tibetans and Tibet's geography hostile and totally foreign to what they were used to so it was largely survival for them, in contrast to the high motivation and determination of the tribals.

There were other distinct and measurable differences that could be attributed to initiative, intuitiveness, determination, self-reliance and other qualities, but all basically stemmed from or were extensions of the Buddhist faith and the joy of freedom so dear to the Tibetans. On the other hand, the Chinese had no such faith or foundation. The lot of the Chinese soldier is not a happy one, for he is treated poorly, trained poorly, paid poorly, led poorly, clothed poorly, housed poorly, is harshly disciplined and motivated primarily by fear. He knows only to blindly follow orders and to obey Party doctrine. These factors may yet serve to the advantage of Tibet and the other formerly free areas swallowed by China, for they are serious flaws not easily corrected by party dogma.

Sadly, the unheeded warnings and dire predictions of the thirteenth Dalai Lama have served as an epitaph for Tibet these past six decades. He was amazingly accurate. Although Tibet will never be the same as it once was, that is not necessarily all bad, for much needed to be changed, as the fourteenth Dalai Lama has often stated. Most of the Tibetans fortunate enough to have escaped have learned much about themselves and the world since becoming refugees. Hopefully this knowledge will continue to be skillfully applied and serve to insure a better future for Tibetans. In this regard, education of all that can be provided with it is totally essential, for professional skills in most of the higher disciplines remains seriously lacking among the thousands of refugees.

That the majority of those in Lhasa who wore the robes of rank in the Buddhist religion and in government were significant and major contributors to Tibet's fall is very sad but factual. Totally unschooled in and all but unknowing about the realities of the outside world of the twentieth century, secure only in what they had learned in their studies or been told by like-minded abbots and lamas, and zealously jealous of any perceived threat to their power and positions, most of the religious leaders in Lhasa and of the monasteries clung to their archaic view of the outside world and remained unwilling to accept changes in Tibet's unique but totally antiquated system of government. Most of the ranking government officials shared these viewpoints.

As noted in Goldstein's book, *A History of Modern Tibet, 1913–1951: The Demise of the Lamaist State*, the jealousies and insecurities of the Lhasans prompted them to repeatedly and successfully challenge and thwart the thirteenth Dalai Lama in his modest attempts to bring a sense of modernization and unity to Tibet. This thinking and attitude also insured that no such ideas would be presented to or pursued by the fourteenth Dalai Lama. The youth of the fourteenth Dalai Lama and the demanding challenges of China abetted the ranking clergy totally, and most of his like-minded tutors. Whereas the thirteenth Dalai Lama had the benefit of British input, the teen-aged fourteenth Dalai Lama had only his close circle of monastics to guide him, until he and they were overwhelmed by the military and political persuasions of Chairman Mao and the less than objective views and perceptions of Prime Minister Nehru. How unfortunate.

Nor did the Dalai Lama choose to listen to his older brothers or to seek advice from others in India whose advice might have been helpful, such as Indira Gandhi, the British or the Americans. Instead, most of what was written at the time reflects that he chose to listen to Ngapo Ngawang Jigme and others who chose the benefits of collaboration over the interests of their country. Thus the Dalai Lama was advised by the untrustworthy and the fearful but high-ranking lamas in Lhasa and the like-minded members of the Kashag, etc., most of whom apparently were more concerned for themselves than for Tibet.

His advisers failed to tell him that Mahatma Gandhi had succeeded by combining passive resistance with repeated, extensive and well executed civil disobedience supported by both Hindus and Moslems. Passivism by itself has not worked, as religious struggles over the centuries have well documented, and as the thirteenth Dalai Lama warned. Unfortunately, history was again ignored. By returning to Lhasa first from Yatung, and then again later from India, the Dalai Lama lost the fleeting opportunity to change the history of Tibet and the world's perception of Chairman Mao's China and India's Nehru.

The Tibet of tomorrow must be different, for governing and government in this and in the next century far exceed the abilities of any one person. Tibet's strength, and her primary industry, has been her religion. The spiritual leader role of the Dalai Lama, and perhaps that of the Panchen Lama as well, need not be changed. But Tibet needs an elected government structure separate from the less than impartial concerns of the lamas and abbots, with the elected being scholars of government in order that they can judiciously implement the will and vision of the people unimpeded by but with the cooperation and support of the religious leaders. This will not be easy to accomplish, for resistance to changes will be strong. But the prosperity and security of Tibet's future is now in the hands of its youth. There need not be nor should there be competition between her government and religious leaders, only mutual understanding, respect and cooperation. And Khambas and Amdos, and all the tribals need to be educated and brought into key roles in the government. The divisive practices of the old ways cannot be repeated. Tibet can no longer be a simple agricultural country under the management of monastic and bureaucratic landlords. This time, history must be heeded.

There are natural riches in Tibet that will require careful development by Tibetans trained in the disciplines related to those riches. But these and other future careers require education in many categories, including doctors, engineers, scientists, ecologists, geologists, teachers, managers, builders, businessmen, architects, communications experts, etc. There need not be any infringement on monastic practices, but neither should there be a return to the days of thousands of monks in thousands of monasteries throughout a Tibet with closed borders and closed minds. Education vital to Tibet's future goals and potential is a priority both vital and urgent, for without it Tibet will be ill-prepared to meet her many future challenges and prospects.

But the immediate goal is for Tibet to regain her autonomy, thereby enabling the Dalai Lama to return to Lhasa. Otherwise, Tibetans might well lose their sense of hope and determination.

Tibet was never a Shangri-La, but neither did it deserve to be the devil's lair that the Chinese have wrought. The Chinese have defiled themselves in what they have done in and to Tibet and in the other regions that China has unjustly seized but none to the extent of the devastation brought to Tibet. The blood of well over one million Tibetans is on China's hands. But like invaluable jewels, Tibet's religion, culture and Dalai Lama remain free, serving the Tibetan people as precious symbols of the past and as hope for the future.

The Chinese yoke of tyranny cannot endure. China's false gods of Marxism and Communism will crumble, just as they did in the Soviet Union. One hopes this will occur before the current Chinese policy and practices in Tibet of assimilation or extermination of Tibetans, better known as genocide, are completed. It may be a close call, for, shamefully, few seem to be willing to challenge China or even to call for an investigation of the issue of abuses of human rights. In the United States, China continues to enjoy the official status and benefits of a most favored nation. Shamefully, politics and corporate business interests have clearly succeeded over sincere humanitarian considerations for the enslaved people that China still controls militarily. In the United Nations there is not a whisper of Tibet, only occasional lip service.

The strength of Tibetan will and purpose can prevail if given a chance, but wise, meaningful and enduring help from the Free World is needed if Tibet and Tibetans are to eventually achieve their rightful place among free nations. The alternative prospects for Tibet — and the influences of the Free World — are not at all encouraging.

Epilogue

Tibet continued to be the scene of more Chinese-caused death and destruction throughout the 1960s, 1970s, and 1980s. Tibetans were especially helpless during the period when Mao's brutal Red Guards ran wild in Tibet under the banner of the so-called "Cultural Revolution." With only a reduced resistance to contend with, the Chinese made no pretense of hiding their obvious intent to totally destroy all aspects of Tibet's religion and thousands more of Tibetans as well. The destruction that had not been completed by the People's Liberation Army prior to the arrival of the Red Guards soon became an art form under the latter's zealous pursuits. There was more raping, destruction of monasteries, mock trials and even instances of armed conflict between competing factions of Chinese military as well as between Chinese communist political entities in Tibet. Caught in the middle of these violent disagreements, as well as being targets themselves, the sufferings and casualties of the Tibetans constantly increased. That Tibet and Tibetans managed to survive at all is surprising and a credit to their steadfastness and to their religion, without which there would have been little to sustain them.

The excesses of the Red Guards in China were less than those in Tibet, for the simple reason that there were fewer restraints on the Red Guards in Tibet than in China. Military commanders, party cadre, Chinese officials, etc., all were intimidated and bullied by these unholy products of Chairman Mao. Although it is a story that has not yet been fully detailed, in his book, *In Exile from the Land of Snows*, John Avedon provides an insightful sample of what transpired in Tibet during the years of siege and terror there by the Red Guards, but they are not the subject of this book and are mentioned only because of their added terror to Tibetans.

The cult of Mao, which, to be more historically accurate, should be known as the Mao dynasty, remains very much alive in China, was and is a reflection of the egocentric ambitions and eccentricities of him and his wife, Jiang Jing. Mao's pursuit of the ill-defined Chinese grail of "Socialism" gave birth to a feeding frenzy of so-called reforms and controls in China that have continued for nearly five decades. Although at a somewhat reduced rate, they still continue.

For example, the high drama of the 1989 demonstrations in Tiananmen

Square followed by the massive and brutal arrests of the gathered students, and then arrests throughout the country of other so-called dissidents, served to expose the naked brutality and unbending political doctrine that still exists in Communist China today.

Mao Tse-tung was originally consumed by visions of extended military greatness, but it appears that the earlier expansionist ambitions that he and most of his inner circle had in the 1950s have, over time, been replaced by defensive and economic concerns regarding their vast empire. These concerns are currently redirected more into the aspirations and ambitions fueled by economic and financial possibilities. But the PLA is also busily trying to modernize its massive military, and its presence throughout the vast reaches of China reminds one and all that it remains the single strongest force in China. Her navy is also expanding and modernizing, as is her air force. Both the so-called "hard liners" and the "soft liners" in China's political arena recognize that the military leadership has a significant position of extensive influence and remains the single most powerful factor even in the Politburo.

The previous "old guard" power brokers are presently few and have little more than a ceremonial input into the policies of the emerging China. Soon none of them will be left. However, most of the old habits, doctrine and policies will likely endure for at least a relatively brief period of time, as will the stringent control factors and fears that have been implanted and established throughout China for nearly fifty years, for they provide needed stability.

The new leadership that will emerge will very likely feel the need to demonstrate its own strength and ability in order to retain and command internal control as well as recognition as a world power and to insure that China can fully realize the economic opportunities the future holds. She will continue to seek international recognition as a leading economic power in world trade, but how the new leadership of China, including her military, will demonstrate stability, power, strength and control remains an unknown at this point in time.

Will the likely saber rattling on the horizon be the seizure of the Spratly Islands in defiance of the competing claims there of Vietnam, Taiwan, Malaysia, Brunei and the Philippines? In 1974 China claimed and drove Vietnam from the Paracel Islands, and in 1988 the Chinese sank three Vietnamese ships in a brief naval battle in the Spratly islands; thus a precedence of sorts has been set. Or will China choose to challenge the United States and dare to attack Chinmen and/or other Chinese Nationalist held islands in the Taiwan Straits? Will China's military threats to Taiwan continue? The ever-flexing Han military tentacles and the Han political ego do not make for a reassuring future, unless the prospects of economic and financial gains persuade the Chinese to forego, at least temporarily, the temptations of demonstrating her military power.

Regardless, China will remain solely under the control and leadership of the party Mandarins, the only question being whether that leadership will be civilian or military, or an uneasy partnership of sorts between the two. For many reasons, including the vital factor of control, the ingredient especially needed by the military and the Party, Communist doctrine (read "discipline") in China is not likely to diminish soon.

As was and is being experienced in the previous Soviet Bloc, vestiges of centralism will likely remain until and unless in the evolution of power the "new" leadership of China decides or is forced to purge the practices and symbols of Communism. There is little prospect that there will be a gradual erosion, for either there is control or not, and the military will likely remain judge and jury on that point. Thus the key question is what will ultimately influence the decision(s) of the Chinese military? Will China remain "Evil Empire II"? Or will her shell crack and break as in the Soviet Union?

As previously noted, China's political structure will of necessity undergo significant changes and restructuring within a decade or less. This metamorphic change will be driven by ever-increasing, and competing, economic, financial and political factors. The economically advantaged and the economically disadvantaged sectors in China will be key factors in these competing considerations and could lead to serious internal fracturing. Add to these problems the continued and serious divisions that exist between the Han and the non–Han Chinese in the more remote "provinces" and it is possible to conclude that extensive civil unrest is distinctly possible, particularly if the Chinese military, in part or total, should become disaffected with the leadership in Peking.

China could easily become a country of economic and military zones, as well as political ones, not unlike China's historic practices and periods of war lords. Such temptations will exist, for no government in Peking can meet the consumer demands or personal aspirations of China's overpopulation once the appetite is whetted. The bicycle prosperity for the masses of today will not satisfy the appetites of tomorrow, and unless revisionist cleansing and deliberate starvation practices are again used against her own people, China's problems will increase as her population grows and economic differences between her areas become more pronounced and difficult to control.

In the meanwhile, all Tibetans continue to suffer, for those in Tibet have had no benefits from the vast military complex installed in their country nor from the exploitation by the Chinese of Tibet's many natural resources, including forests and minerals. China has concerned herself only with China's needs and forced the Tibetans in Tibet to a much lower standard of living than ever before experienced, including starvation caused by food shortages. And the lot of most of the Tibetan refugees in India is not a good one either, except in comparison to those in Tibet.

The development of Tibet by the People's Liberation Army as a military stronghold and as an area for development of China's missile programs was and is a part of the story of China's quest for military supremacy in the East. Her brief and senseless muscle-flexing attacks on India in October 1962 and then years later on the border areas of Russia, and also her attacks on North Vietnam, were more the result of inflated ego trips by the Communist Han political mentality than any well-planned military attempt to add to the vast holdings of the People's Republic. That thousands of Indian and Vietnamese soldiers died and that far more thousands of Chinese died needlessly because of these vain attacks had little impact on the leaders of Communist China. Similarly, her skirmishes with Russian troops along their respective border areas have resulted in the deaths of many on both sides, again with no meaningful purpose.

However, these actions did serve to let the rest of the world, particularly the West, finally recognize China's limited and less-than-modern military abilities, despite its near limitless numbers of soldiers. Tibetan resistance successes had earlier proved and underscored this point, but most of the world's political leaders and military experts failed to recognize or understand it. China also clearly demonstrated to India and the nonaligned nations her lack of moral and diplomatic responsibilities, her disregard for treaty agreements, her near total lack of concern for even her own people, and that the words and promises of the leaders of the PRC cannot be trusted.

Many of these same points were recognized earlier by some of the nonaligned countries, especially by then Singapore's President Lee Kuan-yew, who refused to be intimidated by Mao's huffing and puffing. North Korea's Kim Il-sung, North Vietnam's Ho Chi-minh and Moscow's leadership also recognized China's limited military abilities. And so did China, finally, and these past few years have seen a near frantic activity to modernize and upgrade her military strength. China's borders are many and extensive, requiring a huge commitment of manpower and logistics support to maintain her military presence. This is an expensive undertaking, regardless of the age of the equipment or the size of the force structures involved. And the costs will not diminish so long as China's current policy continues.

Of the three Resolutions by the United Nations General Assembly on Tibet, the first, in 1959, probably had more impact than the succeeding two. It, and the report by the International Commission of Jurists preceding it, surfaced many of the horrible things that Tibetans had suffered at the hands of the Chinese Communists. None of the three resolutions to date have managed to keep an international spotlight on Tibet; however, some world sympathy and support has been generated, but this has not changed the Chinese brutalities in Tibet. The concerns related to the Chinese practices of genocide and human rights violations in Tibet have been noticeably avoided by the leaders of the Free World. No clarion call has been raised, not even support for a proposal for an independent investigation as urged and requested by the Dalai Lama. And sadly, while the Dalai Lama and the plight of the Tibetan people have been embraced privately by many, politically they are largely officially ignored, shunted aside more or less as but another unfortunate international orphan.

Throughout this extended period, the United Nations (and especially its democratic members) only reaffirmed and continued to clearly demonstrate serious inabilities, ineptness and lack of courage, in essence repeating its shameful lack of support to Tibet's original request for help in 1950. As Prime Minister Nehru so aptly labeled it years ago, the United Nations is simply and starkly ineffective. It serves only a few and only in limited ways. Its philanthropic efforts, especially for children, are commendable but could be accomplished equally well, more expeditiously and less costly by the International Red Cross.

The United Nations has little, if any, integrity left; at best it needs a total overhaul and relocation out of the United States. At worst, as demonstrated by its heavy costs and ineffectiveness as a worthy world organization, it is a candidate for the bone pile or simply to be recognized as a center for international debate, with no other powers or functions. Harsh words? Yes. Deserved? Yes.

The problems of any government in exile are many, and those of the Tibetan community are to be expected. The wisdom of continuing a theocracy is but one of many considerations, especially in that there are still few members of the present Tibetan government who are wise in the way of world affairs and the realities of international politics. In simple terms, belief in the Dalai Lama and a free Tibet are the main sustenance for all the Tibetans. Anything less than such a hope will in time result only in serious differences, disintegration and abandonment of that hope, leaving China free to complete her destruction of Tibet and Tibetans.

Unfortunately, there is division among those in Dharamsala in regard to the best policy to pursue with China. There are those that favor an accommodation with China that would allow the Dalai Lama to return to Tibet but with Tibet remaining a Chinese region. Others are strongly opposed to any such arrangement, insisting that the Dalai Lama should return only when Tibet is free. The Dalai Lama has spoken on both sides of the argument, and presently appears inclined to make an accommodation of sorts, with the difference appearing to be one of semantics, degree and interpretation. And his remains the most influential vote.

Part of the problem is the Dalai Lama's oft-expressed interest and belief in Socialism. That is difficult to understand, for it is in conflict with reality. For example, in *Freedom in Exile: The Autobiography of the Dalai Lama*, he writes on page 268: "... Yet the pursuit of Communism has been one of the greatest human experiments of all time, and I do not deny that I myself was very impressed with its ideology at first. The trouble was, as I soon discovered, that although Communism claims to serve 'the people', (it) does not mean everyone, only those who hold views that are held by a minority to be 'the people's views.'" He added, "Some of the responsibility for the excesses of Communism rests squarely on the West. The hostility with which it greeted the first Marxist Government accounts in part for the often ludicrous precautions they took to protect themselves.... However, in as much as I have any political allegiance, I suppose I am still half Marxist. I have no argument with Capitalism, so long as it is practiced in a humanitarian fashion, but my religious beliefs dispose me far more towards Socialism and Internationalism, which are more in line with Buddhist principles. The other attractive thing about Marxism for me is its assertion that man is ultimately responsible for his own destiny. This reflects Buddhist thought exactly."

Yet on the page before those quotes (p. 267), the Dalai Lama wrote, "The truth remains that, since the Chinese invasion, over a million Tibetans have died as a direct result of Peking's policies. When adopting its resolution on Tibet in 1965, the United Nations stated plainly that China's occupation of my homeland has been characterized by 'acts of murder, rape and arbitrary imprisonment; torture and cruel, inhuman and degrading treatment of Tibetans on a large scale.'"

This lack of reality or continuity of thought from one page to another is not easy to understand or to equate. Given the Socialist and Communist accomplishments and "benevolent" practices demonstrated in Russia and throughout the old Soviet Union and the People's Republic of China, North Korea and Tibet, and given the widespread human losses resulting from Marxist/Leninist inspired killings, purges and starvation in all of them, how does one support or forgive such "experiments"? And as for "One World," or "Internationalism," neither allows or provides for freedom and independence, thus are as rife with false promises and ultimate terror as Socialism and Communism. And both are flawed and failed.

To measure the real benefits of these wonders is to compare the numbers of votes cast by the feet of the millions who have fled countries that adopted such philosophies, against the numbers that have left freedom to be a part of the delights of Socialism and Communism. What percentage for the latter? 1 percent? Less? And did not the deaths of more than a million Tibetans leave a message? Or the deaths of some thirty-five to sixty million or more Chinese purged or starved under Mao? Can freedom be treated in such a cavalier manner? How many Tibetan refugees have returned to Tibet as opposed to the number who continue to leave Tibet? And what of the thousands of Tibetans that have been killed while trying to escape from the parade of promises made by the Chinese while forcing Tibet to return to the Great Motherland of China. Tibet is truly China's shame.

China has continued to experience serious problems in Tibet despite her total and overwhelming domination. As reported and shown on TV, there have been many serious outbreaks against the Chinese in Lhasa and other areas in Tibet over the years. Despite the irony of Tibetans now finding themselves to be a minority in their own country, the thousands of Tibetans that are refugees in India and in other countries — and the many more thousands that remain in Tibet — exist on and are sustained primarily by the expectation that the "Red Devils" will eventually leave Tibetan soil and that Tibet will again be free, enabling the Dalai Lama's return to Lhasa.

Obviously, it is not likely that the Chinese will opt to depart Tibet — or any other of her seized non–Han regions — unless or until there are heavy outside influences and persuasive pressures brought to bear on China by other countries. The chances of this happening are slim at best at this point in time, and with China assuming new stature as she commands Hong Kong in 1997 it is not likely that the major bastions of freedom will have the courage to stand up to or challenge China economically or diplomatically, much less militarily. For Tibet, there are no simple solutions.

Further muddying the waters and causing divisions in Dharamsala are the efforts by the Chinese Nationalists and the Kuomintang party (KMT) to influence the Tibetan refugee groups. Through bribes and promises, the KMT has enjoyed some successes, primarily because of the influences of money. Sadly, the KMT reportedly managed to win over one of the survivors of the first group of trainees, who at one time in more recent years enjoyed some political following among the refugees but who is now shunned because of his having become a shill for the KMT. The promise of money now and full autonomy later in exchange for support for the KMT position is a temptation that not all Tibetans can, particularly under their present circumstances, refuse. Like a political commandment, poverty and despair tend to weaken strong political persuasions.

But the main issue within the exile group is independence. "China has said that aside from independence everything between Tibet and China is negotiable; Tibetans answer this by saying that with independence everything between Tibet and China is negotiable. We are willing to negotiate with China, but only as equals."[1]

"What I ceased to have, ... is my faith in our current Government-in-exile's ability to work with the people, and stand up for their rights! What is even more depressing is the fact that we are witnessing the beginning of an era of petty politics, and factional squabbles within the Tibetan community.... It is a fact that the overwhelming majority of Tibetans in Tibet long to live free and independent lives. Anybody who pays any attention to Tibet knows that. Therefore, by the virtue of our being in the free world, is it not the duty of our Government-in-exile to carry out the wishes of the Tibetan people, and wholeheartedly work for Tibetan independence?"[2]

"If we have learned one thing, then it is that our very survival depends upon the achievement of a genuinely free Tibet. The issue, therefore, is independence. Toward this end, our cries will be relentless and our cries will be heard. We will not be silent."[3]

These are brave and moving words. However, without meaningful support for Tibet from the Free World there is little or no hope that the People's Republic of China will soon change. As noted earlier, the United States, driven by economic persuasions, continues to bow to and give China the status of a "Most Favored Nation," while the United Nations simply ignores the status of Tibet. In stark contrast, both the United States and the United Nations were anxious to commit extensive resources and armed forces and to charge onto the continent of Africa, and into Haiti, and into Bosnia waving the banners of freedom and democracy. How inspiring! How absolutely incongruous! How totally political.

And how sad that those who want only to regain their freedom and their country are deafened by the silence of those who choose to do little other than occasionally speak in eloquent terms on the subject of human rights.

APPENDIX A

Text of the Dalai Lama's Cable to the U.N., September 9, 1959

Your Excellency Mr. Hammarskjoeld:

    Kindly refer to the proceedings of the General Committee of the United Nations General Assembly held on Friday, 24th November, 1950, at which it was resolved that the consideration of El Salvador's complaint against the invasion of Tibet by foreign forces should be adjourned in order to give the parties the opportunity to arrive at a peaceful settlement. It is with the deepest regret that I am informing you that the act of aggression by the Chinese forces has not terminated. On the contrary, the area of aggression has been substantially extended with the result that practically the whole of Tibet is under the occupation of the Chinese forces. I and my government have made several appeals for a peaceful and friendly settlement, but so far these appeals have been completely ignored. In these circumstances and in view of the inhuman treatment and crimes against humanity and religion to which the people of Tibet are being subjected, I solicit immediate intervention of the United Nations and consideration by the General Assembly on its own initiative of the Tibetan issue, which had been adjourned. In this connection, I and my Government wish to emphasize that Tibet was a sovereign State at the time when her territorial integrity was violated by the Chinese armies in 1950. In support of this contention, the Government of Tibet urge the following:

    1. No power or authority was exercised by the Government of China in or over Tibet since the declaration of independence by the 13th Dalai Lama in 1912.

    2. The sovereign status of Tibet during this period finds conclusive evidence in the fact that the Government of Tibet concluded as many as five international agreements immediately before and during these years.

    3. The Government of Tibet take their stand on the Anglo-Tibetan Convention of 1914 which recognized the sovereign status of Tibet and accorded the same position to the Tibetan plenipotentiary as was given the representatives

of Great Britain and China. It is true that this convention imposed certain restrictions on the external sovereignty of Tibet, but these did not deprive her of her international position. Moreover, these restrictions ceased to have any effect on the transfer of power to India.

4. There is no valid and subsisting international agreement under which Tibet or any other Power recognizes Chinese suzerainty.

5. The sovereign status of Tibet is equally evident from the fact that during the Second World War Tibet insisted on maintaining her neutrality and only allowed the transport of non-military goods from India to China through Tibet. This position was accepted by the Governments of Great Britain and China.

6. The sovereign status of Tibet has been acknowledged by other Powers. In 1948, when a trade delegation from the Government of Tibet visited India, France, Italy, the United Kingdom and the United States of America, the passports issued by the Tibetan Government were accepted by the Governments of these countries.

Your Excellency, My Government also solicit immediate intervention of the United Nations on humanitarian grounds. Since their violation of the territorial integrity of Tibet, the Chinese forces have committed the following offenses against the universally accepted laws of international conduct:

(1) They have dispossessed thousands of Tibetans of their properties and deprived them of every source of livelihood and thus driven them to death and desperation;

(2) Men, women and children have been forced into labour gangs and made to work on military construction without payment or on nominal payment;

(3) They have adopted cruel and inhuman measures for the purpose of sterilizing Tibetan men and women with a view to the total extermination of the Tibetan race;

(4) Thousands of innocent people of Tibet have been brutally massacred;

(5) There have been many cases of murder of leading citizens of Tibet without any cause of justification;

(6) Every attempt has been made to destroy our religion and culture. Thousands of monasteries have been razed to the ground and sacred images and articles of religion completely destroyed. Life and property are no longer safe and Lhasa, the capital of the State, is now a dead city.

The sufferings, which my people are undergoing, are beyond description and it is imperatively necessary that this wanton and ruthless murder of my people should be immediately brought to an end.

It is in these circumstances that I appeal to you (Mr. Hammarskjoeld) and the United Nations in the confident hope that our appeal will receive the consideration which it deserves.[1]

APPENDIX B

U.N. General Assembly Tibet Resolution, October 21, 1959

On October 21, 1959, the United Nations adopted a joint Malay-Irish resolution on Tibet, which, without naming the Chinese People's Republic, deplored the violation of the fundamental human rights in Tibet and called for their restoration.

Forty-five nations supported the resolution. Nine opposed it. Twenty-six countries, including India, abstained. Two, Guinea and Costa Rica, were absent.

The following is the text of the resolution:

"The General Assembly,

"Recalling the principles regarding fundamental human rights and freedom set out in the Charter of the United Nations in Universal Declaration of Human Rights adopted by the General Assembly on December 10, 1948,

"Considering the fundamental human rights and freedoms to which the Tibetan people, like all others, are entitled include the right to civil and religious liberty for all without distinction,

"Mindful also of the distinctive cultural and religious heritage of the people of Tibet and of the autonomy which they have traditionally enjoyed,

"Gravely concerned at reports, including the official statements of His Holiness the Dalai Lama, to the effect that the fundamental human rights and freedoms of the people of Tibet have been forcibly denied them,

"Deploring the effect of these events in increasing international tensions and embittering the relations between peoples at a time when earnest and positive efforts are being made by responsible leaders to reduce tension and improve international relations,

"1. Affirms its belief that respect for the principles of the Charter and of the Universal Declaration of Human Rights is essential for the evolution of a peaceful world order based on the rule of law,

"2. Calls for respect for the fundamental human rights of the Tibetan people and for their distinctive cultural and religious life."

The voting analysis:

Yes—(45): Argentina, Australia, Austria, Bolivia, Brazil, Canada, Chile, Kuomintang China, Colombia, Cuba, Denmark, Ecuador, El Salvador, Malaya, Greece, Guatemala, Haiti, Honduras, Iceland, Iran, Ireland, Israel, Italy, Japan, Jordan, Laos, Liberia, Luxembourg, Mexico, Netherlands, New Zealand, Nicaragua, Norway, Pakistan, Panama, Paraguay, Peru, the Philippines, Sweden, Thailand, Tunisia, the U.S., Uruguay, Venezuela.

No—(9): Albania, Bulgaria, White Russia, Czechoslovakia, Hungary, Poland, Rumania, Ukraine, Soviet Union.

Abstentions—(26): Afghanistan, Belgium, Britain, Burma, Cambodia, Ceylon, Dominican Republic, Ethiopia, Finland, France, Ghana, India, Indonesia, Iraq, Lebanon, Libya, Morocco, Nepal, Portugal, Saudi Arabia, Spain, Sudan, South Africa, the United Arab Republic, Yemen, Yugoslavia.

Absent—(2): Guinea, Costa Rica.[1]

APPENDIX C

Statement of H.H. the Dalai Lama on the 20th Anniversary of the Tibetan National Uprising of March 10, 1959

This article was received from *News-Tibet* (published by the Office of Tibet in New York, N.Y., Volume XIV, No. 1, 1979) and reprinted in the *Tibet Society Newsletter*, No. 7, Spring 1979.

Today, at this commemoration of the 20th Anniversary of the Tibetan National Uprising, I extend my warm greetings to all Tibetans both inside and outside Tibet. We encompass a variety of ideologies, attitudes, and professions, yet we are united by our common language, race, and traditions.

During the past 20 years, the 100,000 or so Tibetan refugees (the majority in India and the others in 16 countries outside Tibet) have been supporting themselves by agriculture, small business, handicrafts, etc. Their situation is improving and they are becoming self-sufficient. Of special importance are the over 20,000 young Tibetans who, possessing both traditional learning and modern education which are like wings for a bird, are joining the mainstreams of modern life. Our religion and culture, considered "poison" by the communist Chinese, are not only being preserved, but are also spreading among the people in different social strata and races; they are gaining interest and respect in the East as well as in the West.

Cultural and religious institutions are firmly established in Tibetan settlements in India. Politically, we are following a democratic system of government and adhering to principles of freedom and liberty in deed as well as in word. Considering that we were forced from our homeland and scattered in many countries, we have achieved much worth remembering for the society and individual. These achievements must not make us complacent, however, we must strive for greater progress, especially because the main reason we are in exile is our concern for the welfare of the six million Tibetans in Tibet. Hence, while learning from our past experience and without being discouraged by our tragedy, we must persevere in carrying out the struggle until the day when all Tibetans are fully satisfied and happy and when peace and freedom have been restored to our homeland.

The Chinese, of course, not only accuse us of being against progress, against the revolution, and against the Tibetan people, but also of being oppressive and deviant. It is not necessary for us to repeat that these are lies and fabrications; we ourselves do not lie. The free world knows how hard we have tried to follow the path of progress; what we have done to preserve our ancient culture and identity, and how much we have done in terms of justice and impartiality to ensure the well-being of our people. Our actions are as clear as writing on a wall. If friends, enemies, or neutral observers investigate the true situation of the past 20 years, then it will be easy for them to decide who has been telling the truth, who is following the correct path; it will then be obvious who changes from one year to the next, who obscures all under propaganda so unreliable and contradictory that it appears to have been issued by a lunatic.

For instance, we did not suffer from delusions when we challenged the might of the Chinese military. From 1955 to 1959 in desperation the Tibetan populace opposed, resisted, and then rose up in open rebellion against the Chinese, declaring "Chinese quit Tibet; Tibet will be governed by Tibetans." This spontaneous feeling was enunciated by all Tibetans, but the Chinese declared that their opponents in Tibet were the American imperialists (the U.S. was then considered the enemy of China), the Indian expansionists, and just a few Tibetan reactionaries who were fomenting trouble internally and leading the uprising. The Chinese forcibly suppressed the Tibetan national uprising while announcing to the world that the people of Tibet were on the side of China.

In a like manner, in China itself many campaigns were successively launched from 1958 onward such as "the great leap forward," "the cultural revolution," "learn from Tachai" and so forth; it is common knowledge today that these campaigns were failures entailing huge losses and human suffering. Nevertheless, at that time, the Chinese claimed that these campaigns were a success. Moreover, many Chinese leaders involved in these campaigns were purged under various pretexts and vilified, but when conditions necessitated their reinstatement, they were restored with excuses. In a short period, we have seen a Chinese leader who was purged and reinstated again and again with a variety of reasons given for these changes. As a result, the Chinese people, being intelligent human beings, no longer believe the words of their leaders. The same is true vis-a-vis nations; the Soviet Union, previously a close and trusted ally of China, is now regarded as an implacable foe.

For a long time the Chinese economy and system of education have been beset with problems. Until recently, the solution to these difficulties was to drum up propaganda about "great successes"; even workers and common cadres were required to publicize statistics learned by rote. The amount of energy expended on this could have moved mountains and shaken seas, but instead these efforts did nothing but exhaust the people. In order to catch up to the rest of the world, cope with reality, and modernize China, great changes in Chinese policies have taken place recently. Since the creation of imaginary facts through propaganda was not sufficient to solve China's problems, Vice-Premier Teng Hsiao-ping has repeatedly made such statements as "seek truth from facts," "the people of China should have the right to express their long-standing suffering and wishes through wall posters and slogans," "it is no use pretending that one's faults and backwardness do not exist and to act superior," or "we must recognize our mistakes and backwardness." Unlike previous Chinese leaders, Teng often reveals a praiseworthy desire for honesty, modernization, and leniency.

The present Chinese leaders should abandon past dogma, narrow-mindedness, and fear of losing face and should recognize the present world situation. They should perceive and acknowledge their mistakes as well as accept reality and the right of all people to equality and happiness. It is not sufficient to merely put such insights on paper: They should be put into practice. If these insights were strictly translated into practice, then all problems could be solved with honesty and justice.

During the commemoration of the last anniversary of the March 10th uprising, I said that the Tibetans in Tibet who desire to travel abroad should be allowed to do so and that those outside Tibet should be able to visit their country and meet their fellow countrymen. If this freedom existed, then the truth about conditions on both sides would be clearly known by all. This interchange is the right of the Tibetans as well as a practical and humane policy.

The initiation of opportunities for Tibetans to visit families and relatives is a correct and appropriate event, but these visitors must see the actual, ordinary condition of Tibet and not mere show. The pockets of sadness were hidden from the foreigners who recently visited Tibet and such elaborate preparations prior to the visits were made that the tour resembled staged dramas. Such deception may serve its purpose once or twice, but in the end will only bring disgrace as has been clearly demonstrated by recent events in China. I hope that the Chinese will not try such things on Tibetan visitors to Tibet.

In order to determine the truth about conditions in Tibet from visitors, we shall have to investigate whether satisfactory conditions existed for meetings between visiting Tibetans and their relatives or other Tibetans in Tibet. I hope that any Tibetans who desire to travel will be able to do so without restrictions and that such opportunities will not be denied with flimsy excuses or pretexts as have been done in the past.

My statements, based on our experience in the past 20 years, may not be welcomed by the present Chinese occupation forces and some Tibetan cadres at first. Nevertheless, by putting aside bias and chauvinism, by remembering our past experiences as they actually occurred, by not being narrow-minded and egotistical or making such statements as "The east wind will prevail over the west wind," the Chinese must be objective and judge the good and bad aspects and conditions in both the "east" and the "west." I have faith that this address will become the basis for distinguishing truth from falsehood, and thereby effect improvement.

In conclusion, I make special mention at this 20th year of exile of the Government of India's aid to Tibetan refugees, in particular the settlements for our people, education for our youth, and facilities for our religion and culture. The Indian government has a strong humanitarian concern in general, but in particular it is applied to Tibetans because of the centuries of excellent relations between our countries as well as our religious and cultural ties which resemble the relationship between patron and guru. For such assistance and care, I thank the central government of India, the various state governments, and the people of India for all their goodwill during this unprecedented period of tragedy in the history of Tibet. Their efforts will be accorded an important chapter in the history of Tibet and of Buddhism.

APPENDIX D

Text of September 7, 1995, Letter to President Clinton

Written by a Trusted Representative of the Dalai Lama Protesting the State Department Statement Broadcast by Voice of America on August 24, 1995

President Bill Clinton
The White House
Washington, D.C. 20500

September 7, 1995

Dear President Clinton,

    I greatly appreciate your recent efforts to support human rights and freedom of religious expression in Chinese occupied Tibet, including your reception of His Holiness the Dalai Lama. While I applaud your and especially your wife's stand on humanitarian issues in Tibet and China, I would like to express my disappointment with the recent statement by the State Department and broadcast by Voice of America on August 24: "*Like many other countries, the U.S. recognizes that Tibet is part of China.*" This statement does not reflect the position of the U.S. Congress, which in 1991 recognized Tibet as an illegally occupied country, nor does it reflect the democratic ideals of our country and the American people. While I understand that the administration has not yet brought itself in line with the expressed wishes of the Congress, I feel it is counterproductive to broadcast this position over Voice of America. By so doing, you lend your support to the Chinese government's oppressive hand in Tibet. The true nature of the Chinese regime has revealed itself yet again through the harassment and infringements on human rights that have occurred at the United Nations Conference on Women in Beijing. In case you decide not to change your position on the legal status of Tibet, it would be better for the victims of torture and Chinese oppression if you simply leave it unsaid.

    Thank you very much for your attention and good will.

Yours sincerely,*

cc: Vice President Gore

*The signature is not shown here to protect the privacy of the signator.

Glossary

Akshobhya the Buddha of the state of perfect cognition
Amban Chinese political commissioners posted in Lhasa from the early 19th century until 1911 when the Tibetans forced the Chinese from Tibet
Amdo one of the major provinces of Tibet; now Quinghai province
Amdo tribes numerous, widely scattered in and across northeastern Tibet and northwestern China
Blue Chinese the Chinese who relocated into Tibet, primarily in Lhasa, before the Communists assumed to power. The PRC thought them to be pro–Tibetan, thus not trustworthy and forced them to return to China.
Bo (or Po) Tibetan name for Tibet
Bodhisattva a being that compassionately refrains from attaining nirvana until others also attain that state; integral to the Wheel of Life in Buddhism
Buddha the Enlightened One
chang barley beer
Chang Tang plateau covers much of northern Tibet. It is the largest area in Tibet and rich in minerals
Charm Box amulet of good fortune worn by Tibetans
Chorten Tibetan stupa
Chushi Gandrug literally, Four Rivers, Six Ranges; refers collectively to Kham and Amdo and was the adopted name of some of the resistance fighters
coracles lightweight boats made of yak skins
Dapons Tibetan Army commanders
Derge kingdom
Dorje symbolic thunderbolt, with Lotus flowers; indestructible
Dronyerchemmo title of monk official heading the Dalai Lama's personal staff
Dzasak Tibetan rank of general
dzo a gentle animal, half yak, half Indian cow; also known as a Jhabboo
Dzongs location of County/Province governments, usually fortified
Ganden (monastery) the seat of the Gelugpa order (yellow hats)
Gangtok capital of Sikkim
Geshe scholarly monk who has completed the highest degree in the monastic system of education, usually of the Gelugpa order
Golok tribes (major) Butsang, Khangring, Khangsar, Tsangkor; located in eastern Tibet
Kalimpong trading center in northeast India, near Tibet-India border
Kaloons government of Tibet cabinet members
Kashag government of Tibet cabinet
Kham a province located in eastern Tibet; one of the three major provinces of Tibet
Khamba tribes (major) Bachu, Changthang, Horpas, Markham, Nakchu, Nangchen, Rakhi Gumpa, Thargyen, Yadi
Khell 1 khell equals 26 pounds
Koko Nor basin site of Tibet's largest lake, estimated to cover 1,700 miles
Kuomintang Chinese Nationalist Party
Kusang Regiment Dalai Lama's personal bodyguard unit
La Tibetan for mountain pass
Lhasa Convention of 1904 British established a precedent of direct negotiation

with Tibet including the claim of being a most favored nation in Tibet with special interests in Tibet. In return, Tibet agreed not to permit any foreign power to intervene in its affairs.

Ling-kor a five mile path around the Potala considered to be a sacred walk by Tibetans

Manchu Dynasty overthrown in 1911, at which time China became a republic

National People's Congress first session was held in Peking, April 17, 1959

Ngari ancient name for the province of western Tibet

Norbulingka name of the summer palace of the Dalai Lama

Om Mani Padme Hum sacred and popular Tibetan prayer meaning "Hail to the Jewel in the Lotus," or "Hail to the Buddha in Our Hearts"

Oracle one who serves as a medium for protecting deities through practice of trances and divinations

Panchen Lama literally, "great teacher"; associated with Tashilhunpo monastery in Shigatse since the 17th century. Second to the Dalai Lama in religious authority.

Peking Convention of 1906 China confirmed the Lhasa Convention of 1904

PLA acronym for People's Liberation Army

Potala "Abode of the Gods," popularly referred to as the winter palace of the Dalai Lama. Started under the Fifth Dalai, it measures some 1,000 feet high and 900 feet long.

PRC acronym for People's Republic of China

Red Devils a term used by the Tibetans to describe the Chinese invaders

Red Hill located about one mile west of Lhasa

Regent a politically powerful representative of an incarnate lama

reincarnation a phase in the Wheel of Life

Rinpoche a title bestowed on highly revered lamas

Rupon Tibetan Army rank equal to captain

St. Petersburg Convention of 1907 Russia recognized the special interests Britain had acquired in Tibet and both Britain and Russia agreed not to interfere in Tibet. The word *suzerainty* was used for the first time in this convention to designate China's relation with Tibet.

Shape rank of a senior member of the Kashag, the highest government body

Shinje Choegyal the Tibetan Lord of Death

Sikang Chinese province

Simla Conference, October 1913 Tibetan, British and Chinese delegates on equal footing initialed an Agreement that recognized nominal Chinese suzerainty over Tibet. Shortly after, the Chinese government declined to ratify the agreement, thus never formally recognizing themselves as the suzerain power.

Szechuan Chinese province

Tashilhunpo Monastery traditional palace of the Panchen Lama in Shigatse

Tensuk Shapten religious ceremony

Thamzing a coercive process involving forced self-confessions practiced extensively in Tibet by the Chinese

Tibet Autonomous Region established in April 1956 by the PRC

Trunyachemmo one of the four heads of the Yigtsang, the highest order of monks

Tsampa roasted barley flour

Tsang province to the west of U, of which Shigatse is the capital

Tsang-Po the Tibetan name for the Upper Brahmaputra River where it flows eastward and across southern Tibet in Central Tibet

Tsinghai Chinese province

Tso Sung Tibetan charm boxes

U traditional province in Central Tibet, of which Lhasa is the capital

Utsang the provinces of U and Tsang, effectively Central and political Tibet

Younghusband, Sir Francis led the 1904 British military expedition into Tibet which eventually resulted in close relations being established between the British and the 13th Dalai Lama

Notes

Preface

1. M. Huc. *Travels in Tartary Thibet and China.* p. ix.
2. Gompo Tashi Andrugtsang, interview, 1959.
3. John Avedon. *In Exile from the Land of Snows.* p. 1.

Chapter 1

1. "Tibet." Dr. Raghu Vira. April 1960. p. 38.
2. Ibid. p. 41.
3. Ibid. p. 43.
4. Ibid. pp. 41, 42.
5. Ibid. p. 42.
6. "United Asia: Survey on Tibet." January 1959. p. 54.
7. "Tibet." Dr. Raghu Vira. April 1960. p. 47.
8. Chanakya Sen. *Tibet Disappears.* 1960. p. 4.
9. "United Asia: Survey on Tibet." January 1959. p. 154.
10. Ibid. p. 155.
11. Ibid. p. 156.
12. Ibid. p. 156.
13. Peter Fleming. *Bayonets to Lhasa.* 1984. p. 258.
14. Ibid. p. 304.
15. "United Asia: Survey on Tibet." January 1959. p. 157.
16. Ibid. p. 157.
17. "Tibet." Dr. Raghu Vira. April 1960. p. 52.
18. "United Asia: Survey on Tibet." January 1959. p. 157.
19. Chanakya Sen. *Tibet Disappears.* p. 10.
20. "United Asia: Survey on Tibet." January 1959. p. 158.
21. Melvyn Goldstein. *A History of Modern Tibet, 1913–1951: The Demise of the Lamaist State.* 1989. pp. 52–53.
22. Ibid. p. 54.
23. Ibid. p. 54–58.
24. Ibid. p. 59.
25. Ibid. p. 62–63.
26. "United Asia: Survey on Tibet." January 1959. p. 159.
27. Ibid. pp. 159–160.
28. Ibid. p. 161.
29. "Tibet." Dr. Raghu Vira. April 1960. p. 68.

30. Ibid. p. 69.
31. Ibid. pp. 69–71.
32. Goldstein. *History of Modern Tibet.* 1989. pp. 70–73.
33. Ibid. p. 73.
34. Chanakya Sen. *Tibet Disappears.* p. 11.
35. Goldstein. *History of Modern Tibet.* p. 66.
36. Ibid. p. 82.
37. Fleming. *Bayonets to Lhasa.* pp. 305–6.
38. Ibid. p. 306.
39. Goldstein. *History of Modern Tibet.* 1989. p. 89.
40. Ibid. p. 120–21.
41. Ibid. p. 121.
42. Ibid. p. 142.
43. Ibid. p. 144.

Chapter 2

1. Goldstein. *History of Modern Tibet.* pp. 204, 205.
2. Ibid. p. 278.
3. Ibid. pp. 280, 281.
4. Ibid. p. 284.
5. Ibid. p. 287.
6. Ibid. p. 287.
7. Ibid. p. 288.
8. Ibid. p. 288.
9. Ibid. p. 315.
10. Ibid. pp. 324, 325.
11. Ibid. p. 379.
12. Ibid. p. 380.
13. Ibid. p. 390.
14. Ibid. p. 392.
15. Ibid. p. 396.
16. Ibid. p. 398.
17. Ibid. pp. 401, 402.
18. Ibid. p. 409.
19. Ibid. p. 409.
20. Fleming. *Bayonets to Lhasa.* p. 306.
21. "United Asia: Survey on Tibet." p. 162.
22. Chanakya Sen. *Tibet Disappears.* p. 13.
23. Goldstein. *History of Modern Tibet.* p. 266.
24. Ibid. pp. 558, 559.
25. Chanakya Sen. *Tibet Disappears.* p. 13.
26. Ibid. pp. 14, 15.
27. Harrison E. Salisbury. *The Long March: The Untold Story.* 1985. p. 266.
28. Ibid. p. 316.
29. Ibid. pp. 195, 196, 269.
30. Ibid. p. 304.
31. Thubten Jigme Norbu, interview, 1995.
32. Goldstein. *History of Modern Tibet.* p. 642.
33. Chanakya Sen. *Tibet Disappears.* p. 19.

34. Gompo Tashi Andrugtsang, interview, 1959.
35. Goldstein. *History of Modern Tibet.* pp. 180, 181.
36. Gompo Tashi Andrugtsang, interview.
37. Ibid.
38. Chanakya Sen. *Tibet Disappears.* p. 18.
39. Ibid. p. 19.
40. Ibid. p. 21.
41. Thubten Jigme Norbu, interview.
42. Goldstein. *History of Modern Tibet.* p. 735.
43. Chanakya Sen. *Tibet Disappears.* p. 109.
44. Ibid. pp. 110, 111.
45. Ibid. pp. 112, 113.
46. Ibid. p. 114.
47. Ibid. pp. 114, 115.
48. Ibid. p. 116.
49. Ibid. p. 117.
50. Ibid. p. 118.
51. Ibid. pp. 118, 119.
52. Goldstein. *History of Modern Tibet.* pp. 740, 741.

Chapter 3

1. Thubten Jigme Norbu, interview.
2. Michael Harris Goodman. *The Last Dalai Lama.* 1986. p. 183.
3. Thubten Jigme Norbu, interview.
4. Archibald T. Steele. *In the Kingdom of the Dalai Lama.* 1993. p. 96.
5. Thubten Jigme Norbu, interview.
6. Goldstein. *History of Modern Tibet.* p. 759.
7. Ibid. p. 760.
8. Ibid. pp. 762, 763.
9. Roger Hicks and Ngakpa Chogyam. *Great Ocean.* 1984. pp. 78, 79.
10. Goldstein. *History of Modern Tibet.* p. 771.
11. Ibid. pp. 772, 773.
12. Ibid. pp. 796, 798; and Thubten Jigme Norbu, interview.
13. Tenzin Gyatso. *Freedom in Exile: The Autobiography of the Dalai Lama.* 1990. p. 65.
14. Goldstein. *History of Modern Tibet.* p. 813.
15. Gompo Tashi Andrugtsang, interview.
16. Ibid.
17. Chanakya Sen. *Tibet Disappears.* p. 22.
18. Ibid. pp. 22, 23.
19. Geshe Wangyel, a Kalmuk monk (Lama), during many conversations with him about Tibet between 1958 and 1961.
20. Ibid.
21. Gompo Tashi Andrugtsang, interview.
22. Ibid.
23. "United Asia: Survey on Tibet." pp. 166, 167.
24. Gompo Tashi Andrugtsang, interview. (He also made brief reference to some of these same points on pages 34 and 39 of his book, *Four Rivers, Six Ranges.*)

Chapter 4

1. Gompo Tashi Andrugtsang, interview.
2. Ibid.
3. Ibid.
4. Craig Dietrich. *People's China*. 1986. p. 75.
5. Chanakya Sen. *Tibet Disappears*. p. 77.
6. "United Asia: Survey on Tibet." p. 167.
7. Gompo Tashi Andrugtsang, interview.
8. "United Asia: Survey on Tibet." p. 167.
9. Gompo Tashi Andrugtsang, interview.
10. Ibid.
11. Ibid.
12. Hicks and Ngakpa. *The Great Ocean*. p. 90.
13. Ibid. p. 91.
14. Tenzin Gyatso. *Freedom in Exile*. p. 92.
15. "United Asia: Survey on Tibet." p. 168.
16. Ibid.
17. Ibid. p. 169.
18. Ibid. pp. 169, 170.
19. Chanakya Sen. *Tibet Disappears*. p. 120.
20. Ibid. p. 121.
21. Ibid. p. 122.
22. Ibid. p. 123.
23. Ibid. pp. 125, 126.
24. Ibid. p. 127.
25. Ibid. p. 128.
26. Ibid. p. 128.
27. Ibid. p. 128.
28. Gompo Tashi Andrugtsang, interview.
29. Ibid.
30. Ibid.
31. Thubten Jigme Norbu, interview.
32. Gompo Tashi Andrugtsang, interview.

Chapter 5

1. "United Asia: Survey on Tibet." p. 170.
2. Ibid. p. 172.
3. Ibid. p. 168.
4. Gompo Tashi Andrugtsang, interview.
5. "United Asia: Survey on Tibet." p. 170.
6. Gompo Tashi Andrugtsang, interview.
7. "United Asia: Survey on Tibet." pp. 170, 173.
8. Gompo Tashi Andrugtsang, interview.
9. Ibid.
10. Ibid.
11. Jamyang Norbu. *Warriors of Tibet*. 1979. p. 97.
12. Ibid. pp. 106, 107.
13. John Avedon. *In Exile from the Land of Snows*. 1973. p. 44.
14. Gompo Tashi Andrugtsang, interview.

15. Ibid.
16. Ibid.
17. Thubten Jigme Norbu, interview.
18. Ibid.
19. Ibid.
20. Ibid.
21. Ibid.
22. Gompo Tashi Andrugtsang, interview.
23. Thubten Jigme Norbu, interview.
24. Gompo Tashi Andrugtsang, interview.
25. Jamyang Norbu. *Warriors*. pp. 122, 123.

Chapter 6

1. Thubten Jigme Norbu, interview.
2. Michael Harris Goodman. *The Last Dalai Lama*. 1986. pp. 228, 229; Gompo Tashi Andrugtsang, interview; "United Asia: Survey on Tibet." p. 191.
3. Tenzin Gyatso. *Freedom in Exile: The Autobiography of the Dalai Lama*. 1990. p. 105.
4. Gompo Tashi Andrugtsang, interview.
5. Ibid.
6. Ibid.
7. Ibid.
8. "United Asia: Survey on Tibet." p. 171.
9. Thubten Jigme Norbu, interview.
10. Ibid.
11. Gompo Tashi Andrugtsang, interview.
12. Michel Peissel. *The Secret War in Tibet*. 1973. pp. 72, 77.
13. Jamyang Norbu. *Warriors*. p. 117.
14. Ibid. pp. 111, 112.
15. Ibid. pp. 114, 115.
16. Hicks and Ngakpa. *Great Ocean*. p. 102.
17. Gompo Tashi Andrugtsang, interview.

Chapter 7

1. Gompo Tashi Andrugtsang, interview.
2. Gompo Tashi Andrugtsang. *Four Rivers, Six Ranges*. 1973. p. 150.
3. Hicks and Ngakpa. *Great Ocean*. pp. 102, 103.
4. Gompo Tashi Andrugtsang, interview.
5. Tenzin Gyatso. *Freedom in Exile*. p. 105.
6. Gompo Tashi Andrugtsang, interview.
7. Ibid.
8. Ibid.
9. Ibid.
10. Ibid.
11. Ibid.
12. Tenzin Gyatso. *Freedom in Exile*. p. 127.
13. Gompo Tashi Andrugtsang, interview.
14. Ibid.

Chapter 8

1. Gompo Tashi Andrugtsang, interview.
2. Ibid. (There are instances in Gompo Tashi Andrugtsang's book, *Four Rivers, Six Ranges*, where the datum cited differs from that he provided in our discussions in Darjeeling in 1959 on the same or similar topics. I have chosen to cite the information from the interviews since we met not long after he had left Tibet, and he impressed me as being very confident in the details he then provided. In either case, the differences or changes do not detract from or alter the many magnificent achievements of this exceptional man and those of thousands of his fellow Freedom Fighters.)
3. Ibid.
4. Ibid.
5. Ibid.
6. Ibid.
7. Ibid.
8. Gompo Tashi Andrugtsang. *Four Rivers, Six Ranges*. 1973. p. 71.
9. Gompo Tashi Andrugtsang, interview.
10. Ibid.
11. Jamyang Norbu. *Warriors*. pp. 128, 130, 135.
12. Hicks and Ngakpa. *Great Ocean*. p. 105.
13. Ibid. p. 104.
14. Tenzin Gyatso. *Freedom in Exile*. p. 128.

Chapter 9

1. Gompo Tashi Andrugtsang, interview. 1959.
2. Ibid.
3. Ibid.
4. Ibid.
5. Ibid.
6. Ibid.
7. Gompo Tashi Andrugtsang. *Four Rivers*. p. 114.

Chapter 10

1. Roger Hicks and Ngakpa Chogyam. *Great Ocean*. 1984. p. 107.
2. (Tibet) Dr. Raghu Vira. April 1960. p. 79.
3. Roger Hicks and Ngakpa Chogyam. *Great Ocean*. 1984. p. 109.
4. (Tibet) Dr. Raghu Vira. April 1960. p. 79.
5. Roger Hicks and Ngakpa Chogyam. *Great Ocean*. 1984. p. 110.
6. Gompo Tashi Andrugtsang, Athar and Lhotse interviews, 1959. Athar and Lhotse were two of the first six Khambas trained and parachuted into Tibet in 1957. Both escorted the Dalai Lama during his escape from Tibet in 1959. Both later assisted as instructors at the Tibetan training site in Colorado.
7. Ibid.
8. Ibid.
9. Ibid. Also noted in *Great Ocean*. p. 116.
10. Ibid. Also noted in *Great Ocean*. p. 117.
11. Athar and Lhotse, 1959 interviews.

NOTES (pages 186–221)

12. Gompo Tashi Andrugtsang, Athar and Lhotse interviews, 1959.
13. Athar and Lhotse, 1959–1960 interviews.
14. Athar and Lhotse, 1959–1960 interviews.
15. Gompo Tashi Andrugtsang interview, 1959.
16. Roger Hicks and Ngakpa Chogyam. *Great Ocean*. 1986. p. 121.
17. Chanakya Sen. *Tibet Disappears*. 1960. p. 320.

Chapter 11

1. Chanakya Sen. *Tibet Disappears*. p. 129.
2. Ibid. pp. 131, 132.
3. Ibid. pp. 133, 135, 137.
4. *Peking Review*. May 5, 1959 (Special Tibet Number).
5. Ibid.
6. Chanakya Sen. *Tibet Disappears*. pp. 141, 144.
7. Ibid. p. 146.
8. Ibid. p. 149.
9. Ibid. p. 150.
10. Ibid. p. 153.
11. Ibid. pp. 154, 156.
12. Ibid. p. 153.
13. Ibid. pp. 154, 157.
14. Gompo Tashi Andrugtsang, interview.
15. Chanakya Sen. *Tibet Disappears*. pp. 224, 226.
16. Ibid. p. 226.
17. Ibid. pp. 242, 243.
18. Ibid. pp. 294, 304.
19. Ibid. p. 277.
20. Gompo Tashi Andrugtsang, interview.
21. Chanakya Sen. *Tibet Disappears*. pp. 330, 356.
22. Ibid. pp. 154, 158.
23. Ibid. p. 365.
24. Ibid. pp. 470, 471.
25. Ibid. p. 473.
26. Hicks and Ngakpa. *Great Ocean*. 1984. p. 125.
27. Chanakya Sen. *Tibet Disappears*. pp. 412, 413.
28. Ibid. pp. 412, 413.
29. Ibid. pp. 414, 415.
30. Thubten Jigme Norbu, interview.
31. Galbraith, John Kenneth. *A Life in Our Times*. 1981. pp. 395, 396.
32. Thubten Jigme Norbu, interview.

Chapter 12

1. Gompo Tashi Andrugtsang, interview.
2. Gompo Tashi Andrugtsang. interview. A similar version of this is related in John Avedon's *In Exile from the Land of Snows*. 1984. p. 59.
3. Ibid. (Also referred to in Avedon's *In Exile*. p. 234.)
4. Gompo Tashi Andrugtsang, interview.
5. Ibid.
6. Michel Peissel. *The Secret War in Tibet*. p 177

7. Harrison E. Salisbury. *The Long March: The Untold Story*. 1985. p. 326.
8. Gompo Tashi Andrugtsang, interview.
9. Ibid.
10. Ibid.
11. Ibid.
12. Ibid.
13. Ibid.
14. Avedon. *In Exile*. p. 233.
15. Anonymous. (1995 interview with a former Volunteer now living in the United States who requested anonymity.)
16. Ibid.
17. Ibid.
18. Gompo Tashi Andrugtsang, interview.
19. Thubten Jigme Norbu, interview.
20. Anonymous. (1995 interview with a former Volunteer now living in the United States who requested anonymity.)
21. Ibid.
22. Gompo Tashi Andrugtsang, interview.
23. Michael Harris Goodman. *The Last Dalai Lama*. 1986. pp. 263, 268, 273, 274.
24. Tenzin Gyatso. *Freedom in Exile: The Autobiography of the Dalai Lama*. 1990. pp. 121, 122, 126, 127.
25. Avedon. *In Exile*. p. 120.
26. Avedon. *In Exile*. pp. 121–122.
27. Anonymous. (1995 interview with a former Volunteer now living in the United States who requested anonymity.)

Epilogue

1. Thubten Jigme Norbu. "Tibet's Independence." *Tibet: The Issue Is Independence*. 1994. p. 7.
2. Tashi-Topgye Jamyangling. "Independence or Extinction." *Tibet: The Issue Is Independence*. pp. 66, 71.
3. Tashi Rabgey. Tibet: "The Case for Rangzen (Independence)." *Tibet: The Issue Is Independence*. pp. 15, 16.

Appendix A

1. Chanakya Sen. *Tibet Disappears*. 1960. pp. 470, 471, 472.

Appendix B

1. Chanakya Sen. *Tibet Disappears*. 1960. pp. 473, 474.

Bibliography

Andrugtsang, Gompo Tashi. *Four Rivers, Six Ranges.* Dharamsala, India: Information Office of His Holiness the Dalai Lama, 1973.
Avedon, John F. *In Exile from the Land of Snows.* New York: Alfred A. Knopf, 1984.
Danzinger, Nick. *Danzinger's Travels beyond Forbidden Frontiers.* New York: Random House, 1987.
Dietrich, Craig. *People's China.* New York: Oxford University Press, 1986.
Fleming, Peter. *Bayonets to Lhasa.* Hong Kong: Oxford University Press, 1984.
Ford, Robert. *Captured in Tibet.* Hong Kong: Oxford University Press, 1990.
Galbraith, John Kenneth. *A Life in Our Times.* Boston: Houghton Mifflin, 1981.
Goldstein, Melvyn. *A History of Modern Tibet, 1913–1951: The Demise of the Lamaist State.* Berkeley: University of California Press, 1989.
Goodman, Michael Harris. *The Last Dalai Lama.* London: Goodman, Sidgwick & Jackson, 1986.
Gyatso, Tenzin, His Holiness, the Fourteenth Dalai Lama of Tibet. *Freedom in Exile: The Autobiography of the Dalai Lama.* New York: HarperCollins, 1990.
Hicks, Roger, and Chogyam, Ngakpa. *The Great Ocean.* Dorset, England: Element Books,1984.
Huc, M. *Travels in Tartary, Thibet and China.* Chicago: Open Court Pub. Co., 1900.
Kewley, Vanya. *Tibet: Behind the Ice Curtain.* London: Grafton Books, 1990.
Norbu, Jamyang. *Warriors of Tibet. The Story of Aten and the Khambas' Fight for Their Country.* London: Wisdom Publications (Originally Tibet Information Office, Central Tibetan Secretariat, Dharamsala, India, 1979.)
Norbu, Thubten Jigme. *This Is My Country.* New York: E. P. Dutton, 1961.
Peissel, Michel. *The Secret War in Tibet.* Toronto: Little, Brown, 1973.
Salisbury, Harrison E. *The Long March: The Untold Story.* New York: Harper & Row, 1985.
Sen, Chanakya. *Tibet Disappears.* London: Asia Publishing House, 1960.
Steele, Archibald T. *In the Kingdom of the Dalai Lama.* Sedona, Arizona: In Print Publishing, 1993.

Pamphlets and Periodicals

"Facts About Tibet: 1961–1965." Issued by the Bureau of His Holiness, The Dalai Lama, New Delhi, India, 1965.
Peking Review. May 5, 1959. Special Tibet Number. Peking, China.
"Tibet." The Preparatory Bureau, Afro-Asian Convention on Tibet and Against Colonialism in Asia and Africa. New Delhi. April 1960
"Tibet: The Issue Is Independence." Parallax Press, Berkeley, California, 1994. (Excerpts

reprinted from *Tibet: The Issue Is Independence* by Edward Lazar [1994] with permission of Parallax Press, Berkeley, California.)

"Tibet and the United States of America: An Annotated Chronology of Relations in the 20th Century." Second Edition, February 1994. International Committee of Lawyers for Tibet.

"United Asia: Survey on Tibet." *International Magazine of Afro-Asian Affairs* (Bombay) vol. 11, no. 2, 1959.

Index

Abbot of Sa-ca 15
Afghanistan 212
Africa 260
Ahlachak 170
Ahpho (officer) 152
Ahsong (officer) 152
Ahtsar (Ahzar) Lake 159, 172, 173
Ahzin, Captain 160, 165
Aksi Chin 127
All India Convention (on Tibet) 206
Altan Khan 1, 16, 24
Alva, Jaachim 91, 93, 94
Amban (Chinese) 19, 21, 22, 23, 26, 28, 29
Amban Fung 30
Amdo tribe(s) vi, 2, 4, 36, 39, 47, 48, 49, 51, 53, 63, 69, 70, 73, 95, 100, 101, 104, 108, 110, 112, 113, 116, 117, 126, 129, 131, 134, 135, 139, 140, 143, 144, 145, 146, 148, 161, 163, 169, 175, 176, 180, 185, 186, 210, 218, 220, 224, 225, 226, 236, 238, 244, 247, 251
Amdowas 148
Andrugtsang family 142
Anglo-Chinese Convention 29
Anhui 46
Anthony, Mr. 60
Apel Sultrim (Shanam Ma) 129
Army of Tibet 31, 32, 38
Arunchal Pradesh *see* Northeast Frontier Agency/NEFA
Assam 59, 146
Athar, (Tom) 6, 139, 186, 188, 217, 240, 241, 245
Atlantic Charter 42

Australia 56
Ayyangar, Mr. 59

Baba Yeshe (Bapa Gen Yishi) 175, 245, 247
Bachu tribe 161
Bangkok 214
Bangladesh (East Pakistan) 240
Bapa 145, 168, 170, 175
Bapa Phuntsok Wangyal 111
Bathang 28, 101, 104, 111, 113, 126
Bayonets to Lhasa (Peter Fleming) 6
Belgium 212
Bell, Sir Charles 18, 20, 46
Bhutan 17, 44, 94, 142, 146, 167, 191
Birendra, King 247
Black Hat dance 13
Blue Chinese 148
Bodyguard Regiment 38
Bombay 91, 202
Bosnia 260
Brahmaputra River 2, 139, 142, 240
British Military Expedition 19
British Union Jack 44, 71
Brunei 254
Buddhist Red Hats 15, 16
Buddhist Yellow Hats (Gel-ugpa) 15, 22, 23, 32
Bun-Pu-He-u-Tig Hwang Te, King 13, 14
Burma 12, 17, 40, 42, 44, 212
Bush, President George 224

Calcutta 66, 67, 204
Cambodia 212
Camp Hale *see* Colorado
Canada 56

Castle of the Female Dragon *see* Jomdha Dzong
Celestial Empire 43
Central Intelligence Agency (CIA) 4, 5, 6, 139, 186, 213, 214, 234, 235, 236, 237, 238, 239, 240, 241, 242, 244
Central People's Government (Party) 61, 66, 68, 69, 71, 193, 194, 198
Ceylon 44, 212
Chakpori medical school 177, 184
Chakra Pelkhar 168
Chaksam Chupo 172
Chamdo 51, 52, 53, 54, 55, 61, 62, 63, 64, 98, 104, 108, 117, 126, 146, 160, 166, 168, 171, 193, 196, 203, 220, 223
Chamdo Monastery 166
Chang 149
Chang Ching-wu, General 67, 68, 77, 80, 90, 111
Chang Ho-ther, Commander 142, 143
Chang kun-yok 13
Chang Kuo-hua, General 87, 89, 98, 99, 123, 219
Chang Lu 217
Chang-an 12
Changthang 163, 218
Chang-tu *see* Pembar
Chao Erh-feng 19, 74
Chatreng 145, 168, 171
Chatterjee, N.C. 93, 94
Chazo Tashi 145
Chen Yi, Vice Premier 89, 93, 99
Chengtu 9, 45, 105, 127
Chenrezi 14, 16, 222
Chenselinga 34
Che-putsuntanpa 27

283

INDEX

Che-shung-shek 13
Chi Hu Chir 14
Chia Ch'en (year) 26
Chiang Kai-shek 40, 42, 43, 45, 46, 61, 96, 193, 201, 207, 223; *see also* China's Destiny
Ch'ien-Lung, Emperor 16
China's Destiny (Chiang Kai-shek) 43
Chinese Communist Party 46, 48, 71, 72, 89, 98, 99, 105, 123, 125, 156, 201, 217
Chinese Constitution 105, 115, 116, 120, 123
Chinese Military Headquarters, Lhasa 178, 203, 204, 210
Chinese Nationalists 44, 45, 47, 48, 53, 146, 245, 258, 259
Chinese People's National Assembly 81, 82, 178, 221
Chinese People's Republic *see* People's Republic of China
Chinese revolution (of 1911) 20
Chinese State Council 87, 89
Chinese Turkestan 44, 45
Ch'ing Dynasty 24, 53
Chinghai 46
Chinmen 254
Chongay 185
Chophel (officer) 152
Choporgya 232
Chou En-lai 51, 64, 68, 73, 84, 85, 104, 112, 113, 114, 124, 189, 191, 192, 202, 203, 206, 227
Chu Shur 151
Chu Teh, General 61, 64, 221
Chuang(s) 194, 209
Chuba, Major 189
Chuhangmu 199
Chukhor 166
Chulthun 166
Chumbi 24
Chunggyu Woma 160, 175
Chungking 40, 42, 50
Chungpo Karu 171
Chushi Gangdrug vi, 134, 135, 138, 139, 143, 144, 145, 148, 151, 160, 163, 165, 172, 175, 178, 235, 236, 237, 245

Clinton, President Bill 214
Colorado (Camp Hale), resistance fighter training at 5, 238, 243, 245, 246, 247
Commune 119, 120, 121, 124
Communist Chinese Army 101
Costa Rica 212
Cultural Revolution 231, 253
Curzon, Lord 18

Dalai Lama (defined) 16
Dalai Lama, Eleventh 19, 23
Dalai Lama, Fifth (Lobsang Gyatso) 16, 72
Dalai Lama, Fourteenth (Tenzin Gyatso) 1, 2, 3, 4, 6, 7, 27, 36, 37, 39, 40, 43, 46, 47, 49, 50, 51, 57, 63, 64, 65, 66, 67, 68, 71, 72, 73, 75, 77, 81, 82, 83, 84, 85, 86, 87, 90, 93, 94, 95, 96, 98, 98, 100, 101, 102, 109, 111, 112, 113, 115, 117, 118, 119, 129, 132, 133, 135, 137, 139, 143, 146, 148, 156, 163, 164, 169, 172, 173, 174, 175, 176, 179, 180, 181, 184, 185, 186, 187, 188, 189, 191, 192, 194, 195, 200, 201, 202, 203, 205, 206, 207, 208, 209, 210, 211, 212, 213, 214, 215, 216, 217, 218, 221, 222, 224, 225, 226, 227, 228, 232, 236, 238, 240, 241, 245, 247, 249, 250, 251, 252, 256, 257, 258, 259; autobiography of 237; correspondence with Tan Kuan-san 197, 198, 199; and degree of Geshe 177, 178; escape route of 182, 183; and press conference at Mussoorie 201
Dalai Lama, Fourth 1
Dalai Lama, Ninth 19
Dalai Lama, Seventh (Kesang Gyatso) 138
Dalai Lama, Sixth (Tsangyang Gyatso) 16
Dalai Lama, Third (Sonam Gyatso) 16

Dalai Lama, Thirteenth 3, 18, 19, 20, 21, 22, 24, 25, 26, 27, 29, 30, 31, 32, 33, 34, 37, 39, 46, 56, 97, 103, 131, 133, 134, 250, 251; "Political Last Testament" of 37
Dalai Lama, Twelfth 19
Damshang 178
Darjeeling 4, 5, 6, 20, 33, 176, 238
Dartsedo 117
Dawa, Commander 168, 171
Delhi 31, 93
Democratic Centralism 105, 106
Democratic Reforms 102, 103, 104, 108, 109, 111, 115, 120, 123, 124, 125, 127, 128, 131, 134, 136
Dengko 51
de Reincourt, Amaury 44
Derge 28, 104, 108, 126, 156, 168, 169
Derge Yhilung 161
Dharamsala 240, 257
Dhartsedo 107
Digu Tashi Thongmon Dzong 143
Dinching 193
Dip 143
Diplomatic Corps 207
Do Kham 24, 25
Dolan, Lieutenant Brooke 41, 42
Dominican Republic 212
Dorje Phagmo 227
Dorje Yudon 107
Dragon King Pond 195
Drakyab 169
Dramthang 166
Drango 107
Dre Gung (Monastery) 157
Drechu *see* Yangtze River
Drephur 173
Drepung Monastery 6, 26, 33, 100, 111, 133, 137, 185
Dromo *see* Yatung
Dzado 232
Dzong 149

Eden, Anthony 42
Eisenhower, President Dwight 242, 244
El Salvador 56, 57, 261
Engels, Friedrich 200

Ethiopa 212
Exalted Ones 14

Fifth Army 45
Finland 212
First and Second Field Armies 52
"Five Principles of Peaceful Coexistence" 90
Fleming, Peter 6
Ford, Robert 54
Fortune (Indian weekly journal) 91
Four Rivers, Six Ranges (Gompo Tashi Andrugtsang) 152
France 205, 212
Freedom Committee 180
Freedom Fighters (of Tibet) vi, 3, 6, 114, 132, 138, 161, 163, 164, 166, 167, 168, 170, 173, 175, 176, 180, 182, 201, 214, 217, 220, 225, 229, 232, 233, 234, 237, 239, 241, 242, 243, 247, 248
Freedom in Exile: The Autobiography of the Dalai Lama (Tenzin Gyatso) 237, 257

Galbraith, John Kenneth 213, 214
Ganden (Monastery) 15, 100, 111, 133, 137, 149, 177, 185
Ganden-tru-pa 15
Gandhi, Indira 250
Gandhi, Mahatma 52, 91, 214, 250
Gangtok 112, 113
Gartok 98
Gelek Phuntsok Gaba (officer) 152
Gelugpa *see* Buddhist Yellow Hats
Gen Yeshi, Commander 175
Genghis Khan 1, 15, 24, 65
Germany 31, 205
Geshe Wangyel 6
Ghaba Dorjee Gompo 161
Ghana 212
Golmo, prison camp at 224
Golok tribe vi, 73, 93, 95, 100, 101, 104, 108, 126, 127, 135, 163, 218, 244, 247

Gompo Tashi Andrugtsang vi, 5, 6, 110, 111, 129, 132, 133, 135, 138, 141, 142, 143, 144, 148, 149, 150, 151, 152, 160, 161, 165, 167, 168, 170, 171, 172, 176, 183, 217, 236, 238, 240, 241, 242, 244; *see also* Four Rivers, Six Ranges
Gonja 232
Great Britain 17, 18, 19, 30, 31, 34, 40, 41, 42, 44, 46, 47, 60, 66, 67, 90, 96, 201, 205, 212, 213
Great Eastern Prosperity Sphere 43
Great Leap Forward 156, 221, 222, 231
Great Prayer Festival 226
Greece 207
Guam 236, 238
Guinea 212
Gurkhas 17, 247
Gushri Khan 1, 16
Gyado Dhondrup, Commander 168, 171
Gyalo Thondup 6, 43, 64, 113, 124, 238, 240, 244
Gyantse 33
Gyara Chipa 107
Gyari Nima 107, 161
Gyari Tsang 107
Gyasho Bonkhar 171
Gyasho Pengyal 166
Gyato (Walt) Wangdu 6, 139, 188, 217, 236, 240, 241, 245, 247
Gyawa Riksum Gonpo (deity) 143
Gyelton 168
Gyethang 111
Gyeyum Chemmo, Great Mother 178
Gyulo (Nyarong) 162
Gyurme 107

Haiti 260
Han (Chinese) 2, 120, 123, 125, 138, 192, 200, 218, 225, 248, 249
Happy Light Cinema 216
Harrer, Heinrich 36, 64
He Hu Hik Wang Te *see* Bun-Pu-He-u-Tig Hwang Te, King
Himalayas 17, 31

A History of Modern Tibet (Melvyn Goldstein) 6, 167, 250
Ho Chi-minh 256
Hong Kong 55, 56, 108, 164, 208, 213, 223, 226, 259
Horpa tribe 163
Hsi Jao Chia-tso 100
Hsin Hai (year) 26
Hsinka Jigme-dorje 193
Hui(s) 194, 196, 209
Hungary 205
Hwang Te, King 13

I Fan-chen 28
In Exile from the Land of Snows (John Avedon) 6, 237, 253
India 1, 6, 9, 15, 18, 25, 31, 34, 37, 40, 42, 44, 46, 53, 55, 57, 58, 59, 60, 62, 67, 71, 90, 94, 101, 109, 110, 111, 117, 126, 132, 133, 139, 142, 146, 156, 163, 164, 167, 173, 175, 176, 186, 187, 189, 191, 206, 207, 208, 209, 212, 213, 214, 227, 237, 238, 239, 245, 248, 251
Indian Communist Party 203
Indian Foreign and Political Department 39
Indian Intelligence Service 239
Indian Parliament 5, 6, 90, 94, 203, 207
Indonesia 212
Inner Mongolia 28, 71, 75
Inner Mongolian Autonomous Region 209
Inner Tibet 28, 29, 31, 87, 88, 99
International Commission of Jurists 212, 213, 219, 223, 256
International Red Cross 257
Iraq 212
Iron Hill 184

Jago Namgyal Dorje 149, 150, 168
Jama Samphel 168
Jang Lhari 160, 172
Jang Methikha 160
Jang Namtso 156
Jang Yangpa Chen 155, 156

286 INDEX

Japan 18, 32, 40, 43, 44, 46, 206, 213, 214
Japho Jakey 159
Jentzen Dhondrup 4
Jinpa Gyatso 145, 175
Jokhang Monastery (Temple) 23, 29, 85, 177, 184, 196, 197
Jomdha Dzong 107, 108, 17
Jongdung Bhu Dhudul 230
Jongka 232
Jora Gen (Monastery) 175
Jungpo Karnak 168
Jyekundo 52, 127, 232

Kalimpong 23, 74, 101, 109, 113, 126, 132, 191, 193, 203, 207
Kalon Ngapo 68
Kanchung Soanamchiatso 192
Kansu 104
Kanze 101, 168, 170
Kanzeymane 199
Kar-tsen 14
Kashag (Tibetan cabinet) 34, 36, 37, 39, 41, 42, 54, 55, 63, 66, 73, 80, 98, 100, 131, 136, 137, 146, 148, 150, 153, 172, 181, 183, 185, 193, 197, 198, 250
Keng-shi (palace) 14
Kennedy, President John 244
Kenrup Tenzin 63
Kesang Gyatso see Dalai Lama, Seventh
Khache Chazo 143
Khadang Division (Tibetan Army) 138, 142, 173, 175
Kham vi, 2, 9, 29, 31, 36, 38, 41, 45, 51, 52, 53, 54, 64, 98, 100, 101, 104, 106, 108, 110, 111, 112, 113, 115, 116, 117, 127, 128, 129, 132, 134, 135, 139, 140, 142, 143, 144, 145, 146, 148, 149, 150, 153, 161, 163, 165, 166, 172, 175, 176, 179, 180, 185, 186, 210, 218, 219, 220, 223, 229, 232, 234, 236, 237, 238, 240, 241, 242, 244, 245

Khamba resistance fighters vi, 4, 36, 51, 53, 54, 69, 73, 95, 100, 101, 104, 106, 108, 110, 111, 117, 126, 129, 132, 135, 139, 143, 145, 146, 148, 149, 153, 160, 165, 172, 174, 175, 180, 181, 182, 183, 185, 186, 187, 191, 218, 220, 232, 234, 237, 240, 244, 247, 251
Khardag Monastery 175
Khenche Khenrab Phuntsok 23
Khenchung 22
Khensur Losang Choden 149
Khensur Thupten Samten 149
Khotan 127
Khrushchev, Nikita 221
Kiansu 225
Kingsha River 196
Kirong 169
Koko 232
Kong Tse La 158
Kongpo 168, 170, 173
Korea 43, 51, 56, 58, 209
Korean War 236
Kripalani, Acharya 59, 90, 91, 93, 204
Kublai Khan 1, 15
Kumbum Monastery 4, 40, 47, 48, 50, 63
Kuomintang party (KMT) 43, 96, 101, 117, 259
Kuru Sampa 143
Kusang Regiment 180
Kwangsi Chuang National Autonomous Region 209
Kwanming Daily 208
Kyi Chu River 143, 199, 224

Ladakh 17, 38, 44, 59, 238
Lama Tsewang Gyurme 127
Lanchow 46, 47, 99
Lang-dar-ma, King 12, 13
The Last Dalai Lama (Michael Harris Goodman) 236
Lebanon 212
Lee Kuan-yew, President 256
Leh 59
Len, Colonel 128
Lenin 84, 93, 118, 200
Lesang Chozen (officer) 152

Lhalu Shape 53, 54
Lhalu Tsewang Dorje 223
Lhamo Tsering 6, 240, 244
Lhari 170
Lhasa 6, 11, 12, 13, 14, 15, 16, 19, 20, 21, 22, 23, 24, 26, 28, 29, 30, 33, 34, 36, 37, 38, 39, 40, 41, 42, 50, 53, 55, 59, 61, 63, 64, 67, 68, 69, 71, 72, 73, 74, 75, 77, 78, 79, 80, 81, 85, 87, 89, 90, 93, 95, 96, 97, 98, 99, 100, 101, 102, 108, 109, 111, 113, 115, 117, 118, 119, 124, 126, 127, 131, 133, 134, 136, 138, 139, 140, 141, 144, 148, 150, 156, 157, 161, 163, 164, 167, 168, 172, 173, 177, 178, 179, 180, 181, 183, 184, 185, 186, 187, 189, 191, 192, 193, 194, 195, 196, 199, 203, 204, 205, 209, 210, 211, 213, 216, 217, 218, 219, 220, 221, 222, 223, 224, 225, 226, 236, 237, 240, 241, 244, 250, 251, 258, 259
Lhasa Convention 18
Lho Dzong 146, 169
Lhodrak 175
Lhoka (Trigu Thang) 98, 142, 143, 144, 149, 150, 160, 165, 166, 168, 170, 171, 172, 193, 199, 218, 219, 220, 237
Lhotse, (Lou) 6, 139, 186, 188, 217, 240, 241, 245
Lhuntse Dzong 172, 173, 175, 183, 185, 186
Li Wei-han 64, 65
Lien-yu 22, 23, 26
Lin Biao 221
Lingkhor Monastery 54
Lithang 28, 101, 104, 105, 110, 111, 126, 127, 145, 151, 168, 171, 175, 232, 236, 238; monastery in 132
Liu Ba-ting, General 51, 52
Liu Po-chen, General 50
Liu Shao-chi 84, 123, 124, 125, 127, 128, 222
Liu Wen-hu, General 50
Lobsang Gyatso see Dalai Lama, Fifth
Lok Sabha 59, 93, 188, 189, 204

INDEX

Lolo vi, 45, 105, 106, 108
Lonchen Shatra 28
London 42, 43
"Long March" 45, 106, 221, 228; *see also* Yudu
Losar (religious celebration) 178
Lost World — Tibet, Key to Asia (Amaury de Reincourt) 44
Lotse, Commander 170
Ludup (resistance leader) 168
Lybia 212

Ma Chang La 152
Ma Pu-feng 39, 40, 47
Makkul 170
Malaya 42, 213
Malaysia 254
Manchu Empire 24
Manchuria (Manchus) 16, 20, 22, 23, 24, 43, 93
Mandarins 255
Mangmang 187
Mao Tse-tung (Mao/Maoism) 2, 3, 5, 11, 36, 37, 43, 45, 46, 47, 49, 50, 59, 61, 65, 67, 68, 71, 73, 74, 75, 77, 82, 83, 84, 85, 86, 87, 92, 93, 95, 96, 97, 99, 104, 105, 106, 112, 113, 114, 115, 117, 118, 119, 120, 122, 124, 125, 126, 134, 137, 140, 146, 147, 164, 186, 188, 189, 200, 201, 202, 203, 207, 208, 219, 221, 222, 223, 224, 226, 227, 228, 231, 234, 250, 251, 253, 254, 256, 258
Markham Gartok 52, 91, 146, 163, 169, 170, 220, 232
Marx/Marxism (Marxism-Leninism) 74, 77, 78, 79, 83, 84, 85, 86, 93, 115, 118, 146, 200, 205, 206, 252, 258
Masani, Mr. 59
McMahon, Sir Henry (McMahon Line) 28, 31, 42, 59, 191, 238
Mehta, Asoka 93
Menon, K. P. 47
Mhar-Go-La 176
Miao(s) 209, 210
Military Administrative Committee 45, 66

Military Area Headquarters 66, 197, 198, 199, 204
Ming Dynasty 24
Mongolia 1, 15, 16, 18, 21, 23, 25, 27, 28, 42, 43, 46, 48, 72, 73, 75, 83, 194, 200, 208, 209, 210, 248
Monlam (religious) festival 23, 178
Morocco 212
Muja Dapon 51, 52, 53, 54
Mukherjee, Dr. S.P. 57, 58
Mussoorie 201
Mustang (Nepal) 23, 139, 176, 234, 235, 245, 247, 248; Maharajah of 234

Nachen Thang 224
Naduk (resistance leader) 168
Nagchuka (Nakchukha) 23, 157, 171, 193, 232
Nakchu 163, 168
Naksho 169, 171, 232
Namgyal, Commander 168, 170
Namling 232
Nang 232
Nangchen clans 163
Nanking 26, 34, 43
Narayan, Jaya Prakash 188, 189, 204, 205
Nasop 151
Nathula pass 112, 207
National (Tibetan) Assembly 28, 34, 36, 39, 40, 43, 68, 72, 73, 179; *see also* Tsongdu
National Minorities Commission 64
National People's Congress 100, 199, 208, 227
Nehru, Jawaharlal 5, 56, 57, 58, 59, 60, 67, 71, 85, 90, 91, 92, 93, 94, 97, 101, 111, 112, 113, 124, 163, 164, 176, 186, 187, 188, 189, 190, 191, 202, 203, 206, 207, 208, 212, 214, 215, 238, 250, 251, 257
Nel Monastery 175
Nemo Junpa 155
Nemo Lhokhar 152
Nemo River 153
Nemo Shung 153

Nepal 6, 12, 15, 17, 19, 44, 53, 59, 90, 93, 94, 108, 110, 139, 142, 163, 166, 167, 191, 212, 214, 234, 245, 247, 248
Neusha Thubten-Tarpa 193
New China News Agency (NCNA) 50, 54, 59, 61, 87, 89, 100, 101, 108, 123, 199, 208, 219
New Delhi 40, 41, 54, 55, 61, 66, 109, 112, 114, 124, 186, 187, 202, 207, 213, 238
New York Times 7
Ngapo Ngawang Jigme 5, 54, 55, 63, 64, 65, 66, 68, 77, 87, 146, 180, 181, 185, 186, 192, 193, 197, 198, 206, 223, 227, 250
Ngari Korsum 25
Ngatruk, Captain 170
Ngawang Dakpa 135
Ningsia Hui National Autonomous Region 209
Nor 232
Norbulingka 29, 34, 135, 177, 179, 180, 181, 184, 185, 195, 196, 197, 198, 199, 209, 226
North Korea 56, 93, 210, 258
North Vietnam 256
Northeast Frontier Agency/NEFA (Arunchal Pradesh) 31, 40, 94, 214, 238
Nyarong 9, 28, 106, 107, 127, 128, 161
Nyarong Gyulo 162
Nyingma 161

Office of National Policy Making 136
Office of Strategic Services (OSS) 41, 43
Okinawa 236, 240
"One World" ("New World Order") 56
Outer Mongolia 28, 29, 37, 43, 44
Outer Tibet 28, 29, 87, 88

Pakistan 44, 142, 167, 206, 237
Pala 169
Pamirs 12

288　INDEX

Panch Sheel (unity agreement) 112, 204, 206
Panchen Erdeni Ghuji-Geltseng 192
Panchen Kanpo Lija (Committee on Historical and Unsettled Problems) 87
Panchen (Lama) Ngoerhtehni 87
Panchen Lama(s) 3, 16, 25, 26, 27, 30, 34, 36, 37, 38, 50, 65, 71, 73, 75, 82, 84, 85, 87, 89, 98, 111, 114, 115, 186, 192, 206, 210, 219, 220, 222, 225, 226, 227, 251
Pangdatsang family 53, 145, 146
Paracel Islands 254
Patterson, George 163, 189, 190
Peace Conference 41, 42
Pebala Choliehnamje 192
Peking 23, 27, 29, 46, 50, 51, 62, 64, 68, 74, 75, 79, 82, 85, 96, 89, 92, 96, 99, 100, 101, 114, 117, 123, 125, 126, 173, 178, 191, 192, 198, 200, 201, 203, 204, 205, 206, 207, 219, 221, 22, 226, 227, 255, 258
Peking Convention 18
Peking Review 6, 194, 217, 219
Peldhen (officer) 152
Pema 232
Pema Yeshe, Commander 168, 170
Pembar (Chang-tu) 74, 229, 230
Peng Te-Huai 221
People's Daily 208
People's Liberation Army (PLA) vi, 1, 2, 5, 11, 36, 46, 47, 49, 50, 54, 55, 59, 61, 64, 65, 66, 68, 69, 72, 80, 81, 89, 92, 100, 108, 116, 125, 126, 191, 192, 193, 194, 196, 197, 200, 201, 206, 209, 218, 219, 220, 221, 228, 231, 238, 240, 248, 253, 254, 255
People's Liberation Committee 63, 87
People's Liberation Committee of the Chang-tu Area 87

People's National Congress 86, 208, 222
People's Republic of China (PRC) 1, 3, 27, 29, 32, 36, 46, 71, 202, 206, 223, 227, 231, 232, 235, 256, 258, 260
Peter of Greece, Prince 207
Phakpa-la Gelek 227
Phakpa-la Kenchung 179
Pharco Chiso 133
Phari 23
Phewu Tang Tenpa 151
Philippines 206, 236, 254
Phisa 127
Phuntso Tashi 43
Phurpa Trinley 156
PLA Tibetan Military District Command 89, 192, 193, 194, 198
Po 104, 106, 146
Podhopa 168
Portugal 212
Poshokar 169
Posul 232
Potala Palace 16, 17, 23, 25, 29, 135, 177, 179, 180, 181, 184, 185, 195, 196, 225
Potamo 168
Potamo Chunpo Tengchen Rongpo Rapten 168
Powers, Gary 244
Powo Tamo 166
Praja Socialist Party 59
Prasad, Brajeshwar 91
Prasad, Joachim 60
Preparatory Committee for the Autonomous Region of Tibet (PCART) 86, 87, 89, 96, 98, 99, 113, 126, 185, 192, 193, 194

Radio Peking 36, 47, 50, 55, 65, 199, 201
Rakshi Gumpa tribe 163
Ral-pacen, King 13
Ramoche Cathedral 226
Ranadive 59
Ranga, Professor N. G. 58, 60
Rao, Shiva 203
Rapga Pangdatsang 146
Ratuk Ngawang 179
Red Army 45
Red Guards 235, 253
Red Hill 12

Regent (Chinese) 11, 34, 36, 37, 39
Relpa Bhuchung 165, 166, 167
Reting Rinpoche 39
Ribochen 168, 171
Riwoche 52
Rongpo 168, 171
Roof of the World 44
Roosevelt, Franklin D. 41
Russia 17, 18, 19, 28, 29, 56, 57, 60, 91, 205, 256
Russo-Japanese War 18

Sadu Tsang Lhonedrak 168
Saheb, Jam 57
St. Petersburg Convention 18
Saipan 236, 240, 243, 244, 245
Sakya 232
Samdeng Chazo, resistance leader 169
Samphel Jama Tsang 145
Sampo Tsewong-rentzen 193
Sanag Palden 127
Sarteng 166, 168
Saudi Arabia 212
The Secret War in Tibet (Michel Peissel) 145
Sek 171
Sengye-long 168
Sera (Monastery) 15, 29, 100, 111, 133, 135, 137, 185
Serra Jay Pa Monastery 149
Sersum 168
Seventeen Point Agreement 63, 66, 68, 69, 79, 86, 89, 180, 185, 188, 191, 194, 200, 201, 213
Shan Chao 195, 197
Shanam Ma 128, 129
Shang Dadhen Chokhor 150
Shang Gadhen Choling Monastery 153
Shang Gyatso Dzong 153
Shanghai 34
Shao Li-tzu 208
Shartsong Ritro Monastery 49
Shekar-Lhasa road 220
Shekar-Trigu road 220
Shenen Tenzing 149
Shichen Monastery 161, 162
Shigatse 26, 73, 98, 126, 134, 156, 157, 220, 221, 226, 234

INDEX

Shinje Choegyal 217
Shitam Monastery 169
Shiwa Lha Rinpoche 166
Shodor 169, 170
Shol 177, 184
Shota Lhosum 165, 166, 168, 169, 171
Shri Purushotlam Das Tandon 93
Shukden Oracle 142
Shukti Lingka 184
Sikang (Province) 2, 43, 74, 89
Sikang-Tibet highway 74
Sikkim 17, 18, 33, 41, 44, 53, 63, 64, 94, 111, 112, 142, 167, 179, 191, 215, 220, 248
Silum Lokongwa Tsewongrouten 193
Simla 21, 28, 29
Singapore 206, 213, 256
Sinha, Dr. Satya Narayan 91
Sining 16, 21, 39
Sinkiang (Province) 46, 71, 72, 73, 75, 93, 220, 222
Sino-Indian Agreement on Tibet 90, 93, 111, 203
Sino-Tibetan border 21
Snow, Edgar 45
Socialism 99, 106, 118, 119, 124, 201, 253, 257
Sok 171
Sokkhul 168
Sonam Gyatso *see* Dalai Lama, Third
Son-Tsan Gam-Po, King 12
South Africa 212
South Korea 43, 51, 56, 206, 210
South Vietnam 206
Southwest China Military Affairs Commission 50
Southwest School for National Minorities 9, 105
Soviet Union 60, 92, 99, 255; TASS news agency 47
Spain 212
Special Frontier Force 239
Spratly Islands 254
Stalin, Joseph 49, 84, 93, 200, 201, 221, 223
Stam, Betty (missionary) 46
Stam, John (missionary) 46
State Council of the Chinese Government 87, 227

State Oracle of Tibet 2, 57, 67
A Strange Liberation: Tibetan Lives in Chinese Hands (Ama Adhe) 117
Strong, Anna Louise 219, 221
Sudan 212
Sun Yat-sen 27, 53, 54, 146
Surkhang, Tibetan Prime Minister 180
Surkong Wongching-Galei 193
Switzerland 59
Szechuan (Province) 22, 24, 40, 89, 101, 127

Ta Kung Pao 87
Tachienlu 21, 24, 28
Tadrin Tsewang 157
Taiwan 146, 206, 236, 254
Taiwan Straits 254
Takdru Kha 153
Takster Rinpoche 47, 63, 64, 66, 67, 163; *see also* Thubten Jigme Norbu
Taktse (in Amdo) 39, 40
Tan Kuan-san, General 163, 179; correspondence with Dalai Lama 197, 198, 199
T'ang Dynasty 12
Tangu Tu-shi 49, 50
Tashi (Panchen) Lama 34
Tashi Division (Tibetan Army) 173
Tashi Monastery 142
Tashi Norbu 183
Tashi Pelrel, Commander 175
Tashi Phari (Para) 179
Tashi Rama Gang 143
Tashilhunpo (Monastery) 26, 27, 133, 220, 237
TASS (Soviet news agency) 47
Teiji Phunkhang 23
Tekhang Khenchung Thupten Samchok 150
Teng Dzong 169
Teng Hsiao-ping (Deng Xiaoping) 50, 227
Tengchen 169
Tensuk Shapten 133
Tenzin Gyatso *see* Dalai Lama, Fourteenth
Tezpur 187, 199, 200
Thagla Ridge 238

Thailand 206, 213, 214, 238
thamzing 102, 103, 106, 120, 121, 122, 123, 126, 163, 164, 223, 224, 227
Thanghsiung 156
Thangkya 127
Thargya Gonpa 168
Thargye 161, 170
Thau 107
Thi-song-deu-tsen, King 12, 14
Three Precious Ones 14
Thubten Jigme Norbu 4, 6, 47, 48, 64, 163, 164; *see also* Takster Rinpoche
Thupten Woyden Phala 6, 132, 133, 135, 139, 164, 179, 181, 198, 236, 241, 242
Tiananmen Square 253, 254
Tibet Disappears (Chanakya Sen) 6
Tibet Improvement Party 53
Tibetan Communist Party 95, 96
Tibetan Constitution 186
Tibetan Cultural Center 6
Tibetan Foreign Affairs Bureau 41
Tibetan People's Party 74
Tibetan Trade Mission 132
Ti-de-tsen, King 13
Times of India 74
Times of London 34
Tingri Tsang 220
Tokyo 208
Tolstoy, Captain Ilia 41
Topgye Pangdatsang 146
Tramo (resistance leader) 169, 175
Trigu 144, 160, 173, 175, 220, 232
Trikamdas, Purshottam 212
Tromtha 161
Tsaidam Basin 99
Tsalo Karpo, prison camp at 224, 225
Tsang 29
Tsangpo River 193, 199
Tsang-yang Gyatso *see* Dalai Lama, Sixth
Tsawa Pesho 169
Tsedron Jamyang Gyaltsen 23
Tsen-shu-huan 13
Tsepon Namseling 150, 183
Tsethang 164, 168, 173, 219, 232

INDEX

Tsinghai (Province) 39, 43, 49, 65, 72, 73, 87, 99
Tsomo Rak 173
Tsona 150, 173, 175, 199
Tsongdu (Tibetan People's Assembly) 80, 82, 98; *see also* National (Tibetan) Assembly
Tsong-kha-pa 15
Tsuglakhang Cathedral 144, 177, 226
Tuelpa Tsuklak Khang *see* Tsuglakhang Cathedral
Tulku 230
T.V. Soong 42

U vi, 29, 129
Uighur(s) 194, 209
Ulanfu of Inner Mongolia, Vice-Premier 208
United Arab Republic 212
United Kingdom 57; *see also* Great Britain
United Nations 1, 4, 5, 11, 21, 44, 51, 56, 57, 59, 62, 63, 66, 67, 164, 191, 202, 203, 207, 208, 210, 211, 212, 215, 245, 252, 256, 257, 258, 260, 262, 263; Charter of 211, 212; and Genocide Convention of 1948 212; and joint Malay-Irish resolution on Tibet 211
United States 4, 41, 46, 47, 56, 57, 60, 62, 66, 164, 213, 214, 244, 245, 252, 257, 260
Universal Declaration of Human Rights 211
Urga (Ulan Bator) 21, 27, 28, 37
U-Tsang 98, 141

Vietnam 254
Voice of America 214
Volunteer Defense Force 141, 143, 144, 145, 150, 151, 156, 160, 165, 166, 167, 168, 169, 170, 171, 172, 173, 175, 176, 183, 185, 186, 213, 214, 215, 216, 217, 220, 221, 222, 225, 228, 229, 230, 231, 232, 233, 234, 239, 242, 243, 249

Wakho 171
Wallace, Henry 42
Wang Ji-mei, General 108
Wang Peng Yang 14
Warriors of Tibet ([Aten] Rapten Dorje) 9
Western Tibet Reform Party 53
When Serfs Stood Up (Anna Louise Strong) 219
Wongpo Monastery 163
World War I 31
World War II 43, 44, 262
Wulu 9
Wulu Chue 107
Wuyuk 153

Yaan 127
Yabzhi Lingka 195
Yadi tribe 161
Yambulakang Monastery 177
Yamdog Yutso Chinmo 143
Yamdro 220
Yampel Pangdatsang 146
Yangpa Chen 156
Yangtze River 51, 52, 54, 101, 126, 151

Yaphel Tsultrim (officer)152
Yarlung Valley 199
Yarto Thargye 175
Yatung (Dromo) 23, 63, 64, 65, 66, 67, 111, 133, 220, 251
Ye Chun-tang, General 49
Year of the Earth Dog 143
Year of the Earth Hog 169
Year of the Fire Monkey 103
Year of the Iron Dog 22, 24
Year of the Iron Tiger 2
Year of the Water Snake 79
Year of the Wood Dragon 22
Year of the Wood Horse 82
Yemen 212
Yi 45, 101
Yo Wang Hill 195, 196
Younghusband, Sir Francis 18
Yuan Shih-kai 20, 27
Yudu ("Long March," beginning of) 45
Yugoslavia 204, 212
Yunnan (Province) 24, 40, 43
Yuto Chahsidongchu 193

Zachu 161
Zachu River 151, 161
Zachukha 161, 163
Zamdo 161
Zamey Naghdo 161
Zapa-Liru 161
Zasak Monling Pa 149
Zenang Ahker 165, 166, 167
Zhang Guo-tao 45
Zokchen Gompa 161
Zokchen Monastery 161, 162
Zokchen Rinpoche 162, 163

www.ingramcontent.com/pod-product-compliance
Ingram Content Group UK Ltd.
Pitfield, Milton Keynes, MK11 3LW, UK
UKHW041927140426
5217IPUK00014B/356